JOHN HENF

DOCTOR OF T

FAMILY PUBLICATIONS

OXFORD

JOHN HENRY NEWMAN

Doctor of the Church

Edited by Philippe Lefebvre
& Colin Mason

Images courtesy of the Fathers of the Oratory, Birmingham

ISBN 978-1-871217-72-8

FAMILY PUBLICATIONS

6A KING STREET
OXFORD
OX2 6DF

www.familypublications.co.uk

PRINTED IN MALTA

FOREWORD

The literary production of John Henry Newman is so vast and various that it resembles an ocean filled with innumerable gems and caverns, swarming with fish and crawling creatures. Students who begin to sample his writings easily become addicted to them, turning them into a lifelong hobby. Newman's sphere of interest was almost unbounded. He had a passion for geology, gardening, music, and military science. But in his novels and poetry, treatises, sermons, prayers, letters, and diaries, he made it evident that his predominant interest was religion, the theme of the present volume.

In his religious writings Newman explored almost every crucial problem of the past and present. His reflections are of special interest because he thought out his positions from the ground up. Taking nothing for granted, he inquired about the capacity of the human mind to grasp the existence and nature of God. He explained why he believed in God and why that fundamental belief made it necessary for him to be a Christian and, eventually, a Catholic. "I am a Catholic," he wrote, "by virtue of my believing in a God." (*Apologia*, 198)

Fundamental to all of Newman's thinking was the theme of development. Ideas and institutions, he believed, had a life of their own. The Church develops over the centuries, as do her doctrines, structures, and practices. A master of introspection, Newman was able to give an account of how he himself had developed. His intellectual and spiritual life was a microcosm of that of the Church. It grew by trimming away false initiatives and cultivating the implications of insights that were sound. Developments, he recognized, require time to mature. They cannot be rushed.

One cannot sufficiently recommend the reading of Newman's own writings. Exhibiting his thoughts in the process of germination, they are the finest expression of the logic he pursued, a logic of discovery that complements, without replacing, the syllogistic logic of the schools.

Because Newman was so prolific, the student would be ill-advised to plunge into them without a mentor or guide. To read him without direction would be like exploring a continent without a map. One could easily miss the most important sites. Experts on Newman, such as the authors of the present book, are no substitutes for Newman himself, but they are needed to put his work in perspective. They inform us about the persons and events that motivated Newman to write as he did. They warn us against false interpretations and make us aware of the relevance of his thought for our own times.

With prophetic clarity, Newman discerned the mounting challenges to all forms of religious belief in the Western world. Neither fundamentalistic biblicism nor modernistic liberalism, he believed, was a match for the assaults of secularism. But he found a divinely provided remedy in the religion that God had revealed and continued to sustain by His infallible guidance of the Church. The articles in this volume explain how Newman made use of the Catholic tradition to answer his own questions and address the problems of his day. The reader will find good reasons for expecting that Newman will someday be numbered with Athanasius and Chrysostom, Augustine and Aquinas, among the Doctors of the Church.

Fordham University   Avery Cardinal Dulles, SJ
Bronx, New York   25 July 2007

CONTENTS

INTRODUCTION

by Keith Beaumont

This is the second of two volumes published by Family Publications, celebrating the life and work of John Henry Newman. The first, entitled *John Henry Newman – In his time*, presented Newman in connection with various places and contexts, and gave a broad overview of major aspects of his activity. The present volume focuses on Newman the thinker and teacher. The overall aims remain however the same: to appeal to a general readership; to cover aspects of Newman's thought that have not always been covered previously in depth; and to offer the opportunity of publication to a number of emerging young Newman scholars (in this respect, it is an object of particular pleasure to me personally to see three young French and Belgian scholars amongst the contributors).

In this Introduction, readers should note that I have distinguished between Newman's own words and those of the authors of chapters, by putting the former in double quotation marks and the latter in single.

The *Prologue* is formed by my own contribution on 'Newman as theologian and spiritual guide'. Although there are a few excellent studies of this subject (most notably by Fr Charles Stephen Dessain of the Birmingham Oratory), it is an area of Newman's activity which has received far too little attention. For Newman is not only one of the great Christian thinkers of the modern era, and a man the depth of whose personal spiritual experience and holiness is widely recognized, but also one of the great spiritual teachers of our time whose teaching is solidly founded first and foremost on that of the New Testament (the writings of St John and St Paul in particular), on that of the Fathers, and also, doubtless, on his own personal experience of God. This spirituality is however in no way disconnected from his theological

9

thought, quite the contrary – as I have tried to suggest in the title, Newman as 'theologian *and* spiritual guide'. Indeed, his insistence on the importance of 'dogma' derives in part from the realisation that our manner of *thinking about* God determines our manner of *praying* (or not praying) to Him, our manner of *seeking* (or not seeking) Him: our 'spirituality' is thus determined by, and in a measure dependent upon, our 'theology'. Whence Newman's insistence in his preaching upon such key doctrines of Christianity as the Trinity, with a particular emphasis upon the theme of the 'indwelling' of the Holy Spirit by which Christ becomes an interior Presence who 'saves' us here and now from *within*. Yet nothing could be less 'disincarnate' than Newman's spiritual teaching. He proposes almost a programme of what I have ventured to call spiritual 'training', which involves amongst other things self-knowledge, a listening to conscience, faith as trust and obedience, a critical approach to language, the practice of self-denial, and the control of feeling. Ultimately, however, he proposes a spirituality of 'surrender', by which we *allow* Christ to enter into us and to transform us from within.

Part I of the volume then deals with the theme of 'Faith and Reason'. The nature of faith, together with its relation to reason, is a theme to which Newman repeatedly returned all through his life, from the first of his *Oxford University Sermons* to the *Grammar of Assent* and beyond. In 'Newman and the search for a "via-media" between Atheism and Catholicity', Arnella Francis Clamor sets out to examine the significance and the implications of his claim in the *Apologia* that there exists "no medium, in true philosophy, between Atheism and Catholicity" and that "a perfectly consistent mind, under those circumstances in which it finds itself here below, must embrace either the one or the other." To this end, she offers us a penetrating and lucid analysis of Newman's thought, examining his elaboration of a psychology of religious assent, his belief in the importance of 'first principles', his conception of the interconnection between the moral and intellectual life of the individual, and that of the role of conscience, of the primacy of 'dogma', and of the way in which we advance towards faith through the accumulation and convergence of 'probabilities'. She examines also the foundations of Newman's opposition to theological and philosophical 'liberalism'. The author then explores the phenomenon of modern 'atheism', engaging in a dialogue with a wide range of contemporary philosophers and theologians, rightly stressing the ambiguity of the term 'atheism' which covers in reality a broad spectrum of attitudes and dispositions, and asking whether the dialogue with certain 'atheists' may not lead Christians to reflect on and to purify their own faith.

Next, Jane Rupert offers a spirited discussion of Newman's thinking on education. In her view, he 'continues to speak to us with urgency' in that, like an Old Testament prophet, 'he reminds us of perennial principles and premises either forgotten or denied'. By means of an extended comparison between Newman and Rousseau, she contrasts two radically different forms of epistemology and of rationality, which derive from two opposing traditions of which she brilliantly brings out the philosophical and theological implications – the one going back to Classical Antiquity, the other a product of a narrow materialism which, originating in the seventeenth century, underpins the thought of the eighteenth-century Enlightenment and of the mainstream of Western educational thought ever since. Newman defends 'the tradition of universal knowledge or knowledge understood as a complete whole' and the existence of differing forms of reason, each applicable in its own domain but not necessarily in others; he thus views education as a form of intellectual training, requiring method and rigour and leading to the acquisition of a 'connected' view of all things. Rousseau's purely empirical approach, on the other hand, based on the idea that the child must discover everything for himself rather than being taught, leads to a 'closing of the mind', to knowledge becoming 'entirely self-referential', and to the acquisition of a rudimentary, piecemeal and catastrophically truncated view of reality. To an age characterized by a 'narrow idea of reason' which 'permeates contemporary pedagogical practice', and by the 'tyranny of empirical epistemology' (which undoubtedly contribute – one might add – to the pretensions of modern man to self-sufficiency and autonomy), Newman offers an extremely valuable antidote.

In his famous *Biglietto* speech, delivered on the occasion of his elevation to the Cardinalate in 1879, Newman asserted that his entire intellectual career could and should be seen as a struggle against "liberalism in religion" which he characterized as "a great mischief" and "an error overspreading, as a snare, the whole earth". In 'Newman on liberalism in religion', Robert Barron sets out to explore the anomaly that this 'scourge of liberalism' should today be the 'hero' of so many self-proclaimed 'liberals'. All depends, obviously, on definitions.

Newman himself defines the 'liberalism' he attacks as "the doctrine that there is no positive truth in religion, but that one creed is as good as another"; it "teaches that all religions are to be tolerated for all are matters of opinion." According to the author, the liberalism fought against by Newman contains two chief characteristics: its 'denial of an intellectual content to the Christian faith', that is its 'tendency to reduce Christianity to feeling and subjective sentiment'; and 'its insistence that reason appropriately positions and interprets faith'. Through an analysis of *The Idea of a University* and the *Grammar of Assent*, he shows Newman's spirited defence of the intellectual solidity of Christianity – and therefore of the rightful place of theology in a university curriculum – and examines his understanding of the nature of 'reason'. To this end, he discusses Newman's relationship to the philosophy of John Locke, the father of English empiricism, arguing that the interpretative key to the *Grammar* lies in seeing it as 'a sustained argument against Locke's liberal understanding of the relationship between inference and assent' and that 'the refutation of Locke is crucial to Newman's battle with liberalism'. The 'sharp demarcation between faith and reason' advocated by Locke and his followers is, in Newman's eyes, false; for in reality reason and faith 'operate in remarkably similar ways', religious faith being, in Newman's words, "the reasoning of a religious mind".

Part II, 'The Church', opens with a chapter by David Gréa on 'Newman's understanding of the Church' which sets out to examine both his ecclesiology and the contribution which the latter can bring to the search for Christian unity. The author discusses the relationship in Newman's mind between faith and the Church ('faith' being understood here in the widely current modern sense of a body of beliefs, rather than in the Biblical sense of trust or confidence in a person, in the context of a relationship). He traces the development of Newman's ecclesiological views, bringing out his progressive discovery of the 'Visible' Church (as opposed to the 'Invisible', purely 'spiritual' Church of certain Protestant theologians), stressing the importance for Newman of the two key principles of 'apostolicity' – the existence of an unbroken continuity between the Early Church and that of the present day – and 'catholicity' or universality. (The exact relationship between the two principles in Newman's mind is actually more complex than he leads us to believe in the *Apologia*.) The author also briefly examines the manner in which Newman's experience as a Catholic of the functioning of ecclesial authority led him to develop a complex and extremely nuanced understanding of the relationship between the various actors in the Church, and concludes by asking whether the questions posed by the Anglican Newman are not nowadays 'uttered by many a Catholic'. In such a context, he argues, a reading of Newman 'would undoubtedly prove extremely useful to our time'.

In 'Newman, the Church and the world', Andrew Nash explores the manner in which Newman's historical experience as both an Anglican and a Catholic led him to believe in the necessity for the Church to maintain a critical distance between itself and 'the world', that is the political and social realities in the midst of which it found itself. His reading of the Church Fathers and his study of the history of the Early Church – in particular that of the Arian heresy and of the role of St Athanasius, the great champion of orthodoxy in the face of political pressures – pointed in the same direction, leading him to the conclusion that the Church was 'in its origins counter-cultural', something which 'he would understand more profoundly once he became a Catholic'. Indeed, Newman saw 'that the Church must struggle with the world to preserve and teach the truth it has received from Christ'; it must maintain and defend its autonomy, as he put it himself, "against the world". As an Anglican, and even more as a Catholic, he criticized freely the 'worldliness' which he saw in 'establishment Christianity'. Given the fact that, despite our cherished claims to individualism, in reality today 'we live in a more conformist world than ever' in which 'political correctness' tends to subsume other values, Newman has perhaps something still to teach us in this domain.

Edward Miller next undertakes to explore 'Newman's teaching on the Sense of the Faithful', or *sensus fidelium*. In a clear and penetrating study, he outlines the history of this (much abused) term and explores its meaning. Interestingly, though the concept is ancient, the technical term in question did not enter theological vocabulary until the nineteenth century, Newman most probably learning it from his Jesuit professor at the Roman College in 1846-7, Fr Perrone. And Newman himself 'as much as anyone can be credited with retrieving it for productive currency in Catholic thinking, such as happened at the Second Vatican Council'. The author then outlines the circumstances of the publication of Newman's famous but then controversial article 'On Consulting the Faithful in Matters of Doctrine', before examining Newman's own theology in this regard, which seeks to find a balance between *all* the different and complementary sources of authority within the Church. He concludes with an analysis of the fast-growing phenomenon (particularly in Protestant America, but existing also throughout the whole Christian world) of what he calls a 'privatized biblicism', based on the three pillars of 'me, Jesus and the Bible', suggesting that a proper understanding of Newman's approach to the questions of truth and authority can help Christians today to achieve a more authentic and balanced vision.

In 'Newman, the laity, and the Reception of doctrine', Richard Penaskovic examines Newman's contribution to the development of an explicit Catholic theology of 'reception'. Once again, the term is of recent coinage, post-dating even Newman, though the concept is an ancient one, with which Newman himself was fully familiar. The author examines the development of Newman's thought through an analysis of *The Arians of the Fourth Century*, the first volume of the *Via Media* (originally published in 1837 as *The Prophetical Office of the Church*), the little-studied *Newman-Perrone Paper on Development* (in which Newman summarized in Latin, for the benefit of Fr Perrone, the essence of his argument in the *Essay on the Development of Christian Doctrine* of 1845), before looking briefly at the essay 'On Consulting the Faithful in Matters of Doctrine'. He rightly emphasizes that Newman 'did not think of the hierarchy and the laity in opposition to each other' but saw them as working together, using the Latin term *conspiratio*, literally 'breathing together', to describe this relationship. In conclusion, he finds Newman's relevance today to consist in three points: Newman believes that 'one of the main duties of the laity is to strive after holiness', and stresses the role in this of faith and prayer; this condition being fulfilled (and – one is tempted to emphasize – *only* if it is fulfilled), the laity 'are to be consulted in the preparation of a dogmatic definition' because they (too) 'are open to the Holy Spirit'; and thus 'the witness of the laity to the truth of a dogma is an active one'.

In a splendidly clear and well-documented study of 'Newman and the Magisterium', Austin Cooper traces and examines the gradual emergence and development in Newman of a Catholic understanding of the role of the Magisterium. He explores the relationship in Newman's own thought and experience between 'doctrine' (which he considered binding on all Christians), 'devotions' (which may vary with each individual), and 'theology' (which may be the fact of one particular 'school' amongst many). Whilst Newman defended the role of the laity which he saw as 'being involved in the process of the development of doctrine', since 'the faith was given to the whole Church', he by no means denied a special role to the teaching authority of the Magisterium, which possessed in Newman's words "the gift of discerning, discriminating, defining, promulgating, and enforcing" authentic tradition. Lastly, he focuses on Newman's attitude towards the question of papal infallibility, the object of heated debate during the years both preceding and following its promulgation by the First Vatican Council in 1870 as a dogma binding on all Catholics. Whilst himself experiencing no difficulty with the concept, Newman distinguished between the dogma itself and the necessity of its correct interpretation, expressed doubts concerning the opportuneness and the circumstances of its promulgation, and severely criticized the intriguing and 'arrogant' behaviour of its 'clique' of promoters. Here too – as in the 1877 Preface to the republication of the *Via Media*, and as in his spiritual direction – he displayed his profound pastoral concern, in theological questions as elsewhere, his 'consistent attitude' being 'to allow people space and time to develop'. The author emphasizes the 'perennial value' of Newman's 'clear distinction between doctrine and theology'. Alongside (or above) the 'bedrock' formed by the 'dogmatic basis' of Christian life, there exists an 'area of freedom'. He concludes with the following words: 'To hold these two in a productive tension calls for a breadth of vision and a depth of charity. In a world which so often opts for polarization, a Catholic sense of unity and diversity in an atmosphere of mutual respect and love is surely the ideal.'

Finally, Jean Rencki discusses 'Newman and Vatican II'. Given that 'influences' are notoriously difficult to establish, in whatever domain, he wisely restricts himself to demonstrating the manner in which the Council 'vindicated a number of Newman's stances'. This he sees in four areas in particular. The first is that of Christian doctrine, based on Scripture and Tradition, as a living and developing truth: although Newman was not unique in this (his contemporary Johann Adam Möhler, at Tübingen, was working along the same lines), the author argues that the 'historical perspective of Newman is one of his greatest contributions to theology', helping us to understand that 'Tradition is always to be understood as living, not a fossilised or stilted tradition in unchanging forms', and that Vatican II's Constitution on Divine Revelation, *Dei Verbum*, is 'remarkable for its typically Newmanian historical perspective'. A second point concerns Newman's understanding of the Church. His sense of the Church as an organic whole in which all have a role to play is reflected in the very structure of the Dogmatic Constitution *Lumen Gentium*. A third area concerns 'the dignity of the human person', a theme stressed and developed by the Council. At the centre of the thinking of both Newman and the Council there is the doctrine of conscience, the author quoting an extract from *Gaudium et Spes* which speaks eloquently of man's conscience in distinctly Newmanian terms. (He also rightly notes in passing that, thanks to Cardinal Jean Honoré, who wrote the Foreword to the first of these two volumes on Newman, a celebrated statement by Newman concerning conscience has found its way into the *Catechism of the Catholic Church*.) The fourth and final area is that of inter-religious dialogue. Under the influence of the Church Fathers (and in marked distinction to most other theologians of his time), Newman was led to see in 'pagan' religions what the Council (following also the Fathers) would call *semini Verbi*, traces of a Christic presence in which could be detected the workings of the Holy Spirit. The author concludes by suggesting that, if a motto could be attributed to Ecumenical Councils, that for Vatican II would undoubtedly be Newman's own, chosen on his elevation to the Cardinalate: *cor ad cor loquitur!*

Part III is devoted to exploring Newman's teaching on conscience. In the eyes of Pope Benedict XVI, speaking in 1990 as the then Cardinal Ratzinger, Newman's teaching on conscience 'became an important foundation for theological personalism' and made 'a decisive contribution to the renewal of theology'.[1] The subject receives a clear and masterly exposition by Luc Terlinden. He rightly emphasizes Newman's denunciation of the modern, secularized, purely subjective and individualistic conception of conscience, so different from the traditional Christian one, and points to the 'properly religious dimension of conscience' which is 'central to Newman's view'. (Perhaps we could add here that the word 'conscience' as used by Newman retains something of the sense of the French word from which it derives, namely that of *consciousness*: through our 'conscience', we become aware or conscious of a mysterious Other, present in the depths of our own self-awareness.) The author analyses the distinction made by Newman between conscience as a simple

---

[1] In a speech at the Academic Symposium, "John Henry Newman – Lover of Truth", held in Rome in April 1990. See *Benedict XVI and Cardinal Newman*, ed. P. Jennings, Oxford, Family Publications, 2005, pp. 33-4.

'moral sense' (which, notoriously, varies from one individual and one civilisation to another) and what he calls a 'sense of duty': it is this latter which grounds his view of conscience as the 'voice' of God manifesting itself in the 'heart' of man. It is in fact for Newman the experience of conscience which 'makes a real and concrete experience of God possible'. Thus attention to, or neglect of, our conscience is of incalculable importance for our spiritual life, which can either progressively deepen or – alternatively – wither away.

In a penetrating analysis, the author then examines the relationship between 'conscience' and 'reason', stressing the multiple meanings of the latter term. Basing himself on the work of the Canadian philosopher Charles Taylor (the subject, along with Newman, of his recently published doctoral thesis), he discusses the shift which has taken place during the modern era from a 'substantial' to a 'procedural' conception of reason. In the former, 'rationality is linked to the perception of a moral order' and 'practical wisdom consisted in perceiving an order at work in nature'. From Descartes onwards, however, 'it is reason itself which will construct its own order, according to its own norms'. Scientific 'rationality' will increasingly invade all forms of knowledge, usurping the place of all other forms of reason. The rejection of the idea of a pre-existent order of values and meaning will lead to the exaltation of the freedom and autonomy of the individual. Such an attitude was, in Newman's eyes, undermining the very foundations of Christianity. Far from rejecting reason, however, he sought to place it within the context of a 'holistic understanding of the human person', which 'revolves around the ethical-religious experience of conscience'. Finally, to illustrate his ideas Newman brings to light two diametrically opposed attitudes, that of the 'rationalist', for whom 'reason has become the measure of being and of religious truths', and that of the 'religious man', in whom 'reason is integrated in ... the self and [its] essential relationship with God'.

This section concludes with Bernard Mahoney's chapter on 'Newman and moral liberalism', in which he argues that if Newman 'opposed moral liberalism' it was 'because it undermined the judgments of conscience'. The 'moral liberalism' with which he deals here is essentially that of nineteenth-century utilitarianism, which 'rejected the traditional Christian foundation of morality based on the natural law, the foundation of the Christian conscience'. And the theme of conscience is dealt with chiefly in its moral, rather than spiritual, aspect or dimension. He traces the origins of utilitarianism in the

17

thought of a number of philosophers of the previous two centuries, before going on to present, as a contrast to Newman's thinking, the ideas of Jeremy Bentham and John Stuart Mill. He then turns to Newman himself to show how his conception of conscience was radically opposed to that of Mill and other philosophers, and how, in his writings on the subject, he often appears to implicitly conduct a running battle with their ideas.

Finally, *Part IV* deals with various aspects of Newman's teaching on the development of doctrine, which was also declared by the former Cardinal Joseph Ratzinger, in the above quoted speech, to constitute, along with his teaching on conscience, his second 'decisive contribution' to modern theology.

In 'Newman, tradition and development', James Pereiro argues that, whatever the supposed 'influence' of Newman on the Second Vatican Council, 'at least in the area of doctrinal development, the Council made its own ideas he had coined and put into circulation in his 1845 *Essay*', the Council Fathers striving, like Newman, to articulate the two concepts of 'tradition' and 'development'. He stresses Newman's concern with the twin principles of continuity and identity in the context of Tractarian ecclesiology, showing the 'somewhat ambivalent relationship with Tradition' of Newman and the early Tractarians, and the relatively late conversion of Newman to the idea of development. But he also rightly emphasizes that Newman's conception of 'development' contains a personal as well as a general or philosophical dimension. Linking this concept of development with another key Newmanian concept, that of 'realizing', he offers a brilliant analysis of the latter, which cannot be understood apart from Newman's theory of knowledge and which has a bearing also upon his conception of faith: though the moment of 'realizing' may appear 'sudden and unexpected', it involves in reality 'the perception and subsequent conceptual expression of a "new" truth, as the result usually of a long process: the slow maturing of principles already held, accompanied by a deep and vital appropriation of such a truth'. Similarly, Newman's conception of development – which is radically different from the Darwinian concept of 'evolution' – cannot be understood apart from the concomitant concept of 'ethos' which – following the teaching of the Church Fathers – sought to link intellectual searching and moral uprightness. Thus the term 'ethos' designates a 'moral temper' which 'involves openness to God's action in the soul and a humble disposition of mind and heart – opposed to the self-sufficiency of rationalism or the self-righteous confidence of private judgement'.

Finally, in a reference to the contemporary scene, the author argues that in present-day academic theology, the 'connexion between the search for sanctity and theological investigation which was the mark of the Fathers and of the great theologians like Thomas Aquinas, Bonaventure and others is no longer seen as a part of the *bene esse* (well-being) of theology', whereas for Newman it was 'of its very essence' – as was also, in the latter's view, 'humble faith'. Thus, if Newman rejected 'a conception of Tradition fossilized in a particular era of Church history', his 'concept of doctrinal development was as far removed from rationalism as from any form of historicism involving a development without roots, without the anchor of Holy Scripture and Tradition'. The author's own conclusion is eloquent and worth quoting *verbatim*: 'Theology was for Newman a sapiential knowledge, not an exact science; as such, the moral temper of the individual plays a determining role in the direction of his thought. This was a lesson he never tired of repeating. At a distance of one hundred and sixty years from the publication of the *Essay*, Newman keeps reminding us about it.'

In 'Newman, tradition and nineteenth-century Protestant theology', Edward Enright declares at the outset that, apart from Newman and a handful of German Catholic theologians, 'the nineteenth century is the century of Protestant theology'. He therefore sets out to examine Newman's thought on the subject of tradition in relation to that of Friedrich Schleiermacher, recognized as the 'Father of modern liberal Protestant theology', and Adolf von Harnack, the 'Father of modern Church history'. He shows the progressive development of Newman's ideas, dealing in turn respectively with his *Essays Critical and Historical*, his *Lectures on the Prophetical Office of the Church Viewed Relatively to Romanism and Popular Protestantism*, and the *Essay on Development*, before moving on to an examination of the thought of Schleiermacher and von Harnack respectively. What the three men have in common, he argues, is that they 'approached theological issues by historical methodology'. Newman and Schleiermacher share also a common concern with 'the Romantic theme of the organic wholeness of reality'. In contrast to Newman, however, the two Protestant theologians held only a limited conception of tradition, as an interpreter of Scripture. And Newman differs from von Harnack in that the latter, while allowing a concept of doctrinal development, saw it as coming to an end with the Reformation, holding that 'doctrine of any kind was no longer needed after Luther, so that we study the history of dogma in order to be free of it'!

In 'Newman and the crisis of Modernism', Charles Talar offers us a clear, informed and well-documented historical account of the phenomenon of 'modernism', and of the attempts by several of its leading protagonists, in the early years of the twentieth century and in France in particular, to invoke Newman as one of their champions. He rightly emphasizes the complex character of 'modernism' and the over-simplifications expressed in official Church documents condemning it. He discusses the initial French response to Newman during his lifetime, when he was seen as the great figure of the 'convert', and the revival of interest in the 1890s, when two areas in particular of his thought were focussed upon by 'modernists', those concerning the development of doctrine and 'the grounding of faith'. He outlines the interpretation of Newman made by the exegete and theologian Alfred Loisy and the widely-read (but far from accurate) presentation of his thought and character by Henri Brémond, together with the contributions to the debate made by a number of lesser figures. In conclusion, he asks what it was about Newman's work, or the times themselves, that 'called forth so many and such incompatible representations'. He finds an answer partly in the fact that, as Nicholas Lash has suggested, Newman's *Essay on Development* did not present a single theory of development but 'the seeds of a number of such theories'. More important was the question of the relationship between dogma and history, which had by this time become a burning issue, leading amongst modernists to 'a new conception of truth, that of "relative truth" or historical relativity'. Such a conception represented a profound distortion of Newman's thought from which his reputation suffered, so that 'for several decades his name would once again be under a cloud, until his work would be taken up by a new generation of Catholic scholars and impact Vatican II.'

Finally, Thomas Ryba offers us a discussion of the relationship between science and religion, suggesting that Newman's conception of development can be seen as providing a bridge between the two. To this end he examines the ideas of a number of philosophers of science, and focuses in particular on Newman's criteria for distinguishing between 'true' and 'false' developments which he sees as opening up 'new avenues in the dialogue between natural science and religion because of the questions his thought answers'. He then engages in an extended comparison between Newman's concept of 'genuine doctrinal development' and the 'notion of progressive scientific development' put forward by the Hungarian philosopher of science, Imre Lakatos. Along the way, he also examines the validity of Newman's argument in *The Idea of a University* that theology should be considered a 'science'. His conclusion is that 'though certainly not natural science', theology is nonetheless 'a science-like discipline'.

What do these various contributions enable us to conclude concerning the *relevance* of Newman today?

In the domain of spirituality, he can help us to discover or rediscover the importance of the relationship both between 'theology' and 'spirituality' in general, and between our *own* 'theology' and 'spirituality'. He can help us to rediscover the richness of the spiritual teaching both of the New Testament and of the Christian tradition. And, thanks to his lucid and critical realism, he can help us also to avoid a potentially dangerous spiritual 'romanticism' and to engage in an authentic process of spiritual 'training'.

In the domain of theology itself, he invites us to pose the question of whether that discipline is simply an intellectual pursuit, engaging merely the critical intelligence, or whether on the contrary it involves (or *should* involve) also the 'moral temper', indeed the spiritual life, of the individual.

His educational thinking serves to remind us of the importance of 'first principles', and of the necessity of intellectual rigour, of method, and of the acquisition of (or striving towards the acquisition of) a 'connected' view of things.

In the domain of Christian faith, he reminds us that 'faith' is first and foremost not just a body of beliefs but an existential attitude of trust and confidence, involving us in a living personal relationship where true faith is inseparable from hope and love and culminates in a spirituality of 'surrender'. At the same time, his subtle analysis of the workings of the human mind, and of the complex processes by which the mind attains to religious belief – amounting in effect to a psychology and a phenomenology of belief – still has much to teach us. He invites us thus to enter also the domain of epistemology, and to ask the questions: '*how* do we know what we think we know?' and, 'what are the *foundations* of that knowledge?'

His teaching on conscience is a particularly rich source of inspiration also. Newman invites us to see in the phenomenon of conscience not merely a moral dimension, but also, and simultaneously, a spiritual one, inviting us to deepen our interior life in which morality and spiritual experience meet. The experience of God in the depths of our conscience, moreover, common to all men, forms in Newman's eyes the basis of 'natural religion'. His thought in this respect opens up rich perspectives for inter-religious dialogue; but at the same time, he insists that the inchoative nature of the promptings of conscience underlines the need for Revelation in order to complete its insights. Perhaps one might add also that, for all the beauty of the teaching of the Second Vatican Council on conscience (in *Gaudium et Spes*, § 16), the scope and depth of Newman's thought on the subject goes considerably further than that of the Council. In this domain too, he still has much to teach us.

In his ecclesiological thought, Newman throws light on the nature of the complex relationship which exists – or perhaps which *should* exist – between the various actors in the Church, in particular between the laity, theologians and the Magisterium. He proposes in effect a dynamic vision of the Church in which there exists a not merely inevitable, but a necessary and salutary, tension, between each of three 'poles', a creative tension which it is essential to the well-being of the Church to maintain.

He reminds us also of the necessity for the Church as a whole (and for individual Christians) to maintain a critical distance between itself (and themselves) and 'the world' – not in the sense of a rejection of human solidarity, quite the contrary, but in that of a constant vigilance and critical attitude with regard to the values of any given society.

His conception of 'development' – which, despite the title of his *Essay on the Development of Christian Doctrine*, goes beyond mere doctrine to embrace *every* aspect of the life of the Church, as also of that of each individual Christian – invites us to reflect on the true nature of 'Tradition', on the relationship between permanence and change in the Church, and indeed on the personal 'development' of each one of us. Development is, in his view, a permanent feature of the life of the Church and of every Christian; yet this development must be rooted in a stability, a ground, a solidity which nothing can destroy.

Finally, contrary to what we might be tempted to think, Newman's lifelong struggle against what he termed 'liberalism' has far more than a merely historical interest. His description of this 'liberalism' as the belief that 'one creed is as good as another' and that all religions are but a 'matter of opinion' is reminiscent of the 'relativism' consistently denounced by Pope Benedict XVI, which he considers to be the greatest intellectual danger facing Western civilisation today. Perhaps one might add that, behind the emergence in recent centuries of the related phenomena of 'rationalism', 'liberalism' and 'atheism', it is possible to see another, broader development which is a feature of all post-Enlightenment thought – namely the tendency to reduce all religion to a matter of mere *ideas* (which can then be discussed, dissected and eventually rejected). Whereas throughout Christian tradition until then – and for Newman himself – religion was essentially about the search for a direct, personal experience of God.

One might even argue that our contemporary conception of Christianity has itself been strongly influenced by this tendency. When we speak of the 'Gospel', we tend all too often to think simply in terms of a 'message' to be proclaimed, rather than of a 'Mystery' to be explored and personally encountered. Newman renders us an immensely valuable service by reminding us that a full Christian life comprises three complementary dimensions – that being a Christian involves not only believing and acting, but also praying and entering into communion with God in the depths of our own innermost being.

PROLOGUE

Chapter 1

————

NEWMAN AS THEOLOGIAN AND SPIRITUAL GUIDE

by Keith Beaumont

What *kind* of a theologian was Newman? The question may seem surprising. He is after all increasingly recognized as one of the great Christian thinkers of the modern era, whom many see as a precursor of, and a powerful indirect influence upon, the Second Vatican Council (which the French philosopher and close friend of Pope Paul VI, Jean Guitton, once famously described as "Newman's Council"). He was capable of producing a series of powerful and original theological syntheses, as for example in his *Lectures on the Doctrine of Justification* (1838, an unjustly neglected work), his *Essay on the Development of Christian Doctrine* (1845), his *Letter to Pusey* (1865), his *Essay in Aid of a Grammar of Assent* (1870), his *Letter to the Duke of Norfolk* (1875), and the Preface to the third edition of the *Via Media* (1877).

And yet Newman himself resolutely refused the title of 'theologian'. The reasons for this refusal, the expressions of which date chiefly from the period immediately preceding the First Vatican Council of 1870, were multiple. The immediate reason was undoubtedly his reluctance to be drawn into the heated public debates of those years (concerning in particular the issue of papal authority), despite the requests of two bishops (including the leading 'liberal' amongst the French bishops, Mgr Dupanloup of Orléans) that Newman should attend the Council as their *peritus* or theological consultant, and even the express wish of the Pope that he should be present. In a longer term perspective, Newman's refusal of the title of 'theologian' was undoubtedly a reaction of self-defence – his theological orthodoxy had been called into question on a number of occasions, most notably following the publication of the *Essay on Development* in 1845 and even more so that of his essay 'On Consulting the Faithful in Matters of Doctrine' in 1859. But other reasons also can be suggested. Newman perhaps meant to indicate that he had never received any systematic theological training: he was in fact, in theology as in so many other domains, something of an autodidact, a development encouraged by the Oxford system with its emphasis upon wide and intense 'reading' rather than formal instruction. Nor was he in any sense a purely 'academic' theologian, concerned with the systematic elaboration of ideas for their own sake: his theological thinking is essentially pastoral, designed to have an immediate practical application in the lives of his hearers and readers, and all of his theological works, with the partial exception of the *Grammar of Assent*, are (in the French phrase) *oeuvres de circonstance*, written in response to an immediate challenge or need.

But there is perhaps a further reason which caused Newman to reject the title of 'theologian' as this would have been understood at the time. The neo-scholasticism then in vogue in the Catholic Church was an essentially *conceptual* creation, largely disconnected from its Biblical roots, from history and – most important of all in the present context – from *spiritual* experience. Newman's unease with regard to the contemporary understanding of 'theology' reveals in fact one of the central characteristics of all his thinking, his quest for what he calls, in a much-repeated formula of *The Idea of a University*, "a connected view of things".

A brief glance may be useful here at the history of the relationship between 'theology' and 'spirituality'. For the Church Fathers, and indeed during the first twelve or thirteen centuries of Christian thought, no such dichotomy exists as will later develop. The 'theologian' is first and foremost a man who meditates upon Scripture in search of God not simply as an 'object' of reflection, but as the 'subject' of a direct personal encounter and experience. (A celebrated statement by one of the early Desert Fathers, Evagrius of Pontus, even defines the 'theologian' as a man of prayer – the 'theologian' is "one who prays", and "every man who prays is a theologian".) Moral effort is seen not only in terms of a struggle against sin, but as a form of spiritual 'training' (*askesis*) whose object is to prepare the way for a direct personal encounter with God. And 'dogmatic' definitions and formulae have as their principal aim to *orientate* the Christian in this search for God. It was Newman's intuitive grasp of this truth, under the influence of the Church Fathers, which inspired his passionate study of the Arian heresy of the fourth and fifth centuries resulting in his first major historical and theological work, *The Arians of the Fourth Century*. For had arianism triumphed (as, under the influence of political pressures, it very nearly did), Christianity would have rapidly ceased to be a religion based on a spiritual communion between man and God and would have evolved in the direction of a mere well-intentioned moralism – as was increasingly happening in Newman's own day under the influence of an increasingly fashionable theological 'liberalism'.

The progressive loss of this unified (or, to borrow Newman's term, 'connected') vision from the fourteenth century onwards constitutes one of the greatest tragedies to have befallen Western Christianity. The great Christian thinkers of the thirteenth century – St Thomas Aquinas, St Bonaventure – are 'theologians' in both the modern and ancient senses of the word. Thomas, for example, as a faithful son of St Dominic, placed his extraordinary intellectual powers not only in the service of attempting to explain the divine Mystery, but also in that of helping men to come to an actual encounter with God. But from the beginning of the following century, a growing gulf appears between the 'scholastic' (or academic) 'theologians' and the 'spiritual' seekers and writers, the former (forgetting St Paul's warning concerning the dangers of mere 'learning' which can lead to spiritual pride) tending all too often to consider their purely intellectual activity as superior, and to despise the merely 'spiritual' writers – who in their turn express a growing resentment and hostility towards those whom we would today no doubt call 'intellectuals' (the author of the fifteenth-century spiritual classic *The Imitation of Our Lord Jesus Christ* is a typical example). As a result of this growing divide, 'spirituality' came to be seen increasingly in terms of purely personal, 'subjective' experience characterized more by affectivity or emotion than by any properly intellectual content – one distant source, among many, of the present-day confusion surrounding the meaning of the two terms 'spiritual' and 'spirituality'.[1]

It is perhaps useful at this point to reflect on the exact meaning of these two terms. In recent years, they have become increasingly

---

[1] This subject has been studied in detail by Dom François Vandenbroucke OSB in volume 2 of the excellent four-volume *Histoire de la spiritualité chrétienne*, co-authored by Louis Bouyer, Jean Leclercq, François Vandenbroucke and Louis Cognet, and published in France by Les Editions du Cerf between 1960 and 1966.

popular, not to say modish – 'spirituality' frequently enjoying a favour denied to the term 'religion', which in contemporary usage all too often takes on a negative connotation, being associated with 'institutions'. But this popularity has gone hand in hand with an ever increasing vagueness and ambiguity of meaning.[2] The word 'spirituality' in particular has become a catch-all term, reminiscent of Humpty Dumpty's claim that "when I use a word, it means exactly what I choose it to mean"! This is not the place for either a detailed history of the term nor an extended polemic, but a few basic remarks are nonetheless necessary here.

The word 'spiritual' ('spirituality' is a somewhat later creation) derives of course from the Latin *spiritualis* (or *spiritalis*), the equivalent of the Greek *pneumatikos*. Both terms are current in Classical Latin and Greek, but with a relatively weak sense – they refer to the wind, or to the bodily act of breathing, or occasionally to poetic 'inspiration'. But it is the advent of Christianity which – as with so many other key terms – infuses these words with a new and far richer meaning. In the language of the New Testament and of the Church Fathers, the word 'spiritual' refers directly to the workings of the *Holy Spirit*. Thus St Paul, in one of the foundational texts of Christian spirituality in his First Epistle to the Corinthians (2:12 – 3:3), distinguishes three constituent elements present in the true disciple of Christ, which he designates by the terms *sarkikos* (translated in the King James Version by 'carnal'), *psychikos* ('natural'), and *pneumatikos* ('spiritual'). The theme of the 'indwelling' of the Holy Spirit figures prominently in the writings of St John and St Paul, and for the Church Fathers the 'spiritual man' is one in whom the presence of the Holy Spirit dwells. For the next sixteen hundred years, in fact, the word 'spiritual' retains principally this sense: consistently, the 'spiritual' man is seen as one in whom the Holy Spirit dwells. The 'Spiritual Exercises' of St Ignatius of Loyola (the title of which, far from being unique to Ignatius, designated a widely employed and recognized *genre* of the period) employs the word in this sense. In 1646, a disciple of Ignatius, the Jesuit Jean-Baptiste Saint-Jure, published in Paris a work describing the 'perfect' Christian, one in whom the Spirit dwells, under the title *L'Homme spirituel*. And a few years later the founder of the Company

---

[2] In France, at least, certain 'philosophers' have gone so far as to propose a *false* etymology for the word 'spiritual' in order to justify their own use of the term. Thus André Comte-Sponville repeatedly affirms that the word 'spiritual' derives from the Greek *psychikos* and therefore designates all activity of the human *mind*, thereby justifying his claim to a 'secular' or atheistic 'spirituality'.

of St Sulpice, Jean-Jacques Olier, defined the true Christian as "he who possesses within himself the Spirit of Jesus Christ."[3]

The meaning of the word begins to change however from the end of the seventeenth century onwards, betraying an eclipse of the very dimension of Christian experience which it had served to designate: in the philosophical and literary *salons* of eighteenth-century France, the 'spiritual' man is one who is admired for the brilliance of his wit – the outstanding example being supplied by Voltaire! The Christianity of the eighteenth and nineteenth centuries (and also, it must be said, of the greater part of the twentieth century) is, in all the Western churches, Catholic and Protestant alike, increasingly, and often exclusively moralistic in content and tone. 'Faith' in the Biblical sense of confidence placed in a *person*, in the context of a lived relationship, becomes increasingly belief in and adherence to theological *propositions*. The true meaning of the doctrine of the Holy Trinity, which is the very cornerstone of Christian spirituality – God seeks to communicate his very being and life to us, a communication which comes from the Father, through the Son, and in (or by) the Holy Spirit – is increasingly lost. And, as a result, the relationship between man and God is perceived in purely *external* terms: whereas for Saint Augustine, God was "more interior to me than I am to myself", man is now seen as merely standing *before* God, who in turn is perceived above all else as Judge of all things. The 'spirituality' of the age – if indeed such a term can properly be used in this context – is as *un*-spiritual, in the Biblical and traditional sense of the word, as can possibly be.

It is in this context that the teaching of Newman came, for the vast majority of his contemporaries, as a veritable revelation. (Experience of teaching and preaching on Newman reveals that this is often still the case today!) But before outlining that teaching, it is necessary to examine one other aspect of his theological thought – his lifelong insistence upon the importance of 'dogma'. Let us begin by reflecting, yet again, on the meaning of the term. The words 'dogma' and 'dogmatic' have taken on, in popular contemporary usage, a pejorative meaning. But this is a distortion of their true meaning: *dogma* in Greek means 'thought' or 'opinion', the verb *dokeō* signifying 'I believe' or 'it seems to me'. It is in this sense that 'dogmatic theology' is still taught

---

[3] In his *Catéchisme chrétien pour la vie intérieure*, 1656, first lesson. Olier is here implicitly quoting St Paul in Rom 8:9: "Anyone who does not have the Spirit of Christ does not belong to him".

in our faculties of theology: it involves a systematic examination of and reflection upon the intellectual content of 'faith', or upon *that which* we believe.

Yet it was precisely the importance of 'dogma' that was being increasingly called into question in Newman's day, in favour of a religion of sentimental good intentions and mere moralising. Whence Newman's repeated insistence upon the importance of 'dogma': in *Discussions and Arguments*, he affirms that "religion can not be other than dogmatic."[4] In a celebrated passage of the *Apologia* directed against 'liberalism', which from the early 1830s onwards he saw as the chief threat to true religion and which he defined as "the anti-dogmatic principle and its developments", he declares that:

> From the age of fifteen, dogma has been the fundamental principle of my religion: I know no other religion; I cannot enter into the idea of any other sort of religion; religion, as a mere sentiment, is to me a dream and a mockery ... What I held in 1816, I held in 1833, and I hold in 1864.

It was this defence of 'dogma' which was, he maintains in the same passage, the "main principle" of the Oxford Movement, the "fundamental principle of the Movement of 1833."[5] Fifteen years later, in his *Biglietto* speech of 1879, Newman again stated emphatically that all through his long life he had opposed 'liberalism' and sought to uphold 'dogma'.

Yet we must ask what the purpose and function of dogma are for him. It is clearly not (if one may simplify to the point of caricature) a question of simply learning our catechism in order to obtain the approval of some celestial Schoolmaster. As an epigraph to the *Grammar of Assent*, Newman quoted a formula of St Ambrose, "*Non in dialectica complacuit Deo salvum facere populum suum*"[6] – an appeal to look beyond mere reasoning or ratiocination in the quest for God, but also a reminder that mere knowledge *about* or *concerning* God is insufficient in itself. Rather, right *belief* is essential in order to orientate our *spiritual quest* in the right direction. It is in this sense also that – as the above comments on the Oxford Movement clearly suggest – the essential thrust of the Movement was not merely ecclesiological, but spiritual.

---

[4] 'The Difficulties of Latitudinarianism', *Discussions and Arguments*, Longmans ed., p. 134. (Unless otherwise indicated, all quotations from Newman's work are from the 'standard' edition published by Longmans, Green & Co.)

[5] *Apologia pro vita sua*, pp. 48-9.

[6] It was not by dialectics (reasoning, argumentation) that God chose to save his people.

Numerous passages in Newman's writings express this underlying conviction. Thus, in the last of his *Oxford University Sermons*, 'The Theory of Developments in Religious Doctrine', whilst fully recognizing the inadequacy of all theological language to truly define God, he states that such language is essential in order to *direct our minds* to God:

> Creeds and dogmas live in the one idea which they are designed to express, and which alone is substantive; ... the Catholic dogmas are ... symbols of a Divine fact, which, far from being compassed by those very propositions, would not be exhausted, nor fathomed, by a thousand. ... Such sentences as "the Word was God" or "the Only-begotten Son who is in the bosom of the Father", or "the Word was made flesh", or "the Holy Ghost which proceedeth from the Father" are ... *august tokens of most simple, ineffable, adorable facts, embraced, enshrined according to its measure in the believing mind.*[7]

Similarly, in a sermon preached at Christmas 1834, speaking of the function of creeds and dogmas Newman affirms that these are a necessary complement to the Gospels:

> True is it the Gospels will do very much by way of realizing for us the incarnation of the Son of God, if studied in faith and love. But the Creeds are an additional help this way. The declarations made in them, the distinctions, cautions, and the like, supported and illuminated by Scripture *draw down, as it were, from heaven, the image of Him who is on God's right hand* ...[8]

And in the sermon 'The Humiliation of the Eternal Son', he assigns to words and theological formulae the function of "lighting up the image of the Incarnate Son in our hearts."[9]

To resume the argument thus far: our manner of *thinking about* God determines our manner of *praying* to Him (or indeed our inability, or refusal, to pray to Him); our manner of thinking about God determines our manner of *seeking* – or not seeking – Him. Spirituality is not a matter of mere feeling, let alone something vague, or wishy-washy, or sentimental. On the contrary, our 'spirituality' is *determined by* our 'theology'. It is this fundamental insight of Newman's which I have sought to express in the title given to this chapter: Newman as theologian *and* spiritual guide.

What are the sources of Newman's spiritual theology? They are

---

[7] *Fifteen Sermons Preached Before the University of Oxford Between AD 1826 and 1843*, Longmans ed., pp. 331-334. My italics.

[8] 'The Incarnation', PPS, II, n° 3, p. 29. My italics.

[9] 'The Humiliation of the Eternal Son', PPS, III, n° 12, p. 170.

undoubtedly threefold. In the first instance, there is his close reading and intimate knowledge of Scripture, with (as in the case of many truly 'spiritual' writers) a predilection for the writings of St John and St Paul. Secondly, he was undoubtedly influenced by his reading of the Church Fathers. Although Newman rarely if ever quotes his patristic (as opposed to Biblical) sources, and has so perfectly assimilated the thought of the Fathers as to make it his own, it is nevertheless possible in many places to find, if not an echo of, at least a parallel to the thought of, for example, St Augustine, or St Athanasius, or St Basil of Caesarea. Thirdly, a source of Newman's spiritual theology almost certainly lies in his own intimate experience of God. Though he displays all the reserve of the Victorian gentleman with regard to this experience, we can nevertheless catch a glimpse of it from time to time in his writings.

The celebrated passage in the opening pages of the *Apologia* in which he refers to his discovery of 'dogma' and (in the most discreet and indirect of terms) to his simultaneous personal encounter with God – the discovery of "two and two only absolute and luminously self-evident beings, myself and my Creator"[10] – finds an echo in a number of other passages. In the final chapter of the same work, he states that "the being of a God ... is as certain to me as the certainty of my own existence ... Were it not for this voice, speaking so clearly in my conscience and my heart, I should be an atheist, or a pantheist, or a polytheist when I looked out into the world."[11] In one of the first-published of the *Parochial and Plain Sermons*, examining the growth in self-consciousness in the individual mind, he affirms that "we begin, by degrees, to perceive that there are but two things in the whole universe, our own soul, and the God who made it ... To every one of us there are but two beings in the whole world, himself and God."[12] In his personal journal (not intended for publication), he noted during his pre-ordination retreat at St Eusebius in Rome in 1847 that, for all his failings and weaknesses, he had "not lost ... my intimate sense of the Divine Presence in every place, nor the good conscience and the peace of mind that flows therefrom."[13] And he attributes to Charles Reding, the hero of his first novel *Loss and Gain* (1848), the "characteristic, perhaps above anything else" of possessing

[10] *Apologia pro vita sua*, p. 4.
[11] *Apologia pro vita sua*, p. 241.
[12] 'The Immortality of the Soul', PPS, I, n° 2, p. 20.
[13] English translation of Latin notes, in *Autobiographical Works*, London: Sheed and Ward, 1955, p. 247.

"an habitual sense of the Divine Presence; a sense which of course, did not insure uninterrupted conformity of thought and deed to itself, but still there it was – the pillar of the cloud before him and guiding him. He felt himself to be God's creature, and responsible to Him – God's possession, not his own."[14] A parallel theme occurring in a number of passages, which undoubtedly also reflects something of Newman's own experience, is that every man can, in the innermost sanctuary of his own 'heart' or 'conscience', discover himself alone with God, *solus cum solo*. Thus, in a sermon of 1829, he affirms that "in religion each must begin, go on, and end, for himself. The religious history of each individual is as solitary and complete as the history of the world."[15] And in a sermon of 1839, he writes:

> The Christian has a deep, silent, hidden peace, which the world sees not, – like some well in a retired and shady place, difficult of access. He is the greater part of his time by himself, and when he is in solitude, that is his real state. What he is when left to himself and to his God, that is his true life. He can bear himself; he can (as it were) joy in himself, for it is the grace of God within him, it is the presence of the Eternal Comforter, in which he joys. He can bear, he finds it pleasant, to be with himself at all times, – "never less alone than when alone".[16]

Of the various doctrines or 'dogmas' of Christianity, none is more important in the context of Newman's spiritual teaching than that of the Holy Trinity. It is this which, together with the doctrine of the Incarnation, more than anything else sets Christianity apart among the three great monotheistic religions. To speak of the Trinity is to attempt, in our purely human language which can never be fully adequate to the task, to express something of a conception or vision of God as in His very essence *communication*. God seeks to communicate to us something of his own life or being, which is at one and the same time love, and forgiveness, and joy, and a deep inner peace. And he asks of us above all to make ourselves open to and receptive towards such a communication, so that we may indeed enjoy a form of communion with Him. Thus the Christian God is not simply external to man, but the 'subject' of an *interior Presence*.

Newman himself goes so far as to 'almost define' the true Christian in terms of this interior Presence:

> A true Christian, then, may almost be defined as one who has a

---

[14] *Loss and Gain*, Longmans ed., pp. 230-231.
[15] 'Steadfastness in Old Paths', PPS, VII, n° 18, p. 248.
[16] 'Equanimity', PPS, V, n° 5, pp. 69-70.

ruling sense of God's presence within him ... A true Christian ... is he, who, in such sense, has faith in Him, as to live in the thought that He is present with him, – present not externally, not in nature merely, or in providence, but in his innermost heart, or in his *conscience*. A man is justified whose conscience is illuminated by God, so that he habitually realizes that all his thought, all the first springs of his moral life, all his motives and his wishes, are open to Almighty God ... He alone admits Christ into the shrine of his heart; whereas others wish in some way or other, to be by themselves, to have a home, a chamber, a tribunal, a throne, a self where God is not ... instead of His being that true and better self of which self itself should be but an instrument and minister.[17]

And the sermon ends with an impassioned plea for us to recognize this fundamental truth and to allow God to enter into us:

Let us then beg Him to teach us the Mystery of His Presence in us, that, by acknowledging it, we may therefore possess it fruitfully. Let us confess it in faith, that we may possess it unto justification. Let us so own it, as to set Him before us in everything ... In all circumstances, of joy or sorrow, hope or fear, let us aim at having Him in our inmost heart; let us have no secret apart from Him. Let us acknowledge Him as enthroned within us at the very springs of thought and affection. Let us submit ourselves to His guidance and sovereign direction; let us come to Him that He may forgive us, cleanse us, change us, guide us, and save us.[18]

Such is Newman's personal conviction in this regard, and his sense of the importance of this teaching, that he actually suggests in the sermon 'The Religion of the Day' that Satan himself will do everything possible to prevent us from grasping it: "There cannot be a more dangerous (though a common) device of Satan, than to carry us off from our own secret thoughts, to make us forget our own hearts ... and to fix our attention merely on the God who made the heavens."[19]

So central, indeed, is this experience of God to all of Newman's thinking that, in a sermon which echoes St Augustine's celebrated declaration that God has created us for himself alone and that it is only in Him that our hearts will find repose, he affirms that it is only in "the contemplation of its Maker" that the "soul of man" will find true happiness. It is interesting to examine the nature of his argument here. Far from arguing along moralistic lines, Newman

[17] 'Sincerity and Hypocrisy', PPS, V, n° 16, pp. 225-6. The italics are Newman's.
[18] 'Sincerity and Hypocrisy', PPS, V, n° 16, pp. 235-6.
[19] 'The Religion of the Day', PPS, I, n° 24, p. 318.

takes as his starting point a detailed and penetrating analysis of our "affections" and of the nature of true "happiness". He recognizes that "the happiness of the soul consists in the exercise of the affections" and that it lies "in our affections being elicited, employed, supplied." There is no condemnation here of our normal human needs and desires, but merely a recognition that no purely human activity or relationship can satisfy our deepest longings. On the contrary,

> the thought of God, and nothing short of it, is the happiness of man; for though there is much besides to serve as subject of knowledge, or motive for action, or means of excitement, yet the affections require a something more vast and more enduring than anything created. ... He alone is sufficient for the heart who made it. I do not say, of course, that nothing short of the Almighty Creator can awaken and answer to our love, reverence and trust; man can do this for man. Man doubtless is an object to rouse his brother's love, and repays it in his measure. Nay, it is a great duty, one of the two chief duties of religion, thus to be minded towards our neighbour. But I am not speaking here of what we can do, or ought to do, but what it is our happiness to do; and ... our hearts require something more permanent and uniform than man can be ...
>
> God alone is the happiness of our souls ... the contemplation of Him, and nothing but it, is able fully to open and relieve the mind, to unlock, occupy and fix our affections. We may indeed love things created with great intenseness, but such affection, when disjoined from the love of the Creator, is like a stream running in a narrow channel, impetuous, vehement, turbid. The heart runs out, as it were, only at one door; it is not an expanding of the whole man. Created natures cannot open us, or elicit the ten thousand mental senses which belong to us, and through which we really live. None but the presence of our Maker can enter us; for to none besides can the whole heart in all its thoughts and feelings be unlocked and subjected.[20]

To speak of the Trinity, however, is to speak also of the respective 'roles' of the Father, of the Son and of the Holy Spirit. Thus a great many of Newman's sermons explore the different facets of this complex doctrine and their implications for the spiritual life of the Christian. Three aspects in particular of his teaching deserve a brief examination: the 'gift' of the Spirit and the effects of His presence in us; the relationship between the Son and the Holy Spirit; and the role of the Son and the Spirit in our 'salvation'.

The theme of the 'indwelling' of the Holy Spirit was felt by many

---

[20] 'The Thought of God, the Stay of the Soul', PPS, V, n° 22, pp. 315-18.

of Newman's hearers at St Mary's to be the most revelatory of all the elements of his teaching. It lies also at the very heart of the Oxford Movement. According to Newman, for the Christian the Holy Spirit is not merely the subject of occasional and fleeting visits, as was the case for the prophets of the Old Testament, but He becomes a permanent presence in those who prepare themselves to receive Him. Borrowing the Pauline image of the Christian as the 'temple' of the Holy Spirit, he affirms that:

> The Holy Ghost, I have said, dwells in body and soul, as in a temple … He is able to search into all our thoughts, and penetrate into every motive of the heart. Therefore, He pervades us (if it may be so said) as light pervades a building, or as a sweet perfume the folds of some honourable robe; so that, in Scripture language, we are said to be in Him, and He in us. It is plain that such an inhabitation brings the Christian into a state altogether new and marvellous, far above the possession of mere gifts, exalts him inconceivably in the scale of beings, and gives him a place and an office which he had not before. In St. Peter's forcible language, he becomes "partaker of the Divine Nature", and has "power" or authority, as St. John says, "to become the son of God".[21]

The Spirit is the source, in the depths of our 'heart', of a boundless charity: "He lives in the Christian's heart, as the never failing fount of charity, which is the very sweetness of the living waters." The man who "has the gracious presence of [God's] Spirit within him", when he comes to think of himself,

> prays, that he may be enabled to have towards others what God has shown towards himself, a spirit of forgiveness and loving-kindness. Thus he pours himself out on all sides, first looking up to catch the heavenly gift, but, when he gains it, not keeping it to himself, but diffusing "rivers of living water" to the whole race of man, thinking of self as little as may be, and desiring ill and destruction to nothing but that principle of temptation and evil, which is rebellion against God …[22]

It is this presence of the Holy Spirit within us which is the source of the 'holiness' or 'sanctity' to which the Christian aspires, in the eyes of both the Anglican and the Catholic Newman. In the Anglican sermon 'The Gift of the Spirit', we read that "holiness is really the characteristic of that gift which the Holy Spirit ministers now."[23] And in *Discourses to Mixed Congregations*, Newman declares that the saint

---

[21] 'The Indwelling Spirit', PPS, II, n° 19, p. 222.
[22] 'The Indwelling Spirit', PPS, II, n° 19, pp. 230, 226.
[23] 'The Gift of the Spirit', PPS, III, n° 18, p. 259.

"ever lives in the presence of God, and is thereby preserved from evil", his human failings, though real, are but "accidents, and are compatible with the presence of a determinate influence of grace, uniting his heart to God", and so he constitutes "a special witness of the world unseen."[24]

Thus Newman invites us to "contemplate Almighty God" simultaneously "in heaven" and "in our hearts and souls"; such, indeed, he maintains, is the "duty" of all Christians:

> For ourselves, in proportion as we realize that higher view of the subject, which we may humbly trust is the true one, let us be careful to act up to it. Let us adore the Sacred Presence within us with all fear, and "rejoice with trembling." Let us offer up our best gifts in sacrifice to Him who, instead of abhorring, has taken up his abode in these sinful hearts of ours. Prayer, praise, and thanksgiving, "good works and alms-deeds," a bold and true confession and a self-denying walk, are the ritual of worship by which we serve Him in these His Temples ... In this, then, consists our whole duty, first in contemplating Almighty God, as in Heaven, so in our hearts and souls; and next, while we contemplate Him, in acting towards and for Him in the works of every day; in viewing by faith His glory without and within us, and in acknowledging it by our obedience. Thus we shall unite conceptions the most lofty concerning His majesty and bounty towards us, with the most lowly, minute, and unostentatious service to Him.[25]

It is the presence of the Holy Spirit within us which turns our minds to God and enables us to recognize him as our Father, as taught by St Paul:[26]

> The heavenly gift of the Spirit fixes the eyes of our mind upon the Divine author of our salvation. By nature we are blind and carnal; but the Holy Ghost by whom we are new-born, reveals to us the God of mercies, and bids us recognize and adore Him as our Father with a true heart. He impresses on us our Heavenly Father's image, which we lost when Adam fell, and disposes us to seek His presence by the very instinct of our new nature.[27]

But this indwelling of the Spirit raises our minds "not only to the thought of God, but of Christ also."[28] For – as St Paul taught – the Holy Spirit is at once the Spirit of the Father and the Spirit of the

---

[24] 'Saintliness the Standard of Christian Principle', *Discourses to Mixed Congregations*, n° 5, Longmans ed., pp. 96–97.

[25] 'The Gift of the Spirit', PPS, III, n° 18, pp. 269–70.

[26] Cf. Rom 8:26 and Gal 4:6.

[27] 'The Indwelling Spirit', PPS, II, n° 19, pp. 224–5.

[28] 'The Indwelling Spirit', PPS, II, n° 19, pp. 226–7.

Son. Thus Newman reflects at length upon the relationship between the Holy Spirit and the Risen Christ. In a sermon preached on Easter Sunday 1831, entitled 'Christ, a Quickening Spirit', he affirms that:

> He ascended into heaven, that He might plead our cause with the Father ... Yet we must not suppose, that in leaving us He closed the gracious economy of His Incarnation, and withdrew the ministration of His incorruptible Manhood from His work of loving mercy towards us ... Before He went away, He remembered our necessity, and completed His work, bequeathing to us a special mode of approaching Him, a Holy Mystery, in which we receive (we know not how) the virtue of that Heavenly Body, which is the life of all that believe. This is the blessed Sacrament of the Eucharist, in which "Christ is evidently set forth crucified among us;" that we, feasting upon the Sacrifice, may be "partakers of the Divine Nature."[29]

And in a sermon of 1838, entitled 'The Spiritual Presence of Christ in the Church', Newman argues:

> No one, doubtless, can deny this most gracious and consolatory truth, that the Holy Ghost is come; but why has he come? To supply Christ's absence, or to accomplish His presence? Surely to make Him present. Let us not for a moment suppose that God the Holy Ghost comes in such sense that God the Son remains away. No; He has not so come that Christ does not come, but rather He comes that Christ may come in His coming. Through the Holy Ghost we have communion with Father and Son. "In Christ we are builded together", says St. Paul, "for an habitation of God through the Spirit." "Ye are the temple of God, and the Spirit of God dwelleth in you." "Strengthened with might by His Spirit in the inner man, that Christ may dwell in your hearts by faith." The Holy Spirit causes, faith welcomes, the indwelling of Christ in the heart. Thus the Spirit does not take the place of Christ in the soul, but secures that place to Christ ... The Holy Spirit, then, vouchsafes to come to us, that by His coming Christ may come to us, not carnally or visibly, but may enter into us. And thus he is both present and absent; absent in that He has left the earth, present in that He has not left the faithful soul; or, as He says Himself, "The *world* seeth Me no more, but *ye* see Me."[30]

Indeed, in the same sermon Newman even argues that, through his Spirit, this presence of Christ is even *more* real today than in the days of his earthly existence:

---

[29] 'Christ, a Quickening Spirit', PPS, II, n° 13, pp. 144-5.

[30] 'The Spiritual Presence of Christ in the Church', PPS, VI, n° 10, pp. 125-7. The Biblical quotations are from Eph 2:22; 1 Cor 3:16; Eph 3:17; and Jn 14:19.

This, indeed, is our state at present; we have lost Christ and we have found Him; we see Him not, yet we discern Him. We embrace His feet, yet he says, "Touch me not." How is this? It is thus: we have lost the sensible and conscious perception of Him; we cannot look on Him, hear Him, converse with Him, follow Him from place to place; but we enjoy the spiritual, immaterial, inward, mental, real sight and possession of Him; a possession more real and more present than that which the Apostles had in the days of His flesh, *because* it is spiritual, *because* it is invisible ... He enters into us, He claims and takes possession of His purchased inheritance; He does not present Himself to us, but He takes us to Him. He makes us His members.[31]

We find, too, in Newman's spiritual teaching traces of the patristic doctrine of the Incarnation, expressed in the oft-repeated formula that in Jesus Christ, God became man in order that man might be 'deified' or 'divinized':

Such then is our risen Saviour in Himself and towards us: conceived by the Holy Ghost; holy from the womb; dying, but abhorring corruption; rising again the third day by His own inherent life; exalted as the Son of God and Son of man, to raise us after Him; and filling us incomprehensibly with His immortal nature, till we become like Him ...[32]

Finally, in what way does Christ 'save' us? In the Evangelical doctrine from which Newman sought to distance himself from the late 1820s onwards, this 'salvation' was seen as having been effected once and for all by a past action, namely the death of Christ on the Cross, delivered up by God as an expiatory sacrifice for our sins. But the theological debate surrounding this question is by no means resolved today. If contemporary Catholic theology rightly places the emphasis not simply on the death but also on the Resurrection of Christ, we rarely stop to ask exactly *how* it is that Christ 'saves' us today. This is a theme with which Newman grappled over a period of several years. Not only are his insights as relevant now as they were then, but they have profound implications for our spiritual life.

'Salvation', he argues, lies not just in a past event, the death of Christ on the Cross, but in a *present process*. Christ saves each and every one of us, individually, here and now, through our *participation in his Resurrection*. Or, to put it in slightly different terms, through our own *transformation into Him*.

---

[31] 'The Spiritual Presence of Christ in the Church', PPS, VI, n° 10, p. 121.
[32] 'Christ, a Quickening Spirit', PPS, II, n° 13, p. 147.

Newman devoted the whole of one of his major theological works to this question, his *Lectures on the Doctrine of Justification*, given in the Adam de Brome chapel of the church of St Mary's in 1837 and published the following year. In a typical passage, he argues that Christ 'saves' us by transforming us progressively into Himself:

> Christ, who is the Well-beloved, All-powerful Son of God, is possessed by every Christian as a Saviour in the full meaning of that title, or becomes to us righteousness; and in and after so becoming, really communicates a measure, and a continually increasing, measure, of what He is Himself.[33]

Two years later, in one of his finest sermons, 'Righteousness Not of Us, But in Us', he returned to this same theme in an abridged form, arguing that if we are in no way the 'author' of our own salvation – it is Christ who saves us – at the same time this 'salvation' must occur *within us*, through the transforming power of the Spirit of the Risen Christ working in us. But this can only occur *to the extent that we accept and open ourselves up to* this presence and its transforming power; salvation and the spiritual life are thus intimately connected:

> [The] Spirit came to finish in us what Christ had finished in Himself, but left unfinished as regards us. To Him it is committed to apply to us severally all that Christ had done for us. As then His mission proves on the one hand that salvation is not from ourselves, so does it on the other hand that it must be wrought in us. For if all the gifts of grace are with the Spirit, and the presence of the Spirit is within us, it follows that these gifts are to be manifested and wrought in us. If Christ is our sole hope, and Christ is given to us by the Spirit, and the Spirit be an inward presence, our sole hope is in an inward change ...
>
> Let us never lose sight of this great and simple view, which the whole of Scripture sets before us. What was actually done by Christ in the flesh eighteen hundred years ago, is in type and resemblance really wrought in us one by one even to the end of time. He was born of the Spirit, and we are born of the Spirit. He was justified by the Spirit, and so are we. He was pronounced the well-beloved Son, when the Holy Ghost descended on Him; and we too cry Abba, Father, through the Spirit sent into our hearts ... He is formed in us, born in us, suffers in us, rises again in us, lives in us; and this not by a succession of events, but all at once: for He comes to us as a Spirit, all dying, all rising again, all living. We are ever receiving our birth, our justification, our renewal, ever dying to sin, ever rising to righteousness. His whole economy in all its parts is ever in us all at once; and this divine presence constitutes

---

[33] *Lectures on the Doctrine of Justification*, Longmans ed., p. 105.

the title of each of us to heaven ...[34]

We are here, obviously, at the very summit of the spiritual ascent, so to speak. Newman is inviting his hearers and readers to contemplate the ultimate heights to which the disciple of Christ can, through grace, attain. Yet he is no starry-eyed idealist, quite the contrary: nothing could be less 'disincarnate' than Newman's spiritual theology, and he is the sworn enemy of all forms of spiritual 'romanticism'. Indeed, his preaching reveals a tough practical psychology and a down-to-earth realism. If – as we shall see – he rejects the semi-Pelagianism which has characterized the attitude of so many Christians over recent centuries – the idea that we in some way 'earn' or 'merit' our place in heaven – he insists time and again on the necessity of effort and rigour. Yet these are not considered in purely moral terms, but rather in terms of what the early Christians understood by the term *askesis* – a spiritual 'training', akin to the training which they observed all around them being undertaken by soldiers and athletes (again, the origin of the idea is to be found in St Paul). It is one of the paradoxes (not to say contradictions) of contemporary Christianity that we willingly accept (even if we do not use the word) the principle of 'asceticism', with all that it implies of systematic effort, self-discipline and renunciation, in order to achieve success in such domains as sport or academic study, but rarely if ever do we apply it in the domain of spirituality – to the work of 'paving the way' within our souls for the presence of God.

It is possible here only to indicate briefly the key themes of Newman's teaching in this respect. Amongst the most important is that of *self-knowledge*. In the fourth sermon of the first volume of the *Parochial and Plain Sermons*, but the first actually to have been preached, 'Secret Faults', he insists that:

> Strange as it may seem, multitudes called Christians go through life with no effort to obtain a correct knowledge of themselves. They are contented with general and vague impressions concerning their real state ... But exact systematic knowledge they have none, and do not aim at it. When I say this is *strange*, I do not mean to imply that to know ourselves is *easy*; it is very difficult to know ourselves even in part, and so far ignorance of ourselves is not a strange thing. But its strangeness consists in this, viz. that men should profess to receive and act upon the great Christian doctrines, while they are thus ignorant of themselves, considering that self-knowledge is a necessary condition for understanding them ... Thus self-knowledge is at the root of all real religious knowledge; and it is in vain, worse

---

[34] 'Righteousness Not of Us, But in Us', PPS, V, n° 10, pp. 138-140.

than vain, it is a deceit and a mischief, to think to understand the Christian doctrines as a matter of course, merely by being taught by books, or by attending sermons, or by any outward means, however excellent, taken by themselves. For it is in proportion as we search our hearts and understand our own nature, that we understand what is meant by an Infinite Governor and Judge; in proportion as we comprehend the nature of disobedience and our actual sinfulness, that we feel what is the blessing of the removal of sin, redemption, pardon, sanctification, which otherwise are mere words. God speaks to us primarily in our hearts. Self-knowledge is the key to the precepts and doctrines of Scripture. The very utmost any outward notices of religion can do, is to startle us and make us turn inward and search our hearts; and then, when we have experienced what it is to read ourselves, we shall profit by the doctrines of the Church and the Bible.[35]

The theme of *conscience*, which runs through the whole of his writings from beginning to end, constitutes a further key element of this spiritual 'training'. It is important to grasp that the word 'conscience' as used by Newman refers not just to our *moral* conscience, but to our *consciousness* of a mysterious, divine Presence in the very depths of our own consciousness of ourselves. This conscience can be dimmed and finally disappear if we choose to ignore it, just as, if we try to develop our attentiveness to the 'voice' which speaks within us, it can become progressively sharper and clearer. A passage from a sermon of 1834 is particularly revealing of one key aspect of Newman's thought here: in contrast to the modern, secularized, purely subjective conception of conscience, which tends, according to Newman, to enclose us within our own 'selves' – leading ultimately, as he will argue in *The Idea of a University*, to "an intense self-contemplation"[36] – attentiveness to the true voice of conscience leads the "man of religious mind" to "look out of and beyond self", to be "at once thrown out of himself, by the very Voice which speaks within him." Thus we discover God as at one and the same time immanent – present in the depths of our own 'conscience' or 'heart' – and transcendent: the man who is attentive to his conscience "looks out of himself for that Living Word to which he may attribute what has echoed in his heart."[37] (Such expressions as "out of and beyond self" and to be "thrown out of oneself" are of particular importance in Newman's work, and are deserving of a study in their own right.)

---

[35] 'Secret Faults', PPS, I, n° 4, pp. 42–43.
[36] *The Idea of a University*, Longmans ed., p. 192.
[37] 'Faith Without Sight', PPS, II, n° 2, pp. 17–18.

This concept of conscience is closely linked also in Newman's teaching with that of *faith*: faith involves, amongst other things, the readiness to listen to, and to obey, the 'inner voice' which resonates in the depths of our being. Newman urges his hearers and readers to

> learn ... to walk *by faith* ... Let us aim at, let us reach after and (as it were) catch at the things of the next world. There is a voice within us, which assures us that there is something higher than earth. We cannot analyze, define, contemplate what it is that thus whispers to us. It has no shape or material form. There is that in our hearts which prompts us to religion, and which condemns and chastises sin. And this yearning of our nature is met and sustained, it finds an object to rest upon, when it hears of the existence of an All-powerful, All-gracious Creator. It incites us to a noble faith in what we cannot see. Faith and humility are the only spells which conjure up the image of heavenly things into the letter of inspiration; and faith and humility consist, not in going about to prove, but in the outset confiding on the testimony of others ... Faith and obedience are the main things; believe and do, and pray to God for light, and you will reason well without knowing it.[38]

As the closing words of this extract indicate, alongside faith the theme of *obedience* also takes on a particular importance. This 'obedience' is to be understood both in terms of self-discipline and rigour, and in terms of attentiveness, the verb 'to obey' deriving from the Latin *ob-audire*, to listen attentively. But faith is understood by Newman also as a fundamental disposition: it is at once a *habit* of mind, a recognition of our *dependence* upon God, and ultimately the expression of a desire to place ourselves totally *in his hands*:

> What is meant by faith? it is to feel in good earnest that we are creatures of God; it is a practical perception of the unseen world; it is to understand that this world is not enough for our happiness, to look beyond it towards God, to realize His presence, to wait upon Him, to endeavour to learn and to do His will, and to seek our good from Him. It is not a mere temporary strong act or impetuous feeling of the mind, an impression or a view coming upon it, but it is a *habit*, a state of mind, lasting and consistent. To have faith in God is to surrender one's-self to God, humbly to put one's interests, or to wish to be allowed to put them into His hands who is the Sovereign Giver of all good.[39]

A further illustration of Newman's hard-headed realism can be seen in his repeated criticisms of a Christianity which is merely a

---

[38] 'Faith Without Demonstration', PPS, VI, n° 23, pp. 339–41.
[39] 'Faith and Obedience', PPS, III, n° 6, pp. 79–80.

matter of *words* and abstract *ideas*. Nothing is easier, he argues, than to mistake mere words for the reality which they serve to designate or towards which they point. A whole sermon is devoted to the dangers (expressed in the title) of 'Unreal Words', and numerous passages in other sermons denounce the trap into which we so easily and so commonly fall in this regard: "There cannot be a more fatal mistake than to suppose we see what the doctrine means, as soon as we can use the words which signify it."[40] "We are apt to speak of soul and body, as if we could distinguish between them, and knew much about them; but for the most part we use words without meaning."[41]

Another frequently recurring theme is that of the necessity, for the Christian, of the practice of *self-denial*. Self-denial, Newman tells us,

> of some kind or other is involved ... in the very notion of renewal and holy obedience. To change our hearts is to learn to love things which we do not naturally love, to unlearn the love of this world; but this involves, of course, a thwarting of our natural wishes and tastes. To be righteous and obedient implies self-command; but to possess power we must have gained it; nor can we gain it without a vigorous struggle, a persevering warfare against ourselves. The very notion of being religious implies self-denial, because by nature we do not love religion.[42]

Elsewhere, Newman presents this self-denial as the essential criterion of the authenticity of our spiritual life:

> A rigorous self-denial is a chief duty, nay ... it may be considered the test whether we are Christ's disciples, whether we are living in a mere dream, which we mistake for Christian faith and obedience, or are really and truly awake, alive, living in the day, on our road heavenwards. The early Christians went through self-denials in their very profession of the Gospel; *what are our self-denials*, now that the profession of the Gospel is not a self-denial? In what sense do *we* fulfil the words of Christ? Have we any distinct notion what is meant by the words "taking up our cross"?[43]

And a little further on in the same sermon, he adds that we are not called on to perform great heroic acts, but to practise self-denial in the little details of everyday life:

> According to Scripture, the self-denial which is the test of our faith must be daily. "If any man come after Me, let him deny himself, and take up his cross *daily*, and follow Me." ... Accordingly, it seems that

[40] 'The Immortality of the Soul', PPS, I, n° 2, p. 17.
[41] 'The Resurrection of the Body', PPS, I, n° 21, p. 273.
[42] 'The Duty of Self-Denial', PPS, VII, p. 86.
[43] 'Self-Denial the Test of Religious Earnestness', PPS, I, n° 5, p. 66. The italics are Newman's.

> Christian obedience does not consist merely in a few occasional
> efforts, a few accidental good deeds, or certain seasons of repentance,
> prayer and activity ... Thus to take up the cross of Christ is no great
> action done once and for all, it consists in the continual practice of
> small duties which are distasteful to us.[44]

He insists over and over again on the importance of *time*, which
implies also regular self-discipline maintained over many years:

> Reading in Scripture how exalted the thoughts and spirit of
> Christians should be, we are apt to forget that a Christian spirit is
> the growth of time; and that we cannot force it upon our minds,
> however desirable and necessary it may be to possess it ... whereas,
> if we strove to obey God's will in all things, we actually should be
> gradually training our hearts into the fulness of a Christian spirit.[45]

He criticizes severely – doubtless with the 'Evangelical' Christians
of his time in mind, but the words are as relevant today as they were
then – the over-emphasis placed on mere *feeling* or on emotionalism,
both in general and more especially in the context of the Evangelical
conception of 'conversion'. Certain Christians, in the emotional
fervour which frequently accompanies such 'conversion',

> look upon the turbid zeal and feverish devotion which attend their
> repentance ... as the substance and real excellence of religion.
> They think that to be thus agitated is to be religious; they indulge
> themselves in these warm feelings for their own sake, resting in
> them as if they were then engaged in a religious exercise, and
> boasting of them as if they were an evidence of their own exalted
> spiritual state.[46]

And then when, as inevitably occurs, the emotional fervour subsides,
they imagine that "they are losing their faith, and falling into sin again."
Indeed, often "they do fall away, for they have no root in themselves.
Having neglected to turn their feelings into principles by acting upon
them, they have no inward strength to overcome the temptation to
live as the world, which continually assails them." Or else, "they seek
for potent stimulants to sustain their minds in that state of excitement
which they have been taught to consider the essence of a religious life,
and which they cannot produce by the means which before excited
them. They have recourse to new doctrines, or follow strange teachers,
in order that they may dream on in this their artificial devotion ... ."[47]

[44] 'Self-Denial the Test of Religious Earnestness', PPS, I, n° 5, p. 66-7. The italics are again
Newman's. The biblical quotation is from Luke 9: 23.
[45] 'Obedience the Remedy for Religious Perplexity', PPS, I, n° 18, pp. 232-3.
[46] 'The Religious Use of Excited Feelings', PPS, I, n° 9, pp. 118-19.
[47] 'The Religious Use of Excited Feelings', PPS, I, n° 9, pp. 119-20.

True spiritual progress involves not just feeling, but the role also of the *will*; it is the will alone which is the principal agent in all religious 'training': we too easily forget that "by giving utterance to religious sentiments we do not become religious, rather the reverse; whereas, if we strove to obey God's will in all things, we actually should be gradually training our hearts into the fulness of a Christian spirit."[48]

Another element of Newman's teaching concerns the subject of *love*. He criticizes severely those who confuse 'love' with mere feeling, together with those for whom it remains nothing more than a mere idea or abstract notion. Those who "talk magnificently about loving the whole human race with a comprehensive affection" are simply deluding themselves and others. Such declarations merely reveal "that such men have certain benevolent feelings towards the world, feelings and nothing more; nothing more than unstable feelings, the mere offspring of an indulged imagination, which exist only when their minds are wrought upon, and are sure to fail them in the hour of need … This is not to love men, it is but to talk about love. The real love of man must depend on practice, and therefore, must begin by exercising itself on our friends around us, otherwise it will have no existence … the love of our private friends is the only preparatory exercise for the love of all men."[49] Similarly, the love of God has its roots in human love and friendship; and the mutual love between husband and wife constitutes an excellent training ground for that same love of God.

An attitude of *humility* is also strongly urged by Newman (as indeed by all true spiritual guides and masters). An extract from a talk to his fellow-Oratorians contains an eloquent example of such an exhortation:

> I would beg for you this privilege, that the public world might never know you for praise or for blame, that you should do a good deal of hard work in your generation, and prosecute many useful labours, and effect a number of religious purposes, and send many souls to heaven, and take men by surprise, how much you were really doing, when they happened to come near enough to see it; but that by the world you should be overlooked, that you should not be known out of your place, that you should work for God alone with a pure heart and single eye, without the distractions of human applause, and should make Him your sole hope, and His eternal heaven your sole aim, and have your reward, not partly here,

---

[48] 'The Religious Use of Excited Feelings', PPS, I, n° 9, pp. 232-3.
[49] 'Love of Relations and Friends', PPS, II, n° 5, pp. 54-5.

but fully and entirely hereafter.[50]

Newman's teaching embraces also the subject of *prayer* and *worship*. In consequence of his spiritual theology, he recognizes, following St Paul, that at the deepest level of our being it is the Holy Spirit Himself who prays in us, and that

> as our bodily life discovers itself by its activity, so is the presence of the Holy Spirit in us discovered by a spiritual activity; and this activity is the spirit of continual prayer. Prayer is to spiritual life what the beating of the pulse and the drawing of the breath are to the life of the body. It would be as absurd to suppose that life could last when the body was cold and motionless and senseless, as to call a soul alive which does not pray. The state or habit of spiritual life exerts itself, consists, in the continual activity of prayer.[51]

But he also urges us to make of prayer a form of spiritual *discipline*, with specific and regular times and places devoted to it. Prayer is for the Christian a 'duty', willingly embraced in order to gain a 'privilege'.[52] It is the sole resource available to he who is "desirous of gaining comfort to his soul, of bringing Christ's presence home to his very heart, and of doing the highest and most glorious things for the whole world."[53] In opposition to the Protestant practice of *ex tempore* prayer, which tends – through the sustained creative effort which it demands – to turn us inwards upon ourselves, Newman recommends the use of set 'forms' of prayer which calm the mind and centre our attention on God rather than on ourselves.[54] Prayer, together with 'watching', constitutes the hallmark of the early Christians as the Bible shows them to us:

> This is the very definition of a Christian, – one who looks for Christ; not who looks for gain, or distinction, or power, or pleasure, or comfort, but who looks "for the Saviour, the Lord Jesus Christ". This, according to Scripture, is the essential mark, this is the foundation of a Christian from which every thing else follows ...
>
> Hence it follows, that watching is a special mark of the Scripture Christian, as our Lord so emphatically sets before us: "Watch therefore, for ye know not what hour your Lord doth come ... Be ye also ready, for in such an hour as ye think not the Son of man cometh" [Mt 24:42, 44] ...

---

[50] 'The Mission of St. Philip – Part 2', *Sermons Preached on Various Occasions*, n° 12, Longmans ed., p. 242.

[51] 'Mental Prayer', PPS, VII, n° 15, p. 209.

[52] 'Times of Private Prayer', PPS, I, n° 19, p. 245.

[53] 'Religious Worship a Remedy for Excitements', PPS, III, n° 23, p. 348.

[54] Cf. 'Forms of Private Prayer', PPS, I, n° 20, pp. 257 ff.

> And accordingly, prayer, as St. Peter enjoins in the last text [1 Pt 4:7], is another characteristic of Christians as described in Scripture … This habit of prayer then, recurrent prayer, morning, noon, and night, is one discriminating point in Scripture Christianity, as arising from the text with which I began, "our conversation is in heaven".[55]

As for public prayer or worship, a passage from an early sermon sees in this, and not – as was the then current view – in preaching, the principal *raison d'être* for attending religious services:

> Now if I were to ask, what is the chief reason we come to Church, many persons, I conceive, would answer without hesitation, we come to hear the preaching of the word of God – but this is a very incorrect statement … Men in this day speak as if hearing so called preaching was *the* great ordinance of the Christian religion, whereas the great ordinance, the difficult ordinance, and the most blessed and *joyful* ordinance of the Gospel is prayer and praise, and that not of one by one, but joint prayer and praise, of many together. Christ promises a special *blessing* on *joint* prayer which he has not pronounced on private prayer, and, though both public and private prayer are in one sense means of grace, yet it is the peculiar office of *public prayer* to bring down Christ among us – it is as being collected into one, that Christ recognizes us as His. And this then, and nothing short of this, is the great reason of our meeting together in Church for common prayer; – preaching (i.e. public instruction) being added, but only as a means of our praying better and living better. But prayer is an end, for it is devotion, an acceptable sacrifice, the Christian's life itself.[56]

To those who would make a distinction between 'believing' and 'practising' their faith, to the neglect of the latter, Newman invites them to regard regular collective worship not as a mere moral obligation but as a form of spiritual discipline and as a 'preparation' for our ultimate encounter with God:

> Now observe, that it is scarcely a sufficient answer to this question to say that we must strive to obey [God], and so to approve ourselves to Him … appearing before God, and dwelling in his presence, is a very different thing from being merely subjected to a system of moral laws, and would seem to require another preparation, a special preparation of thought and affection, such as will enable us to endure His countenance, and to hold communion with Him as we ought. Nay, and, it may be, a preparation of the soul itself for His

---

[55] 'The Apostolical Christian', *Sermons on Subjects of the Day*, n° 19, Longmans ed., pp. 278-281.
[56] *Sermons 1824-1843*, vol. I, edited by Placid Murray OSB, Oxford: Clarendon Press, 1991, p. 25. The italics are Newman's.

presence, just as the bodily eye must be exercised in order to bear the full light of day, or the bodily frame in order to bear exposure to the air ... And in the worship and service of Almighty God, which Christ and His Apostles have left us, we are vouchsafed means, both moral and mystical, of approaching God and gradually learning to bear the sight of him ... Direct intercourse with God on their part now, prayer and the like, may be necessary to their meeting Him suitably hereafter: and direct intercourse on His part with them, or what we call sacramental communion, may be necessary in some incomprehensible way, even for preparing their very nature to bear the sight of Him.[57]

Yet the rigour of this teaching – particularly evident in the early sermons – is tempered, increasingly, by a gentle Christian humanism, for which Newman will find a parallel and an inspiration, in his Catholic period, in the figure of St Philip Neri. The final chapter of *The Idea of a University* deals with the relationship between religion and secular culture, and closes with a panegyric of St Philip who, in contrast to the violent zeal of a Savonarola,

preferred, as he expressed it, tranquilly to cast his net to gain [men's souls]; he preferred to yield to the stream, and direct the current, which he could not stop, of science, literature, art, and fashion, and to sweeten and to sanctify what God had made very good and man had spoilt.[58]

In a sermon of 1838, Newman recognizes – not without a certain wry humour – that our very errors and failings can, in the end, if corrected, lead us to God:

We advance to the truth by experience of error; we succeed through failures. We know not how to do right except by having done wrong. We call virtue a mean, that is, as considering it to lie between things that are wrong. We know what is right, not positively, but negatively; we do not see the truth at once and make towards it, but we fall upon and try error, and find it is *not* the truth. We grope about by touch, not by sight, and so by a miserable experience exhaust the possible modes of acting till nought is left, but truth, remaining. Such is the process by which we succeed; we walk to heaven backward; we drive our arrows at a mark, and think him most skilful whose shortcomings are the least.[59]

Frequent also in his writings is a restatement of the old scholastic

---

[57] 'Worship, a Preparation for Christ's Coming', PPS, V, n° 1, pp. 6-8. The image of the eyes which must be 'exercised' or 'trained' to bear the light of the sun – and thus the divine Light – is frequent in the writings of such Church Fathers as Augustine and Athanasius.
[58] *The Idea of a University*, Longmans ed., p. 235.
[59] 'The State of Innocence', PPS, V, n° 8, pp. 107-8. The italics are Newman's.

adage – which the Jansenist-inspired pessimism of recent centuries had tended to cause to be forgotten – that *gratia perfecit naturam*,[60] grace is not opposed to nature and, in order to work, does not destroy it, but transforms it, bringing nature to perfection. In a chapter address of June 1848, Newman exhorts his fellow-Oratorians (all of them former Oxford men like himself) in the following terms:

> Aim at being something more than mere University men, such as we have all been. Let grace perfect nature, and let us, as Catholics, not indeed cease to be what we were, but exalt what we were into something which we were not.[61]

And in a lecture given in 1854, he states that "grace … has innovated upon nature, not destroying or suspending it, but bringing it to a higher order."[62] In a sermon devoted to St Paul, he sees the latter as a shining example of those, "of the highest order of sanctity",

> in whom the supernatural combines with nature, instead of superseding it, – invigorating it, elevating it, ennobling it; and who are not the less men, because they are saints. They do not put away their natural endowments, but use them to the glory of the Giver; they do not act beside them, but through them; they do not eclipse them by the brightness of divine grace, but only transfigure them … Thus they have the thoughts, feelings, frames of mind, attractions, sympathies, antipathies of other men, so far as these are not sinful, only they have these properties of human nature purified, sanctified, and exalted; and they are only made more eloquent, more poetical, more profound, more intellectual, by reason of their being more holy.[63]

And in another sermon – again not without a degree of wry humour – Newman meditates on "the means which God has provided for the creation of the Saint out of the sinner":

> He takes him as he is, and uses him against himself: He turns his affections into another channel, and extinguishes a carnal love by infusing a heavenly charity. Not as if He used him as a mere irrational creature, who is impelled by instincts and governed by external incitements without any will of his own, and to whom one pleasure is the same as another, the same in kind, though different in degree … it is the very triumph of His grace, that He enters

---

[60] 'Gratia perfecit naturam': grace perfects nature.

[61] In *Newman the Oratorian. His Unpublished Oratory Papers*, ed. Placid Murray, Leominster: Fowler Wright Books, (1968) 1980, p. 221.

[62] In *Newman the Oratorian. His Unpublished Oratory Papers*, ed. Placid Murray, Leominster: Fowler Wright Books, (1968) 1980, p. 276.

[63] 'St Paul's Gift of Sympathy', *Sermons Preached on Various Occasions*, n° 7, Longmans ed., pp. 92-3.

into the heart of man, and persuades it, and prevails with it, while
He changes it. He violates in nothing that original constitution of
mind which He gave to man: He treats him as man; He leaves him
the liberty of acting this way or that; He appeals to all his powers
and faculties, to his reason, to his prudence, to his moral sense, to
his conscience: He rouses his fears as well as his love; He instructs
him in the depravity of sin, as well as in the mercy of God; but still,
on the whole, the animating principle of the new life, by which it
is both kindled and sustained, is the flame of charity.[64]

In conformity with such principles, in his spiritual direction, practised
abundantly through his correspondence, Newman appeals consistently
to the inner resources of each person. Writing in 1846 to the wife
of his recently deceased intimate friend, John Bowden, inclining
to conversion to Catholicism, he expresses his total refusal to exert
pressure on her, issuing instead the following invitation:

Use the means which God has given you, as you have hitherto done.
As far as I know your course, you have almost grown of yourself
into what you are – in the course of many months, first by the
example of myself and others, next by your own judgment on the
present state of things, further by the general impression made on
you by history, and, not the least, by your knowledge of the gradual
tendencies of dear John. Here is the legitimate way in which you
are called upon to use your reason. God will bless you in such a
calm spontaneous use of it.[65]

To Magdalena Helbert, a woman also inclining to conversion but
troubled by innumerable scruples, Newman writes that "[God] does
not call you to join the Church till you know it is the Church – He
has helped you hitherto, and He will help you still."[66] And to the
intellectually demanding daughter of his friend Sir John Simeon, he
writes urging her to use her own intellectual powers in the search
for religious truth, honestly recognizing the difficulties that may exist
along the way:

You must begin all thought about religion by mastering what is
the fact, that any how the question has an inherent, irradicable [sic]
difficulty in it … If we say, "Well, I will not believe any thing",
there is a difficulty in believing nothing, an intellectual difficulty.
There is a difficulty in doubting; a difficulty in determining there is
no truth; in saying that there is a truth, but that no one can find it

---

[64] 'Purity and Love', *Discourses to Mixed Congregations*, n° 4, Longmans ed., pp. 71-2.
[65] To Mrs J. W. Bowden, 27 June 1846, *Letters and Diaries of John Henry Newman* [hereafter L&D],
XI, pp. 131-2.
[66] To Mrs Helbert, 30 August 1869, L&D, XXIV, p. 323.

out; in saying that all religious opinions are true, or one as good as another; a difficulty in saying there is no God; that there is a God but that He has not revealed Himself except in the way of nature; and there is doubtless a difficulty in Christianity. The question is, whether on the whole our reason does not tell us that it is a duty to accept the arguments commonly urged for its truth as sufficient, and a duty in consequence to believe heartily in Scripture and the Church.[67]

But at the same time, Newman urges upon his correspondent that mere intellect does not suffice to establish religious truth and that she must take into account also the testimony of conscience – inviting her to enter into the depths of her own self in search of God:

Another thought which I wish to put before you is, whether our nature does not tell us that there is something which has more intimate relations with the question of religion than intellectual exercises have, and that is our conscience ... You must not suppose that I am denying the intellect its real place in the discovery of truth; but it must ever be borne in mind that its exercise mainly consists in reasoning, – that is, in comparing things, classifying them, and inferring. It ever needs points to start from, first principles, and these it does not provide ... In physical matters, it is the senses which gives [sic] us the first start – and what the senses give is physical fact – and physical facts do not lie on the surface of things, but are gained with pains and by genius, through experiment ... it is the senses which *enable* the intellect to act, by giving it something to act upon. In like manner we have to ascertain the starting points for arriving at religious truth ... To gain religious starting points, we must in a parallel way interrogate our hearts, and (since it is a personal, individual matter,) our *own* hearts, – interrogate our own consciences, interrogate, I will say, the God who dwells there.[68]

Finally, Newman – for all his sympathy with the monastic life of 'separation' from the world – recognizes that the vast majority of Christians are called upon to 'contemplate' Christ *in* the world, in the midst of their everyday activities:

He [the Christian] will endeavour to discern and gaze (as it were) on the countenance of his Saviour. He will feel that the true contemplation of that Saviour lies *in* his worldly business; that as Christ is seen in the poor, and in the persecuted, and in children, so is He seen in the employments which He puts upon His chosen, whatever they be; that in attending to his own calling he will be

---

[67] To Louisa Simeon, June 25 1869, L&D, XXIV, pp. 274-6.

[68] L&D, XXIV, pp. 274-6. Continuation of the previously quoted passage. The italics are Newman's.

meeting Christ; that if he neglect it, he will not on that account enjoy His presence at all the more, but that while performing it, he will see Christ revealed to his soul amid the ordinary actions of the day, as by a sort of sacrament. Thus he will take his worldly business as a gift from Him, and will love it as such.[69]

And yet the *means* to this end remain the same for all Christians: they lie in what is traditionally known as a spirituality of 'surrender' to God. The Christian must 'surrender' himself to God, not in the sense simply of seeking actively to discern and to do his will, important though that may be, but in the sense of *allowing* the Spirit of God to enter into him and to work in him, slowly but progressively transforming him from within. Newman's very conception of 'faith', as we saw earlier, leads to such a disposition: having "faith in God" is, amongst other things, "to surrender one's-self to God."[70] And his insistence upon the recognition of God as our 'Creator' signifies, in terms of our spiritual life, the willingness to *allow* ourselves to be 'created' – or 'recreated' – by Him.

Yet Newman is at the same time perfectly conscious of the difficulty which even the most sincere Christians have in entering fully into such dispositions. In the sermon 'The Testimony of Conscience', he offers a devastatingly lucid analysis of our *resistance* to God despite all our professions of obedience, and of our reluctance to 'let go' of our own selves in order to receive Him fully into us and to allow his Spirit to work in us and thereby transform us:

> We are by nature what we are; very sinful and corrupt, we know; however, we like to be what we are, and for many reasons it is very unpleasant to us to change. We cannot change ourselves; this too we know full well, or, at least a very little experience will teach us. God alone can change us; God alone can give us the desires, affections, principles, views, and tastes which a change implies: this too we know; for I am all along speaking of men who have a sense of religion. What then is it that we who profess religion lack? I repeat it, this: a willingness to *be* changed, a willingness to suffer (if I may use such a word), to suffer Almighty God to change us. We do not like to let go our old selves; and in whole or in part, though all is offered to us freely, we cling to our old selves. ... We do not like to be new-made; we are afraid of it; it is throwing us out of all our natural ways, of all that is familiar to us. We feel as if we should not *be* ourselves any longer, if we do not keep some portion of what

---

[69] 'Doing Glory to God in Pursuits of the World', PPS, VIII, n° 11, p. 165. The italics are Newman's.
[70] 'Faith and Obedience', PPS, III, n° 6, pp. 79-80.

we have been hitherto; and much as we profess in general terms to wish to be changed, when it comes to the point, when particular instances of change are presented to us, we shrink from them, and are content to remain unchanged.

But such an attitude will not do; only one of total 'surrender' to God will enable us to receive his Presence into us, and thus to be 'saved'. The passage continues, not without (yet again) a touch of wry humour:

> But when a man comes to God to be saved, then I say, the essence of true conversion is a surrender of himself, an unreserved, unconditional *surrender*; and this is a saying which most men who come to God cannot receive. They wish to be saved, but in their own way; they wish (as it were) to capitulate upon terms, to carry off their goods with them; whereas the true spirit of faith leads a man to look off from self to God, to think nothing of his own wishes, his present habits, his importance or dignity, his rights, his opinions, but to say, "I put myself into Thy hands, O Lord; make Thou me what Thou wilt; I forget myself; I divorce myself from myself; I am dead to myself; I will follow Thee".[71]

[71] 'The Testimony of Conscience', PPS, V, n° 17, pp. 240-1. The italics are Newman's throughout.

PART I

FAITH AND REASON

Chapter 2

NEWMAN AND THE SEARCH FOR A 'VIA-MEDIA' BETWEEN ATHEISM AND CATHOLICITY

by Arnella Francis Clamor

A. Introduction: In Search of a 'Via Media'

In his autobiographical work, *Apologia Pro Vita Sua* (1864), John Henry Newman (1801-1890) proffered an enigmatic statement that eventually solicited much controversy:

> And thus again I was led on to examine more attentively what I doubt not was in my thoughts long before, viz. the concatenation of argument by which the mind ascends from its first to its final religious idea; and I came to the conclusion that there was no medium, in true philosophy, between Atheism and Catholicity, and that a perfectly consistent mind, under those circumstances in which it finds itself here below, must embrace either the one or the other.[1]

What is perhaps disconcerting in this statement is the stark disjunction claimed by a writer reputed for his extraordinary ability to perceive the subtle nuances in an issue, as well as to judiciously hold the polarities of an intellectual position. For the Anglican Newman was a man of the *via media*, always in search of a middle ground, of a broader perspective in order to view a problem. It took him almost ten years, however, before he realized the implausibility of his ecclesiological theory for the Anglican Communion as a *via media* between Protestantism and

---

[1] *Apologia Pro Vita Sua: Being a History of His Religious Opinions*, ed. Martin J. Svaglic (Oxford: Clarendon Press, Reprint 1990), pp. 179-80.

Catholicism.[2] Did his conversion to Roman Catholicism transform Newman into a man of the extreme position? Or was it a long and arduous gestation of thought that finally drove Newman to declare the impossibility of an intermediary position between Atheism and Catholicity?

Newman's statement, of course, cannot be justified without doing an injustice to the testimony and the defence of the faith undertaken by other religious traditions, both Christian and non-Christian alike. The theological value of this statement, we believe, lies in its revealing the logic of Newman's reflections on both religious formation and the development of unbelief. The very density of this statement conceals a lifelong struggle against the growing influence of anti-religious ideas and values in nineteenth-century British society in particular, and in educated society in general. Few of Newman's contemporaries understood the threat that liberalism posed to religion. Few of his contemporaries understood their faith in the depths in which Newman fathomed it. Newman had to confront the extremely complex multi-confessional world of nineteenth-century England. The lack of both a spiritual and theological compass made Newman pose the question: how does one avoid scepticism in religion? How does one find the subjective and objective criteria for truth in matters of religion? This was a question Newman struggled with all through his life. His reflection on this question will find an answer in his encounter with Catholicism.

The search for a *via media* between Atheism and Catholicity receives renewed interest when we consider the pedagogical problem of the transmission and reception of the faith in our contemporary secularized society. Practical questions arise: how is freedom structured by a cultural milieu that is marked by religious and ideological pluralism? How to transmit religious principles and values? How to update moral and theological formation? This chapter intends to re-examine the system of *first principles*, the moral and intellectual ethos, sentiments, mode of argumentation, practical expectations, etc., that govern the way to Catholicity and the way to Atheism, respectively, according to Newman.

---

[2] Newman thus wrote about this startling realization: "Protestantism and Popery are real religions; no one can doubt about them; they have furnished the mould in which nations have been cast; but the *Via Media*, viewed as an integral system, has never existed, except on paper." See Newman's *The "Via Media" of the Anglican Church*, ed. H. D. Weidner, Vol. 1 (Oxford: Clarendon Press, 1990), p. 13.

B. Newman's Method of Investigation

How does one concretely advance from theism to Christianity, and from Christianity to Catholicity? How does one concretely appropriate religious ideas? What form of development do these ideas take? In a letter to a friend Newman explains the three great principles that lead the believer, by an almost inexorable logic, from belief in God to belief in the divine authority of the Church:

> I have been accustomed to say that there are three grand principles; the first leading to the Second, the second to the third; 1 There is God and a Moral Governor, 2 that He has revealed Himself in Christianity, 3 and that this revelation is contained in the Catholic Church − hence in one thing I wrote now out of print I say 'Let a man but master this one doctrine (the Being of God) and he is already three fourths of the way towards Catholicism' that is, by the logical force of those true principles of belief which made him a theist.[3]

Newman, however, would describe the process whereby a person apprehends the idea of the living God from a predominantly psychological perspective. His distinctive psychology of religious assent would follow through the process by which the real apprehension of the living God in conscience is cultivated until the believer is led from theism to Christianity, and, in Newman's case, from Anglican Christianity to Catholicity.[4]

What was an intuition since his conversion to dogmatic religion at age fifteen was given fuller elaboration later in his long life. In his *Essay in Aid of a Grammar of Assent* (1870), written twenty-five years after his conversion to Roman Catholicism, Newman explained that the reception of religious truth is determined by the personal appropriation and application of what he calls an *organum investigandi*, or instrument of investigation, which constitutes the practical, personal

---

[3] *The Letters and Diaries of John Henry Newman*, ed. Charles Stephen Dessain, et al., Vol. 29 (Oxford: 1973-77), p. 317. Letter to Miss Lambert (November 1880).

[4] Newman explains his predilection for the psychological approach as a need for modesty in intellectual endeavours in which theory is so much linked to life: "I begin with expressing a sentiment, which is habitually in my thoughts, whenever they are turned to the subject of mental or moral science ... that in these provinces of inquiry *egotism is true modesty*. In religious inquiry each of us can speak only for himself, and for himself he has a right to speak. His own experiences are enough for himself, but he cannot speak for others: he cannot lay down the law; he can only bring his own experiences to the common stock of psychological facts. He knows what has satisfied and satisfies himself; if it satisfies him, it is likely to satisfy others; if, as he believes and is sure, it is true, it will approve itself to others also, for there is but one truth." (*Grammar of Assent*, pp. 384-85.)

way of giving an account of one's faith, and advancing in it. Newman explains:

> There is a certain ethical character, one and the same, a system of first principles, sentiments and tastes, a mode of viewing the question and of arguing, which is formally and normally, naturally and divinely, the *organum investigandi* given us for gaining religious truth, and which would lead the mind by an infallible succession from the rejection of atheism to theism, and from theism to Christianity, and from Christianity to Evangelical Religion, and from these to Catholicity.[5]

Newman was well aware of the complex process and the convergence of elements – sentiments and tastes, system of first principles, mode of arguing, etc. – that lead to the attainment of conviction in religion, or to descent into unbelief. We shall give a schematic presentation of the salient features of these antithetical orientations in the forthcoming sections.

C. The Way to Catholicity: Newman's Psychology of Religious Assent

This is perhaps Newman's most important contribution to theology and to religious education: the elaboration of a psychology of assent. With his *Essay in Aid of a Grammar of Assent* (1870) Newman has succeeded in articulating the intimately personal character of the reasoning process that leads to religious assent.

C. 1 Moral and Intellectual Antecedents: Conscience and Truth

The way to Catholicity involves, first of all, certain moral and intellectual preparation. For Newman these represent the moral and intellectual *antecedents* to religious assent: the education of mind and heart, the search for truth, the formation of and fidelity to conscience, etc. These are a prerequisite for any religious undertaking, for –

> Truth there is, and attainable it is, but that its rays stream in upon us through the medium of our moral as well as our intellectual being ... that perception of its first principles which is natural to us is enfeebled, obstructed, perverted, by allurements of sense and the supremacy of self, and, on the other hand, quickened by aspirations after the supernatural.[6]

Of these elements, the most important for Newman is *conscience*.

---

[5] *An Essay in Aid of a Grammar of Assent*, Note II, p. 499.
[6] *Grammar of Assent*, p. 311.

Newman sees conscience, not as an irrational instinct, but as a "constituent element of the mind" whose operations could be scrutinized. He also regards conscience as a special *feeling* of awe and reverential fear which, accompanying the consideration or commission of particular acts, imply the presence of an all-seeing Judge and Moral Governor. The originality of the Newmanian argument, however, lies in its elaborating the double aspect of conscience: moral sense *and* sense of duty, judgment of reason *and* magisterial dictate, the critical *and* judicial offices, personal apprehension of the Divine Law *and* the moral imperative to obey its transcendent injunctions.

It is the "sense of duty" experienced in conscience, however, that gives us a real apprehension of the presence of a transcendent and personal God. It is because our Conscience *obliges* us to do what we judge to be right, and to avoid what we judge to be evil, that we acquire an awareness of God's all-seeing Presence and Providence. Newman says that this authoritative voice − "or the echo of a voice, imperative and constraining"[7] − imposing demands over and beyond personal interests, possesses a tonality that one recognizes as always belonging, not to things, but to persons and to the order of personal relations. For Newman this intimate image of God in conscience is a global and synthetic image bearing within itself the divine attributes in an implicit manner.[8] What are otherwise partial aspects or disparate attributes on the notional order come together into a synthetic whole on the relational order: the gradual discovery of a God who is the ultimate object of all human longing and striving. Newman's heroine *Callista* gives expression of her personal experience of God in conscience:

> I feel that God within my heart. I feel myself in His presence. He says to me, 'Do this, don't do that'. You may tell me that this dictate is a mere law of my nature, as is to joy or to grieve. I cannot understand this. No, it is the echo of a person speaking to me. Nothing shall persuade me that it does not ultimately proceed from a person external to me. It carries with it its proof of its divine origin. My nature feels towards it as towards a person. When I obey it, I feel a satisfaction; when I disobey a soreness, − just like that which I feel in pleasing or offending some revered friend ... the echo implies a voice; the voice a speaker. That speaker I love and I fear.[9]

---

[7] *Grammar of Assent*, p. 107.

[8] See *Grammar of Assent*, pp. 113–14.

[9] See Newman's novel *Callista: A Sketch of the Third Century* (1855), p. 174.

For Newman, it is the cultivation of the personal capacity for relation with a transcendent being that underlies personal synthesis in religion, hence the importance of education in faith and conscience formation at an early age. Moreover, it is the fidelity to conscience that allows one to touch a higher power that eventually transforms one's vision of life and of the world. For Newman *religion* is not an abstract idea, but a personal encounter with the living God in human history. And the place of that encounter is not Impersonal Reason but the interiority of *conscience*: "The Heart speaks to the heart."[10]

C. 2 *First Principles in Revealed Religion: The Primacy of Dogma*

Secondly, Newman's psychology of religious assent involves what he calls religious *first principles*. In Newman's theory of knowledge, these are non-demonstrable primary judgments that ultimately ground all religious judgment and orient theological reasoning.[11] Because *first principles* are the dynamic motors of thought, they are responsible for the growth and the development of religious ideas.

If the central idea of Christianity is the Incarnation, then there is a whole system of principles that proceed from it. In his *Essay on the Development of Christian Doctrine* (1845) Newman enumerates the basic principles of Christianity:[12]

(1) Newman first mentions the principles related to the life of the believing intellect: *dogma*, *faith* and *theology*. God reveals Himself – in the history of the chosen people, in the Scriptures, in the life of the Church – and *faith* is our response to God's self-revelation. *Theology* is essential to the life of the believer as it serves to deepen the understanding of our faith.

(2) There are also the moral principles: the *malignity of sin*, the need for *grace*, the demand for *asceticism*, the possibility of the *sanctification of mind and matter*.

(3) Newman cites the *mystical interpretation of Scripture*[13] as well as

---

[10] St Francis de Sales' *Cor ad cor loquitur* was the motto chosen by the old Newman for his Cardinal's coat of arms.

[11] *Grammar of Assent*, p. 60. No one starts with a *tabula rasa* in theological and religious reasoning. Even atheist philosophers base their arguments on an epistemological paradigm: God does not exist. Why then do people still believe in God when there is no God to believe in? Hence, those who profess themselves *atheists* try to explain – philosophically, sociologically, psychologically, even bio-chemically – the upsurge and genesis of this 'religious' phenomenon.

[12] *An Essay on the Development of Christian Doctrine*, 6th edn (Notre Dame, IN: University of Notre Dame Press, 1989), pp. 324–26.

[13] Newman's notion of the *mystical* principle, unfortunately, was limited to the spiritual

the *sacramental* character of both Nature and Scripture.[14]

(4) Newman also added a tenth element, an ecclesial principle: the *development of doctrine*, a deepening of the Church's self-understanding as expressed in her doctrines. With this ecclesial principle of development, Newman's own spiritual and theological itinerary – his labours for the renewal of the Church of England in the Oxford Movement, and his subsequent conversion to Roman Catholicism in 1845 – adds an autobiographical note to his manner of elaborating the psychology of assent.

All these principles – intellectual and moral, mystical and sacramental, dogmatic and ecclesial – are interconnected. One principle cannot be overemphasized at the expense of the others without falling into heterodoxy. Any real theologizing must keep in mind this interconnection between the doctrines of faith and moral life (*nexus doctrinae*) as essential to orthodoxy.

For Newman, however, the most important is the *dogmatic principle*. The dogmatic principle affirms that there is an objective reality to the divine object of our faith, independent and prior to our willing it. Now, prior to the creedal propositions and dogmatic formulae that give a partial view of the divine mysteries, Newman claims that the Divine Self-revelation is first apprehended in a synthetic image-idea or vivifying intuition that is the very source of ecclesial life. Newman calls this 'implicit' master vision the *Christ-idea*.[15] This Christ-idea finds

---

interpretation of Scriptures. But while this spiritualistic reading of the biblical text is open to excesses, his great insight was that this mystical interpretation – because based on a life marked by a striving for holiness – heals the spiritual atrophy caused by a literalist and positivist reading of the Bible.

[14] Newman thus explains the *sacramental principle*: "Nature was a parable. Scripture was an allegory. Pagan literature, philosophy, and mythology, properly understood, were but a preparation for the Gospel. Without Revelation, the visible world would still remain without its divine interpretation; Holy Church in her sacraments will remain, even to the end of the world, only a symbol of those heavenly facts which fill eternity. Her mysteries are but the expressions in human language of truths to which the human mind is unequal." (*Apologia*, p. 27.)

[15] In the *Grammar of Assent* (p. 464), Newman identifies this "Christ-idea" to be an "imprint" of the image of Jesus Christ in the depths of our being: "A temporal sovereign makes himself felt by means of his subordinate administrators, who bring his power and will to bear upon every individual of his subjects who personally know him not; the universal Deliverer, long expected, when He came, He too, instead of making and securing subjects by a visible graciousness or majesty, departs; – but is found, through His preachers, to have *imprinted the Image or idea of Himself in the minds of His subjects individually*; and that Image, apprehended and worshipped in individual minds, becomes a principle of association, and a real bond of those subjects one with another, who are thus united to the body by being united to that Image; and moreover that Image, which is their moral life, when they have been already converted, is also the original instrument of their conversion. It is the image of Him who fulfils the one great need of human

65

synthetic expression in the Person of Christ united to His Church, and gradually comes to explicit awareness through catechesis and theology, prayer and meditation, as well as through active participation in the liturgical and community life of the Church.

C. 3 Method of Reasoning: The Cumulation and Convergence of Probabilities towards Certitude in Religion

The third component in the way to Catholicity is the method of reasoning. Newman explains the passage from unbelief to faith through a process of *informal* reasoning. Over and above *explicit*, discursive reasoning based on proofs and evidence, Newman emphasizes what he calls *implicit* reason, very much like Pascal's "reasons of the heart." In the process of assent, the imagination also plays an important role in making *real* for us what would otherwise remain as a *notional* apprehension of the divine mysteries.

In the *Grammar of Assent* Newman outlines his method of the *cumulation* of *probabilities,* the process of bringing together multifarious elements – life instances and events, profound desires and moral choices, personal experiences and reflections, contacts with spiritual persons and life in community, etc. – that lead to a religious conclusion. The *convergence* of these apparently independent probabilities constitutes the process of informal reasoning which – in spite of the paucity of proof or direct evidence – culminate in religious conviction.[16]

It is important to note that for this process of assent, the *mediations* of the Christ-idea play a cardinal role. For Newman, these are not just a support for faith, as some religious writers construed it, but the normal way by which the Christ-idea – i.e. the Person of Jesus Christ united to His Church – is mediated to us. These mediations of the Christ-idea include: the Church and the Sacraments, Scripture, authority, tradition, personal testimony and influence. One cannot expect a deepening of faith without cultivating a moral and spiritual life, or participating in the life of the Church. Personal influences and authentic witnesses are of prime importance, too. Moreover, in the mediation of the Christ-idea, the study of the works of sacred authors fulfils a role analogous to that realized by personal influence in the propagation of Gospel truth.[17] As the writings of the sacred authors

---

nature, the Healer of its wounds, the Physician of the soul, this Image it is which both creates faith, and then rewards it."

[16] See *Grammar of Assent*, pp. 288, 293.

[17] See Newman's 'Personal Influence, the Means of Propagating the Truth,' in *Fifteen Sermons*

present a personal synthesis of the Christian doctrine, the authentic witness reveals a personal synthesis of the Christian character.

The object of this process of bringing together different probable evidences is, of course, the attainment of *certitude* or conviction in religion. Newman, however, concedes that while "certitude is the result of arguments that are but *probabilities*,"[18] much depends on the personal appropriation of right or false reason, good or bad theism; hence, the importance of acquiring the right moral and intellectual attitude, of correctly understanding religious first principles or premises, and of applying the appropriate method of reasoning.

D. The Way to Atheism

The anti-religious orientation is not as systematically investigated in Newman's writings. Modern atheism was still at a nascent stage during Newman's time. Although Newman had predicted already in the 1850s its terrible advent,[19] he did not foresee the complex global configuration of the phenomenon that is modern atheism. The elements that, for Newman, constitute the way to atheism are subsumed under a broader phenomenon. What Newman portrays is a physiognomy of unbelief seen through the prism of liberalism, and its result, scepticism in religion.

Newman's writings on liberalism, however, are mostly polemical in nature and cover several decades. They portray the complexity and diversity of liberalism in England – from Low Churchmen to Platonists, from non-Christian theists (pantheists) to atheists – and indirectly reflect the general situation of unbelief in the European continent. Liberalism as socio-historical fact is a highly complex phenomenon.[20] Most of the liberalistic first principles which Newman outlined in his works on liberalism are also peculiar to the Victorian age: the overly optimistic view of human nature, absolute faith in science and progress,

---

Preached before the University of Oxford between AD 1826 and 1843, 3rd edn (Notre Dame, IN: University of Notre Dame Press, 1997), pp. 75-98.

[18] *Grammar of Assent*, p. 293.

[19] The French theologian and philosopher Maurice Nédoncelle points out that Newman even preceded Nietzsche in predicting the "black tide" of unbelief and its impact on the whole of society. Nietzsche's *The Gay Science* appeared only in 1882. See Maurice Nédoncelle's preface to Jean-Guy Saint-Arnaud's *Newman et l'incroyance* (Québec: Les Éditions Bellarmine, 1972), pp. 7-8.

[20] A comprehensive study of Newman's thought on liberalism is beyond the scope of this chapter. This topic is discussed in greater depth and detail elsewhere. See, for instance, Terrence Merrigan, 'Newman and Theological Liberalism', *Theological Studies* 66 (2005), pp. 605-21.

JOHN HENRY NEWMAN DOCTOR OF THE CHURCH

excessive emphasis on rationalism, etc. Newman, however, had the perspicacity to point out that certain anti-religious presuppositions or first principles – i.e. a certain scepticism concerning the objective status of religious truth, or that of Revelation, etc. – do determine the orientation and outcome of the arguments for or against belief in God.

For this section, we shall take *atheism* to refer to a vision of the world and of human history that denies the existence of a personal God who is Creator of the universe and Governor of the moral order: eternal, omnipotent, omniscient, benevolent and loving, personally interacting with the universe and with the lives of the beings He created. We shall briefly present how the way to atheism, through liberalism according to Newman, broadly parallels the way to Catholicity on the level of antecedents, first principles, and method of reasoning.

D. 1 Anti-Religious Antecedents: The Anti-Conscience Principle

When Newman was named cardinal by Pope Leo XIII in 1879, he reiterated in his speech what he believed to be his lifelong mission:

> For thirty, forty, fifty years I have resisted to the best of my powers the spirit of liberalism in religion. Never did Holy Church need champions against it more sorely than now, when, alas! it is an error overspreading, as a snare, the whole earth; and on this great occasion, when it is natural for one who is in my place to look out upon the world, and upon Holy Church as in it, and upon her future, it will not, I hope, be considered out of place, if I renew the protest against it which I have made so often.[21]

What does liberalism represent for Newman and why his lifelong battle against liberalism in religion? For Newman liberalism represents, on the level of moral antecedents, the *anti-conscience principle*: it denies the reality of sin and evil, and reduces the experience of conscience to mere aesthetic sense, expediency or utility. Contrary to the moral principles of Christianity – which emphasize the sense of sin, and the utter incapacity of humankind to achieve its own salvation and, hence, the need for grace – liberalism proclaims the post-Enlightenment view of the intrinsic goodness of human nature and its inherent capacity for self-salvation. It is the overly optimistic view of human nature in liberalism that renders it naive and impervious to the testimony

---

[21] *Addresses to Cardinal Newman with His Replies, Etc., 1879-1882*, ed. William P. Neville (1905), p. 64.

of conscience and of human history regarding the manifestations of evil as personal and social sin. Liberalism ignores what the Newman scholar Yearley calls the "negative theophany" of conscience:[22] the existential experience of the abyss that exists between the sanctity of God and the sinfulness of the human person.

D. 2 Anti-Religious First Principles: The Anti-Dogmatic Principle

On the level of first principles, Newman calls liberalism the *anti-dogmatic principle* because its principles are inimical to revealed religion. In presenting a list of eighteen liberalistic tenets in the *Apologia*,[23] Newman shows the naturalistic way in which liberalism conceives the relationship between reason and faith, between personal freedom and God's transcendent authority (as it is manifested in conscience, Divine Revelation and the living Church). Liberalism ultimately rejects the vital link between conscience and the dogmatic principle, which Newman succinctly explains in his *Essay on the Development of Christian Doctrine*:

> What Conscience is in the history of an individual mind, such was the dogmatic principle in the history of Christianity. Both in the one case and the other, there is the gradual formation of a directing power out of a [transcendent] principle.[24]

While the religious experience of conscience reveals one's relationship

---

[22] Lee H. Yearley, *The Ideas of Newman: Christianity and Human Religiosity* (University Park and London: The Pennsylvania State University Press, 1978), p. 99.

[23] *Apologia*, Note A, pp. 294-96. Here is a sampling of some of the basic propositions of religious liberalism according to Newman:

– No religious tenet is important, unless reason shows it to be so.

– No one can believe what he does not understand. There are no mysteries in true religion.

– No theological doctrine is any thing more than an opinion which happens to be held by bodies of men.

– It is dishonest in a man to make an act of faith in what he has not had brought home to him by actual proof.

– It is immoral in a man to believe more than he can spontaneously receive as being congenial to his moral and mental nature.

– No revealed doctrines or precepts may reasonably stand in the way of scientific conclusions.

– There is a right of Private Judgment: that is, there is no existing authority on earth competent to interfere with the liberty of individuals in reasoning and judging for themselves about the Bible and its contents, as they severally please.

– The Civil Power has the right of ecclesiastical jurisdiction and administration.

– Virtue is the child of knowledge, and vice of ignorance.

[24] *An Essay on the Development of Christian Doctrine*, 6th ed. (Notre Dame, Indiana: University of Notre Dame Press, 1989), p. 361.

with a God who governs personal life, the assent to dogma – i.e. the ecclesial formulation of divinely revealed truths – reveals the Church's communion with the Holy Spirit who orients growth in ecclesial self-understanding.[25]

What makes liberalism the anti–dogmatic principle? Liberalism takes Divine Revelation to be mere *manifestation* – "i.e. a series of historical works conveying a representation of the moral character of God"[26] – and not *mystery*. Its interpretation is based on subjective individual perception. The objectivity of the fact of revelation is thus denied, because of varying interpretations.[27] The liberalistic ethos purports to address the problem of the plurality of interpretations by taking private judgment to be the ultimate gauge particularly in matters of religion and morality:

> Our private judgment is made everything to us, – is contemplated, recognized, and consulted as the arbiter of all questions, and as independent of everything external to us. Nothing is considered to have an existence except so far forth as our minds discern it.[28]

Religious truth is likewise reduced to personal interpretation or private opinion. Consequently, all authority and tradition are excluded. Submission to authority is considered the most debasing of attitudes because it demeans human freedom.[29]

D. 3 Anti-Religious Method: Rationalism unto Scepticism (The Anti-Faith Principle)

Liberalism is dominated by a rationalistic method often divorced from moral and religious antecedents. This type of rationalism exemplifies the *anti-faith principle* because it pretends to substitute itself for the normal channels by which Revelation is mediated to us: the inspiration of Scriptures, the witnessing of holy persons, and the testimony of the living Church in her doctrines and traditions. Newman describes how

---

[25] See the Dogmatic Constitution on Divine Revelation *Dei Verbum* (18 November 1965) § 8.

[26] *Essays Critical and Historical*, 10th ed., Vol. 1 (London: Longmans, Green, and Co., 1890), pp. 69-70.

[27] Newman, for his part, offers this clarification: "We must distinguish between a revelation and a reception of it, not between its earlier and later stages. A revelation, in itself divine, and guaranteed as such, may from first to last be received, doubted, argued against, perverted, rejected, by individuals according to the state of mind of each. Ignorance, misapprehension, unbelief, and other causes, do not at once cease to operate because the revelation is in itself true and in its proofs irrefragable." (*Essay on the Development of Christian Doctrine*, p. 82.)

[28] *Essays Critical and Historical*, Vol. 1, p. 34.

[29] *Discussions and Arguments on Various Subjects*, 5th ed. (London: Longmans, Green, and Co., 1888), p. 259.

the rationalistic spirit reduces revealed religion to a religion within the limits of reason:

> It is Rationalism to accept the Revelation, and then to explain it away; to speak of it as the Word of God, and to treat it as the word of man; to refuse to let it speak for itself; to claim to be told the *why* and the *how* of God's dealings with us, as therein described, and to assign to Him a motive and a scope of our own; to stumble at the partial knowledge which He may give us of them; to put aside what is obscure, as if it had not been said at all; to accept one half of what has been told us, and not the other half; to assume that the contents of Revelation are also its proof; to frame some gratuitous hypothesis about them, and then to garble, gloss, and colour them, to trim, clip, pare away, and twist them, in order to bring them into conformity with the idea to which we have subjected them.[30]

In Newman's time, moreover, the general adoption of the ideal of rationality of the empirical sciences served to neutralize the idea of a personal God in theology.[31]

How does the rationalistic method lead to atheism? Newman's intuitions find confirmation in the history of philosophy. In his brilliant book *At the Origins of Modern Atheism* (1987), the American Jesuit philosopher Michael Buckley traces the dialectical origins of modern atheism to bad theology. And by bad theology Buckley means a way of theologizing fraught with the internal contradiction between content and form.[32] The theological enterprise degenerates into atheism when the religious inquirer dissociates theological theory from living faith, form (language and method of reflection) from content, method of investigation from the divine object of faith. When the experience of conscience is bracketed as evidence to be explored, and when rational argument – rather than assent, communication, witnessing – is taken to be the dominant form for expressing religious truth, the

---

[30] *Essays Critical and Historical*, Vol. 1, p. 32.

[31] The history of British empiricism, for example, manifests the different stages of the neutralization of the God-principle. Francis Bacon (1561-1626) made a strict separation between the natural and supernatural spheres. Thomas Hobbes (1588-1679) proposed to concentrate philosophical investigation only on the material world. John Locke (1632-1704) pegged religious proofs on the capacities and limits of human knowing. David Hume (1711-1776) reduced all supernatural impressions to sense impressions. Consequently, the naturalism of Bacon, the empirical theism of Hobbes and Locke, and the scepticism of Hume contributed to emptying the God idea of any reference to a transcendent deity. See James Collins, *God in Modern Philosophy* (London: Routledge & Kegan Paul Ltd., 1959), especially Chapter IV: 'Empiricism and the Neutralizing of God', pp. 90-125, and Notes, pp. 422-25.

[32] See Michael Buckley SJ, *At the Origins of Modern Atheism* (New Haven and London: Yale University Press, 1987).

focus of the theological investigation is eventually displaced. Since the common ground between theology and philosophy is the study and contemplation of the material universe, immanent, impersonal nature becomes – instead of conscience – the evidence for a transcendent, personal God. Buckley comments on the irony of this position: "The God of these theologians is Christian in the absence of Christ and religious in the absence of religious experience."[33]

The result of the self-alienating process engendered by bad theism and bad theology, as Newman predicted, is scepticism in religion. In its ambition to explain away the mysteries of faith, rationalism blocked and destroyed the key to authentic religious knowledge. This 'blockage' in reason is scepticism, the avowal of the utter incapacity of secular reason to penetrate the mysteries of life and to mediate ultimate meaning. While rationalism searches for reasons instead of plunging into the mysteries of faith, scepticism "[refuses] to be satisfied with reasons there where they should satisfy."[34] Newman believes that scepticism, the "bottomless pit" of doubt,[35] is the most corrosive form of rational unbelief because of its propensity to corrupt spiritual interiority.

Thus, when Newman speaks of Atheism and Catholicity, he thinks of the internal rationality of their antecedents and rational first principles and of the logical process that leads to their conclusion.

E. The 'Religious' Function of Modern Atheism

Is the way to Atheism only diametrically opposed to the way to Catholicity? This seems to be Newman's conclusion if one consistently works out the internal rationality of their respective first principles to their logical end. In absolutely separating the ways to Catholicity and to Atheism, however, Newman perhaps fails to see how atheism could itself be a critical tool in the service of religion.

Beyond Newman's claim of the impossibility of a middle ground between Atheism and Catholicity, contemporary theologians and philosophers of religion seek to elaborate a possible interface. The French phenomenologist Paul Ricœur offers another perspective to viewing the problem:

Atheism does not exhaust itself in the negation and destruction of

---

[33] Buckley, *Origins of Modern Atheism*, p. 356.
[34] *Essays Critical and Historical*, Vol. 2, p. 85.
[35] See Newman's article 'The Development of Religious Error', in *The Contemporary Review* (October 1885), p. 672.

religion; rather, that atheism clears the ground for a new faith, a faith for a postreligious age.[36]

How can atheism purify and engender a renewed faith? We shall see in this section the 'religious' uses of modern atheism.

The American philosopher Merold Westphal thinks that we should first identify the kind of atheism that is addressed: *Evidential Atheism* or the *Atheism of Suspicion?*[37]

On the one hand, Evidential Atheism – let us call it the Atheism of Scepticism – refutes the rationality of religious beliefs and practices. For Westphal, the adequate Christian response to Evidential Atheism is to refute it, to show that there is sufficient rational evidence to warrant religious belief and practice. The psychology of religious assent that Newman elaborated in his *Grammar of Assent* is a response to this type of atheism grounded on scepticism.

On the other hand, the Atheism of Suspicion – represented by the 'unholy' triumvirate of Freud, Marx, and Nietzsche – probes into the psychological motives of the believer.[38] The latter type of atheism is more insidious, because one confronts not only the problem of 'bad faith' but also of *false consciousness*. It is perhaps the inability, indeed, the refusal of classical scholastic theology to confront this real psychological problem that has rendered it ineffective.[39] Paradoxically, for Westphal, the Atheism of Suspicion – concerned not so much with doctrine, but with the psychology that underlies belief – fulfills an important function in the service of religion. It represents a critique of the false consciousness that animates inauthentic religion. Westphal thus summarizes the critique of religion of the Masters of Suspicion:[40]

---

[36] Alasdair MacIntyre, and Paul Ricœur, *The Religious Significance of Atheism* (New York: Columbia University Press, 1969), p. 59.

[37] Merold Westphal makes an important distinction between scepticism and suspicion: "Skepticism is directed toward the elusiveness of things, while suspicion is directed toward the evasiveness of consciousness. Skepticism seeks to overcome the opacity of facts, while suspicion seeks to uncover the duplicity of persons ... It seeks to discredit the believing soul by asking what *motives* lead people to belief and what *functions* their beliefs play, looking for precisely those motives and functions that love darkness rather than light and therefore hide themselves." See Merold Westphal, *Suspicion and Faith: The Religious Uses of Modern Atheism* (New York: Fordham University Press, 1998), pp. 13-14.

[38] Westphal, *Suspicion and Faith*, pp. 13-14.

[39] Thus Peter Homans asks appositely in *Theology After Freud* (Indianapolis: Bobbs-Merrill, 1970), p. x: "Has theology's preoccupation with philosophy in effect obscured its capacity to engage those contemporary modes of thought and experience that are predominantly psychological in character?"

[40] See Westphal's brilliant summary in *Suspicion and Faith*, p. 229.

(1) For Sigmund Freud (1856-1939) religion is "ontological weakness seeking consolation." For Freud, the image of God embodies the projection of our desires. Our feelings of deep insecurity and alienation in this world lead us to fabricate a divine father-image, representing both ideal (the embodiment of authority) and illusion (protection against a hostile world). Religion, for Freud, is but infantile wish fulfillment, arising from repressed, unconscious infantile longings for protection and security.

(2) For Karl Marx (1818-1883), religion is "sociological power seeking legitimation." Marx calls religion the "opium of the people"[41] because it distracts the human person from the real and ultimate demands of history and society by its illusory promises of an eternal heaven. The "slaves" – the people, the masses, the oppressed, the underprivileged – rely on the consolations of religion to deal with their condition of poverty and powerlessness. The "masters" – the powerful, the ruling classes, the political elites – use the sanction of religion to assuage their guilty consciences. Religion, Marx claims, becomes very easily a political and ideological tool, used by those in power to justify or legitimize the status quo with its social injustices. Hence, for Marx, the critique and overthrow of religion becomes a moral imperative in order to regain authentic humanism.

(3) For Friedrich Nietzsche (1844-1900), religion is "sociological weakness seeking revenge." For Nietzsche, the main animating force in the history of ideas and mores is not absolute reason but an irrational cosmic will: the *will to power*. There is no absolute truth or universal moral order, only an infinite variety of human aims and interpretations. The only pervasive trait of this ocean of passions and meanings is the capacity to creatively harness and perfect this primal energy, a singular talent that distinguishes "masters" from "slaves". On the level of the individual ethics, the good is that which serves my self-interests. For "masters", revenge is even a virtue because it protects the master's position of domination and eliminates all opposition. For "slaves", the only plausible moral option is "to make a virtue out of necessity" – that is, to "imaginatively" transform one's position of weakness and subordination into a position of (spiritual) power and (moral) superiority. In their *resentment* for their condition as "slaves", these learn to transform their non-value into value, compensating by "spiritual" revenge, imagining an eschatological future when "justice" will finally be meted out.

---

[41] Karl Marx and Friedrich Engels, *On Religion* (New York: Schoken Books, 1964), p. 42.

Westphal proposes a different method of response to the Atheism of Suspicion: to take its critique as "prophetic voices that challenge believers to take seriously the critique of religion generated by suspicion and to lead the way in using it as an aid to personal and ecclesial self-examination."[42] For the Atheism of Suspicion expresses in secular language the biblical critique of inauthentic religion:

> The hermeneutics of suspicion in the hands of modern atheists is not only a secular theology of original sin; it is also a secular version of the prophetic message.[43]

Atheism, as it was developed by the Masters of Suspicion, thus uncovers an orientation diametrically opposed to that described by Newman in the inferential process that leads from 'simple' to 'complex' (or mature) assent. The Atheism of Suspicion reveals the mechanism of false consciousness, in the complexity of its psychological, moral or social ramifications. However invaluable its service to religion, this type of atheism remains only at the threshold of real religion because it rejects the existence of a God beyond the caricature proffered by false religious consciousness. In its most religiously tolerant stance, atheism concedes the inconceivability of God, thus becoming simply agnostic. But in ceding to agnosticism, atheism becomes merely sceptical. We cannot, however, remain on the level of this parody of religion. Parody must be overcome by a renewal of Christian prophetism. And it is here that we turn to Newman to help us retrieve the inner resources of religious rationality and of Christian spirituality in order to respond to the challenge of our contemporary age.

F. In Aid of a Revival of Assent: Newman's Dogmatic Principle and Illative Sense

Can we still apply Newman's method of investigation to the faith problems of our contemporary period, which is characterized as 'post-Christian', even 'post-atheist'? Indeed, the militant anti-theism of the past century has had its heydey. After the debacle of atheist humanism and the collapse of totalitarian atheist regimes, we are witnessing a resurgence of religion in the twenty-first century.[44] With the demise of faith in the unity of reason and the viability of dogmatic

---

[42] Westphal, *Suspicion and Faith*, p. 16.

[43] Westphal, *Suspicion and Faith*, p. 213.

[44] See, for example, Peter L. Berger (ed.), *The Desecularization of the World: Resurgent Religion and World Politics* (Washington, D.C. and Grand Rapids, MI: Ethics and Public Policy Center and William B. Eerdmans Publishing Company, 1999).

interpretation, however, religion in the contemporary age has taken on a more secular configuration: non-metaphysical, non-dogmatic, non-institutional.[45]

Gianni Vattimo (born 1936) is perhaps one of the best representatives of this contemporary way of thinking. His "weak thought" philosophy (*il pensiero debole*) contends that such secularization – i.e. the weakening of the "sacred" construed as absolute, power, dominion, authority, dogmatic "violence" – is a process internal to Christianity.

For Vattimo, secularization heralds the kenotic or nihilistic destiny of Christianity. And the only limit to religious secularization is charity. Inspired by the German philosopher Martin Heidegger, Vattimo claims that the task of theology is to think faith without object, without dogma, and without the Church.[46] The future of religion tends inexorably towards a "secular" or "religionless" Christianity.

Vattimo contends that the traditional dogmatic search for "objective" truth conceals a will to power. The Christian principle of charity alone could lead us to a more "human-friendly" notion of truth. For Vattimo the love of neighbour is concretely translated as the "weakening of all claims to the literal validity of biblical texts and to the peremptoriness of the churches' dogmatic teaching,"[47] as well as "an active commitment to diminish violence in all its forms."[48] The 'praxis' of charity for Vattimo is lived as openness to a plurality of interpretations. This truth-as-charity is the vocation that is given to us Christians by virtue of the event of the Incarnation. Charity alone helps us understand that the message of the Christian God

---

[45] In his keynote address at the North American Conference of Associates and Religious (NACAR) annual meeting in 2006 (Cincinnati, OH), theologian and spiritual writer Ron Rolheiser OMI, identifies the characteristics of our present "ecclesial moment": (1) *Radical freedom* in terms of "over-choice" renders commitment to marriage, vocation, and career extremely difficult. (2) *Atheism and agnosticism* become more and more part of our everyday consciousness. The absence of any vestige of God in our homes, work and recreation places, obliges believers to personally develop a deep inner religious directedness. (3) An *intoxicating materialistic culture* presents hyper-stimulated emotions – ambition, restlessness, greed, sex, anger, etc. – as "expected" behaviors. (4) *Excessive individualism* leads to the death of public and ecclesial life, and results in greater loneliness and restlessness. (5) A *bewildering pluralism* (religious, cultural, ideological, etc.) makes people embrace religious and moral relativism uncritically. See Leah Curtin, 'Living Waters from Within: NACAR 2006', accessed March 2006 from <http://www.franciscansisters.org/english/news/NEWS/sfplife_ LeahCurtin_ NACAR.htm>.

[46] Gianni Vattimo, *After Christianity*, trans. Luca D'Isanto (New York: Columbia University Press, 2002), p. 134.

[47] Vattimo, *After Christianity*, p. 49.

[48] Vattimo, *After Christianity*, pp. 51-52. See also Vattimo, *Belief*, trans. Luca D'Isanto and David Webb (Cambridge: Polity Press, 1999), pp. 44, 88.

is a word to be interpreted, not a dogma to be explained or to be imposed: "Revelation does not speak of an objective truth, but of an ongoing salvation."[49] It is through this ongoing interpretation of the Word of God that God's self-revelation in history and in cultures continues. Only this principle of charity, Vattimo claims, could allow us to be reconciled to our Christian past and heritage, in spite of its dark history of crusades, inquisitions, and dogmatic absolutizations.[50]

A fundamental question remains, however. If, as Vattimo contends, there is a kenotic itinerary and nihilistic destiny of the Christian religion, where then do we find the true kenotic face of Christianity? Surely not in persons or ideological parties who bear resentment against Christianity in general, and the Catholic Church in particular. Our religious sense obliges us to look elsewhere and to consider the lives of the contemporary icons of charity: the French Carmelite Saint Thérèse of Lisieux (1873-1897), Doctor of Charity; the Polish Franciscan Conventual Father Maximilian Kolbe (1894-1941), Martyr of Charity; the Albanian Apostle of Charity in India, Mother Teresa (1910-1997); Frère Roger Schutz (1915-2005), the Swiss Founder of Taizé who spearheaded an Ecumenism of Charity; Jean Vanier (born 1928), the lay Canadian founder of L'Arche and Foi et Lumière communities, an international ministry in the service of handicapped persons and the families who take care of them. What do we witness in these contemporary icons of Christian charity? One striking quality: all are persons who, in Newman's words, are prepared to "live and die upon a dogma."[51] Christian truths and first principles animated and gave form to their charity. Here Newman's dogmatic principle reasserts itself.

For Vattimo, charity is the limit to secularization, to the de-theologizing of religion. For the Christian saints, charity is the starting point of theology, and is the heart of dogma. Thus, contrary to Vattimo's "foundationless" theology, Newman's dogmatic principle (the Person of Christ united to His Church) is at the heart of Christian charity and mysticism.

The theological and existential question is posed anew: Is the way of true religion beyond, or within the tension between Atheism and Catholicity? Otherwise put, could the serious Christian believer just

[49] Vattimo, Belief, p. 48.
[50] See Michel Collin, 'Le Christianisme 'post-métaphysique' a-t-il un avenir?' Kephas (janvier-mars 2005): 13-36, p. 26.
[51] Newman, Grammar of Assent, p. 93.

step outside the tension between faith and unbelief? Spiritual theology examines the antinomies experienced in the heart of belief, of which the most profound antinomy is experienced in the contemplation of the incarnate God. Accordingly, the great French Jesuit theologian Henri de Lubac speaks of the need to bear the *paradoxes of faith*.[52]

Could the Christian theologian, in re-thinking Christianity in the postmodern twenty-first century, simply forego the tension between metaphysics and nihilism, between the immanence of the Word and the transcendence of God? It seems that the great ferments underlying the secularism of our contemporary age are marked by three great tensions. The Canadian theologian and spiritual writer, Ron Rolheiser, OMI, goes as far as saying that our contemporary secularism is marked by "three great divorces":[53]

(1) Spirituality versus Ecclesiology: we witness an upsurge of new spiritual movements in Western countries where we see a marked decline in church membership and parish participation.

(2) Life versus Wisdom: the forces of life (desire, intelligence, innovation, humour, wit, etc.), especially in our young people, draw their creative energies elsewhere, and seem to be disconnected from the traditional sources of Christian wisdom which deal with the ultimate questions of life and meaning, love and communion, suffering and death.

(3) Justice versus Piety: private piety rarely seems to express itself in committed social action; conversely, the passion for justice hardly translates itself into mature devotion.

A re-appraisal of Newman's theological method at the end of this chapter enables us to see how Newman has himself mastered the creative tensions in the heart of theology and in the life of faith.

On the level of the intellectual and moral preparation for the assent of faith, the religious élan involved, for Newman, an antecedent task of maintaining the tension between the experience of God in conscience and the impression of God's absence in human history, of courageously posing himself between the self-evidence of "myself and my Creator" and God's non-evident presence in the world.[54] How does Newman

---

[52] See Henri de Lubac, *Paradoxes*, *Oeuvres complètes* XXXI (Paris: Les Éditions du Cerf, 1999) and *Autres Paradoxes* (Namur: Éditions Culture et Vérité, 1994).

[53] See Fr Ron Rolheiser's Kelly Lecture "Hope and Concern – The Church and the Culture on the Eve of a New Millennium" delivered at St. Michael's College, Toronto, Canada (March 25,1999), accessed March 2006 from <http://www.ronrolheiser.com/pdfs/hope_and_concern.pdf>.

[54] In his *Apologia* (pp. 241-42), Newman describes, in a gripping fashion, the unfathomable

reconcile the antinomic images of the living God in conscience, on the one hand, and of the world in which God seems to be absent, on the other? A merely philosophical or scientific attitude could only arrive at this Manichean conclusion: that evil has as much right as the good to exist in the world, and that it even has broader jurisdiction and greater victories on the whole. Not so, Newman claims, with the religious imagination formed by conscience and nourished by a life of prayer:

> [The religious imagination] has a living hold on truths which are really to be found in the world, though they are not upon the surface. It is able to pronounce by anticipation, what it takes a long argument to prove – that good is the rule, and evil the exception. It is able to assume that, uniform as are the laws of nature, they are consistent with a particular *Providence*. It interprets what it sees around it by this *previous inward teaching*, as the true key of that maze of vast complicated disorder; and thus it gains a more and more consistent and luminous vision of God from the most unpromising materials. Thus *conscience* is a connecting principle between the creature and his Creator; and the firmest hold of theological truths is gained by *habits of personal religion*.[55]

Perhaps the reduction of conscience to mere moral or aesthetic sense, or to a mere sense of expediency or utility is, at heart, a practical refusal to live this tension at the heart of the religious quest? Religious educators know too well that effective catechetical instruction involves the formation of a Christian conscience.

On the level of religious first principles, Newman was careful to maintain the balance and the unity among the fundamental principles of Christianity contained in the central doctrine of the Incarnation. Speaking of the interconnection between the doctrines of faith in the *Grammar of Assent*, Newman writes:

---

mystery of iniquity that is evident in the profound alienation of the world: "To consider the world in its length and breadth, its various history, the many races of man, their starts, their fortunes, their mutual alienation, their conflicts; and then their ways, habits, governments, forms of worship; their enterprises, their aimless courses, their random achievements and acquirements, the impotent conclusion of long-standing facts, the tokens so faint and broken of a superintending design, the blind evolution of what turn out to be great powers or truths, the progress of things, as if from unreasoning elements, not towards final causes, the greatness and littleness of man, his far-reaching aims, his short duration, the curtain hung over his futurity, the disappointments of life, the defeat of good, the success of evil, physical pain, mental anguish, the prevalence and intensity of sin, the pervading idolatries, the corruptions, the dreary hopeless irreligion, that condition of the whole race, so fearfully yet exactly described in the Apostle's words, 'having no hope and without God in the world,' – all this is a vision to dizzy and appal; and inflicts upon the mind the sense of a profound mystery, which is absolutely beyond human solution."

[55] *Grammar of Assent*, p. 117. Emphasis added.

> The matter of revelation is not a mere collection of truths, not a philosophical view, not a religious sentiment or spirit, not a special morality, – poured out upon mankind as a stream might pour itself into the sea, mixing with the world's thought, modifying, purifying, invigorating it; – but an authoritative teaching, which bears witness to itself and keeps itself together as one, in contrast to the assemblage of opinions on all sides of it, and speaks to all men, as being ever and everywhere one and the same, and claiming to be received intelligently, by all whom it addresses, as one doctrine, discipline, and devotion directly given from above. In consequence, the exhibition of credentials, that is, of evidence, that it is what it professes to be, is essential to Christianity, as it comes to us; for we are not left at liberty to pick and choose out of its contents according to our judgment, but must receive it all, as we find it, if we accept it at all.[56]

Orthodoxy in this Newmanian sense is not a matter of blind obedience, but of personally appropriating and bearing the intellectual and moral tension between the different principles of Christianity.[57] In his study of the history of the councils in the early centuries of the Church, Newman discovered that heterodoxy resulted when theologians absolutized one idea – the humanity of Christ over his divinity (Arianism), the invisible character of the Godhead over His Self-Revelation in the flesh (iconoclasm), etc. – to the detriment of the other Christian principles:

> Here we see the ordinary mistake of doctrinal innovators, viz. to go away with this or that proposition of the Creed, instead of embracing that one idea which all of them together are meant to convey; it being almost a definition of heresy, that it fastens on some one statement as if the whole truth, to the denial of all others ... [58]

Effectively, heresy is the option for this absolute theological idea at the cost of breaching ecclesial unity. Newman studied in depth the origins and causes of the Christological Arianism of the fourth century. Did he foresee its resurgence in the twenty-first century as ecclesiological Arianism, the reduction of the Church to mere human institution?

On the level of the concrete application of the theological and psychological method of assent, the Newman professor Terrence

---

[56] *Grammar of Assent*, p. 387.

[57] Pope Benedict XVI's first encyclical *Deus Caritas Est* (25 December 2005), for example, shows admirably well how the tensions between *eros* (worldly, possessive, romantic love) and *agape* (love grounded in and shaped by faith, Christian charity), flesh and spirit, humanity and divinity, love of God and love of neighbor, etc., are transcended in the Incarnation of the Word.

[58] *Fifteen Sermons Preached before the University of Oxford between AD 1826 and 1843*, 3rd ed. (Notre Dame, Indiana: University of Notre Dame Press, 1997), p. 337.

Merrigan describes Newman's theological thought as a creative keeping together of polarities: real and notional, explicit and implicit, formal and informal, theology and religion.[59] Newman's *illative sense* is the practical capacity of holding the tension between the various probabilities and evidences that present themselves to the believer as material constituting religious assent. What is the illative sense perfected by the believing intellect but human judgment purified, elevated and enlightened to such an extent that it is able to penetrate the mysteries of the Spirit?

More important perhaps than cultivating the capacity to creatively bear the tensions between the different poles of faith and theology, is the theologian's duty to bear the tension inherent in the theological act: to behold the abyss that exists between our concepts and the mystery of God. The great temptation, the Belgian Jesuit Albert Chapelle writes, is to reduce the intellectual work in theology to mere knowledge, possession, or power.[60] This danger is found not only in the theological enterprise, but in the heart of contemporary thought. Is there finally a theological method that is commensurate with the object of theology? No one could be more keenly aware of the insuperable distance that exists between God and the human person than the mystics. Even mysticism itself remains always on the threshold of atheism, because the very transcendence of God opens up an abyss between the human spirit and the mysteries of faith. Even for the most fervent of believers, the temptation to disbelieve will always remain present.[61] Like Newman, Chapelle claims that only a spirit of adoration and humility, of constancy and fidelity in prayer, of trust and audacity can enable us to live this unbearable tension.

The living example of our contemporary icons of charity manifests not only a remarkable penetration of Christological doctrine, but also an extraordinary capacity to synthesize the paradoxes of faith.[62] This

---

[59] See Terrence Merrigan, 'Clear Heads and Holy Hearts,' *Louvain Theological and Pastoral Monographs*, 7 (Louvain: Peeters Press, 1991).

[60] Albert Chapelle SJ, *Au creux du rocher: Itinéraire spirituel et intellectuel d'un jésuite. Mémorial* (Bruxelles: Les Éditions Lessius, 2004), p. 151.

[61] The father of the boy possessed by a dumb spirit in St Mark's gospel expresses for us all the cry of the believer: "I believe; help my unbelief!" (Mark 9:24)

[62] The mysterious "trial of faith" of St Thérèse of Lisieux, for example, is a very poignant example of how the antinomies of faith are lived out in anguish: without consolation, but not without certitude. Some months before she died, she entered into a "night of faith," experiencing the moral and mental anguish of unbelievers in the face of death. And here she embraced the great antinomies: God's Infinite Grandeur *and* her extreme poverty, the darkness of sin *and* the Light of Divine Love. St Thérèse's discovery of the drama of human freedom and of sinful refusal made

reveals a "theological interiority" that is solidly grounded on dogma. Contrary to this, Vattimo's argument for a liberation from dogmatic Christianity – inspired, without doubt, by Jacques Derrida's option for "religion without religion" – seems to be a mere apologia for a more liberal theology and a more relativistic morality.

These questions ultimately remain: Can faith exist without grounds or without an object?[63] Can Christian charity develop without a dogmatic core and without ecclesial communion? In refusing to articulate a response, Vattimo's nihilism in the end manifests not so much the qualities of what he calls *pensée faible* (*pensiero debole*), but rather the inanities of what, in the last analysis, is but *pensée fatiguée*. We shall let Newman sum up our argument:

> Nothing would be more theoretical and unreal than to suppose that true Faith cannot exist except when moulded upon a Creed, and based upon Evidence; yet nothing would indicate a more shallow philosophy than to say that it ought carefully to be disjoined from dogmatic and argumentative statements. To assert the latter is to discard the science of theology from the service of Religion; to assert the former, is to maintain that every child, every peasant, must be a theologian. Faith cannot exist without grounds or without an object ... [64]

Conclusion: The Cross as the Place of Prophecy

In our contemporary period, the need to re-inflame the religious imagination of Christianity – new saints, the witnessing of a greater kenotic charity, the renewal of Christian mysticism – cannot do away with this dogmatic core. In the end, this kenotic mysticism – experiencing the cross of secularism and unbelief, living in depths the drama of the human situation – is at the service of Christian charity. And the life and witnessing of the saint becomes truly a mediation of the Person of Christ in the heart of the world, indeed, the triumph of charity and of illuminating grace.

The spiritual icons of our age – Pedro Arrupe, Mother Teresa, Jean Vanier, etc. – all speak of the need to assume the cross of our age.

---

her understand, at the same time, the mystery of God's Merciful Love and her vocation in the heart of the Church. Beyond a mere purification of faith, St Thérèse's trial took on a redemptive character, participating, as it were, in the Passion of Jesus. See Guy Gaucher, OCD, *La Passion de Thérèse de Lisieux (4 Avril-30 Septembre 1897)*, nouvelle édition revue et augmentée (Paris: Éditions du Cerf et Desclée de Brouwer, 1993).

[63] See *Oxford University Sermons*, p. 254.

[64] *Oxford University Sermons*, pp. 253-54.

For these spiritual masters, the place of prophecy is there where the cross is present, that is, there where the weak and the poor, the marginalized and rejected of society find themselves. But the Cross – symbol of the tensions at the heart of faith – has to be personally appropriated. Only then could it offer new hope and engender spiritual rebirth. And this, Newman was well aware, is ultimately the work of grace. The faith vision attained by Newman's illative sense is not an intellectual achievement, but the living synthesis realized by assimilating the Person of Christ and receiving His Spirit.

We thus conclude this chapter with Newman's reflections in his *Lectures on the Doctrine of Justification* (1838):

> Christ's Cross does not justify by being looked at, but by being applied; not by being gazed at in faith, but by being actually set up within us, and that not by our act, but by God's invisible grace. Men sit, gaze, and speak of the great Atonement, and think that this is appropriating it; not more truly than kneeling to the material cross itself is appropriating it. The Cross must be brought home to us, not in word, but in power, and this is the work of the Spirit. This is justification; and when imparted to the soul, it draws blood, it heals, it purifies, it glorifies.[65]

---

[65] *Lectures on the Doctrine of Justification*, 4th ed. (London: Rivingtons, 1838), Chapter 7, p. 203.

Chapter 3

———

NEWMAN AND THE TYRANNY OF METHOD IN CONTEMPORARY EDUCATION

by Jane Rupert

U nlike educational theorists such as Rousseau in the preceding century, Newman's convictions regarding education were rooted solidly in practice. His first role as an educator was as a young tutor at Oriel College at Oxford. In mid–century, he was responsible as rector for establishing the new Catholic University of Ireland; at this institution in Dublin he both defended the tradition of liberal education and included subjects in arts and science then new to the university. After leaving the Catholic University in 1858 to return to his religious order's foundation in Birmingham, at the request of Catholic families in England he established a Catholic school for boys. Here, when beyond his sixtieth year, in addition to administrative responsibilities, Newman taught religious knowledge and marked the notebooks for classes of sixth-form students.

Newman's work on education continues to speak to us with urgency in our own period because like an Old Testament prophet he reminds us of perennial principles and premises now either forgotten or denied. In our historical moment when the very nature of reason has been compromised by the monopoly of a scientific outlook, Newman recalls reason to itself. In *The Idea of a University*, he defends two kinds of reasoning rejected by modern educational reformers and by the empirical Enlightenment's inductive concept of mind that is foundational to their thought: first, the converging rationality typical of literature and, secondly, theoretical deductive reasoning which connects received ideas to specific instances.

Newman recognized that two fundamental assumptions in education prevalent from antiquity to the modern era were in peril: the tradition of universal knowledge or knowledge understood as a complete whole and the principle that the various domains of universal knowledge are known through different kinds of reason, each adapted to its own task. Because knowledge is now fragmented, the idea of it as an entire or complete whole is almost alien to us. However, in the nineteenth century, Newman understood the need to defend the foundational importance of this idea. In his discourses in *The Idea of a University* he resisted those who would break up the unity of knowledge by privileging the applied sciences and who from the point of view of these sciences considered that graduates in the humanities were characterized by elegant imbecility. He also resisted career-oriented education which connected education from the earliest years to a profession following the pattern of John Locke's seventeenth-century treatise on educational philosophy. Locke outlines how a boy might be trained for the business world, emphasizes social skills, considers languages important only for their value in business communication, and generally omits anything not directly connected to business success. Under these utilitarian pressures and in the absence of the foundational idea of the interconnected unity of knowledge, Newman says that disciplines at the university would be displayed like wares in a market with students opting for courses in this or that with no connection between them.

Yet more gravely, underlying these two utilitarian ideas of education familiar in our own time is a still more fundamental threat to reason itself through the monopoly exercised by the inductive method common to both. In experimental science reason proceeds inductively from sense observation to ideas. In the empirical Enlightenment's concept of reason, we know only through the immediate sense experience of things; ideas are derived only from a comparison of our own sensations; only our own conclusions are valid. Because both this philosophy and science reduce reason to the empirical intellect, Newman spent his life defending the other kinds of reason oppressed through their imperial pressures. From an early sermon in 1826, in *The Idea of a University* (1852), to his final book, *An Essay in Aid of a Grammar of Assent* (1870), he argued the cause of the other kinds of reason that are cultivated traditionally through liberal studies and are also engaged by religious reflection.

The same assumptions that Newman confronted in the nineteenth century are even more embedded in our own system of education through a methodology that holds reason hostage. The importance of Newman's voice to our era will become apparent as we listen to his arguments in *The Idea of a University* for the unity of knowledge and diversity of methods and as we follow their implications for education in his dramatization of classroom practice. By contrast, the limited and narrow idea of reason that permeates contemporary pedagogical practice will emerge through its prototype: that is, in the eighteenth-century educational philosophy of Jean-Jacques Rousseau which recognizes only the physical world. The similarities between Rousseau's philosophy of education and the methodology mandated for teaching in our own classrooms today will demonstrate the profound disturbance caused in education by the tyranny of empirical epistemology and its exclusion of the two other principal kinds of reasoning championed by Newman.

In *The Idea of a University,* when Newman maintained that the foundation of education is in universal knowledge, he represented an idea assumed since antiquity but increasingly alien by his own period. The idea of knowledge as an entire whole underpinned the studies in Aristotle's Lyceum in the fourth century BC; in the first century BC the Roman orator, Cicero, claimed that the field of rhetoric included all knowledge human and divine understood as a whole. A millennium and a half later, when the universities were being founded in twelfth-century Europe, this idea of knowledge understood as a whole was still assumed. Newman argues for this same idea of the unity of all knowledge from both a philosophical and theocentric perspective. In his evocation of the cosmic unity of knowledge, he dispels any assumption that only the physical world is of consequence as the empirical enlightenment or modern science might claim. Rather, he represents knowledge as a monumental structure, divine, human, and physical, that the mind can take in as a whole only by viewing it in parts from various angles.

This structure is known through its various aspects represented in the many disciplines or sciences where each discipline is at once in control of its own domain and part of a larger whole. The science of theology, the science of grammar, or the science of geology each operates according to its own principles and its proper integrity without interference with these principles or this integrity by any other science. This means that just as the science of theology is not to interfere with Galileo's mathematics and experimental observations, so the method of sense observation belonging properly to the physical sciences is not to be imposed on the study of language or religion.

At the same time as operating within their own province, since the sciences are parts of "one large system or complex fact,"[1] they are also all interconnected and incomplete portions converging and contributing towards the mass of knowledge as a whole. Here in this unity of knowledge understood as whole, the philosophy of education meets a theology of education. In the tradition of education in which Newman writes, the complex unity of knowledge is theocentric; it is grounded in God as first and final cause, at the very opposite pole from the sensate materialist philosophy of Rousseau as well as from any exclusive study of the physical sciences and of secondary causes. Newman finds in God as Creator and Sustainer the common source of all knowledge: in both the physical realm and the social and moral human domain. And equally importantly, in God, too, he finds the source of the laws that constitute the mind as the various keys that open for us a knowledge of the universe. Quite simply, God is the Source and Guarantor of universal knowledge and of its coherent intelligible unity, the philosophical ground of knowledge.

In *The Idea of a University*, Newman describes the Creator and Sustainer, the Warrant of universal knowledge, as at once a divine Person distinct from the world and implicated in it. Newman asserts that God is an "invisible, intelligent Being," an invisible Agent: not only "behind the veil of the visible universe ... acting on and through it, as and when He will," but also "absolutely distinct from the world, as being its Creator, Upholder, Governor, and Sovereign Lord." And so of the animal creation Newman writes: "His are the tribes and families of birds and beasts ... His are all beings, visible and invisible, the noblest and the vilest of them." Because of an intelligent Creator, material creation can be investigated according to intelligible principles: "the primary atoms of matter, their mutual action, their disposition and collocation, electricity, magnetism ... are the work of His hands."

As Creator or invisible Agent, God is also the source of intelligibility in the order of humankind. Newman continues: "And so in the intellectual, moral, social, and political world, Man, with his motives

---

[1] John Henry Newman, *The Idea of a University* (University of Notre Dame Press: Notre Dame, 1982) p. 33.

and works, with his languages, his propagation, his diffusion, is from Him." Viewed from the perspective of Providence, the intelligible pattern of history is from Him: "the periods and eras ... not the incidental sin, over-abundant as it is, but the great out-lines and the results of human affairs, are from His disposition." So, too, theoretical or speculative truth and principles in human affairs, the received starting-points of deductive reasoning disdained by the inductive materialist philosophers are from God: proverbs, "the majestic precepts of philosophy, the luminous maxims of law, the traditionary rules of truth, justice, and religion, even though imbedded in the corruption, or alloyed with the pride, of the world, betoken His original agency, and His long-suffering presence."[2]

And, finally, the gifts of the intellect, our various modes of reasoning, and the elements of the mind are from God. In the *Grammar of Assent* (1870), Newman emphasizes the theocentric origin of the various laws of the mind as keys to knowledge of the universe with the important caution regarding the use of the right method for the matter at hand. He writes that we have God's blessing when we follow the method proper to our subject-matter, whether the way of observation or of experiment, as in the physical sciences, of speculation or of research, when the principles of things and their consequences are important, or of demonstration and of probability.[3]

The assumption in this tradition of a coherent, interconnected world accessible to the various operations of the mind has a direct bearing on teaching in its intelligible connection of particulars. In his brief reference to methodology in *The Idea of a University*, Newman asserts: "I hold very strongly that the first step in intellectual training is to impress upon a boy's mind the idea of science, method, order, principle, and system; of rule and exception, of richness and harmony."[4] Even from a child's first years in school, accuracy, thoroughness, and attentiveness to detail are to be cultivated according to the pedagogical maxim of "a little well," the *multum non multa* of the Latin proverb.

What Newman meant by "a little well" is clearly illustrated in sample entrance exams in Greek and Latin grammar that he published for university candidates when he was Rector at the Catholic University of Ireland in the 1850s. Grammar was not neutral terrain.

---

[2] Newman, *Idea*, pp. 46-9.

[3] John Henry Newman, *An Essay in Aid of a Grammar of Assent* (University of Notre Dame Press: Notre Dame, 1979) pp. 275-6.

[4] Newman, *Idea*, pp. xliv.

On the one hand, the study of Greek and Latin grammar was still connected to the long tradition in classical education that was then just starting to change with the introduction of new subjects to the university like fine arts and the modern languages. On the other hand, the study of grammar had been under seige in educational theory since the seventeenth century; in the second half of the nineteenth century, as universal primary education was established, the study of grammar was again rejected by empirical reformers.

The seventeenth-century educational theorists who promoted the empirical inductive method and rejected both the deductive and literary reasoning of the language disciplines are well represented by Comenius, a Czech who briefly joined similar-minded educators in England in 1641-2. Comenius believed that the inductive method for empirical science described by Francis Bacon would, with some refinement, become a universal method leading to world-wide certitude and light. For the puritan English educational reformers, education was meant for the advancement of science and its alleviation of human suffering and need endured since the Fall; education was to inculcate exclusively the empirical inductive method proceeding from sense observation to general laws. Languages, too, had to conform to this method. Although access to certain classical texts like Pliny's work on the natural sciences was still considered important, the deductive reasoning of grammar which begins with abstractions rather than sense observation had to be eschewed. To teach Latin without grammar and to cultivate sense observation in this scientific program, Comenius devised textbooks that circulated for the next centuries throughout Europe. In them labelled woodcuts illustrated such things as tools and useful occupations accompanied by descriptive sentences in both Latin and vernacular languages like English. Nineteenth-century thought on the education of children was informed by similar principles. In the same period as *The Idea of a University*, Herbert Spencer speaks in his work on education of the intensely stupid custom of teaching grammar to children.

Newman's sample oral exams in Latin and Greek grammar for university candidates proceed, then, from very different premises than those of seventeenth and nineteenth-century reformers. They illustrate the cultivation of the two kinds of reasoning excluded by the reformers' programs: deductive and literary reasoning. The science of grammar proceeds not through sense observation but includes deductive reasoning from observed rules abstracted from examples in the language itself. Disciplines like grammar were valued also for their strengthening in the individual of the power of deductive reason. In comments in the university newspaper on geometry, Newman refers similarly to the strengthening of deductive reasoning through the study of geometry which was considered an asset to the verbal arts of writing and speaking, to logic and metaphysics. When Newman was preparing for his Oxford fellowship exam in 1822, which involved especially Latin composition, he records that he made the study of mathematics "his principal subject because of the general strength it imparts to the mind."[5]

In contrast to Rousseau's sensate empirical model, the grammar exams also affirm the idea that disciplines are intelligibly structured. As Newman explains, an entrance exam is itself a reflection of the idea that education and the sciences that comprise it are a connected system based on fixed principles, building up, part by part, methodically, towards a definite end. The entrance exam ensures that students might profit from university lectures by having an elementary knowledge on which to build: failure to master fractions before studying square roots will lead to frustration.[6]

A final important distinction between the tradition represented by Newman's grammar exams and the empirical educators lies in the humanist connection of grammar to literature. Unlike the reformers' scientific program where language is connected to the sense observation of material things, language is studied instead in conjunction with the expression of thought: that is, through literature in its broadest sense, a world reflected through the filter of an author's mind and heart such as Cicero's reflections in his correspondence with his friends. Here on this field of literature or letters the second kind of reasoning typical of the humanities is developed: that is, the converging, congruent rationality of literature. Unlike either the inductive or deductive sciences that operate within single fields, the reasoning characteristic of literature draws from various quarters: from any discipline related to the understanding of an author's thought. For this reason, Newman insisted that history is little better than a storybook if it is disconnected from the chronology and geography that anchor it in time and place.

During the oral entrance exam Newman demonstrates the

---

[5] Newman, *Autobiographical Writings*, pp. 59-61.
[6] John Henry Newman, *The Catholic University Gazette* (James Duffy: Dublin, 1854-5) p. 7.

converging rationality of literature through the exchange of question and answer in the classic triad of teacher, text, and student; questions range from the meaning of words, to an author's philosophical school, to geography and history. In the entrance exam in Greek, after asking the candidate to translate the title of the *Anabasis*, Xenophon's account of a Greek conflict in Asia Minor, the examiner then asked basic collateral questions about history and geography. He asks questions on the implications of the title's prefix, *ana* (up), in the context of the movement of the Greek troops up through Asia Minor towards the Persian capital, Susa; he attempts to elicit from the student the capital's name, the name of the Persian emperor, Xerxes, and information about the empire's dates and its extent. He directs the candidate to the text itself to see that the point of departure of the Greek troops was from Sardis and he asks what countries they would pass through on their way up from the coast of Asia Minor to Persia. The basic factual questions regarding history and geography not only make the reading more fully real but illustrate the preference Newman had for socratic questioning, even in university lectures, on the grounds that learning is neither passive nor impersonal and follows a different trajectory for different people.

And so, as the sample entrance exams invite us into a university room and into an exchange where classroom practice is animated, we enter into into a demonstration of the two kinds of reasoning associated with liberal studies. These exams are meant to demonstrate that the converging reasoning of literature and the deductive connection of rules to examples not only lead to a command of other languages and to an understanding of texts; they also develop the habit of connecting ideas to specific instances and to a healthy distrust of unsubstantiated generalizations or claims. Newman writes of the schoolboy: "Let him once gain this habit of method, of starting from fixed points, of making his ground good as he goes, of distinguishing what he knows from what he does not know, and I conceive he will be gradually initiated into the largest and truest philosophical views."[7]

Newman believed that this training in the exact use of language connecting the general to particular instances was a training in independent thought. The accurate understanding and use of words was a protection against intellectual quackery or against accepting the latest unexamined assumptions paraded in catchwords and slogans. Those trained in the exact use of language would not be drawn in by

---

[7] Newman, *Idea*, pp. xlv.

shallow theories through what Newman calls the misty and inexact use of words and phrases, particularly in politics and religion: words like 'civilization' and 'progress' or 'freedom of conscience', or 'the Gospel'. Rather than being controlled by words, they would have a command both of language and of the thought conveyed by it.

Even as Newman was writing and delivering lectures in Dublin on the idea of a university in the 1850s, the fledgling system of elementary education in England was being established according to the same empirical philosophy that he resisted with his full intellectual strength for more than forty years. Matthew Arnold, who was not only a poet but also a school inspector for thirty years in this new system of elementary education, records in school reports his dismay at the tyranny exercised by what was then called the concrete method. This method, grounded in empirical philosophy, rejected deductive reasoning or rule-teaching in favour of teaching things in the concrete rather than in the abstract; for example, the abstract rules of grammar. This method also suppressed the literary imagination, marginalizing the literature that both teaches and delights; instead, children were given passages to read on subjects like the new gas lighting in the streets. This separation of language from literature contributed to the children's limited vocabulary which distressed Arnold. Because inductive reasoning from sense observation was privileged, the methodology traditional to the language disciplines was discouraged; memory work such as learning poetry by heart was disparaged, Arnold says, as an old-fashioned, unintelligent exercise.[8] The concrete method which limits the mind to one way of knowing endured in Britain until 1914. After a hiatus, it returned in the reforms of education that began in the 1960s. In our own systems of education, it is with us yet.

Nineteenth-century popular education, as our own, was influenced by the inductive method not only as advocated by the English seventeenth-century reformers but also as exacted by the philosophical premises and concept of mind of the empirical Enlightenment. Newman was categorical in his denunciation of the assumptions of its philosophers who recognized only one operation of the mind. He described the empiricist, David Hume, and the utilitarian philosopher, Jeremy Bentham, as simply a disgrace. Among the empirical philosophers, no one exercised more influence than Rousseau on the elements and principles of the culture of the inductive

---

[8] Matthew Arnold, *Reports on Elementary Schools 1852-1882* (Eyre and Spottiswoode: London, 1910).

method prevalent in education in our own era. His philosophy of education is the inverse of the tradition that Newman represents: a tradition grounded in a Creator uniting all knowledge divine, human, and physical and recognizing all the operations of the mind including deductive, inductive, and converging reasoning. Rousseau's philosophy of education was neither Christian nor humanist but materialist; that is, it recognized only the physical world. As a consequence, there was only one way of knowing, through the comparison of one's own sensations derived from the physical observation of things or from one's own experiences. In other words, in this empirical philosophy, the inductive method meant for the physical sciences was transmuted into an epistemology.

Ironically, in Rousseau's connection of the inductive method of science to materialist philosophy even the goal of empirical scientific reasoning was redirected. In his philosophy of education, the cultivation of the empirical method was diverted from its end in the common good as envisioned by seventeenth-century educational reformers. Its *telos* was located instead at the opposite pole; that is, in the interests of the individual. As for the two kinds of reasoning associated with the humanities, they were simply eliminated. The luminous starting-points of principles and ideas that are the signposts and guides for deductive reasoning were dismissed as prejudice and prejudgment. This means that in pedagogical method, as Matthew Arnold found, reasoning from rules was forbidden. Similarly, as Arnold observed, literature was excluded.

To appreciate the closing of the mind effected by this materialist philosophy and its narrow epistemology, Rousseau's educational thought must be understood within its sources in the neo-epicureanism introduced into the empirical Enlightenment tradition by Pierre Gassendi (1592-1649).[9] Unlike Newman's theocentric tradition, for Epicurus (341-270 BC) the goal of life was to maintain

---

[9] Like Francis Bacon (1561-1626), Pierre Gassendi (1592-1649), Provençal abbot, philosopher and teacher of mathematics, was repulsed by the method of Aristotelian verbal logic and its domain of speculative truth which was counter to the new orientation of the age represented by astronomers like Galileo, and to the kind of logic or method needed for empirical observation in the physical sciences. In *On the Aristotelian Logic* (1624), Gassendi wrote typically of the lack of utility of verbal method in arriving at truth; that dialectic has no necessity or utility; that definition or division in artificial language is useless in distinguishing the true from the false. In 1626 Gassendi began his work on Epicurus in whose ideas he found a philosophy more congenial to the empirical tendency of his age. His work culminated in the *Syntagma philosophiae Epicuri* (Treatise on Epicurean Philosophy), a commentary on the work of the third-century biography of Epicurus by Diogenes Laërtius, which was published posthumously in 1659.

personal serenity or tranquility through both an economic and inner self-sufficiency or freedom (*eleutheria*). This state of bodily health and freedom from psychological distress was to be attained through the avoidance of pain and the pursuit of pleasure and through knowledge of the natural limits of both. For Epicurus, the perturbation of personal serenity through the two great fears, fear of the gods and fear of death, was eliminated through the atomist physical theory of Democritus. According to this prescient theory of physics from antiquity, everything was begotten and dissolved by the motion of an infinite number of atoms, travelling through the void with great swiftness, combining and colliding. As a result, in the words of the Roman epicurean poet, Lucretius (c. 95-55 BC), "nature is seen to be free at once and rid of proud masters, herself doing all by herself of her own accord, and having no part or lot in the gods."[10] Mind and spirit born in living creatures, like the body, are mortal. Virtue is what is useful to individual tranquility. Removed from the register of right and wrong, from religious sources of morality, as well as from universal or perennial ideas and definitions, justice is based on mutual advantage. Friendship is an egotistical pleasure.

Rousseau mirrors exactly this epicurean telos and its tenets in his first work on education. In the conclusion of his *Discourse on the Sciences and Arts* (1750), he says that true philosophy lies in knowing how to be content with ourselves. Here, couched carefully in the terms of disapproval made necessary by eighteenth-century censorship, he writes of a philosophy that claims that only matter exists, that there is no God but this world, that neither vices nor virtues exist, and that good and evil are dreams. To forward neo-epicurean philosophy and its materialist method, Rousseau also repudiates the fine arts and the humanism of the Renaissance. Throughout his work, he disparages the liberal tradition in literature and philosophy whose literary and deductive modes of reasoning do not fit sensate epistemology and materialist assumptions. He associates the arts and sciences with luxury, idleness, and the corruption of wealth, and he praises the virtuous simplicity of life before the advent of the arts and sciences in primitive and rustic peoples.

In Rousseau, then, we find a radically different idea from the tradition Newman represents in antithetical views on the nature of knowledge, the mind, and the goal of education. Instead of an objective world whose coherence and intelligibility are guaranteed by

---

[10] Lucretius, *De Rerum Natura* (William Heinemann: London, 1924) p. 7.

a Creator, knowledge is entirely self-referential. In Rousseau's works on education, the goal is in self-sufficiency through attunement to the material world of nature, independent not only from God but as much as possible from others. Our self-sufficient beatitude lies in "amour de soi"; that is, in self-esteem or self-love effected through our relation to the material world of things, our true teacher. In this forerunner of child-centred education, the goal of self-sufficiency and self-esteem means that we are to be masters of ourselves, not of others, neither tyrants nor slaves. In the relation between parent and child or between teacher and pupil, the words command and obey have no place; pupils are to obey only what is taught to them through the neutral world of things. To maintain contentment in the equilibrium between our faculties and our desires in relation to the world of things, the imagination is to be suppressed; only humankind, Rousseau explains, has superfluous faculties.

In *Emile* (1762), Rousseau's second and best-known work on education, his narrow theory of mind and his materialist philosophy are illustrated through the framework of child-rearing and the education by a tutor of a fictional character called Emile. A lesson by Emile's teacher on refraction through the example of a stick partially submerged in the water is at the same time an illustration both of his theory of mind and of the empirical method, the only pedagogical method that his epistemology will allow, the same method that dominated in Matthew Arnold's time and has monopolized our own.

Although the purpose of the lesson is to teach refraction, abstractions are to be avoided like in the nineteenth-century concrete method. There is to be neither hypothesis before investigation nor verbal conclusion at the end of it. While Emile's teacher is aware that he has taught the principle of refraction, for Emile it is enough to have absorbed the lesson in the concrete. In an illustration of how judgment is based on a comparison of sensations, Emile and his teacher walk around the submerged stick making observations from different angles. They notice that the break in the stick turns as they do; looked at from straight above, the stick is no longer curved; when they stir the water's surface, the stick follows the undulations of the water; and when the water flows out, the stick straightens out as the water goes down. Guided by his teacher, Emile will discover for himself the idea of refraction without actually articulating it in words.

In this phase of Emile's education, all is to be learned through the same method of compared sensations, the only way we know. Unlike the intelligibly sequential and systematic tradition represented by Newman, for Rousseau's pupil learning is incidental, almost random, because knowledge is embedded in the concrete. Since reason is connected to immediate sense experience no further effort is required once an idea is reached; nothing has to be learned, nothing is to be memorized; no direct teaching is to take place. Instead, the role of the teacher is limited to contriving situations that facilitate Emile's observation of things in which alone authority rests and from which he is to draw his own conclusions. In accordance with the epicurean concern for the self, Emile's own desire to learn will be his motivation; when needed, the teacher is to arouse this desire by interesting him in materials which should be of immediate practical utility or relevance to him. Emile will simply learn to read on his own when sufficient motive is provided, such as receiving a letter from his father. Rather than teaching world geography through maps, Emile will learn geography through his own observations by making a map of the area between the city where he lives and his father's country house. Rousseau exults: "See the difference there already is between your pupils' knowledge and mine's ignorance! They know maps, and he makes them."[11] As for history, because words are known only in relation to things, Emile will not even know the word.

Although the second phase of Emile's education has exerted the most influence on our own pedagogical method, the first is significant for indicating what is considered unimportant. In Rousseau's theory of child development, prior to the second phase that begins with adolescence, education consists in sharpening sense perception. Unless connected to sense, all knowledge is hollow. The sensate method connected to things in the first phase of education eliminates everything taught to children in the traditional verbal culture Newman represents; neither languages and grammar, nor history, nor geography, nor poetry, nor religious knowledge enter into Emile's education. For him, Rousseau says, the present will not be sacrificed to the future as in other schools where children are made into galley-slaves. He will be concerned only with his immediate palpable interest and will learn only what he feels to be of present utility.

Neither the literary imagination, the converging reason of literature, nor deductive maxims have any place in young Emile's education. There is no place for the delight Newman describes in his reading as

---

[11] Jean-Jacques Rousseau, *Emile or On Education*, trans. and intro. Allan Bloom (Basic Books: New York, 1979) p. 171.

a boy Aesop's fables and the stories of *The Arabian Nights*. In the first phase of education for Rousseau, the tradition of teaching children through fables like the fox and the crow is dismissed on the grounds that what the poems describe lies outside of Emile's experience: for example, a talking fox and the poetic word order. Even when Emile is allowed to read La Fontaine's fable in the final phase of his education, the moral at the end is to be omitted because he is never to accept the reasoning of other people. Indeed, in general books are boring; they do not teach us to reason according to Rousseau's empirical model of reasoning; they teach us the reason of others.

However, the single most serious consequence for education in Rousseau's philosophy is its denial of the diversity of methods assumed in Newman's tradition. Instead, a universal method is assumed as a key to all knowledge and exercises absolute control over it. Incredible as it may seem that a theory rejecting most of the faculties and operations of the mind might dominate whole systems of education, yet such in fact is presently the case. All disciplines are affected by this monopoly of method: the sciences and mathematics are estranged; languages, literature, religious knowledge, and the arts are alienated.

If the school system is a laboratory for testing the validity of philosophy, then the claims for a universal method by inductive empirical philosophy are demonstrably absurd. We do well to heed Newman's theocentric view of the various ways we know and of the blessings derived from following their paths, or Aristotle's view that knowledge of the right method was just as important as a knowledge of ideas. If the teaching of second languages is in disarray through the application to it of an alien method, other subjects, too, must suffer from the imperial designs of a method that claims to be universal. Has Rousseauian epistemology beginning with sense observation influenced the method of teaching reading through the visual observation of words and through guessing words in a book from visual clues in pictures? Has this epistemology's categorical rejection of memorization dictated the downplaying of learning by heart multiplication tables in arithmetic? Does the Rouseauian premiss that morality is learned through a comparison of experiences influence the teaching of religious education through a group sharing of experiences. Does Rousseauian pedagogy that forbids direct teaching affect the teaching of history through the project method that assigns students to collect data for themselves? These questions are important as methods are not neutral; a method meant for material investigation and applied to the humanities or religion cannot rise above its own limits.

If Newman is considered a nineteenth-century prophet and sage, it is in part because he understood the importance of the elemental distinctions between methods which, along with an understanding of the principles of the various disciplines, assure that education keeps on the right path. The usurpation of reason by one mode of thought that he observed in the nineteenth century has become an unconscious assumption in our own era. Newman's recognition of the disorder of the intellect, his analysis of the illness, his arguments for the various modes of reasoning that constitute our humanity make him a much-needed doctor for the ailments in our present systems of education. In those afternoon lectures delivered in the late spring of 1852 to his Dublin listeners and in his reflections on method in his University Sermons and *The Grammar of Assent*, we find for our own times and our own classrooms both an alarm rung and a path made clear.

Chapter 4

"A GREAT MISCHIEF":
NEWMAN ON LIBERALISM IN RELIGION

by Robert Barron

Introduction

Some years after he had elevated John Henry Newman to the college of Cardinals, Pope Leo XIII ruefully commented to an English visitor: "*Il mio Cardinale* (my very own Cardinal)! It was not easy, it was not easy. They said he was too liberal."[1] To be sure, some of the resistance to Newman's elevation was personal, but the Pope's remark indicates the very real ideological opposition to one who had operated so often outside of the customary framework of Catholic thought. To many of his traditionally-minded contemporaries, Newman was indeed a progressive, an ally of such questionable figures as Lord Acton and Ignaz Döllinger. Moreover, in the decades immediately following his death, Newman was often claimed as an inspiration by some of the leading Catholic modernists. George Tyrell was a self-described Newman 'disciple', and Alfred Loisy, who kept a portrait of Newman in his home just outside of Paris, invoked the Cardinal's teaching on the development of doctrine frequently in his own writings.[2] And in the years just prior to the Second Vatican Council, many theologians of a more progressive stripe – Congar, Bouyer, Balthasar, de Lubac, among others – were deep admirers of Newman. Finally, if one surveys the writings of liberal Catholics today, one sees certain key ideas of Newman – doctrinal development, the consultation of the laity, a

---

[1] Quoted in Ian Ker, *John Henry Newman: A Biography* (Oxford: Oxford University Press, 1988), p. 715.
[2] Marvin O'Connell, *Critics on Trial: An Introduction to the Catholic Modernist Crisis* (Washington, DC: Catholic University of America Press, 1994), p. 183.

somewhat restrained understanding of papal authority – frequently cited and enthusiastically explored.

And yet, in his *Biglietto* speech of 1879, delivered upon reception of the letter formally announcing his appointment as Cardinal, Newman said that his entire intellectual career – both as an Anglican and Roman Catholic – should be interpreted as a steady struggle against "liberalism in religion."[3] Allowing for no ambiguity in regard to his attitude, he characterizes liberalism as a "great mischief" and "an error overspreading, as a snare, the whole earth."[4] How can we begin to explain the anomaly that a hero of so many liberals should be the scourge of liberalism? Happily, Newman himself goes a long way toward resolving the dilemma through his careful definition of the famously slippery and multivalent term. In the *Biglietto* speech, he states, "liberalism in religion is the doctrine that there is no positive truth in religion, but that one creed is as good as another ... it is inconsistent with any recognition of any religion as *true*."[5] Making this characterization even more precise, he asserts that, for liberals, "revealed religion is not a truth, but sentiment and taste."[6] Then he draws some practical implications from this definition. First, "it (liberalism) teaches that all religions are to be tolerated for all are matters of opinion ... Men may go to Protestant Churches and to Catholic, may get good from both and belong to neither."[7] In accord with what some have named the modern "peace treaty", the liberal society tolerates religion as long as it remains a private matter, insuring that any religion's claim to cultural relevance is seriously attentuated. In Newman's terms, "since then religion is so personal a peculiarity and so private a possession, we must of necessity ignore it in the intercourse of man with man."[8] The liberal program was not, he felt, utterly devoid of merit. In fact, it inculcated the virtues of "justice, truthfulness, sobriety, self-command, and benevolence." But Newman makes the rather stark observation that this whole range of liberal precepts and virtues was designed to "supersede, to block out religion," and that, therefore, "there never was a device of the Enemy so cleverly framed and with such promise of success."[9] The

---

[3] John Henry Newman, *Biglietto* speech (see Appendix).
[4] Ibid.
[5] Ibid.
[6] Ibid.
[7] Ibid.
[8] Ibid.
[9] Ibid.

very attractiveness and nobility of the liberal program made it an especially insidious opponent of traditional religion.

In his great intellectual autobiography *Apologia pro vita sua*, Newman provides a brief characterization, very much in line with his observations in the *Biglietto* speech: "my battle was with liberalism; by liberalism I meant the anti-dogmatic principle and its developments." He goes on to specify that, though his mind had changed in regard to many things in the course of his lifetime, in this opposition to liberalism, he had remained firm: "From the age of fifteen, dogma has been the fundamental principle of my religion ... I cannot enter into the idea of any other sort of religion; religion, as a mere sentiment, is to me a dream and a mockery."[10] In an appendix to the *Apologia*, we find a much more detailed account of the phenomenon of liberalism, culminating in eighteen carefully worded propositions meant to delineate its salient features. What emerges as central here is liberalism's elevation of autonomous reason to a position of interpretive primacy in regard to the affirmations of faith. Proposition one runs as follows: "no religious tenet is important, unless reason shows it to be;" and proposition number two articulates a corollary: "no one can believe what he does not understand."[11] Propositions four and five bring us quite close to the central argument of *A Grammar of Assent*, for they articulate the position on religious assent that Newman directly opposed in his late-career masterpiece: "it is dishonest in man to make an act of faith in what he has not had brought home to him by actual proof," and "it is immoral in a man to believe more than he can spontaneously receive as being congenial to his moral and mental nature."[12]

If we take these statements from the *Biglietto* speech and from the appendix to the *Apologia* as a guide, we can identify Newman's two major concerns in regard to liberalism. First, its denial of an intellectual density to the Christian faith, or to state it somewhat differently, its tendency to reduce Christianity to feeling and subjective sentiment. This is the type of religious liberalism on display in Schleiermacher and his army of disciples in the nineteenth and twentieth centuries. Second, its insistence that reason appropriately positions and interprets faith. This mode of liberalism can be seen in practically every major

---

[10] John Henry Newman, *Apologia pro vita sua* (Garden City: Image Books, 1956), pp. 163-164.
[11] Ibid., Appendix A.
[12] Ibid.

modern philosopher who took an interest in religion: Spinoza, Leibniz, Hegel, Jefferson, and Emerson, to name just a few. But it was no more evident than in the writings of Immanuel Kant. In his *Religion Within the Limits of Reason Alone* (a title which fairly gives away the game), Kant argued that a purely Biblical religion can exist alongside a rational religion as long as they don't seriously conflict; but he insisted that, were they to fall into tension, the former would have to cede to the latter. What I propose to do in the remainder of this chapter is to explore in some detail Newman's refutation of these two forms of "the great mischief."

The Properly Intellectual Character of Christian Religion

Though the intellectuality of Christianity is a central theme in a number of Newman's writings, it receives its fullest treatment in the discourses that he gave in connection with his appointment as rector of the Catholic University of Ireland in 1852, later collected as the text, *The Idea of a University*. The practical issue that inspired Newman was the increasing prevalence of excluding theology from the curriculum of university studies. For the first time since the founding of universities in the Middle Ages, it was being proposed, in the mid nineteenth century, that religion did not belong in the circle of academic disciplines, along with the physical sciences, literature, mathematics, etc. In the second of the Dublin lectures, Newman engages this issue head on, proposing the following syllogism: by its very nature, a university professes to teach universal knowledge; theology is surely a branch of knowledge; therefore theology must be taught in any university worthy of the name. His argument will hinge, therefore, on the defense of the minor premise.[13]

The advocates of the exclusion of theology from the university have proposed, says Newman, a number of restrictive criteria for determining the intellectual validity of a system of thought, and they have, in light of these principles, found religion wanting. For example, some say that the only legitimate sciences are those that are based on sense experience and that the supernatural claims of religion, which cannot be verified sensibly, are therefore not scientific. Others maintain that abstract reasoning is the test of authentic intellectuality and that, consequently, the historically-based doctrines of Christianity

---

[13] John Henry Newman, *The Idea of a University* (Notre Dame: University of Notre Dame Press, 1986), pp. 14-15.

cannot possibly be intellectually dense. Still others hold that since real knowledge is what is given through immediate intuition, the dogmas of Christianity, which transcend experience, are not matters for properly intellectual exploration.[14] But Newman answers these objections with a neat *tu quoque*. If the criterion of sense experience were strictly applied, then ethics would be excluded from the circle of disciplines; if abstract reasoning were the benchmark, then physics would be set aside; and were immediate intuition the litmus test for intellectual respectablity, then history would be eliminated. In short, these various attempts to justify the marginalization of theology are grounded in an irrationally restrictive set of criteria. Then Newman turns the tables on these critics. Is it not the case, he asks, that God's existence is indeed testified to in sense experience (as Thomas Aquinas showed in his famous five proofs), in the intuition of the conscience, and in the testimonies of historical witnesses? Therefore, he concludes, it is by an altogether arbitrary (and finally unreasonable) edict that the liberal organizers of university curricula advocate the exclusion of theology.

Other critics are more subtle, in the measure that they speak for the exclusion of religion from the university precisely on religious grounds. They maintain, in the Schleiermacherian mode, that religion consists, not in knowledge, but in feeling. To be sure, religious faith is indispensible to human well-being and to the satisfaction of a desire for security and union with the sublime, but, they argue, it would as unreasonable to have a chair of religion at a university as to "demand a chair of fine feeling, a sense of honor, patriotism, gratitude, maternal affection, or good companionship."[15] In this context, Newman cites a British politician to the effect that religious belief is akin to "peculiarities, idiosyncracies, accidents of the individual," over which a person has no real control, and he draws attention to a British educator who held that the purpose of religious instruction is to cultivate one's feelings and "to teach the poetry of devotion, the music of well-ordered affections."[16] But this sort of subjectivism, Newman insists, turns God into a vague short-hand for "the forces of nature" or "fate" or "the universe considered as a totality" and thus becomes repugnant to an authentic monotheism which holds God to be a reality utterly distinct from the world. More to it, it undermines the

---

[14] Ibid., p. 19.
[15] Ibid., p. 22.
[16] Ibid., p. 24.

classical Christian conviction that faith is an intellectual relationship to this objective divine being. Therefore, both sets of critics are wide of the mark, and there exists, in point of fact, no real justification for the liberal exclusion of religion from the circle of university sciences.

At the beginning of the third discourse, Newman considers a compromise position, forwarded by some educators, viz. that religion, though objective and scientific, ought to be cultivated in private and not in the public context of a university.[17] In response, Newman argues that Truth, the proper object of the mind, is tantamount to the knowledge of the infinitely complex relations among existing things. In its proper sphere and in accord with its peculiar methodology, an individual science legitimately pores over an aspect of reality, but, for that very reason, it cannot therefore aspire to speak for the whole, to provide, on its own, access to the Truth. When it attempts such an imperialistic grasp, it is led, necessarily, into falsehood. Thus, for example, were a chemist to claim for chemistry a vision of the whole, he would, perforce, deny the existence of the free will. Truth is served only when each particular science respects the dignity and legitimacy of the others. Therefore, the exclusion of theology from the public discourse of the university will have a deleterious effect on the intellectual conversation, the pursuit of Truth. But the consequences of this exclusion would be particularly devastating, precisely because theology speaks of that reality which impinges so directly on the whole of finite existence.[18] According to traditional theology, God is not one being among many, a supreme instance of the genus "being". Rather, God is the creator of all things, the reason why there is something rather than nothing, the condition for the possibility of contingent reality. Consequently, though God is other than the world, he necessarily presses upon every aspect of the world with unconditioned power. He is the ground of the physical world and hence has to do with the physical sciences; he is the beauty which inspires all artists and writers; he is the good who stands behind every human action and endeavor; he is spoken of, directly or indirectly, by the poets and philosophers of every culture and every age. Given the nature of God, it is impossible therefore to admit that the exclusion of the science of God from the circle of university disciplines would have anything but a negative effect on the quest for Truth. Newman's conclusion: "religious truth is not only a portion, but a condition of

---

[17] Ibid., p. 33.
[18] Ibid., p. 52.

general knowledge. To blot it out is nothing short, if I may so speak, of the unravelling of the web of University Teaching."[19]

In discourse number four, Newman makes explicit a point that was implicit in the previous speech, viz. that the compromising of the intellectual density of theology will conduce in short order to the dangerous imperialism of a rival discipline. The only science that can legitimately hold a central place in the circle of university subjects is theology, since, as we saw, it speaks of the Creator God who grounds the whole of finite being. Once theology has been demoted and marginalized – as it must be in liberalism – another science will necessarily move into the controlling position, and this will conduce toward the skewing, not only of that particular science, but of the entire university enterprise. As a first example of this process, Newman mentions the manner in which music, art, and architecture became decadent and extravagent once they lost their relationship to religion and declared themselves self-sufficient.[20] Another instance is the cognitive totalitarianism of economics in the Marxist mode, whereby our knowledge of the whole of society – art, literature, the army, politics, business – is reduced to economic principles and thereby distorted. We find something very similar today, of course, in so much of postmodern philosophy, which holds to the primacy of power relationships in practically every aspect of life. Newman helpfully sums up this final argument: "supposing theology be not taught, its province will not simply be neglected but will actually be usurped by other sciences, which will teach without warrant conclusions of their own in a subject matter which needs its own proper principles for its due formation and disposition."[21]

The style of argumentation used in discourses three and four is indirect. Whereas in the second speech, Newman had rather straightforwardly demonstrated the intellectual character of theology, in the next essays, he showed that the fundamental drive of the mind – the quest for a coherent grasp of the whole – would be fatally compromised were theology, in the liberal manner, allowed to devolve into a species of subjectivism.

---

[19] Ibid., p. 53.
[20] Ibid., p. 59.
[21] Ibid., p. 74.

Faith as the Reasoning of a Religious Mind

We recall that the second feature of liberalism that Newman highlighted was its tendency to allow for the positioning of faith by secular reason. So many of the avatars of the Enlightenment construed religion as fundamentally irrational and therefore dangerous; what they proposed as a corrective was a rationalized, and hence universalized, religion. This taming and domesticating of Christian faith is an aspect of the liberalism that Newman consistently fought. One of the clearest expositors of the modern, rationalist approach to religion was an English philosopher for whom Newman had great respect, viz. John Locke. As a grounding for his proposal of a "reasonable" Christianity, Locke articulated a powerful critique of the traditional stance of faith. In his writings on the theory of knowledge, he held that there must be a strict correspondence between the assent to truth and the logical inference which grounds that assent. One should not, he felt, give a proposition any more credence than the proposition can bear, so that if the inferential support for a claim is weak, one's assent should be weak, if the inferential support is absolute, one's assent should be absolute. To contravene this principle is not only epistemologically irresponsible but unethical: "it is not only illogical, but immoral to carry our assent above the evidence that a proposition is true ... to have a surplusage of assurance beyond the degrees of that evidence."[22] Though it seems, *prima facie*, safely reasonable, this classically liberal proposal, Newman saw, amounted to a frontal assault on the primacy and independence of faith as a mode of knowing religious truth. For if inference and assent are tied as tightly as Locke claimed they are, then many of the creedal affirmations of classical Christianity are made illegitimately and irresponsibly. An interpretive key to Newman's *A Grammar of Assent* is to read that great text as a sustained argument against Locke's liberal understanding of the relationship between inference and assent.

Newman takes it as basic that, *pace* Locke, we frequently give unconditional assent to propositions and ideas for which we can muster far less than utterly convincing inferential arguments. For instance, we unhesitatingly assent to what Newman calls "the furniture of the mind," that is to say, that full range of basic beliefs, assumptions, convictions, etc., in light of which we navigate our way through the

---

[22] Cited in John Henry Newman, *An Essay in Aid of a Grammar of Assent* (Notre Dame: University of Notre Dame Press, 1979), p. 138.

world.[23]   But who among us could mount a clear and convincing argument for the conviction that the law of gravity will hold today as yesterday, that space and time will continue to be the framework of experience, or that fire is dangerous to the touch?   In regard to these foundational assertions, assent and inference are not in tight correlation.   Or again, our assent to a given proposition might fail, even though the reasons for making that assent remain unassailed. We can find our minds suddenly changed, due to events in our personal lives, to the cross word or critique of a colleague, to the influence of the company that we keep – and not at all due to shifts in the argumentative base. Or, on the contrary, despite strong and persuasive arguments for a position, we sometimes fail to give assent. Newman observes in this context, "we sometimes find men loud in their admiration of truths which they never profess" and "a man convinced against his will is of the same opinion still."[24]   To be sure, certain demonstrations or inferences, if they are short and luminously clear, command assent by themselves, but Newman thinks that such arguments are rare, outside of the area of mathematics. Normally, the process of coming to assent must be supplemented by a wide range of other influences. The upshot of these observations and examples is that the relationship between assent and inference is far more subtle than Locke thought. Indeed, unconditional assent is so typically given without unconditional inferential support that we can formulate a kind of law of the mind to the effect that we accept propositions as true which lie "outside the narrow range of conclusions to which logic, formal or virtual, is tethered."[25]

Now none of the above should lead us to the conclusion that logic and inference have no role to play in the act of coming to assent. In point of fact, argues Newman, formal inference – usually reducible to some configuration of the Aristotelian syllogism – is an indispensible guide to correct thinking. To the extent that names and logical symbols can capture the range and variety of individual things, syllogisms function well. "All men have their price; Fabricius is a man; therefore he has his price." That pithy argument is valid in the measure that the abstraction "man" includes and corrals that utterly unique individual Fabricius. It is certainly true in general that human beings can be bought and bribed,

---

[23] Ibid., p. 141.
[24] Ibid., p. 143.
[25] Ibid., p. 150.

but perhaps Fabricius is the one great exception to that rule, in which case, the syllogism will fail. "Thus it is," Newman concludes, "that the logician ... turns rivers, full, winding, and beautiful, into navigable canals. To him, dog or horse is not a thing which he sees, but a mere name suggesting ideas."[26] He is suggesting that syllogisms by themselves can never reach definitive conclusions because they can never attain to the level of the particular. Because they commence with abstractions, they can end only with some type of general indication, not definitive proof. Even in the "exact" physical sciences, Newman holds, there is room for error because general natural laws cannot reach every possible case. Therefore neither abstract logic nor the natural sciences "prove" in the strict sense, but they do indeed open up vistas and perspectives, pointing toward the right answer: "though it (the syllogism) does not go so far as to ascertain truth, still it teaches us the direction in which truth lies ... Nor is it a slight benefit to know what is probable and what is not so ..."[27]

If, therefore, inferential reasoning is valuable but insufficient, how do we explain the fact of unconditional assent? If Locke is wrong, how do we get from inference to assent? Newman's answer to these questions, found in the section on informal inference, constitute the heart of *A Grammar of Assent*. We come to be certain about concrete, finite matters, he says, through "the accumulation of probabilities, independent of each other, arising out of the nature and circumstances of the particular case ... probabilities too fine to avail separately, too subtle and circuitous to be convertible into syllogisms ..."[28] As an illustration of this process, Newman proposes the manner in which we come to unconditional certitude in regard to the proposition that Great Britain is an island. No one thinks that an air-tight syllogism or strict logical argument for the truth of this claim could be constructed; nevertheless, only mad people would hesitate to affirm it with complete assurance. What gives us the serene confidence that goes beyond logical warrant? We have, argues Newman, in a largely unconscious way, culled and arranged a whole series of probable arguments that converge in the direction of affirming Great Britain's insularity. We have been taught from childhood that Britain is an island; it has been so described on every map that we have ever seen; everyone who speaks of Britain assumes that it is an island; the entire history of Great

---

[26] Ibid., p. 215.

[27] Ibid., p. 228.

[28] Ibid., p. 230.

Britain implies and assumes it; in our own explorations of Britain, this presumption has been borne out, etc.[29] Similarly, why am I convinced that one day I will die? Even the famous syllogism "all men are mortal; I am a man; therefore, I am mortal" is not utterly convincing in itself, for it is just possible that I am that one great exception to the general rule. The syllogism certainly points me in the direction of the truth, but I assent to the proposition because I can see everywhere around me the process of decline and aging; I know that people have died; I have never met or heard of anyone who has attained, say, 150 years. These probable arguments, converging toward the same point, lead me to unconditioned assent. Signalling the indirect and largely instinctual nature of this process, Newman recalls the story of a judge who always handed down his rulings with great confidence and authority but never gave the explicit rationale for his judgments. Newman observes approvingly, "his decisions were likely to be right, but his reasons sure to be unsatisfactory."[30]

What is the faculty of mind by which these converging probable arguments, hunches, intuitions, experiences, and examples are arranged? Coining a term on the basis of the Latin word for carrying, Newman called it the "illative" sense. The illative sense is the instinct by which the judgment is carried across the gulf that separates inference from assent. What is the sanction or justification of this faculty? It is accepting ourselves, epistemologically, as we are and not as we might wish to be. A consistent mark of the modern theory of knowledge – evident, for example, in both Descartes and Locke – is a tendency toward angelism, but Newman is not an angelist. In a higher world it might be the case that assent is flawlessly conformed to inference, but here below, we reason in a messier, less exact, more complex way. And what precisely is the nature of the illative sense? It is, says Newman, the intellectual counterpart to *phronesis* or right moral judgment, what Thomas Aquinas called "prudence", the capacity to see how the moral law applies in a given situation. Just as prudence deftly assesses motive, situation, circumstance, consequences, and nature of the act in itself in order to make a coherent moral choice, so the illative sense surveys and sizes up the wide range of evidences – both rational and non-rational – in order to make a right intellectual judgment concerning the truth of things.[31]

---

[29] Ibid., p. 234.
[30] Ibid., pp. 240-241.
[31] Ibid., p. 277.

Having surveyed the central argument in the *Grammar of Assent*, we are now in a position to understand more clearly how this refutation of Locke is crucial to Newman's battle with liberalism. Part of the liberal agenda was to control and domesticate faith by relegating it to a secondary and subservient level vis-à-vis reason. What Newman has demonstrated is that the sharp demarcation between faith and reason advocated by Locke and his colleagues is false, that in point of fact, reason and faith operate in remarkably similar ways, through a subtle process of assessing both inferential and non-inferential evidence. By undercutting the claim to a qualitative difference between reason and faith, Newman effectively placed in question the liberal assertion that reason properly orders and positions faith. In one of his University Sermons, Newman neatly summed up this argument with the pithy formula that faith is nothing but the reasoning of a religious mind.[32] In other words, the faithful person is not irrational (as more extreme versions of liberalism would have it), but rather rational in regard to the things of revelation. Faithful people assent with complete assurance to propositions for which there is insufficient inferential support, but so do secular scientists and philosophers.

Conclusion

I commenced this chapter by observing the tension between Newman the critic of liberalism and Newman the hero of liberals. I further specified that what liberals of Newman's time and ours have found attractive in his theology is a certain stress on doctrinal development, the active role of the laity, and a nuanced understanding of papal authority. Obviously, within the confines of this brief chapter, I cannot even begin to do justice to Newman's treatment of these subtle issues, but I hope that my clarification and explanation of Newman's understanding of liberalism has served to resolve the apparent tension at least to some degree. To claim that the meaning of doctrine unfolds as it is assessed by "lively minds" is by no means to call into question the integrity and objectivity of the truthfulness of Christianity, just the contrary. And to hold that ecclesial authorities may "consult" the faithful – in the manner of a physician consulting the pulse of his patient – in order to determine how and what one dimension of the body of Christ believes is certainly not to question the intellectual integrity of doctrine; it is rather to presuppose it. And to defend the

---

[32] Cited in Ker, p. 261.

relative freedom of a theological inquirer against a too aggressive exercise of ecclesial authority is hardly to allow faith to be positioned by reason; it is, instead, to allow the reasoning of the religious mind to operate within proper bounds and with helpful resistance. Perhaps it is truest to say that the apparent tension between Newman the liberal and Newman the scourge of liberalism is born of an insufficient grasp, on our part, of the range and subtlety of the thought of this nineteenth century master of Catholic theology.

PART II

THE CHURCH

Chapter 5

NEWMAN'S UNDERSTANDING
OF THE CHURCH

by David Gréa

The Church and Unity

It is sometimes argued that Newman made a real contribution
towards Christian unity in that, once he had become a Catholic, he
republished most of his Anglican writings. This seems to indicate that
a Christian who is led by faith and by a properly informed conscience
can develop a theology that is accepted by different communions. Yet,
isn't it surprising to call as a witness to ecumenism a Christian who
definitively left Anglicanism to join the Catholic Church?

While a study of Newman's life and work can undoubtedly offer
considerable support for ecumenism, it would be a pity however, as
much for ecumenism as for the knowledge of Newman's work, to
overlook the fact that the former Fellow of Oriel was convinced,
after 1845, that only one Church deserved to be called Catholic, and
that this was the Church of Rome: "The Catholic religion is given
from God for the salvation of mankind, and all other religions are but
mockeries."[1]

In this chapter, we will pay tribute both to Newman's genuine
Christian journey and to the crux of the matter that led him to join
the Catholic Church – the faith that leads to salvation. To do so, we
will look at the interaction and evolution of the ideas that Newman
had of the faith and of the Church. This might help us to understand
Newman's ecclesiology, and we believe that Christian unity will also
find a source of inspiration and motivation here.

---

[1] *Discourses to Mixed Congregations*, p. 20. For Newman's quotations, see www.newmanreader.
org.

1. 1801-1833: from his conversion to the beginning of his struggles

Before the autumn of 1816, the faith of young John Henry Newman was shaped by an Anglican upbringing based on Bible reading and catechism lessons. When he was fifteen, Newman realized that the God that was spoken of in the Bible existed for him, that He was his Creator. This knowledge of the existence of God, whom he knew as a person, developed in the wake of Anglican evangelicalism – which was mainly built on a Calvinist theology – and found its expression in the Athanasian Creed which the Anglicans often used in their liturgy. As salvation in Jesus revealed that God is triune, Newman undertook to collect passages from Scripture providing evidence for the dogma of the Trinity.[2] He soon considered the Christian faith as doctrines that are defined,[3] and once he had become a Catholic he wrote: "From the age of fifteen, dogma has been the fundamental principle of my religion: I know no other religion; I cannot enter into the idea of any other sort of religion; religion, as a mere sentiment, is to me a dream and a mockery."[4]

The doctrines of faith

His conception of the Church was influenced by his readings as well as by some of the persons he met and by his personal experiences. Once he was ordained a priest in the Church of England on Sunday May 29 1825, it did not take long for the newly ordained cleric to notice that the evangelical ideas that went along with his faith did not match reality and were not applicable in a parish: "that was unreal ... Calvinism was not a key to the phenomena of human nature, as they occur in the world."[5] At the same time he understood, thanks to Dr Hawkins, that "the sacred text was never intended to teach doctrine, but only to prove it, and that, if we would learn doctrine, we must have recourse to the formularies of the Church; for instance to the Catechism, and to the Creeds."[6] Newman developed this idea in his first book *Arians of the Fourth century*, as a fundamental doctrine calling into question the Protestant principle of *scriptura sola*. Of course, Scripture remained for Newman the source for preaching, the basis

---

[2] *Apologia pro Vita Sua*, p. 5.
[3] *Parochial and Plain Sermons*, Vol. 2, pp. 256, 258.
[4] *Apologia*, p. 49.
[5] *Autobiographical Writings*, p. 79.
[6] *Apologia*, p. 9.

for any evidence and the ultimate verification for any doctrine, but it was not sufficient to teach or to formulate the fundamental doctrines contained in the Athanasian Creed.

One of the temptations in our time consists in following a religious sentiment detached from any Creed, as if a dogma would reduce God to formulae. Newman did not fall prey to this fear because he considered the revelation of God and His existence as more certain than the flux of his personal emotions. The Creed manifested this exteriority of God who lets Himself be known according to His own ways and far beyond our understanding. However, if there was a Creed, a legitimate authority was also required to formulate it and guarantee its interpretation.

The Church takes shape in Newman's faith

After his conversion of 1816, Newman considered the Church as a necessary institution, but without any specific meaning. However, upon reading Butler's *Analogy*, he was struck by the demonstration that was given about the Church visible and the sacraments which she delivered.[7] For many years, he considered that the true Church was invisible and that it comprised the saved, whereas the Church visible was necessary for the life of Christians, yet without any possibility of identifying her members with those of the Church invisible.

In dialogue with Dr Whately from Oriel College, Newman learnt how to consider the existence of the Church as a living body, with real existence, not simply de facto but as a body endowed with a mission and an ecclesiastical government. It was at that time that he understood the importance for the Church to be independent from the State. In 1829, once he had been appointed vicar of St Mary's, he stated in a sermon why there had to be an authority in the Church and why Christians had to submit to it:

> If we had a living head upon earth, such as once our Saviour was with His disciples, teaching and directing us in all things, the visible Church might so far be dispensed with. But, since we have not, a form of doctrine, a system of laws, a bond of subordination connecting all in one, is the next best mode of securing the stability of sacred Truth.[8]

---

[7] *Apologia*, p. 10.
[8] *Parochial and Plain Sermons*, Vol. 3, pp. 198-99.

The Church, visible and invisible

At the time when the influence of his friend Richard Hurrell Froude was increasing and was imparting to him a certain admiration for the Church of Rome, John Henry Newman began to consider the Church of Antiquity as the model for the Church and for Christian living. Research work for his book *Arians of the Fourth Century* comforted him in this conviction and, from then on, he never ceased to read, translate and comment on the Fathers, particularly the Greek Fathers through whom the idea of the Church visible, her importance and her primary role for the faith gradually took hold of him. He would write in 1833: "Scripture makes the existence of a Visible Church a condition of the existence of the Invisible."[9] Newman also demonstrated that the sacraments, which are necessary for salvation as the catechism puts it, were in the hands of the Church visible, a durable society in continuity with that of the Apostles.

On the eve of the Oxford Movement, Newman believed that the Church had been divinely instituted to guarantee the faith of the Apostles and the promises of Christ. He gradually came to identify the Church visible with the assembly of the baptized (one becomes a member of the Church through baptism that justifies) while still speaking of the Church invisible, either to signify that baptism alone does not guarantee salvation,[10] or to include the Church in heaven. As a visible institution, she had a structure and a government that should enable her to keep the deposit of faith jealously and with no compromising with the State. Her rites and sacraments were the channels of grace.[11]

2. 1833-41: promotion of catholic doctrines – the Oxford Movement

In 1833, a few academics from Oxford, of which Newman soon became the leader, gathered together to find the means to fight erastianism[12] and liberalism. By liberalism, Newman meant

> the mistake of subjecting to human judgment those revealed doctrines which are in their nature beyond and independent of it,

---

[9] Tract 11, pp. 2-3, end of 1833.

[10] Newman was disconcerted by the incoherent behaviour of many of the baptised. He had to clarify what regeneration, justification, holiness and faith meant, and how they were related to one another, in order to resolve this problem. See *Lectures on Justification*.

[11] Cf. *Advertisement* to the 2nd Volume of the *Tracts for the Time*, p. v.

[12] A theory that unites Church and State and subordinates the former to the latter.

and of claiming to determine on intrinsic grounds the truth and value of propositions which rest for their reception simply on the external authority of the Divine Word.[13]

Through the *Tracts for the Time*, they aimed their arguments against the position that implied that people should believe whatever they think is right, even though they run the risk of not believing in God as His Revelation presents Him to us. In order to do this, the Tractarians set about to expound the proofs of the great catholic doctrines[14] which were vindicated by the Fathers of the Church and the Anglican divines.

The Tractarians against Rome

The prejudices of the Tractarians against the Church of Rome were sufficiently well established to maintain both that this church was a legitimate branch of the Catholic Church and that it contained and encouraged devotions which bore witness to the corruption of some of her doctrines.[15] Furthermore, to consider the Church of Rome as Antichrist was an Anglican principle:

> It was then a thought of genius, and, as I think, preternatural genius, to pitch upon the expedient which has been used against the Church from Christ's age to our own; to call her, as in the first century, Beelzebub, so in the sixteenth, Anti-Christ; it was a bold, politic, and successful move [...] the charge that Christ is Anti-Christ must not only be made, but must be sustained. ... Falsehood then has ever been the indispensable condition of the impeachment which Protestants have made.[16]

However, to answer the suspicion of Papism that was weighing heavily against the Tractarians, Newman developed a theory called the *via media*, of Anglicanism as a middle way between Protestantism (which in his view was leaning towards heresy and ran the risk of leading Christians into atheism) and Roman Catholicism (whose doctrinal corruptions seemed obvious to him). In 1837, he published a book, entitled *Lectures on the Prophetical Office of the Church,* which touched upon the question of the authority of the Church in matters of faith: "Both we and Roman Catholics hold that the Church Catholic

---

[13] *Apologia*, p. 288. (see the chapter on Newman and Liberalism).

[14] For the Tractarians, the term 'catholic' encompassed the Anglican, Roman and Orthodox churches. The catholic doctrines were those inherited from the Apostles and delineated by the Fathers of the Church.

[15] Tract 20, p. 1.

[16] *Present Position of Catholics in England*, pp. 224-25.

is unerring in its declarations of faith, or saving doctrine; but we differ from each other as to what is the faith, and what is the Church Catholic."[17]

The crux of the matter: the faith

Newman had thus put his finger on the crux of the debate: ecclesiology depended on the faith. The claim of the Catholic Church to be infallible made of her the only Church to claim the exclusivity to be catholic. She attributed to herself the prerogatives of the undivided Church. Going against the Church of Rome who considered with St Augustine that those who were separated from the body of the Church were *ipso facto* deprived of the inheritance of Christ, Newman affirmed that holiness and universality had not been actual since the schisms – the separation of the Greek church and the schism of the 16th century. He pleaded for the primacy of the principle of the purity of the faith over the principle of the unity of the Church. To defend this position, the Anglicans had to assume a development of doctrines, since the doctrines of the first centuries of the Church did not fully contain the Anglican system. Such an argument however could be used equally by Roman theologians. Newman concluded in the *Apologia*:

> I had the whole state of the question before me, on which, to my mind, the decision between the Churches depended. [...] After all, in my view the controversy did not turn upon it [the ministry of the pope]; it turned upon *the Faith and the Church*. This was my issue of the controversy from the beginning to the end. There was a contrariety of claims between the Roman and Anglican religions, and the history of my conversion is simply the process of working it out to a solution.[18]

The heart of Newman's interior debate could be summed up in these terms: catholicity versus apostolicity. The problem did not depend directly on a theological argument, but rather on the question of the faith and the Church. We will see later on that this question critically came to the fore once he had become a Catholic. Facing this problem head on, Newman realized that a clear distinction had to be made between the current state of customs in the countries in communion with Rome and the formal dogmas of that Church. While maintaining his accusations against Rome, Newman wanted to find arguments in

---

[17] *Via Media*, Vol. I, p. 212.

[18] *Apologia*, pp. 111–112. (Emphasis is mine.)

favour of the Anglican communion. He now had to give evidence that the *Thirty-nine Articles* which defined the Anglican faith were not opposed to a Catholic interpretation. If Anglicanism was indeed presenting the faith of the first centuries – otherwise she was not teaching the faith – a reading of the *Thirty-nine Articles* according to the catholic doctrines should prevail over the original intentions of their authors. This is what Newman set out to do in Tract 90.

3. Faith and Church: denouement

After its publication in 1841, Tract 90 was condemned by the very bishops whose authority Newman was striving to found on the Church of Antiquity. He then started to have qualms about the authenticity of the Church of England, fearing that it had never been a church.[19] However, as some of his prejudices against the Church of Rome were still as fierce, he had no intention of joining her. Years later he would look back on these prejudices in a very perceptive analysis of how they worked.[20]

In 1840, Newman had settled in Littlemore, a village located a few miles from Oxford, to pray and to be free from controversies. He gradually retired from his academic functions and pastoral duties as Vicar of St Mary's with a view to joining the Anglican laity.

When reading sermons by saints of the communion of Rome, Newman realised that nothing in the Catholic system interposed itself between the soul and its Creator:

> The Catholic Church allows no image of any sort, material or immaterial, no dogmatic symbol, no rite, no sacrament, no Saint, not even the Blessed Virgin herself, to come between the soul and its Creator.[21]

From 1843 onwards, he therefore undertook a close scrutiny of the principle of development in the doctrine of the Christian Church in order to understand how one could discern between an orthodox doctrine and its corruption. This study was clearly leaning in favour of the Roman church. Difficulties vanished one by one as he was making progress on his *Essay on the Development of Christian Doctrine,*

---

[19] *Apologia*, p. 158: "For myself, this only I see, that there is indefinitely more in the Fathers against our own state of alienation from Christendom than against the Tridentine Decrees." The reading of an article by Wiseman, his own study about Arianism, and the crisis of the Jerusalem bishopric justified this fear. (See *Apologia* chapter III.)

[20] *Present Position of Catholics in England.*

[21] *Apologia*, p. 195.

and he ceased using the term Roman Catholics and began to call them "Catholics". Before even finishing this book, Newman had resolved to be received into the Catholic Church. If one admitted that the Church was divinely guided, one could find that the doctrines she taught were already clearly delineated in the early Church "so that the question simply turns on the nature of the promise of the Spirit, made to the Church."[22] Newman deduced from this that there was no middle-ground between atheism and Catholicism and he concluded in these terms: "I hold this still: I am a Catholic by virtue of my believing in a God."[23]

Faith in the infallibility of the Church

Since Christianity is alive, it is natural for faith to develop and for there to be an authority to confirm the authenticity of these developments. Newman showed that it was legitimate to expect God to have established the Church so that faith would be safeguarded, according to the promise made to Peter. So when Newman became a Catholic, he made a new and decisive act of faith: "That the Church is the infallible oracle of truth is the fundamental dogma of the Catholic religion; and 'I believe what the Church proposes to be believed' is an act of real assent."[24] From then on, Newman considered the Church with the eyes of the Catholic faith: a supernatural yet very real vision of the Church. It was not enough to believe what the Church teaches to become a Catholic; it was also necessary to believe in her infallibility, that is to say in what she has not yet defined: "A convert comes [to the Church] to learn, and not to pick and choose."[25]

After 1845, Newman wrote that the power of the Church came from her very being and purpose: to fulfil her divine mission, the mission to fight mankind's rebellion against God. The Church had been instituted to fight against sin and she sacrificed nothing to that mission. This provides an explanation for the whole of the Church's teaching and action. She considers that human nature is not irredeemable, and that the restoration of each person is achieved not only through teaching and preaching, but also through a spiritual

---

[22] *Apologia*, p. 197.

[23] *Apologia*, p. 198. Contrary to what Newman implies in *Apologia* p. 10, it was only after 1845 that he used the word 'oracle' on a regular basis to qualify the Church. See for example *Discourses to Mixed Congregations*, Chapters 3, 8, 10, 11, 13, 17, 18.

[24] *Grammar of Assent*, p. 153.

[25] *Difficulties of Anglicans*. Vol. II, p. 18.

power and inner grace received from above and channelled through the Church. Newman was professing his faith in what the Church guaranteed, taught and decided. He denied the idea that infallibility would render the use of reason illicit and, on the contrary, he underlined the fact (verified historically) that the energy of human intelligence grows when confronted with opposition. The object of the Church's power was not to restrain the freedom or the vigour of thought, but to contain it and to control its excesses, as the history of the fight against heresies illustrates. During the process of investigation and deliberation that would culminate in an infallible decision, individual reason was always dominant.[26] Such a method tended to develop not only the freedom, but also the courage, of theologians or private controversialists. Furthermore, Catholicity offered a vast array of cultures, societies and methods, which protected the Church from being narrow-minded. Besides, Newman acknowledged the guidelines to the infallibility of the Church: the great truths of moral law, natural religion and apostolic faith; the Church should always be able to declare that she is guided by Scripture and Tradition.

From the notion of the Church to her reality

When he became a Catholic, Newman found himself in a body where all he had unceasingly been looking for and trying to demonstrate for years was accepted and lived out.[27] He went thus from a theory of the Church to a concrete experience of her. It might be thought that nothing had changed for Newman, that his passage to the Catholic Church was but the coherent consequence of the ideas he had been defending with his friends in the Oxford Movement. However, to move from one idea which could not find an embodiment for the life of this idea, to the reality of what you hold to be certain, modifies your ecclesiology, in so far as experience inspires and informs ideas.

---

[26] *Difficulties of Anglicans*, Vol. I, p. 301: "There is nothing to hinder his having his own opinion, and expressing it, whenever, and so far as, the Church, the oracle of Revelation, does not speak." See p. 312.

[27] *Difficulties of Anglicans*, Vol. II, p. 3, Newman remembered that he felt he was outside the family of St Athanasius and St Basil while he was studying them as an Anglican. "I recollect well what an outcast I seemed to myself, when I took down from the shelves of my library the volumes of St. Athanasius or St. Basil, and set myself to study them; and how, on the contrary, when at length I was brought into Catholic communion, I kissed them with delight, with a feeling that in them I had more than all that I had lost; and, as though I were directly addressing the glorious saints, who bequeathed them to the Church, how I said to the inanimate pages, 'You are now mine, and I am now yours, beyond any mistake.' "

To think is one thing. To experience and to live out concretely what you think is another. By experiencing the idea he had of the Church, Newman understood her, discovered her, sensed unforeseen connections and inner workings.[28] Shortly after joining the Catholic Church, while the Real Presence lay in the tabernacle of the chapel next to his room, he wrote:

> I could not have fancied the extreme, ineffable comfort of being in the same house with Him who cured the sick and taught His disciples, as we read of Him in the Gospels, in the days of His flesh.

Whereas before becoming a Catholic,

> I did not know, or did not observe, the tabernacle Lamp – but now after tasting of the awful delight of worshipping God in His Temple, how unspeakably cold is the idea of a Temple without that Divine Presence! One is tempted to say what is the meaning, what is the use of it?[29]

This turning point in Newman's faith is remarkable. What he had always been looking for, the presence of Christ, the contemplation of God, the promised graces, was now given to him. To a certain extent, one could say that his quest, thanks to his journey in the Church of England, had led him to have a truthful desire and a sound understanding of the faith, but that it had only become real when he had taken the decisive step in October 1845. This is the message he endeavoured to get across to his audience in lectures he gave in 1850: "When Catholics speak of faith they are contemplating the existence of a gift which Protestantism does not even imagine."[30] Newman drew his distinction between two conceptions of the faith from his own experience. This is how he underlined the contrast between Catholicism and Anglicanism:

> Still a great difference, for the Catholic Church [is] a body, a society such as no body of men is. Enumerate particulars. – (1) Not able to believe what they please, not knowing what they are pledged to; strictness of confession, the Church having a hold upon them. ... But this is the strength as well as the difficulty, for it is a body or society which has privilege.[31]

This is what would frighten his former colleagues, and what people tend to minimise or to reject today. He also stated from the pulpit:

---

[28] Cf. I. Ker, *John Henry Newman. A Biography*, Oxford, Oxford University Press, 1988, p. 351.
[29] *Letters & Diaries*, Vol. XI, p. 131, to Mrs J. W. Bowden, March 1/46.
[30] *Difficulties of Anglicans*, Vol. I, p. 269.
[31] *Sermon Notes*, pp. 4–5, 22 July 1849.

"It is not the Church enforces on them faith, but faith obliges them to take the Church."[32] For Newman, faith and the teaching of the Church were no longer conflicting. The Church seemed to be the final destination reached by Newman's theology, as can be noticed in the famous sermon he preached on July 13 1852 in Birmingham, entitled *The Second Spring.*[33]

4. Catholic ecclesiology
Lay people and the Magisterium: Authority in the Church

Once he had reached the port,[34] Newman did not cease being active. On several occasions he asserted that since he had become a Catholic he was at peace with his religion. Never did he regret or come to doubt his position. Leaning on the principles which led him to join the Church, he soon started to promote the commitment of an educated laity in society, as he was convinced that their influence would be decisive to rid the English people of its prejudices against the Church.[35] In May 1859, in an article in *The Rambler*, he stated that if the laity had been consulted on matters relating to dogmatic decisions "as lately in the instance of the Immaculate Conception,"[36] it was all the more appropriate to listen to their opinions in matters relating to their areas of expertise. On seeing that the notion of consulting the laity in dogmatic matters (which he had touched upon in his article) was criticized, he replied in the same magazine: "The body of the faithful is one of the witnesses to the fact of the tradition of revealed doctrine, ... their consensus through Christendom is the voice of the Infallible Church."[37] Newman had joined the Church thanks to the Catholic faith seen at work in the history of the Church, and, in the name of this same faith, he was now upsetting the standard

---

[32] *Sermon Notes*, p. 77, 27 April 1851.

[33] *Occasional Sermons*, p. 169: "The Catholic Church, that great creation of God's power." See also *Occasional Sermons*, pp. 123, 129.

[34] *Apologia*, p. 238: "It was like coming into port after a rough sea; and my happiness on that score remains to this day without interruption."

[35] *Present Position of Catholics in England*, p. 390: "What I desiderate in Catholics is the gift of bringing out what their religion is; it is one of those 'better gifts,' of which the Apostle bids you be 'zealous.' You must not hide your talent in a napkin, or your light under a bushel. I want a laity, not arrogant, not rash in speech, not disputatious, but men who know their religion, who enter into it, who know just where they stand, who know what they hold, and what they do not, who know their creed so well, that they can give an account of it, who know so much of history that they can defend it."

[36] *The Rambler*, p. 122, May 1859.

[37] *The Rambler*, p. 205, July 1859.

ecclesiology of his time. The controversy had serious consequences in the relationship that the Oratorian had with the Catholic hierarchy, from England to Rome. It left him wounded, and he wrote in his diary at the time:

> It has made me feel that in the Blessed Sacrament is my great consolation, and that while I have Him who lives in the Church, the separate members of the Church, my Superiors, though they may claim my obedience, have no claim of my admiration, and offer nothing for my inward trust.[38]

What can be noticed here is that the certainty of belonging to the unique Church of Christ did not shield the Oratorian from the human and spiritual struggles any Christian has to put up with, who endeavours to live out his faith concretely within the Church and in the world. For Newman, the criterion for discerning the legitimacy of the Church and of her authority did not come from a human feeling of well-being or from the fraternal expression of community, but from her divine origin and her charisms. As an Anglican, he was already stating that the Church, as in one of the parables of the Kingdom of heaven, was filled with good and bad fish.[39] It was not the individual quality of Christians which ensured the faithfulness of God to his promises, but the Holy Spirit. This distinction between the charism and the person enabled Newman to remain faithful to the living Magisterium of the Church while his faith remained unscathed by the faults and shortcomings of his superiors. The fact that there existed a gift of infallibility in the Catholic Church did not entail that the members of the Church that received it were infallible in all their actions. There was in fact a risk, which the Oratorian denounced, of an act of authority being imposed in a tyrannical fashion. In Newman's mind there was no confusion between authority and infantilism. To believe in doctrines did not mean for him having to conform to all sorts of devotions, nor to overstate the Church's authority on all subjects.[40]

---

[38] *Autobiographical Writings*, pp. 251-52, January 8 1860.

[39] Mt 13:47-50. Cf. *Difficulties of Anglicans*, Vol. II, p. 81.

[40] A Letter Addressed to the Rev. E. B. Pusey…, in *Difficulties of Anglicans*, Vol. II, p. 28: "The faith is everywhere one and the same, but a large liberty is accorded to private judgment and inclination as regards matters of devotion." A Letter Addressed to the Duke of Norfolk …, in *Difficulties of Anglicans*, Vol. II, p. 256: "Conscience being a practical dictate, a collision is possible between it and the Pope's authority only when the Pope legislates, or gives particular orders, and the like. But a Pope is not infallible in his laws, nor in his commands, nor in his acts of state, nor in his administration, nor in his public policy. Let it be observed that the Vatican Council has left him just as it found him here."

The organic Church

In 1847, Newman and his companions decided to become Oratorians, in the footsteps of Saint Philip Neri. The Oratory took into account and respected the diversity of the charisms of its members and offered great flexibility as far as mission was concerned. This acknowledgement of the complementarity of charisms in the Church was one of the characteristic features of Newman's ecclesiology. This organic dimension of the Church, however, could sound beautiful in theory and turn out to be more confused in practice, as the history of the Church teaches us. In Newman's view, the Church was fulfilling her work, even though this may not seem obvious at first glance. In 1877 Newman had the opportunity to take up his book *Lectures on the Prophetical Office of the Church,* which we have already mentioned, with a view to republishing it. Since he was denouncing, in the first edition, the excesses of both the Roman Catholics and the Protestants as opposed to the wisdom of the *via media*, he wrote a Preface for the edition of 1877, and added numerous footnotes, from which one can measure the abyss that there was between the author's conception of the faith and the Church first in 1837, and then after his conversion. In this lengthy Preface, he answered the Anglican objections which he had formulated, at the time of the first edition, against the Church of Rome. He now developed an organic vision of the Church in her offices of Priest, Prophet and King. He specified how their respective spheres of authority were clear, determined and ordered organically, so that the Church may receive vitality and impetus from the Spirit, in her faithfulness to the dogmas, and in the manner she lives them out, teaches and understands them at each period in history. But beyond this demonstration, Newman came back to the necessity of faith to recognize and understand the Church:

> We need not feel surprise then, if Holy Church too, the supernatural creation of God, is an instance of the same law, presenting to us an admirable consistency and unity in word and deed, as her general characteristic, but crossed and discredited now and then by apparent anomalies which need, and which claim, at our hands an exercise of faith.[41]

One should not trust appearances, nor should one try to understand the life of the Church without the faith.

---

[41] *Via Media,* Vol. I, p. xciv.

To return to where we started

In this study, by trying to show the particular links Newman established between the faith and the Church, we have necessarily emphasized the differences or oppositions he brought to light between the Anglican and the Catholic positions. However, it should be stressed before concluding this chapter that the Oratorian's intellectual rigour, as well as his personal knowledge of Anglicanism and his empathy with the Anglicans' questions, gave him legitimacy and earned him a gratitude that was publicly expressed for the first time when he was asked to become the first honorary fellow of Trinity College in Oxford.

When Newman was created a Cardinal by Leo XIII on May 12 1879, it was his work as well as his life that was given recognition. In the wake of that event, Newman received congratulations from all sides, and one of his friends, an Anglican priest, wrote to him:

> I wonder if any man, at least of our time, was ever so loved by England – by all religiously minded England. And even the enemies of faith are softened by their feeling for you. And I wonder whether this extraordinary and unparalleled love might not be – was not meant to be – utilized, as one means to draw together into one fold all Englishmen who believe. I can conceive no more powerful nor truer eirenicon.[42]

This last quotation bears favourable witness to the ecumenical impact of Newman's life and work.

Conclusion

It is not altogether true to claim that there is continuity in Newman's ecclesiology without mentioning the real break to which he kept alluding from October 1845 onwards. Yet, it is clear that his becoming a Catholic came at the end of a process, starting with a spiritual experience which he interpreted within the evangelical mindset, and whose thirst he later slaked at the wellspring of the Anglican divines. He was gradually led to give a real assent to the Catholic Church, instituted by Christ, under the influence of the Holy Spirit, guided by Scripture and faithful to antiquity. It is his faith in this Church that gave him the criteria to understand the developments of her dogmas, of her structure and inner life. It is this faith that preserved the divine origin of the Church and ensured the reception of God's promises. It is this faith in God, and therefore in the Church, that enabled him to

---

[42] *Letters & Diaries,* Vol. XXIX, p. xvi, 6 October 1879 from Octavius Ogle.

understand her hierarchical and organic organisation. This faith, far from denying individual conscience and the use of reason, illuminates them and enables them to deploy their faculties in fruitful tension.

It is notable that Newman's works remain highly relevant today. Indeed, the Anglican objections, which he set out to answer, seem nowadays to be uttered by many a Catholic. Reading Newman would undoubtedly prove extremely helpful to our time.[43]

Newman's journey helps us to understand how important it is for Catholics to be formed within the Church, so as to know their common faith and to be able to account for it. Far from turning them in on their own identity, this faith opens them up and enables them to discern the work of the Holy Spirit in others. As for Anglicans, Newman kept calling them to act in accordance with their principles, announcing to them time and again that he had found the living expression and the reality of the Church – as he was presenting her up to 1845 – in the Catholic Church, which was in communion with the Pope. It is precisely through faith and for his salvation that Newman joined in full communion with the Catholic Church. [44]

---

[43] We particularly recommend reading the *Essay on the Development of Christian Doctrine* and the *Apologia pro Vita Sua.*

[44] *Letters & Diaries*, Vol. XXI, p. 315, letter to E. B. Pusey, Nov 25/64: "I think that to be in communion with Rome is to be united to the Church of the promises, of grace and of salvation."

Chapter 6

NEWMAN, THE CHURCH
AND THE WORLD

by Andrew Nash

It is one of the ironies of Newman's life that the movement which was ultimately to project him into the Catholic Church began as a defence of the Church of England. In the 1830s reform was in the air, and the privileges of the Established Church were coming under the critical gaze of unfriendly politicians. Churchmen had been alarmed by Catholic Emancipation in 1828 under the Tories, and now the Whigs were in power. Fresh from the overwhelming victory of the Reform Act of 1832, they were now turning their attention to the anomaly of the Established Church in Ireland which was paid for by the taxes of a resentful Irish Catholic population. The finances of the Church of England would be the next target. For Newman and his High Church friends, all this was the unacceptable encroachment of the State on the rights of the Church. It was in this atmosphere of 'the Church in danger' that John Keble preached his Assize Sermon of 1833, 'National Apostasy'[1], which Newman always regarded as the beginning of the Oxford Movement.

To the modern secular historian, all such resistance to reform seems purely reactionary, and obviously no Catholic has sympathy with a rearguard defence of the Protestant Ascendancy. Certainly the churchmen lost in this struggle, and the liberal reformers carried all before them, gradually but irreversibly bringing about the transformation of British society – part of the wider pattern of the evolution of Western civilisation which has produced today's liberal democratic culture. So the specific issues which so alarmed

---

[1] Readers may most easily access this via the internet, e.g. http://anglicanhistory.org/keble/keble1.html.

Keble, Newman, Pusey and their followers now seem antiquated and irrelevant. Yet Catholics and some other Christians today may find that Keble's sermon still has resonances because it deals with the fundamental question of what we today call secularism – the ideology that civil society should completely exclude any public role for religion. Keble noted

> the growing indifference, in which men indulge themselves, to other men's religious sentiments. Under the guise of charity and toleration we are come almost to this pass; that no difference, in matters of faith, is to disqualify for our approbation and confidence, whether in public or domestic life.

Keble saw this relativising of belief as evidence of a fundamental rejection by British society of its former claim to be a Christian nation, paralleling it with the Israelites' rejection of God at various times in the Old Testament. The much more developed secularising of our society since then, most notably the rapid abandonment of Christian sexual morality, may in fact make Keble now appear more prophetic than reactionary.

Newman and the other churchmen who formed the Oxford Movement were thus responding to a new hostile cultural climate. The great issue was: what is the relationship between the Church and society? The Church of England was supposed to be just that – the nation together in one church. True, English history since the Reformation had been littered with battles about the rights of 'dissenters', i.e. non-Anglican protestants, but at least all were Christians (who were united in their hostility to Catholics). The Church of England was established by law and woven into the fabric of the nation's cultural and political institutions. As a state church it was subject to the Crown and therefore to Parliament. So, presumably Parliament could reform or change the Church as it thought fit. Or could it? Did the Church not have rights of its own, as a divinely instituted body?

Although Newman's conversion as a young man had been to the Evangelical school of Christianity, he had gradually moved towards a more High Church position. Crucial in this process had been his reading of the Fathers of the early Church. Here he found a Church which was at first surrounded by a hostile state which persecuted it. The Church was thus in its origins counter-cultural – something which he would understand more profoundly once he became a Catholic. But even after the conversion of the Emperor Constantine, when the Church emerged from the catacombs it found itself in a fraught relationship with the state which now wished to embrace it. Newman's first book, *The Arians of the Fourth Century*,[2] brings this home forcefully.

Arianism was a heresy which struck right at the heart of what Christians believe about Jesus. For Arius and his followers, Jesus was 'like God' and could even be termed the 'Son of God', but he wasn't actually God from God and consubstantial with the Father, as the Creed was ultimately to define. As we read Newman's narrative of the tumultuous events which Arianism provoked, we see how much the struggle was affected by the Church's recent emergence into its public role in Roman society. No sooner had Constantine proclaimed toleration of Christianity than he was interfering in it. The Arians had the ear of the imperial court, and whatever Constantine really believed (or even understood) about Christological doctrine, he was determined that there should be peace on this matter throughout the Church. To gain influence, the Arians courted the secular power which in turn did not hesitate to use force to get rid of those who upheld the traditional orthodox faith. The great champion of orthodoxy, Saint Athanasius, was repeatedly banished from his See. Perhaps most painful of all to the Catholic reader is the fall of Pope Liberius, himself in exile for upholding the orthodox faith. The imperial power tempted him to give in, using the argument that it was for the good of the Church – an argument 'enforced by the threat of death as the consequence of obstinacy'[3] – together with the offer that he could return to his See. Tragically, Liberius succumbed, agreeing to condemn Athanasius and to sign an ambiguous confession of faith which, while it could be interpreted in an orthodox sense, could also accommodate the Semi-Arians. He later regretted what he had done under this pressure – but it's hard to find a worse example in the history of the Church of the baleful power of the state, even against the papacy itself, to promote heresy.

So Newman saw that the Church must struggle with the world to preserve and teach the truth it has received from Christ:

> the Christian Church, as being a visible society, is necessarily a political power or party. It may be a party triumphant, or a party under persecution; but a party it always must be, prior in existence

[2] The critical edition is published by Gracewing/Notre Dame, 2001, edited with an introduction by Rowan Williams (before he became Archbishop of Canterbury) who finds much evidence in the text of Newman's preoccupations with the state of the Church of England.
[3] Op. cit., p. 321.

to the civil institutions with which it is surrounded, and from its latent divinity formidable and influential, even to the end of time. ... In truth, the Church was framed for the express purpose of interfering, or (as irreligious men will say) meddling with the world. It is the plain duty of its members, not only to associate internally, but also to develop that internal union in an external warfare with the spirit of evil, whether in Kings' courts or among the mixed multitude; and, if they can do nothing else, at least they can suffer for the truth, and remind men of it, by inflicting on them the task of persecution.[4]

Studying Arianism also made Newman aware of the role of the laity in upholding the Faith. Later, when he was a Catholic, he was delated to Rome (though ultimately cleared) for his article 'On Consulting the Faithful in Matters of Doctrine', and today liberal Catholics like to cite Newman in support of a concept of 'reception' by which they mean that a doctrine is only true if laity decide they agree with it. But this is to misunderstand Newman's context – it was the ordinary Christian faithful who instinctively rejected Arianism which was very much a heresy of the educated. Arians were those who were most at home in the intellectual world of the late Empire, Greek-speaking sophisticates who looked down on the conservative Latins as backwoodsmen who didn't understand theological nuances. Arianism was a doctrine which was in tune with the spirit of the age, promoted by prelates and emperors. But it was wrong because it destroyed the central Catholic tenet of the Incarnation. As Newman was later to put it: 'The Catholic people, in the length and breadth of Christendom, were the obstinate champions of Catholic truth, and the bishops were not.'[5]

It had been 'Athanasius *contra mundum*', and the prolonged Arian crisis showed Newman how essential was the autonomy of the Church 'against the world'. In his writings for the Oxford Movement, Newman more and more expressed his discomfort with the way that the Church of England compromised with 'the world'. In 1842 the church agreed to team up with Prussian government and institute a Protestant bishopric of Jerusalem which would alternate between England and Prussia and preside over Calvinists, Lutherans and Anglicans alike – with the handy side-effect of giving England

---

[4] Ibid., p. 258-9.

[5] Ibid., p. 445; this is from the extract from Newman's article in the *Rambler* magazine of July 1859 which he added as an Appendix to the edition of *Arians* republished towards the end of his life.

and Prussia political clout in the Holy Land. To Newman, for whom the apostolic succession was an article of faith, this subordination of a church principle to political pragmatism was deeply shocking. It was evident that the church was being treated as an arm of the state.

But it was not just the constitutional subordination of the church to the government that worried Newman and his fellow Tractarians; it was also the invasion of worldly culture into the church. It was partly a matter of style, but style can be very expressive of underlying attitudes and beliefs. For instance, in an article he wrote for the *British Critic* (the house magazine of the Tractarians) Newman brings out how different the ethos of the early Church was from that of respectable English Protestantism, contrasting the ancient practice of alms-giving with the modern church bazaar:

> much might be said of the potent influence exerted on such occasions by the young ladies who ofttimes take their station at the booths and vend their charity. Aged bishops are said, of old time, to have exerted an arm of force, and to have compelled others to enjoy the privileges, and undertake the duties of the Christian Church; – but now-a-days, bright eyes and tasteful bonnets are found more effective.[6]

Newman's gentle mockery points up the way that religion has become a matter of fashion and social occasions – in a word, it has become worldly. Popular Protestantism had developed a secular culture of its own which was utterly at odds with the Church of the Fathers:

> The Temple of this new system is Exeter Hall [the London venue for large anti-Catholic public meetings]: its holytide is "the London season;" its chancel is a platform; its cathedral throne is the chairman's seat; its ministers are the speakers; for holy salutations it uses "Ladies and Gentlemen;" for benedictions it has "cheers;" for a creed it maintains the utility of combination; and for holy services and godly discipline it proclaims civil and religious liberty throughout the world.[7]

To our ears 'civil and religious liberty' are of course admirable objectives. But Newman is making the point that these have become a substitute for the preaching of the Gospel. A modern parallel might perhaps be the environmental movement which, while doubtless having vitally important aims, has become for many people a substitute for religious belief (even adopting formerly religious vocabulary about 'saving the world').

The problem with fashionable causes – even laudable ones – is

---

[6] 'Exeter Hall', *The British Critic*, XXIV (July 1838), p. 197.
[7] Ibid., p. 198.

that they can be easily supported by those who are comfortably off, those today sometimes termed the 'chattering classes'. Religion, on the other hand, should not be too comfortable. Newman's journalism during the Oxford Movement included some effective satire on the religious habits and attitudes of the middle and upper classes. For example, in an article on the 'The American Church' Newman noted the dangers in this episcopalian sister-church of Anglicanism becoming so attractive to the 'respectable' classes in the United States:

> If this view of things is allowed a footing, a sleek gentleman-like religion will grow up within the sacred pale.

On the comfortably furnished American churches he comments with irony:

> we think we may say without fear of mistake, that pews, carpets, cushions and fine speaking are not developments of the Apostolical Succession.[8]

This may sound a long way from defending the Faith in a relativistic age, but Newman is warning about what happens when the Church becomes too accommodated to the world.

Once Newman became a Catholic, he gave even freer rein to his critique of worldliness in establishment Christianity. His novel *Loss and Gain* is best known as a fictionalized account of the difficult conversion experience which members of the Oxford Movement had been through, so it has lengthy passages of theological discussion. But it also has much humour in Newman's depiction of religion which compromises itself with the world. We are introduced to the hero's Tutor, Mr Vincent, who, like all Oxford dons at that time, is an Anglican clergyman:

> he was of a full habit, with a florid complexion and large blue eyes, and showed a deal of linen at his bosom, and full wristbands at his cuffs. Though a clever man, and a hard reader and worker, and a capital tutor, he was a good feeder as well; he ate and drank, as he walked and rode, with as much heart as he lectured in Aristotle or crammed in Greek plays. [...] Beside this he preached a good sermon, read prayers with unction, and in his conversation sometimes had even a touch of evangelical spirituality. The young men even declared they could tell how much port he had taken in Common-room by the devoutness of his responses in evening-chapel.[9]

---

[8] *Essays Critical and Historical*, vol. I, p. 302.
[9] *Loss and Gain.*, p. 74.

Newman satirises the way Mr Vincent gives a religious gloss to his comfortable lifestyle, as the college Manciple presents him with the next meal's menu for approval:

> "Watkins," he said, giving it back to him, "I almost think to-day is one of the Fasts of the Church. Go and look, Watkins, and bring me word." ...
>
> Watkins returned sooner than could have been expected. He said that Mr. Vincent was right; to-day he had found was "the feast of the Apostles."
>
> "The Vigil of St. Peter, you mean, Watkins," said Mr. Vincent; "I thought so. Then let us have a plain beefsteak and a saddle of mutton; no Portugal onions, Watkins, or currant-jelly; and some simple pudding, Charlotte pudding, Watkins – that will do." [10]

This absurd compromise with the real traditions of the Church extends to Anglican doctrine. Mr Vincent goes on to warn the book's hero, Charles Reding, against "pushing things *too far*" in his theological views and gives a lengthy encomium on the Church of England's *lack* of doctrinal unity:

> Even our greatest divines differed from each other in many respects; nay Bishop Taylor differed from himself. It was a great principle in the English Church. Her true children agree to differ.

This reaches its climax in a description of the church of England as a tree which

> sheds its fruits upon the free earth, for the bird of the air and the beast of the field, and all sorts of cattle, to eat thereof and rejoice. [11]

What is effective here is Newman's linking of the food motif with the theological disunity and the pseudo-Biblical rhetoric of the establishment Protestantism of his day. Later in the novel, Charles explains to his sister:

> "I cannot bear the pomp and pretence I see everywhere. ... Here are ministers of Christ with large incomes, living in finely furnished houses, with wives and families, and stately butlers and servants in livery, giving dinners all in the best style. ... There is a worldly air about everything, as unlike as possible the spirit of the Gospel. I don't impute to the dons ambition or avarice; but still, what Heads of houses, Fellows, and all of them evidently put before them as an end is, to enjoy the world in the first place, and to serve God in the second. Not that they don't make it their final object to get to heaven; but their immediate object is to be comfortable, to marry,

[10] Ibid., p. 80.
[11] Ibid., pp. 84-5.

to have a fair income, station, and respectability, a convenient house,
a pleasant country, a sociable neighbourhood."[12]

It would of course be easy to find many examples of worldly Catholic
prelates. Newman's contemporary, Cardinal Nicholas Wiseman, was
famous both for his pomp and his corpulence and was said to have
observed Lenten abstinence by having four courses of fish. There
are human weaknesses which have always been with the Church and
always will be. The danger comes not so much from personal failings
as from the adoption of the attitudes of the world. Whatever the
failings of her members, the Church must preach the Gospel in season
and out of season. The Church of England, in Newman's view, was
incapable of doing this because it was perpetually chasing after the
spirit of the age. His *Lectures on the Difficulties of Anglicans* of 1850
were aimed at showing his former Oxford Movement colleagues
how inconsistent their position was as Anglicans. They claimed to
believe in the Church's divine authority, but a state church such as
the Church of England must reflect the changing will of the nation
which is simply the will of 'the world'.

> It is as little bound by what it said or did formerly, as this morning's
> newspaper by its former numbers. ... While the nation wishes an
> Establishment, it will remain, whatever individuals are for it or
> against it; and that which determines its existence will determine
> its voice. ... As the nation changes its political, so may it change its
> religious views; the causes which carried the Reform Bill and Free
> Trade may make short work with orthodoxy.[13]

The history of Anglicanism since Newman's time has shown this to
be true – in the eyes of many both inside and outside the Church
of England, it has been one of continued compromise with the
changing beliefs of the world. The birth control movement becomes
influential in the 1920s and 30s, and the Church of England abandons
the traditional Christian opposition to contraception. The social
revolution of the 1960s arrives, and an Anglican prelate appears as
a witness for the defence in the landmark *Lady Chatterley's Lover*
pornography trial. Some women want to be ordained as priests? The
Church of England must adopt the feminist agenda. And currently the
worldwide Anglican communion cannot make up its mind whether
or not it is in accordance with the Gospel to have a practising lesbian
as a bishop. Newman would not have been surprised at these logical

[12] Ibid., p. 257.
[13] Ibid., pp. 8-9.

developments of Anglicanism's spirit of accommodation with the world.

The world will always want things to fit in with its way of thinking and behaving. As Newman put it:

> it is not enough for the State that things should be done, unless it has the doing of them itself; it abhors a double jurisdiction, and what it calls a divided allegiance; *aut Cæsar aut nullus*, is its motto, nor does it willingly accept of any compromise.[14]

Today we like to tell ourselves that modern society has escaped from the strict conventionality of the Victorian age, but actually we live in a more conformist world than ever. The values of Western liberal society claim precedence over everything else. Not for nothing is the prevailing cultural orthodoxy known as political *correctness* – there is no room for suggesting that it might be incorrect. This is in fact no different from the assumption of imperial superiority that we now so excoriate in the Victorians.

The underdog, counter-cultural, status of the Catholic Church in nineteenth century England reminded Newman of the early church, and becoming a Catholic gave him a critical distance from the culture of his time, enabling him to stand aside from it and view it with detachment. This can be seen most clearly – and entertainingly – in his liveliest work, the *Lectures on the Present Position of Catholics in England* of 1851.[15] These were popular lectures delivered in the Birmingham Corn Exchange in the wake of the anti-Catholic agitation that followed the restoration of the Catholic hierarchy in England in 1850. In the nineteenth century, the average Englishman (and woman) was an anti-Catholic bigot of a kind we today only associate with the Celtic fringes of the British Isles. Anglican clergy denounced the Catholic Church from their pulpits as the Whore of Babylon and the Pope as the Antichrist. When Pope Pius IX gave English Catholics their own territorial bishops for the first time since the Reformation, this was denounced as 'papal aggression' in a campaign headed by no less than the Prime Minister himself, Lord John Russell. This was no outbreak of working class sectarianism. The campaign was masterminded by the British Reformation Society, the Protestant Association and the Evangelical Alliance, whose membership was

---

[14] *Difficulties of Anglicans*, p. 175.
[15] For more detail on what follows, see the Introduction to my critical edition of the *Lectures*, published by Gracewing/Notre Dame, 2000.

solidly middle class.[16] These were the progressives in English society: Russell was a Whig, not a Tory; the anti-Catholic campaigners were those who saw themselves as the vanguard of social improvement. It was also highly respectable, even genteel. In fashionable Cheltenham, the leading evangelical cleric, Rev Francis Close, (after whom Dean Close School was later to be named) delivered a sermon so rousing that his hearers set fire to the local Catholic church. Anti-Catholic legislation was rushed through parliament, and one peer wanted the Royal Navy to bombard the Vatican.

Once things quietened down, Newman took the opportunity to deliver a highly effective analysis of the culture of anti-Catholicism which had allowed it all to happen in the midst of civilized nineteenth century England. These lectures are to be recommended for those who think Newman is all heavy theology or demanding sermons. In a series of entertaining passages Newman depicts the blinkered prejudices of the Protestant Englishman. His audience, which included non-catholics, laughed aloud. Some of the funniest passages concern the 'Prejudiced Man' who is so sure that he knows all about Catholics, how wicked and deceiving they are, and who is incapable of overcoming his preconceptions.[17] This culminates in a wonderfully ignorant description of Benediction written by a 'Protestant Scripture Reader' which Newman took from a real-life anti-Catholic magazine. This earnest observer thinks that the benighted Catholics are being induced to worship a star on a stick (actually the monstrance containing the Blessed Sacrament) and that they marvel at a 'miraculous' tinkling sound which the crafty priest is secretly making from a concealed bell – the Scripture Reader has failed to spot the attendant server who is of course ringing a bell as the blessing is given, as every Catholic present knows.

Although these Lectures make us laugh, they are also dealing with real problems of which we can recognize the modern counterparts. One such was *The Awful Disclosures of Maria Monk*, a popular anti-Catholic work which purported to be the real memoirs of a former nun in Canada. Her story told of sexual corruption in the convent, with novices raped by priests and the resulting babies strangled and buried in the cellars. The book was in fact a form of pornography, and its fraudulent nature had long been exposed. Newman analyses

---

[16] See Paz, D.G., *Popular Anti-Catholicism in Mid-Victorian England* (Stanford, 1992), pp. 124-127; and Wolffe, J., *The Protestant Crusade in Great Britain* (Oxford, 1991); pp. 163-5.

[17] Op. cit., pp. 236ff.

how such anti-Catholic propaganda works: the book contains lots of description of actual Catholic practices which it depicts as hypocritical externals behind which lurks the worst possible vice. And so, Newman explains:

> When a person, who never was in a Catholic church or convent, reads such particulars ... and then afterwards actually sees some Catholic establishment, he says to himself, "This is just what the book said;" "here is quite the very thing of which it gave me the picture;" and I repeat he has, in consequence of his reliance on it, so associated the acts of the ceremonial, the joined hands or the downcast eyes, with what his book went on slanderously to connect them, with horrible sin, that he cannot disconnect them in his imagination; and he thinks the Catholic priest already convicted of hypocrisy.[18]

We have the same technique used today in popular depictions of corrupt Catholic priests in films and television dramas. *The Da Vinci Code*, for instance, depicts members of the well-known Catholic association Opus Dei as monks who murder, lie and steal. This is of course a gross calumny (and in any case there are no monks in Opus Dei). Yet it is now established as a stereotype. A recent BBC television drama again featured members of Opus Dei as self-serving hypocrites committing adultery and murder, and even quality newspapers now routinely refer to Opus Dei as a 'sect'. The image is now firmly established in the public mind by association – just in the way that Newman had shown that 'Maria Monk' worked. Anything which the real Opus Dei says or does is automatically connected in the public's imagination with the evil acts of the stereotype.

Newman also points out the immense difficulties that face a Catholic who tries to respond to such false accusations against the Church. He gives an example of a claim by an anti-Catholic writer that a certain monk left a written confession after his death that he had murdered several people. This is of course part of the long anti-Catholic tradition of 'monkish hypocrites' (which continues today). A Catholic decides to research this accusation. What happens?

> Well, after a great deal of trouble, after writing about to friends, consulting libraries, and comparing statements, let us suppose him [the Catholic] to prove most conclusively the utter absurdity of the slanderous story, and to bring out a lucid, powerful, and unanswerable reply; who cares for it by that time? who cares for the story itself? it has done its work; time stops for no man;

---

[18] Ibid., pp. 169-170.

it has created or deepened the impression in the minds of its hearers that a monk commits murder or adultery as readily as he eats his dinner. Men forget the process by which they receive it, but there it is, clear and indelible. Or supposing they recollect the particular slander ever so well, still they have no taste or stomach for entering into a long controversy about it; their mind is already made up; they have formed their views; the author they have trusted may, indeed, have been inaccurate in some of his details; it can be nothing more. Who can fairly impose on them the perplexity and whirl of going through a bout of controversy, where "one says," and "the other says," and "*he* says that *he* says that *he* does not say or ought not to say what he does say or ought to say?" It demands an effort and strain of attention which they have no sort of purpose of bestowing. The Catholic cannot get a fair hearing; his book remains awhile in the shop windows, and then is taken down again.[19]

This continues to be the case today – indeed the difficulty of responding to an anti-Catholic calumny is exacerbated in today's world of instant media reaction when reports of a speech or publication can be flashed round the world, seizing the headlines and being taken up immediately by people who have never read the original accusation and certainly have no means of evaluating its truth. A good example is the accusation that Pope Pius XII collaborated with the Nazis which, despite scholarly refutation, is now becoming an accepted part of the world's view of Catholicism.

What advice does Newman give us in the face of such a hostile world? Towards the end of his life, nearly fifty years after Keble's sermon on 'National Apostasy', Newman, long a Catholic and now receiving his Cardinal's hat from the Pope, returned to Keble's analysis of society when he made his *Biglietto* speech in Rome:

For thirty, forty, fifty years I have resisted to the best of my powers the spirit of liberalism in religion. Never did Holy Church need champions against it more sorely than now, when, alas! it is an error overspreading, as a snare, the whole earth; and on this great occasion, when it is natural for one who is in my place to look out upon the world, and upon Holy Church as in it, and upon her future, it will not, I hope, be considered out of place, if I renew the protest against it which I have made so often. [...] Hitherto the civil Power has been Christian. Even in countries separated from the Church, as in my own, the *dictum* was in force, when I was young, that: "Christianity was the law of the land". Now, everywhere that

---

[19] *Lectures on the Present Position of Catholics in England*, p. 96.

goodly framework of society, which is the creation of Christianity, is throwing off Christianity.[20]

Echoing Keble, he terms this phenomenon 'this great *apostasia*' and thinks that 'it threatens to have a formidable success; though it is not easy to see what will be its ultimate issue.' Perhaps surprisingly, he downplays it as a threat to the Church:

> I lament it deeply, because I foresee that it may be the ruin of many souls; but I have no fear at all that it really can do aught of serious harm to the Word of God, to Holy Church, to our Almighty King, the Lion of the tribe of Judah, Faithful and True, or to His Vicar on earth. Christianity has been too often in what seemed deadly peril, that we should fear for it any new trial now.

The horrors of the twentieth century's totalitarian atheist regimes were beyond his imagination, though he was at least right that England would escape such barbarity. He concluded that:

> Commonly the Church has nothing more to do than to go on in her own proper duties, in confidence and peace; to stand still and to see the salvation of God.

It may disappoint us that Newman does not suggest a more radical programme for the Church in its engagement with the hostile, secularizing world. After all, at the turning point of his life from Anglicanism to Catholicism, he had given the Church a ground-breaking new apologetic in his *Essay on the Development of Christian Doctrine*; and in its Introduction he had boldly stated the case for such new thinking:

> The assailants of dogmatic truth have got the start of its adherents of whatever Creed; philosophy is completing what criticism has begun; and apprehensions are not unreasonably excited lest we should have a new world to conquer before we have weapons for the warfare. … An argument is needed, unless Christianity is to abandon the province of argument; and those who find fault with the explanation here offered of its historical phenomena will find it their duty to provide one for themselves.[21]

His point here is in the last sentence: it is a challenge to Anglicans to face up to the dynamic of his argument which led to Rome. The alternative was to hand the field over to the sceptics. Doubtless today there are other new arguments which need to be developed, new apologetics for an age in which scientific phenomena are interpreted as evidence for atheism by such as Richard Dawkins.

---

[20] See Appendix 1, p. 313.
[21] Christian Classics edn., 1968, p. 31.

But the aged Newman's advice that the Church 'has nothing more to do than to go on in her own proper duties, in confidence and peace' acts as a useful corrective to those who think that the Church should adopt an ever more radical programme of liberalization to make itself acceptable to the modern world. Such liberals – like the Arians – are often in positions of influence. They sometimes even invoke Newman's name to give weight to their ideas. Nothing could in fact be further from Newman's keen sense of the critical relationship between the Church and the world.

The social position of the Church has changed enormously since Newman's day. The 'present position' of Catholics in England is that the Church has become closely interwoven with contemporary culture: we have an almost wholly government-funded Church education system, and Catholics to be found in all areas of public life. The appointment of the late Cardinal Basil Hume was seen by some as English Catholicism finally attaining social acceptability; towards the end of his life the Queen was widely reported as referring to him as 'my cardinal'. The Pope himself has taken tea at Buckingham Palace. Newman – who earlier had found himself convicted of criminal libel by a biased court as a result of one of his *Present Position* lectures – made a contribution towards this change in attitudes; and towards the end of his life he accepted worldly honours such as the honorary fellowship given him by his old Oxford college. But he was under no illusions about the true nature of the society of his time. Today we see contradictory reactions by the world towards the Church, such as the extraordinarily sympathetic coverage of Pope John Paul II's death and funeral by a media which had relentlessly attacked his moral teaching. The world is always fickle, and the reality is that the Church today is in an increasingly precarious position in Western society. Numerically declining, enormously damaged by the clergy sexual abuse scandals, and now – as the gay adoption crisis has shown – beginning to lose its freedom of social action, the Church would be foolish to be optimistic about its relationship with the world. We would do well to keep Newman's clear-eyed analysis before us:

> when our Lord came, it was with the express object of introducing a new kingdom, distinct and different from the kingdoms of the world, and He was sought after by Herod, and condemned by Pilate, on the very apprehension that His claims to royalty were inconsistent with their prerogatives. Such was the Church when

first introduced into the world, and her subsequent history has been after the pattern of her commencement; the State has ever been jealous of her, and has persecuted her from without and bribed her from within.[22]

---

[22] *Difficulties of Anglicans*, p. 175.

Chapter 7

NEWMAN'S TEACHING ON THE SENSE OF THE FAITHFUL

by Edward Miller

Many have heard of Newman's *Apologia pro Vita Sua*, an autobiographical classic ranking with St Augustine's *Confessions*. University undergraduates likely have met up with portions of his *Idea of a University*, either in literature or education courses. And many have likened Newman's *Essay on Development of Doctrine* in its sphere to Darwin's *Origin of Species* in another sphere. It is unlikely, however, that these readers are familiar with Newman's writings on "sense of the faithful," despite the fact that it is no less important for those religious matters to which it pertains.

'Sense of the faithful' is a tricky English phrase. We ask, "What is your sense of things?" and we mean, "What is your opinion?" Newman's phrase does not signify this usage. Someone's sense can also be her sentiment, or it can refer to one of his sensory organs as when we claim that our senses were impaired when the accident occurred. Neither do these instances capture the phrase. Our English words translate theology's *sensus fidelium*, and it is this chiseled expression in the background. When Newman came to publish an article on this topic in a magazine for lay people, he, ever the adroit writer who tended to shun technical words and Latin phrases except when necessary, chose as his title, 'On Consulting the Faithful in Matters of Doctrine'.[1] Of course, he was left with needing to explain what consulting entailed, as we shall see.

---

[1] The essay appeared in the July 1859 issue of the *Rambler*. Newman never brought the essay into the *Uniform Edition* of his works, although a portion of it appears in the appendix to *Arians of the Fourth Century* (1871) as Note V. It was reprinted in *On Consulting the Faithful in Matters of Doctrine*, ed. John Coulson, (London: Chapman, 1961), but it is now out of print. German translations of Newman's essay have appeared, as in *Hochland* 40:401-14, 49-57.

Before presenting Newman's explanation of sensus fidelium, I want to situate the phrase in a wider context in terms of its history and its relationship to similar theological matters. Then, after completing Newman's explanation of sensus fidelium, I wish to apply his teaching to a contemporary problem that I label 'privatized biblicism.'

The wider context

In most general terms, sensus fidelium attempts to describe a sort of instinct possessed by baptized persons for knowing the mystery of God inhabiting them, that is, they are able to recognize their faith. Our technical expression, sensus fidelium, is more recent, but the reality it describes is rooted in the New Testament. The faithful are able to recognize the Lord's voice (Jn 10:4). They can distinguish between Christ and Antichrist (1 Jn 2:18-27). For Paul, the baptized interpret spiritual matters (1 Cor 2:10-16). In the earliest liturgical texts, the baptized are anointed and have the insights of prophets (*Didascalia*, chap. 9, the *Apostolic Tradition*, chap. 1). Fr Yves Congar has collected the testimonies of third and fourth century church fathers to this same sort of instinct for the faith.[2] Different phrases have been used to describe this baptismal instinct. 'Sensus ecclesiae' [sense of the church] and 'sensus fidei' [sense of faith] are terms belonging to different moments of church history. The latter was favored by St Thomas Aquinas (1225-1274), and he described personal faith as possessing an instinctive ability to adhere to its "proper objects" (to God and God's revelation).[3] A later disciple of Aquinas and fellow Dominican, Melchior Cano (1509-1560), is credited with making this baptismal instinct an approved theological instrument or source – he termed it in Latin a *locus* – for arriving at insights into revelation. At this stage sensus fidelium seems to enter church vocabulary as a working term.

For certain, it does not become a key working term in Counter-Reformation Catholicism. In articulating the faith, priority is accorded to the teachings of the popes and to the consensus positions among vetted theologians, the latter being called the *auctores probabi* [the approved authors]. The term sensus fidelium will come to Newman

---

[2] Yves Congar, *Lay People in the Church* (Newman Press: Westminster, 1967), Appendix 2. Congar faults the Protestant Reformation for elevating the personal witness of Christians into a church structure in itself to whose judgment even church authorities are subject. See p. 279. Newman would fully agree.

[3] *Summa Theologiae*, II-II, q. 1, articles 1 and 3.

by way of Giovanni Perrone (1794–1876), a Jesuit professor at the Roman College. Perrone himself was influenced by the great German theologian of Tübingen, Johann Adam Möhler, whose research returned to importance the work of the Holy Spirit in the church and in individuals.[4] But Newman did not read German, and so it was this Italian Jesuit theologian who provided Newman with the acceptable Catholic terminology of sensus fidelium. This grounding enabled Newman to make his famous case about consulting the faithful and to use, as evidence for it, his own vast knowledge of earlier church history. Although Newman inherits the term sensus fidelium, he as much as anyone can be credited with retrieving it for productive currency in Catholic thinking, such as happened at the Second Vatican Council.[5]

As a final context for the term sensus fidelium, which at the same time provides a link to Newman's important essay on consulting the baptized laity, I need to mention two matters about the nature of Catholicism. In my own nation, where democracy and voting rights are practically shibboleths of being American, the use in religious matters of the term 'consulting' evokes images of Protestant Congregationalism. The congregation 'calls' ministers to the pulpit, and it terminates them, too. Doctrinal matters are decided by votes of the delegates elected to go to the periodic convocation (the 'convention' for Baptists, the 'presbytery' for Calvinists, the 'annual conference' for Methodists, etc.). Plebiscite is laudably democratic but it is ill-fittingly Catholic. Catholicism is not a democracy, and Catholicism contends that the biblical church was not, either. On the other hand, were one to think that the antithesis of a democratic congregationalism is an autocratic Catholicism, this, too, ill fits Catholicism. Even were I tempted to simple solutions, I could not say that the role of authority in Catholicism lies half way between democracy and autocracy. The understanding of authority in Catholicism does not measure out in this simplistic manner. And so I need to explain my second matter about Catholicism more fully.

---

[4] Yves Congar has documented the influence of Möhler on the Roman theologians in L'Église – de saint Augustin à l'époque moderne (Paris: Cerf, 1970), pp. 417–35. See also Cardinal Walter Kasper's doctoral thesis, Die Lehre von der Tradition in der Romischen Schule (Herder: Freiburg, 1962).

[5] A number of studies have documented Newman's influence on Vatican II, some going so far as to call Newman the absent conciliar father. His shadow seems evident in the Dogmatic Constitution on the Church, para. 12, where one reads that "the body of the faithful as a whole, anointed as they are by the Holy One, cannot err in matters of belief."

Some people, especially non-Catholics, have been misled into thinking that the pastoral authorities in the Catholic Church, the pope and the other bishops, are the source and depositories of the truths of revelation in the manner similar to elderly relatives in a family who possess knowledge (memories) of earlier generations known only to them. These elderly relatives are teaching authorities for younger family members because the older relatives possess items of knowledge within themselves alone. The younger members have no awareness at all of these items until they are taught them, as it were. Some people view the pope and bishops – in technical language they are called the *magisterium* or the church's teaching office – in this same light in respect to the laity in the church. It is as if the magisterium had access to knowledge that others do not possess at all. It is as if the bishops have access to books containing the truths of revelation or had unique access to their own seminary teachers who passed on to them what is to be taught to the church's faithful.

This is an inaccurate view of the church feature, crucial to Roman Catholicism, called magisterium. Explaining it only as much as would provide a proper but clear enough context for the topic of this chapter, I would make three brief observations about magisterium. First, it is a charism, that is to say, a gifting from God to certain members of the church (the bishops) to discern what has been "revealed for our salvation" and then to teach it to others. Second, the process of discernment does not take the bishops to some sequestered locations that are blocked off to all others, analogous to my example above where an elderly relative retreated to the recesses of her memory that was inaccessible to younger relatives. No, the bishops do not go to certain books or prized seminary notes or even into the personal recesses of their own minds – here my analogy with the elderly relative falls away – in order to discern God's revelation. They must go to a living thing, the faith of the church. Newman likened this faith of the church to an "idea" that lived and developed within all the baptized members of the church, clergy and laity alike. ('Idea,' for Newman, is not merely a conceptual construct; it is like an animating force, like a soul within a human body.)

Before using this second point to set the context for the chapter's topic, I must make a third observation about magisterium, one that is even more misunderstood than the second point by many non-Catholics and not a few Catholics themselves. The charism to discern leads to the charism of the bishops to teach. Pastors teach. This is a most important thing they do. But the charism does not necessarily mean that each and every instance of teaching, by this or that bishop, or even by a preponderant number of them, is protected by an infallibility that precludes error in every teaching utterance. When the charism of the teaching "enjoys infallibility" – this is the verb used technically in Catholic tradition – then God does protect from erroneous pronouncement what is meant "for us and our salvation." But there are rules for when "infallibility" is assumed to be operative and to what types of teaching it is meant to be surrounding protectively. (Newman was much concerned with these rules, following the First Vatican Council, but this is another topic from mine.)

In the Roman Catholic scheme, all episcopal and papal teaching enjoys a presumptive truthfulness, and for this reason it is called 'authoritative' magisterium. In fact, most of the official teaching happening in the Catholic Church does not invoke the protection of infallibility, and yet it is authoritative and instructive and enriching (and presumptively true). For example, nothing from the Second Vatican Council was taught infallibly in the manner in which ecumenical councils of the past solemnly so taught, yet the recent Council teaches matters for the renewal of the church that one ought to judge are divinely intended steps forward. Nevertheless, there can be instances of error in episcopal teaching, as happened, in Cardinal Newman's judgment, in the fourth century when Arianism was rampant in the church. Popes, too, have erred. Newman was constantly being asked about the case of Pope Honorius (+638) and monothelitism.[6]

The error I have in mind with my third point is the view that every single teaching of magisterium is infallible. This is simply not so. This is not the contention of Catholicism itself. The error associated with my second point had to do with how popes and bishops obtained the matters that they then taught to the Catholic people. As I said above, it is more misunderstood than correctly appreciated. Newman did appreciate it, and in reference to this second point (the locations the official teachers go to discern what is to be officially taught), I wish to locate Newman's teaching on sensus fidelium, because it is a privileged repository of the living faith of the church.

There are a number of 'sources' that are to be mined, that is to say, to be discerned, in order to come to know what God has revealed. The bible is obviously a source, but it is not a source in the manner that a text book or catechism can unambiguously impart doctrines.

---

[6] Monothelitism is the view that there is only one will in Christ.

The bible cries for rightful interpretation. Because I will conclude my essay with an application of Newman's teaching on sensus fidelium to biblical understanding, I merely mention the bible as one source, albeit a uniquely normative source preeminent to all others, and I proceed to describe other sources.

The liturgy of the church is a source of coming to know the faith. Is it true that Jesus is really and truly present after the consecration of the bread and wine? This is a most important question about what is revealed, because some Christians in recent centuries have come to deny it. An unlettered Catholic might answer quite simply: "Listen to the words of the Mass. 'Through the action of the Holy Spirit, may these elements become for us the body and blood of Christ.' The prayers of the liturgy are an avenue to the answer. Another source of knowing revelation is the solemn (infallible) teachings of past ecumenical councils, such as the Council of Ephesus's "Mary is rightly termed the Mother of God (theotokos)." The consistent teachings by the 'Fathers' of the church (Cyril, Athanasius, Basil, Ambrose, Augustine, etc.) are yet another source. (This was a feature dear to Newman. When Edward Pusey, John Keble, and he sought to reclaim the English Church as 'Catholic,' and when Newman left the Church of England because it could never be Catholic, the referent for being Catholic was patristic life and teaching.)

The sense of the faithful is a source of knowing what has been revealed, too. To present Cardinal Newman's teaching about sensus fidelium from his famous essay of 1859, it is necessary, first, to tell the story behind the essay.

Newman's 1859 essay 'On Consulting the Faithful in Matters of Doctrine'

Newman's essay originated painfully for him. The full story involves some tribulations of the *Rambler* magazine.[7] The magazine was a layman's initiative from the start, and during an era of strong hierarchical controls on Catholic life and thought, this feature of the magazine unsettled some persons, but not Newman. It was begun in 1848 by John Moore Capes, an Anglican convert, as a well-crafted literary outlet to express Catholic interpretations on contemporary affairs and books. In 1857 it came under the direction of Richard Simpson,

---

[7] Some of the following materials are borrowed from my book, *John Henry Newman on the Idea of Church* (Shepherdstown: Patmos Press, 1987).

another convert, who as editor was joined by Sir John Acton. Acton came from an "old Catholic family" and was educated in Germany under the celebrated church historian, Ignaz von Döllinger.

The critical tone of some of Simpson's articles displeased the bishops, but it was not until the appearance of one of Acton's book reviews that the bishops took action. In arguing the point that no Catholic is as perfect as the Catholic religion, Acton averred that St Augustine, besides being the church's greatest doctor, is also the father of Jansenism. A storm ensued, and Acton asked his former professor for help. Döllinger's letter, "The Paternity of Jansenism," appeared in the December 1858 issue of the *Rambler*. The letter was sent to Rome for censure, and the bishops put pressure on the magazine to fold.

It was in such roiled waters that Scott Nasmyth Stokes (convert, Trinity College Cambridge graduate, Government Inspector of Schools) contributed an unsigned article, "The Royal Commission on Education," to the January *Rambler*. The article criticized Catholic laity and particularly the bishops for refusing to cooperate with the Newcastle Commission investigating educational possibilities for all youths; no Catholics were on the commission, and Cardinal Wiseman ordered all his clergy to be uncooperative. The author was accused of 'disloyalty.' The February issue carried the retort from Stokes wondering why the bishops "were displeased by the loyal expression of opinions entertained by many Catholics and supported by arguments that cannot be met."[8] Unaccustomed to such direct criticism, the bishops threatened censure. Both sides appealed to Newman. The bishops would not censure the *Rambler* if the editorship changed hands; Acton and Simpson would step down only if an editor sympathetic to open journalism was appointed. Newman, the only person acceptable to both sides, agreed reluctantly to become editor in March.

In the "Contemporary Events" column of his very first issue (May 1859), Newman wrote some anonymous comments on the Newcastle Commission question, and with these comments Newman's painful involvement began.

> This leads us to our second remark. Acknowledging, then, most fully the prerogatives of the episcopate, we do unfeignedly believe, both from the reasonableness of the matter, and especially from prudence, gentleness, and considerateness which belong to them personally, that their Lordships really desire to know the opinion

---

[8] *The Letters and Diaries of John Henry Newman*, (London: Nelson, 1969), Vol. 19, p. 17, n. 2. Hereafter LD.

of the laity on subjects in which the laity are especially concerned. If even in the preparation of a dogmatic definition the faithful are consulted, as lately in the instance of the Immaculate Conception, it is at least as natural to anticipate such an act of kind feeling and sympathy in great practical questions.[9]

Newman's analogy with the 1854 dogma of the Immaculate Conception led theology professor John Gillow of Ushaw Seminary to label as *haeresi proxima* [nearly heresy] the opinion that bishops needed to consult laity in order to formulate an infallible dogma. Newman's commentary and other features in the issue unnerved Newman's own bishop, Bernard Ullathorne, to such an extent that he accepted readily Newman's resignation of editorship after just one issue. But before transition to new leadership could be had, the July issue needed to appear. Newman decided to bring together all his thoughts on the relationship between the laity, the church's revealed faith, and the hierarchy's role in teaching this faith, in his final chance to set matters straight. Newman's motive in writing the famous essay did not derive from an argumentative personality that needed to "get the last word in" but from his pastoral concern to "open up" within the Roman Catholic Church certain theological matters that struck him as underdeveloped or neglected or too one-sided.[10]

Newman begins the famous July 1859 essay asking whether it is correct to say that the laity can be consulted on matters of the faith. Mindful of Dr Gillow's accusation of 'nearly heresy' and the fact that Gillow and other seminary theologians work with Latin terms, Newman distinguishes the word 'consulting.' The Latin sense of the word denotes taking counsel and requesting a judgment from the persons consulted. The English sense of the word may mean the same, but it can also connote an inquiry into a factual matter, as when someone consults a barometer to get the weather. Newman uses a physician/patient example to clarify this double sense: a physician consults a patient's pulse, but it is in another sense that a patient consults a physician for a diagnosis. The laity's beliefs can indeed

---

[9] LD 19:129, n. 3. It is a coincidental side note that Nasmyth Stokes's nephew was among the first seven boys enrolled in Newman's Oratory School, whose operations began in May 1859, also.

[10] People advocate different paradigm images of Newman: promoter of 'Catholic' principles, champion of church authority, spiritual director *par excellence*, founder of the English Oratory, and so forth. My paradigm image is of a person who used a God-given talent for writing in order to open up issues, and his book, *Grammar of Assent*, is a palmary example. In order to open up topics, he needed to be the enemy of one-sidedness of viewpoint, and *Idea of a University* is its great illustration.

be consulted in the former sense as a "testimony to that apostolic tradition, on which alone any doctrine whatsoever can be defined" (p. 55),[11] and this is quite other than implying that the laity are judges of revelation.

Newman follows with a question: Can consulting the laity for its sensus fidelium be a preliminary to an infallible definition of a dogma?[12] Newman claims that it can, because the laity as a group is one of the witnesses to what are the revealed doctrines in the church's tradition, and its "*consensus* through Christendom is the voice of the Infallible Church" (p. 63). Newman frequently employs 'consensus fidelium' in place of sensus fidelium to carry the flexibility of the English sense of consulting. Revelation, as if the single soul animating the body the church, expresses itself variously: in the teaching of the episcopacy, in the settled positions of theologians, in the liturgy, and in the sensus fidelium. Accordingly, no witnessing source ought to be disregarded as a testimony to the apostolic tradition of the church.

Some persons will stress one or another of these testimonies, but Newman chose to accent the sensus fidelium because certain doctrines in their earliest stages of development had a clearer basis in it than in other channels of testimony.[13] Newman suggests five ways of understanding the special channel of testimony that he calls the sensus fidelium of the laity: (1) as a witness to the existence of an apostolic teaching, (2) as a sort of instinct, or *phronema*, deep in the heart of the church itself, (3) as an impulse of the Holy Spirit, (4) as an answer to the laity's own prayer life, (5) and as a jealousy of error such that a false articulation of the faith would beget in the laity feelings of scandal. In illustration of the last phenomenon, the unsigned 1859

---

[11] Page references are to the Coulson edition (see note 1) and are provided directly in the narrative for ease of reading and to avoid constant footnoting.

[12] Newman has in mind the recent dogma of 1854. Before Pius IX's infallible teaching, the Pope, in his encyclical of 1847, *Ubi Primum*, queried all Catholic bishops to assess the devotion of their clergy and laity about Mary's Immaculate Conception. See LD 13:81–82 for Newman's sense of the query.

[13] Here Newman follows Perrone's position and relies on his theological stature that the silence of other testimonies can be compensated for by the sensus fidelium. In researching the historical roots of the idea of Mary's Immaculate Conception, Peronne unearthed the local Marian festivals, the scattered liturgical texts prayed willingly by the faithful, and the Marian devotions of the laity. See his *De Immaculato V. Mariae Conceptu*, (Rome, 1847), p. 139. But Newman, by 1859, writes of a more active sense to the sensus fidelium. For Perrone, the laity witness the faith by being exact reflections of what bishops taught them. For Newman, God's revelation penetrates the minds and hearts of the faithful. Therefore, the laity are a testimony to what their faith means to them when it unfolds within them. What the laity have been taught plays an important role in this inner vitality but not the only role.

essay references *The Arians of the Fourth Century*, Newman's book of 1833. Although the fourth century was an age of learned churchmen – Athanasius, Ambrose, Jerome – nevertheless, "in that very day the divine tradition committed to the infallible Church was proclaimed and maintained far more by the faithful than by the episcopate," and "the body of the episcopate was unfaithful to its commission, while the body of the laity was faithful to its baptism" (pp. 75-76).

The essay draws two final conclusions from the years of Arian turmoil, whose reverberations will be shown shortly. During the sixty-year period between the Council of Nicea and the First Council of Constantinople, individual bishops taught inconsistently and argued with each other. Newman, not mincing words, concludes that "there was a temporary suspense of the functions of the 'Ecclesia docens' [the church's magisterium] (p. 77). Furthermore, localized episcopal synods of the period were pitted against one another, with the result that "general councils said what they should not have said, and did what obscured and compromised revealed truth" (p. 76).

I have been content to describe the uncomfortable origins, for Newman, of the 1859 essay in order to situate his notion of sensus fidelium. I leave to another in this book to describe the painful consequences he suffered after the July issue of the *Rambler* appeared, especially the essay's delation to Rome for censure by Bishop Thomas Brown of Newport.[14] I wish, however, to draw two consequences from the essay, especially for readers new to Newman, as these consequences attach to a proper grasp of sensus fidelium.

The first consequence recalls my earlier contextual observation about magisterium and the location of sources of revelation. Newman is to be credited with retrieving sensus fidelium in its fully active sense. It is true that Fr Perrone brought him to view the testimony of the laity as an 'instrument' of revealed tradition when other sources were unclear. Perrone enabled Newman to move beyond his Anglican self of 1837 – I refer to the Newman who wrote *Lectures on the Prophetical Office of the Church* – who then relied on St Vincent of Lerins' ancient rule that true doctrines are those beliefs taught "everywhere and by everyone all the time." Yet many later doctrines of the church lacked such clear Vincentian warrants in the earlier teachings of the church and theologians. Perrone provided a doorway out of the fog.[15] Still,

---

[14] See LD 19:207, n. 1, 19:240, n. 2, and 19:279-283 concerning Brown's delation and Newman's memo.

[15] Newman met Perrone when Newman came to Rome in 1847 to study for priestly ordination.

Perrone had not the fully active sense of sensus fidelium that Newman came to have, as I hope the following image clarifies.

Against Dr John Gillow's contention that infallibility resides 'exclusively' in the magisterium and nowhere among the laity, Newman quoted with approval Fr Perrone's metaphor of a signet and wax in order to express a more unified view of infallibility. Infallibility resides in the laity and hierarchy in a unitary fashion just as a figure is contained simultaneously on the seal and on the wax the seal uses. But the wax of the Perrone's metaphor can be viewed quite passively. The indent on the wax reflects only what is engraved on the seal, and the wax plays no active contribution at all to the effect; it is simple impressionable. For Newman, the image works successfully to counter Gillow's contention of exclusivity, but the "merely being stamped" feature of the wax metaphor falls short for him in describing the resiliency and durability of the laity's faith. In various writings Newman describes baptismal faith as robust and discerning. It can withstand attacks, and not only at the level of martyrdom. Thus, for Newman, sensus fidelium testifies to the faith of the baptized as a robust actor on its own behalf and not merely as a passive reflector of ideas, as if only parroting others.

The second consequence to be drawn from Newman's essay refers to the other contextual observation I made earlier concerning magisterium and whether it never errs. This consequence also addresses whether Newman's 1859 essay is orthodox Catholic teaching itself. A noted theologian of the day, with far more stature than John Gillow of Ushaw Seminary, found certain statements in the essay quite dangerous. Johann Baptist Franzelin, SJ, was professor of dogmatic theology at the Gregorian University in Rome and a consultant to several Vatican congregations.[16] He objected to the three statements: that there had ever been suspense in the role of the 'Ecclesia docens' [the church's magisterium], that the 'body' of bishops failed to witness to orthodoxy during the Arian crisis, and that general councils have erred. To prove his orthodoxy, Newman would have to answer

---

Newman wished the Jesuit's support for his recently published book on *Development of Doctrine*, itself Newman's final doorway from Anglicanism to Roman Catholicism. So Newman wrote a synopsis of the book in Latin for Perrone, *De Catholici Dogmatis Evolutione*, now reprinted in *Gregorianum* 16 (1935):404-444.

[16] Franzelin's objections were never published but were expressed in his lectures at the 'Greg.' Somehow they found their way to Newman. Newman responded when he republished *Arians* in 1871. See note 1. Franzelin, in later years, wrote the first draft of Vatican I's constitution on faith and reason, *Dei Filius*.

Franzelin point by point.

Newman's British empirical bent always led him to go by the facts of a case, what the late renowned Newman scholar, Professor Jan Walgrave of Louvain, termed his penchant for "the nature of things."[17] Newman's decision to republish his 1833 book about fourth-century Arianism gave him the opportunity, in an appendix to the 1871 edition, to marshal the statements of fourth-century synods and bishops into a display of discord and disagreement that could not be denied. Those were the uneasy "facts" of the fourth century. On the other hand, the laity in this period were "the obstinate champions of Catholic truth, and the bishops were not."[18]

By the suspense of the church's teaching office, Newman showed that the period between Nicea (AD 325) and Constantinople (AD 381) was marked with intense doctrinal confusion within the hierarchy. A clear and consistent teaching from the bishops was lacking because many of them were Arian. He was not, he claimed, saying that the teaching office broke down, because the teaching office, in the official style people understand it to be, was not utilized until the Council of Constantinople. As to his reference to the failure of the 'body' of the bishops to represent orthodoxy, he thought Franzelin misunderstood him to be claiming that the bishops – what we today after Vatican II call the 'college' of bishops – erred during a conscious universal expression of magisterium (i.e. in an ecumenical council or in what is today termed 'ordinary infallible magisterium'). Newman said he meant that the "great preponderance" of bishops, considered in their individual actions but nevertheless amounting to a sizeable number of themselves, did not witness to the orthodox faith whereas the body of the Catholic laity did, in spite of episcopal discord. Finally, his phrase, erring "general councils," did not refer to what are now termed ecumenical councils, but rather to those somewhat large yet regional gatherings of bishops (synods) that indeed can err and have, in fact, erred at times.[19]

It is important to appreciate fully this second consequence of Newman's teaching about sensus fidelium. The better defense of the rightful authority of the church's magisterium is to recognize the absence of those specific conditions required for an infallible teaching

---

[17] See his "John Henry Newman," *Encyclopedia of Religion*, 2nd ed., (Detroit: Thomson Gale, 2005), Vol. 10:6510-6512.

[18] *Arians*, p. 445.

[19] *Arians*, p. 467.

and to acknowledge that church teaching can and has erred in other cases. This does not happen very often, but it has happened, as in church pronouncements from the past about usury and about slavery. It is a worse and self-defeating defense of authority to deny flaws and slips doggedly. The stronger defense of magisterium acknowledges the possibility of error in certain circumstances, identifies the conditions for infallible pronouncement when a church teaching claims the assent of faith from the baptized, and urges an attitude of docility and reverence for all teachings of the magisterium, in principle.[20] This was Newman's understanding of church authority ever since becoming a Roman Catholic in 1845, and the essay of 1859 is of a piece with this understanding and uses it as its linchpin argument. And, most importantly, Newman has a fully orthodox understanding of the role and exercise of authority in the Catholic Church. Theologians whose theology is suspect are not created cardinals, and it was important to Pope Leo XIII in 1879 to name Newman a cardinal in his very first consistory, to remove any lingering suspicions about the events of 1859.

Applying Cardinal Newman's teaching to a contemporary phenomenon

The American phenomenon I am envisioning possesses a kind of battle cry and shibboleth: "I don't need the institutional church. Just 'me, Jesus, and the bible' is all that's necessary." The phenomenon is on the increase; the fastest growing segment of Christianity in America is nondenominational Christianity. Even when one sits in a "megachurch" on Sundays, with a hundred-person choir and TV cameras as background, this born-again Christian is reading his bible as the preacher perorates. This camera-ready assembly is only, by a stretch, a church. It has no traditions, as would the United Methodist Church and the Church of England, for example. Its functioning authority, if one discounts the preacher's short-lived influence, is the bible, just the bible. Even when someone of this phenomenon remains in one of the traditional churches – and I have met them in certain prayer groups in my own Roman Catholic Church – the person's

---

[20] The Second Vatican Council teaches that the faithful owe an *obsequium religiosum* to the church's authentic magisterium. It is almost impossible to translate the phrase as briefly as it appears in Latin. Everything Newman wrote to people about docility and respect for church authority and about having a 'implicit faith' for what will yet be taught by the church captures what the Latin phrase means.

inner life is being nurtured by a bible study group more than Catholic sacramental life, in his or her opinion. Other phrases and images of the phenomenon are tell-tale: the inner light, the gift of the Holy Spirit, being 'anointed,' 'when I was first saved,' for example. Here in America, the mainstream Protestant churches, such as the United Methodist Church, the Presbyterian Church USA, and the Episcopal Church of the United States, are losing congregants precipitously. Roman Catholicism is losing its Spanish-speaking members in alarming numbers to Hispanic Pentecostal storefront churches (read: 'me, Jesus, and the bible' Christianity). I suspect these features of the phenomenon duplicate in other parts of the English-speaking world.

Newman never encountered the nondenominational aspect of the phenomenon, because the Christians he met were "located" somewhere: in Anglicanism, in Roman Catholicism, in the Scottish kerk, in the congregations of "dissenters," such as the Quakers. But even the dissenters had traditions that defined them and into which new members were socialized. In other words, new Quakers think and act like older Quakers! However, akin to our phenomenon today, Newman spoke of a 'bible Christianity' that described many Christians he knew, particularly the evangelical wing of the English Church. He criticized it, of course, and the criticism was based on one of those 'facts' that so constructively channeled his empirical way of thinking. He would say something like "the bible cannot explain itself and was never meant to."[21] And his supporting fact was simple: Put bibles in front of a Unitarian and a Trinitarian and have them read cover to cover. The Unitarian will remain Unitarian when finished, and so will the Trinitarian! Newman's inference from this fact is equally simple: the bible is meant to be read within a tradition, and the tradition guards it from self-imposed interpretations.

To the mentality, 'me, Jesus, and the bible,' which I wish to call hereafter a 'privatized biblicism', the rejoinder can certainly be that genuine Christianity requires church authority, indeed an infallible church authority. Newman makes this very case in his essay on *Development of Doctrine*, where infallibility insures the adjudication of doctrines, and also in that marvelous fifth chapter of the *Apologia*, where the "immense energy of the aggressive, capricious,

---

[21] Newman's study of the Arians has convinced me that Arius was the first biblical fundamentalist. He threw at his opponents texts like "The Father is greater than I" (Jn 14:28) and "Yahweh begot me [Wisdom], the firstborn of his ways" (Prv 8:22). So if Jesus the Word is less the Father and is begotten at the start of creation, Jesus is not divine, Arius argued.

untrustworthy intellect" of sinful persons requires the checking power of infallibility in religious matters.[22] But this approach, this appeal to church authority, would not work with the privatized biblicism that is met today, one that differs sufficiently from Newman's experience and one that places one's own gift of the Spirit in opposition to needing church authority as a guide.

Catholicism has, perhaps, a more persuasive approach to this mentality from the manner in which Newman understands sensus fidelium. The claimed strength of a privatized biblicism is the possession of the Holy Spirit that obviates that person's need for external authority. If someone wanted to criticize such a mentality, one would have a skewed version of Christianity indeed to deny that the Holy Spirit inhabits individuals, and it would be self-defeating to merely assert the need for an authority external to the bible person we are envisioning. The better approach to this mentality is to affirm the role of the Holy Spirit (a good thing) and to question the privatizing of the Spirit (a bad thing), and I believe we can thank Cardinal Newman for the suggestion.

The sensus fidelium has two key properties: (1) It is brought about by the possession of the Holy Spirit by the laity. This is a non-hierarchical statement. It is quite inner and very individually personal. It sounds like the claimed strength of privatized biblicism. When one converses with such persons and wishes to offer a better understanding of the bible to them, one is at least using the same kind of language as they use, when using the language of sensus fidelium. The conversation can get going. But the conversation will stand on surer footing because of the second characteristic of sensus fidelium. (2) The *fidelium* [Latin plural for 'believers'] of this theological phrase suggests immediately the collective feature of the Holy Spirit as inner gift to a particular person. To be Spirit-filled is not only to 'be godly,' but to 'be with others.' God's presence brings one into league with other Spirit-filled persons. The New Testament frequently uses collective language for having been reborn in God. Believers live 'in Christ,' they confess 'one Lord, one Faith, one Baptism,' and believers belong to the 'one Body of Christ,' to use the language of St Paul.

These things, of course, "reborn Christians" confess, too. They point about themselves to other Spirit-filled bible people in the congregation. But the fidelium, in Newman's sense of the word, which was also a sense espoused by Perrone, Möhler and others who

---

[22] *Apologia*, p. 246.

championed sensus fidelium, refers not only to a localized expression of the laity but also to laity outside one's immediate culture and, most importantly, to the laity outside one's time period. Sensus fidelium makes a wide-ranging appeal to the experiences of the laity all over and from other times. Summing up this strategy of approach to bible-only Christians of today, one would ask them, "How do other Christian laity, now and in times past, experience this or that issue of which you speak from the bible? For you would not want to deny to them the gift of the Spirit that you so cherish for yourself. Ought not your understanding of the Spirit be in concert with theirs?" Notice that one does not seek to persuade with the language of 'hierarchy' or 'authority.' It is, rather, the language of other 'laity' and of the 'Holy Spirit.' I am but applying Newman's sense of sensus fidelium to this phenomenon.

The application, however, is not quite complete. Against the strategy suggested above, someone might remark that this stands no more chance of swaying our "me and the bible" mentality than does the language appealing to church authority for interpretations of the bible. Newman's style of going by a 'fact,' especially an awkward fact, is once again helpful. And as Newman so often does in writing up a fact for imaginative consideration, I, too, would like to paint a situation that will make our application more complete.

There is an interesting resurrection appearance scene in Mark 16. The risen Jesus commissions the gathered disciples to go to the whole world to preach the gospel. "Whoever believes and is baptized will be saved; whoever does not believe will be condemned. These are the signs of believers: they will exorcise demons, they will speak new languages, they will pick up serpents, and if they drink any deadly thing, it will not harm them." If there was ever a text to warm the hearts of bible Christians, this is it. Only faith saves you, and here are the signs of having it. Now there are churches in Tennessee that take this text very prescriptively. In the Sunday service, the laity handle deadly snakes and some of them sip strychnine periodically. Imagine a conversation between one of these Tennessee men and a sophisticated attendee of a megachurch in Beverly Hills, California. He asks her, "Are you being saved, sister?" She responds, "Of course, I believe in Jesus my Savior, and I have been anointed by the Spirit," "Well," he asks, "do you handle copperhead snakes?" She appears horrified at the suggestion and gasps, "Of course I don't." He retorts, "But don't you believe in the bible?" She seems befuddled by the

THE SENSE OF THE FAITHFUL

question and hesitates, and in the most evangelistic tones he instructs her about Jesus' very words in Mark 16. She stammers, "That's not what the words mean," and he responds in the stentorian cant of one sent to evangelize the whole world, including Beverly Hills, "Hear ye the word of the Lord and obey what is clearly written."

She has no way to answer him that is logically consistent with her own religious convictions. After all, she rejects infant baptism on the grounds that "it's not in the bible, and I believe only what's in the bible." Mark 16 becomes her problem because "it's in the bible." Problems presented by the text lurk for him, too, such as the implications of the "Thou art Peter and upon this rock" text. I want to focus on her conundrum, however. Something tells her that Christianity is not about brandishing snakes, even though the only text is on "his side." And she is right. Her 'sense' of the faith is correct. But it is a sense without moorings other than being anchored in her own private subjectivity. It is also quite unchristian for our Tennessee visitor because, as I just said, the one and only bible text is on "his side" of the argument.

The only possible answer to him is to assert that Christianity has never understood discipleship to entail snakes and strychnine until "your church came along." At this point, all the texts – I refer to the texts reporting the devotional life of the laity – are on her side and not his. Therefore, "me, Jesus, and the bible" has to move away from the bible in order to save the bible from caricature. Expressed in the language of sensus fidelium, her sense of the faith has to move beyond herself and her megachurch and seek solidarity with Christian laity elsewhere and especially with Christians from the first century onwards. This, then, is the second property of Newman's description of sensus fidelium. It is its property of 'location.' It locates itself in the universal church. Sensus fidelium is within the individual as personal faith, and it is beyond the individual as the collective faith of fellow Christians. Sensus fidelium must be both personal and ecclesial, both my faith and our faith, both what the Spirit says to me and what the Spirit has been saying to us for so very long.[23]

---

[23] Besides the 'ecclesial' dimension of what has been the faith of the laity across the ages, there is also the 'ecclesiastical' complement to sensus fidelium, which is the magisterium. If anything said above would seem to suggest any divorce between magisterium and sensus fidelium, as if the seal and the wax have meaning apart from relationship to one another, then Newman is being misconstrued. That there might, from time to time, exist a tension between them is another matter. Newman's thinking on complex religious realities always left room for tensions. Otherwise, he could never have written the essay of 1859.

Such, then, is Newman's understanding of sensus fidelium, and we hope a new audience of readers will appreciate this side of Newman as much as they may his more celebrated achievements.[*]

[*] Research for this essay was supported by the Earhart Foundation of Ann Arbor, Michigan.

Chapter 8

NEWMAN, THE LAITY, AND THE RECEPTION OF DOCTRINE

by Richard Penaskovic

What happens when an ecumenical council is over and its participants travel home? Do its decisions automatically become part of the life of the Church? If they do, how is this done? And when does reception occur? Merely when they are received by the local churches or does reception only really occur when a doctrinal text has become part of the teaching tools in use for the theological education of seminarians? These are some of the questions dealing with what theologians refer to as reception. My chapter consists of three parts. First, I reflect on the notion of reception in general. Second, I speak of reception in the thought of John Henry Newman. And third, I speak to the relevance of Newman's thought today in regard to the laity.

What is reception? The term, reception, may be understood in the historical or classical sense as a spiritual process by which the decisions of a council are assimilated into the life of the local church. This is how Newman understood reception. I speak of reception as a *spiritual process* because it ties in with a person's faith and that of the Church as a communion of believers. In receiving the dogmas of an ecumenical council, for example, the local church considers the decisions of the council to be consonant with the apostolic faith. Newman would say that the whole Church ratifies a definition as authentic. In saying this Newman did not mean that the subsequent reception by the whole Church was a necessary condition for a dogmatic decision.[1]

The process of reception concerns the entire faith community,

---

[1] Ian Ker, *John Henry Newman: A Biography* (Oxford University Press: Oxford and NY, 1990), p. 681.

that is, the bishop, the priests, and the laity. Another way of stating this is to say that this reception occurs on several levels: at the level of church government (the bishop), at the theological level (theologians and approved authors), and at the level of the laity. Keep in mind that reception involves a *process*, one that may last for centuries.

Some Definitions

In Newman's day the term 'reception' was virtually unknown. In fact, I cannot find any mention of the term 'reception' at the First Vatican Council in 1870. However, there are passing references in the speeches of the bishops to a doctrine that has been 'received' by the Church. This means that the idea of reception was certainly known. However, it was not discussed using the word 'reception' as such. Newman himself was not acquainted with the term 'reception' in the technical, theological sense. He did certainly know the concept of reception, speaking of it in terms of the 'faith of all the believers' (*sensus fidelium*) and 'the consent of the faithful' (*consensus fidelium*).

Contemporary theologians distinguish between 'the sense of the faith' or *sensus fidei* and the 'faith of all the believers' or *sensus fidelium*, although Newman does not always make this distinction. The 'sense of the faith' refers to the faith of the individual believer. It involves making sense or meaning of one's entire life as viewed through the eyes of faith. The sense of the faith functions as an instinct or active sense ever on the lookout for God's fingerprints in one's life. Newman understands the sense of the faith as a critical capacity that senses what is, and what is not, of God. It's the believers' reception of their faith in terms of their particular circumstances, abilities, culture, and life experiences. The sense of the faith would most likely be captured if I, a Christian, had to explain my faith to my Muslim friends.[2]

The *sensus fidelium* or 'the faith of all the believers' has reference to the whole of the Christian people's acceptance of the faith. Newman uses the phrase 'the consent of the faithful' or *consensus fidelium* as synonymous with the phrase *sensus fidelium*. The 'consent of the faithful' refers to the unified expression of the faith of all believers, which results from faith. If the 'sense of the faith' or *sensus fidei*, is an instinct for the faith or an organ of faith, the 'consent of the faithful'

---

[2] For an excellent treatment of the 'sense of the faith' see John J. Burkhard, '*Sensus Fidei*: Theological Reflection since Vatican II: I. 1965-1984,' *The Heythrop Journal* 34 (1993): 41-59 and '*Sensus Fidei*: Recent Theological Reflection (1990-2001),' Part II, *The Heythrop Journal* 47 (2006):38-54.

assumes the existence of the 'sense of the faith.' The 'consent of the faithful' has to do with the agreement which arises among the faithful as a result of the sense of faith vis-à-vis specific items of faith. It is the situation in which the entire body of believers (from the bishops down to the laity) share the same belief.[3]

Newman, the Laity, and the Consent of the Faithful

Let me briefly describe how theology works. All of theology is a reflection on the Word of God or scripture. Scripture (interpreted ecclesially) is the final and ultimate norm of all theology, or what theologians call the *norma normans non normata*. However, each age reflects on and interprets the scriptures anew. Theologians call this tradition or the interpretation of scripture down through the ages. In the early centuries of the Church, theologians were interested in the spiritual sense of scripture, that is, how can the word of God nourish the prayer life of the individual Christian. In the Middle Ages, on the other hand, theologians used scripture to prove certain doctrines. We see this later development in the *Summa Theologica* of Thomas Aquinas.

In addition to scripture there are other sources of theology. First, we have the understanding of the faith which theologians possess. Second, there's the statements of the teaching office (magisterium) of the Church. Third, we have theological reason or the attempt to use our minds to understand what faith means. Fourth, one may speak of the *sensus fidelium* or 'the faith of all the believers' and the *consensus fidelium* or 'the consent of the faithful,' which finds expression in the liturgy or worship of the Church.

In a previous chapter of this book Dr Miller has analyzed at length Newman's famous essay, 'On Consulting the Faithful in Matters of Doctrine'. I would like to take another tack. I begin by analyzing the book, *The Arians of the Fourth Century* and the *Via Media I* for Newman's thoughts on the laity. Then, I make reference to the *Newman-Perrone Paper on Development* and make some brief remarks about the essay, 'On Consulting the Faithful in Matters of Doctrine', in search of a theology of consultation.

As noted above, Newman does not speak explicitly of reception as a technical term in theology. Rather, he speaks instead of the 'faith of all the believers' (*sensus fidelium*) and the 'consent of the faithful'

---

[3] Francis A. Sullivan, SJ, *Magisterium: Teaching Authority in the Catholic Church* (Paulist Press: Mahwah, NJ, 1983), p. 23.

(*consensus fidelium*). How did Newman learn about these terms? Not long after his conversion to Roman Catholicism in 1845 Newman went to Rome to update himself theologically. He took courses from Professor Perrone, the best known theologian in Rome at the time. Perrone made Newman aware of these terms, the *sensus* and *consensus fidelium*. However, Perrone never gave these terms a definite place in his work, the *Praeelectiones*. Why not?

Perrone held that the 'faith of all the believers' (*sensus fidelium*) was at the basis of all other expressions of the Church's tradition such as prayer, the worship of the Church, and definite events of church history. He also argued that prayer, the liturgy and the like were, in the final analysis, mere reflections of the doctrine proposed by the pope and bishops. Newman, however, took another view of the matter. He realized that the 'faith of all the believers' (*sensus fidelium*) was a relatively independent source of tradition and could be named along with the other witnesses of tradition.

What allowed Newman to go beyond his own teacher, Prof. Perrone, in this matter? Newman was much better versed in patristics or the thought of the Church Fathers than his esteemed teacher. Already in 1828 Newman began to read the Church Fathers systematically. In writing his book on the Arian heresy he again read the Church Fathers carefully in 1831. Generally speaking, the laity were forced by the magistrates in the fourth century to join themselves to the heretical party, the Arians, who doubted that Jesus was equal to the Father. Newman was particularly taken with the remarks of Hilary of Poitiers who said of the laity subject to Arian teaching that their own piety allowed them to interpret expressions religiously which were originally invented as evasions of correct doctrine.

From his study of the Arian heresy Newman drew three conclusions. First, he saw clearly that the laity generally preserved the Catholic faith during the Arian heresy although some orthodox bishops at the time sided with the Arians. Second, Newman noticed that creedal formularies developed partly as a result of the need for instructing the laity in the faith. Third, Newman realized that the laity need not be up-to-date theologically. Rather, it was more important that they have a robust faith. Newman later modified this view somewhat in his *University Discourses* and in his essay, 'On Consulting the Faithful in Matters of Doctrine' while yet managing to maintain his thesis that holiness in the laity is more important than knowledge.[4]

---

[4] Richard J. Penaskovic, *Open to the Spirit: The Notion of the Laity in the Thought of J.H. Newman*

Via Media I (1837)

The *Via Media I* is an important text for understanding Newman's thoughts on the laity and the reception of doctrine. Here Newman distinguishes between two traditions in the Church, the episcopal tradition and the prophetical tradition. The episcopal tradition is the official teaching of the Church and has the nature of a written document. The creed, for instance, is 'received' by the laity on the basis of the episcopal tradition. It has evidence of its apostolic origin similar in kind to that adducible for scripture. Later on as a Roman Catholic Newman would say that a papal encyclical forms part of the episcopal tradition.

On the other hand, we have the prophetical tradition which Newman calls 'the mind of the Spirit.' It is the thought and principle which breathes in the Church, the way the Church views things, the body of its 'received' notions and practices. The prophetical tradition finds expression in the liturgy and worship of the Church, in the theological schools such as the Dominican and the Franciscan schools of theology in the Middle Ages, and in the *sensus fidelium*. The laity are part and parcel of the prophetic tradition in the Church by reason of their sharing in the worship of the Church, in their partaking of the sacraments, and in their devotional practices.

How does this tie in with the notion of reception? The laity must believe all that the episcopal tradition proposes for belief. The laity must have an active faith not only for the creed but in regard to the prophetical tradition in the Church. Newman would say that no matter how far the creed is extended, the laity have the duty of obedience if not of active faith. The Church, for her part, speaks her mind in her prayers, services, and sacraments. When the Church so speaks, the whole Church, learned and unlearned, must respond. Another word for this response is faith. In sum, the laity receive in faith what the episcopal tradition presents to them. Newman feels that the members of the Church must either believe what the Church holds as true or silently acquiesce in the whole of it.

The Newman-Perrone Paper on Development

Newman wrote the *Newman-Perrone Paper on Development* (hereafter as *Newman-Perrone Paper*) in Latin to acquaint Father Perrone in Rome with the main ideas of his book, *An Essay on the Development*

(Werner Blasaditch Verlag: Augsburg, Germany, 1972), p. 20.

of Christian Doctrine. I see the *Newman-Perrone Paper* as a vital link between Newman's *Essay on Development* and the essay, 'On Consulting the Faithful'. In the *Newman-Perrone Paper* Newman argues that the word of God may be called 'objective' insofar as it resides in the mind of the Holy Spirit and in the understanding of the Roman Church, where Peter is present. The laity have to do with 'subjective' tradition in the Church, viz. that which is handed down from one generation to another, unanimously and spontaneously. This happens without conscious planning and without regard to any doctrinal definition.[5]

In the *Newman-Perrone Paper* Newman assigns a place to the faithful in the development of doctrine provided their minds are filled with divine light (grace). When Newman speaks of the faithful he includes not only the laity but also the doctors and teachers of the Church. They are to reflect on the word of God and when they do they begin to see the relationship between the various truths of the faith. The faithful deepen their knowledge of the faith under the guidance of the Holy Spirit in a manner not reducible to human logic. In this connection Newman makes an analogy between the mind of the individual Christian and the mind of the whole Church. The word of God has exactly the same history in the mind of the Church as a whole that it has in the mind of the individual believer. God's word becomes an inner sense as it is reflected upon by the teaching Church (the hierarchy) and the listening Church (the laity).[6]

This reflection and rumination on the word of God carried on by the teaching Church and the listening Church makes the subjective word of God objective, that is, it eventually passes into dogma. Until the time the Church actually puts a particular part of its faith into dogmatic form, the Church herself may not be fully conscious as to what she actually thinks on a particular subject. The laity in the Church contribute to the development of doctrine by their prayers, adoration, and worship or 'dogma in action.' Newman calls worship the special province of the laity in the Church.

Newman sees meditation as another factor in the development of doctrine. Meditation on the part of the laity in the fourth century resulted in the dogma of Mary's dignity as the Mother of God. For Newman meditation functions as a springboard for new dogmatic definitions. A dogmatic definition performs three functions: it removes

---

[5] The Latin text, *De Catholici Dogmatis Evolutione,* of the *Newman-Perrone Paper on Development* is now reprinted in *Gregorianum* 16 (1935): 404-434.

[6] Penaskovic, *Open to the Spirit*, p. 102.

doubt, a dull intellect, and a double tongue. At the same time it teaches and strengthens the laity in the faith.

Newman remarks that the fullness of the truth of the Holy Spirit lodges within the 'Catholic mind' which includes that of the laity. This truth contained in the Catholic mind is not reducible to certain dogmatic statements. However, it is manifested in formulas written for that very purpose. Newman could so strongly emphasize the role of the laity in the Church precisely because he sees them as led by, and open to, the Holy Spirit. We may speak of a 'Catholic mind' because the Holy Spirit takes up residence in the mind of the laity, coloring their perception of reality.[7]

In sum, Newman argues that the laity are not only the recipients of church doctrine but are in a sense co-creators of church doctrine by virtue of their living out the faith and reflecting on its meaning. They can perform this dogmatic function inasmuch as they are led by the Holy Spirit. I now turn to Newman's famous essay, 'On consulting the Faithful in Matters of Doctrine'.

On Consulting the Faithful

Allow me to make some brief remarks about Newman's famous essay, 'On Consulting the Faithful in Matters of Doctrine' where Newman makes some telling remarks about the laity and the reception of doctrine. The faithful are consulted in the preparation of a dogmatic definition for several reasons: 1) The laity are witnesses to the tradition of revealed doctrine so that their consent is the voice of the infallible Church. 2) The Church's tradition manifests itself in various ways, that is, in the bishops, the doctors or theologians, and in the people by means of their history, liturgy, and rites. 3) The 'consent of the faithful' can make up for deficiencies in regard to various points of doctrine on the part of the Fathers of the Church. 4) The universal conviction of pious Catholics is part of the argument in favor of the doctrine of the Immaculate Conception.

Dr Ed Miller in another chapter of this book has commented on this essay extensively. I wish to make two points. First, as Newman observed in the *Newman-Perrone Paper* and again in his famous essay, the laity witness to the truth of a dogma by their devotion, worship, in fact by their entire lifestyle. This witness of the laity is not merely a passive process on the part of the laity, but rather an active one. Think

---

[7] Penaskovic, *Open to the Spirit*, p. 122.

of the witness of the laity as similar to communication satellites today which boost a message while simultaneously passing it on.

Second, Newman did not think of the hierarchy and the laity in opposition to each other. Rather, he felt that the teaching Church and the Church taught work marvelously together, hand in glove. Together they are a twofold testimony, never to be divided, working together in partnership. Newman uses the Latin word, *conspiratio*, to describe this relationship. *Conspiratio* has the sense of 'breathing together' much like we humans use two lungs working together to breathe. Newman's great contribution to the notion of reception is this: the faith is transmitted and received by the faithful working totally in concert with the church hierarchy.[8]

The Non-Reception of Doctrine

So far I have spoken about the reception of church doctrine by the laity. The question naturally arises whether there can be a non-reception of doctrine by the Church and by the laity. In this connection the notion of heresy or the denial of church doctrine comes to mind. This is the most blatant case of the non-reception of doctrine by members of the Church. There were some individuals and groups of people who rejected the definition of papal infallibility at the time of its proclamation in 1870. They formed a schismatic church. However, not all cases of the non-reception of doctrine result in heresy.

Did Newman weigh in on this matter of papal infallibility? Yes, he did. John T. Ford, a noted Newman scholar, points out that even after the definition of papal infallibility was approved by Vatican I, Newman was unsure whether Catholics were *bound* to accept it or not.[9] Newman based his hesitation on the lack of moral unanimity at the Council, pointing out that opposition to defining the dogma had resulted in the exodus from the council of more than eighty bishops before the actual vote on papal infallibility was taken. What, in fact, happened is this: the bishops failed to persist in united opposition as a body, so that there was no justification for resisting the definition.

More importantly, Newman felt that if the definition were received by the entire body of the faithful, then too, it would claim our assent by virtue of the principle that 'the general acceptance or judgment of Christendom suffices,' (*Securus judicat orbis terrarum*). For

---

[8] Paul G. Crowley, 'Catholicity, Inculturation, and Newman's *Sensus Fidelium,' The Heythrop Journal* 33 (1992): 171.

[9] John T. Ford, 'Newman on the Reception of Doctrine,' *CTSA Proceedings* 36 (1981), p. 188.

Newman the Church as a whole is the primary subject of infallibility. The Pope is then the crystallization point of the infallibility of the whole Church.[10]

Professor Ford observes that Newman felt moved to sketch out a more acceptable interpretation of the doctrine of infallibility than that advanced by Cardinal Manning and the strong supporters of papal prerogatives at the time, the Ultramontane party. This group was very disappointed that the definition of papal infallibility could not be used to rigorously enforce the encyclical of Pope Pius IX, the *Syllabus of Errors*.[11] Newman notes that if a person accepts the doctrine of papal infallibility this does not necessarily imply acceptance of the process leading up to its formulation as a dogma. He also believed that a later council or pope may correct the one-sidedness of a previous one. In regard to a council, Newman was prescient. Vatican II did provide a corrective or balance to the notion of papal infallibility by emphasizing the notion of episcopal collegiality.

Newman's Relevance Today

Newman's relevance today may be summarized in three points:

1. Throughout his many writings Newman believes that one of the main duties of the laity is to strive after holiness. Newman makes this point in the *Parochial and Plain Sermons*. In raising the level of religion in their own hearts, the laity automatically raise it in the world at large. The laity are to realize the unseen or spiritual world which is as real as the material world all around us. Part of realizing the unseen world is for the laity to have a deep prayer life, making Christ the axis on which their world turns. For Newman the laity are signposts which show the world the true meaning of Christianity. In some ways the idea of Christianity itself is an abstraction. This abstraction comes to life in the lives of the people of God.

In pursuing their vocation the laity will often find themselves at odds with the secular world. This should be no surprise because the Christian and those of the world see life differently. The latter look to reason alone to find out how to live. The laity, on the other hand, are also led by faith, which gives them a different view of reality. Faith may be compared to a glass of water, without color, odor, or taste. Yet when held up to the light of day it's a prism that both reflects and

---

[10] Ker, *John Henry Newman*, p. 682.
[11] Ker, *John Henry Newman*, p. 658.

captures all the beauty, mystery, and wonder in the entire universe. Faith gives the Christian new eyes. It's like the plastic lens we put on to view a movie in three dimensions. If we take the lens off, the images on the screen look blurred. So too, if we do not look at life through the lens of faith, our vision of reality is cloudy. For this reason Newman underscores the importance of faith on the part of the laity.

2. The laity are to be consulted in the preparation of a dogmatic definition because they are open to the Holy Spirit. The divine indwelling is the theological reason why the laity are to be consulted. In his own personal life Newman discovered a saving relationship with the Father, Son, and Holy Spirit when he was fifteen years old. From then on his religion and his theology became person-centered. Newman's entire theology of the laity is the attempt to help other Christians discover the deeper roots of their Christian heritage, namely, open to, and led by, the Holy Spirit.[12]

3. The witness of the laity to the truth of a dogma is an active one. It manifests itself in prayer, devotions, meditation, and the worship of the Church. The witness of the laity is similar to today's communication satellites which boost a message while simultaneously passing it on.

---

[12] Penaskovic, *Open to the Spirit*, p. 253.

Chapter 9

NEWMAN AND THE MAGISTERIUM

by Austin Cooper

A s an adolescent, Newman was deeply aware of Church teaching. He recorded that "(when) I was fifteen ... I fell under the influences of a definite ... Creed, and received into my intellect impressions of dogma which, through God's mercy have never been effaced or obscured."[1] By the 1830s, when the Oxford Movement began, he was able to articulate his basic religious belief:

> First was the principle of dogma ... Secondly, I was confident in the truth of a certain definite religious teaching based on this foundation of dogma: viz. that there was a visible Church, with sacraments and rites which are the channels of invisible grace ... And further (there was) the Episcopal system, I founded it upon the Epistles of St Ignatius ... My own Bishop was my Pope; I knew no other; the successor of the Apostles, the Vicar of Christ.[2]

Newman very early expressed his "attachment to the doctrine and discipline of the Church."[3] Indeed the Oxford Movement was noted for its insistence on the faithful observance of fast days, the daily recitation of Matins and Evensong and more frequent celebration of Holy Communion, this latter being made possible through the ministry of the historic episcopate. Such an attitude was akin to what Catholics mean by the ordinary Magisterium of the Church. For one must "hear" the Church which is the "pillar and ground of truth."[4] Newman was adamant on the need to obey his bishop but he saw the

---

[1] John Henry Cardinal Newman *Apologia Pro Vita Sua Being a History of His Religious Opinions*, Edited with an Introduction and Notes by Martin J Svaglic (Oxford: The Clarendon Press, 1967) pp. 15.14; 17.20.

[2] *Ibid.*, pp. 54.17, 55.5 and 56.21.

[3] Newman to R.I. Wilberforce 29/10/33 Ian Ker and Thomas Gornall SJ Eds *The Letters and Diaries of John Henry Newman* (LD), Volume IV (Oxford: Clarendon Press, 1980) p. 74.

[4] Newman to *The Record* 31/10/33 LD IV 33 and Newman to *The Record* 14/11/33 LD IV p. 102.

dilemma: this was all very well in the case of the generally sympathetic Bagot of Oxford, but what if his Ordinary was the Bishop of Chester?[5] However he regarded himself absolved from obedience if the bishop was clearly heretical.[6] Despite such a hypothetical case, he expressed a consistent belief that "the Holy Church nowhere, whether in England or elsewhere, can do wrong — she is the immaculate Spouse — then only can you say the Church has gone wrong when and in Council assembled she has done it."[7] However the Church does not necessarily find this assurance in an individual bishop for "only in Synod do they prescribe doctrine."[8] Needless to say there was a unique role for a general council when the Holy Ghost was present.[9] Once again one finds in the early Newman clear indications of what developed into an acceptance of the extraordinary Magisterium. For this was to be the means for expressing that great reassurance: *securus judicat orbis terrarum.*

Newman's succinctly stated belief in obedience to a teaching authority might easily blur the cost of discipleship involved. In 1838, when Bishop Richard Bagot of Oxford, made some (admittedly mild) criticism of the *Tracts for the Times*, Newman expressed the view that he would give up the series of which he was clearly the leading mover: he professed that "a Bishop's lightest word *ex cathedra* is heavy. His judgment on a book cannot be light."[10] However when one looks at Newman's correspondence behind this terse comment, one sees something of the great difficulty he felt in being obedient to ecclesiastical authority.[11] This is hardly surprising: religious obedience is not necessarily a military like response to orders, or even the dutiful reaction of someone like the prophet Isaiah. For many there is a struggle, like that experienced by that other Old Testament colossus, Jeremiah. Newman's years in the Church of England were to witness other trials of obedience: especially the crisis over Tract 90. And his sensitive nature was to be repeatedly put to the test in his Catholic days.

---

[5] Newman to A.W. Hadden, 15/1/42 in Gerard Tracey Ed. *The Letters and Diaries of John Henry Newman* Volume VIII (Oxford: Clarendon Press, 1999) p. 425.
[6] Newman to John Keble February 19 1842 LD VIII p. 466.
[7] Newman to S F Wood 23/3/38 Gerard Tracey Ed. *The Letters and Diaries of John Henry Newman* Volume VI (Oxford: Clarendon Press, 1984) p. 219.
[8] Newman to J R Hope-Scott 17/10/41 LD VIII p. 300.
[9] Newman to B Harrison 24/11/35 in Thomas Gornall Ed. *The Letters and Diaries of John Henry Newman* Volume V (Oxford: Clarendon Press, 1981) p. 168.
[10] *Ibid.*, p. 78.8.
[11] Several letters regarding this see LD VI pp. 285–302.

Throughout these various trials Newman's own theological position was maturing: the notion of development is a central motif of his life. As he was working on his great work on this very topic, he wrote to Mrs William Froude:

> I have always held a development of doctrine, at least in some great points in theology. E.g. I have thought that the doctrine of the Holy Trinity and Incarnation are intellectual developments of the inspired declarations of Scripture – but I used to think either that this development was made in the Apostles' life time and given by them traditionally to the Church, or at least that it was made by the Church in the *first* ages.[12]

Much later Newman claimed that he would not have become a Catholic without this idea of development.[13] Gradually he came to the conviction "founded on my study of early Church history (that) the Church of Rome in every respect (is) the continuation of the early Church. I think she is the early Church *in* these times, and the early Church is she in these times."[14]

It was precisely this that challenged him to the most profound act of obedience to the authority of the Church. In a letter written to his sister Jemima he expressed something of the pain involved in his move to the Catholic Church:

> A clear conviction of the substantial identity of Christianity and the Roman system has now been on my mind for a full three years. It is more than five years since the conviction first came to me, though I struggled against it and overcame it. I believe all my feelings and wishes are against change. I have nothing to draw me elsewhere. I hardly ever was at a Roman service, even abroad – I know no Roman Catholics. I have no sympathy with them as a party. I am giving up everything. I am not conscious of any resentment, disgust, or the like to repel me from my present position – I have no dreams whatever, far from it, of what I could do in another position. Far from it indeed – I seem to be throwing myself away.[15]

It is difficult to appreciate the position of the Catholic Church in 1845. In one of his most evocative passages, Newman gives us a feel

---

[12] Newman to Mrs William Froude June 9 1844 in *The Letters and Diaries of John Henry Newman*, Volume X, Edited by Francis J McGrath FMS (Oxford: University Press, 2006) pp. 264-5.

[13] Newman to Alfred Plummer April 3 1871 in *The Letters and Diaries of John Henry Newman*, Volume XXV, Edited by Charles Stephen Dessain and Thomas Gornall SJ (Oxford: Clarendon Press, 1973) p. 308 and Newman to David Moriarty Bishop of Kerry April 11 1971 in *ibid.*, p. 315.

[14] Newman to Richard Westmacott July 11 1845 LD X p. 729.

[15] Newman to Mrs John Mozley November 24 1844 LD X p. 435.

for the contemporary scene:

> 'The Roman Catholics;' – not a sect, not even an interest, as men conceived of it, – not a body, however small, representative of the Great Communion abroad, – but a mere handful of individuals, who might be counted, like the pebbles and detritus of the great deluge, and who, forsooth, merely happened to retain a creed which, in its day indeed, was the profession of a Church. Here a set of poor Irishmen, coming and going at harvest time, or a colony of them lodged in a miserable quarter of the vast metropolis. There, perhaps an elderly person, seen walking in the streets, grave and solitary, and strange, though noble in bearing, and said to be of good family, and a 'Roman Catholic.' An old-fashioned house of gloomy appearance, closed in with high walls, with an iron gate, and yews, and the report attaching to it that 'Roman Catholics' lived there; but who they were, or what they did, or what was meant by calling them Roman Catholics, no one could tell; – though it had an unpleasant sound, and told of form and superstition. And then, perhaps, as we went to and fro, looking with a boy's curious eyes through the great city, we might come today upon some Moravian chapel, or Quaker's meeting-house, and tomorrow on a chapel of the 'Roman Catholics': but nothing was to be gathered from it, except that there were lights burning there, and some boys in white, swinging censers; and what it all meant could only be learned from books, from Protestant Histories and Sermons; and they did not report well of 'the Roman Catholics,' but, on the contrary, deposed that they had once had power and had abused it.[16]

However clear and logical Newman's argument concerning the development of doctrine might have been, entering the Church was an act of obedience nothing less than heroic. And he was quite clear that he had come to Rome "to learn my religion."[17]

His approach to doctrine through an historic lens was to stand him in good stead as a Catholic. Time and again he was to be able to see doctrinal and theological issues both as a systematized view of the faith, and also as an historic reality. This was evident in his ready defence of the doctrine of the Immaculate Conception. He supported Bishop Ullathorne's writings on the topic, celebrated the definition at the Catholic University and asked Frederick Faber to write some verses for the occasion. Throughout he was clear about the theological principles involved. He explained to Mrs William Froude that:

---

[16] John Henry, Cardinal Newman 'The Second Spring' *Sermons Preached on Various Occasions* (London: Longmans, Green & Co., 1908) pp. 172-3.

[17] Newman to Richard Stanton 15 August 1855 in Charles Stephen Dessain *The Letters and Diaries of John Henry Newman*, Volume XVI, (London: Nelson, 1965) pp. 526-7.

There is a marked contrast in Catholicity between the views presented to us by doctrine and devotion respectively. Doctrines never change, devotions vary with each individual. Catholics allow each other, accordingly, the greatest licence, and are, if I may so speak utter *liberals*, as regards devotions, whereas they are most sensitive about doctrine. That Mary is the Mother of God is a point of faith – that Mary is to be honoured and exalted in this or that way is a point of devotion. The latter is the consequence indeed of the former, but a consequence which follows with various intensity, in various degrees and in various modes, in various minds ... As far as I can make out from history and from documents St Chrysostom had not the devotion to Mary, which St Bonaventura had or St Alfonso – but they agreed together most simply and absolutely that she was the Mother of God.[18]

This distinction between doctrine and devotion was to be complemented by his clear distinction between doctrine and theology. And in articulating these very basic differences he was to be greatly assisted by his ability to view the historic experience of the Church. Newman was able to place this in the widest possible ecclesial context, with a sure sense of historic perspective. Commenting on the dogma of the Immaculate Conception he explained:

Had St Paul been asked whether our Lady's conception was immaculate, or whether she was born in original sin, is it wrong to say that he would have been puzzled by the words 'conception', 'immaculate', and 'original sin'? Is it detracting from his perfect knowledge of all that which the Church in after times has developed and shall develop to the end, if I allow he would have kept silence and have left the question unanswered? Is it more than saying, that scientific phraseology was not among the languages which were comprised in the Pentecostal gift? – But if he had been asked, whether or not our Lady had the grace of the Spirit anticipating all sin whatever, including Adam's imputed sin, I think he would have answered in the affirmative. If he never was asked the question, I should say he had in his mind the decision of the Church in 1854 in confuso or implicate.[19]

The action of the pope in this definition seemed a clear articulation of the deposit of faith. In contrast to the definition of papal infallibility, he took consolation in the fact that there was "nothing sudden, or secret ... it had been talked about years out of mind."[20] The Marian

---

[18] Newman to Mrs William Froude January 2 55 LD XVI pp. 341-2.

[19] J. Derek Holmes Ed. *The Theological papers of John Henry Newman, Newman on Bliblical Inspiration and on Infallibility* (Oxford: Clarendon Press, 1979) p. 159.

[20] Newman to Orestes Brownson 13 April 1870 LD XXV p. 97.

definition was clearly the expression of the faith of the whole Church: once again *securus judicat orbis terrarum*. This definition also witnesses to Newman's own development. Given his Anglican criticisms of Catholic attitudes to Mary, so clearly expressed in *Apologia*, he now readily accepted this definition, and penned some deeply devotional Marian prayers.[21] In his own growth doctrine, theology and devotion are all interwoven.

Far more contentious were Newman's hassles with ecclesiastical authority over the issue of the role of the laity in the Church. This should be viewed in the context of Newman's consistent willingness to respect the individual conscience. This was to find its final articulation in his celebrated defence of the freedom of conscience. Needless to say this was by no means the same thing as an individual right to choose between alternative offerings as in a democratic election. Several aspects of the rights of conscience emerge from Newman's letters in which we see his pastoral approach to individuals. His having come to a strong conviction that he should join the Catholic Church did not involve any hint of intolerance or judgment of those who differed. He reassured his sister Jemima: "I believe the Church of Rome to be true ... In saying this, I am not saying another is wrong, who does not do the same."[22] And of course the truth appeals differently to different people: "I think that in every age every man may find a sufficient evidence in his own line of thought. One aspect of the Church will be the instrument of conversion with one man, another with another; but some or other for everyone."[23] In his correspondence there is a very sensitive pastoral approach that respects the individual. He was prepared to wait patiently for individuals to develop. However his interest in the laity was not merely as people being taught, but as being involved in the process of the development of doctrine. Newman had long held that the faith was given to the whole Church. He expressed this in a letter to Jemima as early as 1837:

> I hold most decidedly, that where Catholic Truth is denied (where it is, when men deny the grace of Baptism) any one, layman, woman, child, has a right to hold up the standard of faith against Bishops, Archdeacons, and Clergy. It is a mere question of *expediency* how far they should do this – a mere question of the *manner* of doing it, the time, place, towards whom etc., but they have the right, and are

[21] John Henry Newman *Meditations and Devotions* (London: Burns & Oates, 1964) pp. 108–150.
[22] Newman to Mrs John Mozley 22 December 1844 LD X pp. 467-8.
[23] Newman to an unknown correspondent June 19 1870 LD XXV p. 147.

bound, under these discretionary limits, to exercise it.[24]

In his first book, *The Arians of the Fourth Century*, Newman asserted the role of the laity in keeping alive the true faith. He made the startling assertion that

> the episcopate, whose action was so prompt and concordant at Nicæa on the rise of Arianism, did not, as a class or order of men, play a good part in the troubles consequent upon the Council; and the laity did. The Catholic people, in the length and breadth of Christendom, were the obstinate champions of Catholic truth, and the bishops were not.[25]

He was to draw on this theme later in his controversial article 'On Consulting the Faithful'. This essay, published in *The Rambler*,[26] returned to Newman's oft repeated idea of an original deposit of faith which develops:

> I think I am right in saying that the tradition of the Apostles, committed to the whole Church in its various constituents and functions *per modum unius*, manifests itself variously at various times: sometimes by the mouth of the episcopacy, sometimes by the doctors, sometimes by the people, sometimes by liturgies, rites, ceremonies, and customs, by events, disputes, movements, and all those other phenomena which are comprised under the name of history.

However, this by no means denied the special role of the teaching authority of the Magisterium:

> It follows that none of these channels of tradition may be treated with disrespect; granting at the same time fully, that the gift of discerning, discriminating, defining, promulgating, and enforcing any portion of that tradition resides solely in the *Ecclesia docens*.[27]

In a very lucid example he described what he meant by 'consulting':

> We talk of 'consulting our barometer' about the weather: – the barometer only attests the *fact* of the state of the atmosphere. In like manner, we may consult a watch or a sun-dial about the time of day. A physician consults the pulse of his patient; but not in the same sense in which his patient consults *him*.[28]

Newman was confident that consultation had taken place prior to the

---

[24] Newman to Mrs John Mozley Sept 11 37 LD VI p. 127.

[25] John Henry Cardinal Newman *The Arians of the Fourth Century* (London: Longmans, Greene & Co., 1908) p. 445.

[26] John Henry Newman 'On Consulting the Faithful in Matters of Doctrine' *Rambler* I (New Series), Part II, (July 1859) pp. 198–230.

[27] 'On Consulting the Faithful' p. 206.

[28] 'On Consulting the Faithful' p. 200.

definition of the Immaculate Conception. In defending his article he wrote to Bishop Ullathorne:

> I meant to state, what I think was the case, that, out of the condescension of the Holy See, the Christian people at large were consulted on the *fact* of the *tradition* of the Immaculate Conception in every part of the Catholic world. The fact of the tradition, I conceive, was one chief ground of the Definition being possible.[29]

Unfortunately this article was to test Newman's patience and obedience, leaving him under a cloud for some years. He was delated to Rome by Bishop Brown of Newport for apparently suggesting failure on the part of the teaching authority of the Church. In a theological note Newman explained that, during the turbulence of the Arian controversy,

> there was a temporary confusion, arising out of a number (of bishops) who got puzzled or were deceived or were timid or were heretics as such, that, as a cloud obscures the heavens, so the testimony of all was for a time suspended ...[30]

The matter of Newman's orthodoxy devolved into a complicated series of manoeuvres which amounted to a lack of communication.[31] He vainly sought to obtain a clear statement of official Roman objections, asking Cardinal Wiseman's intervention to secure three things:

1. The passages of the Article, on which the Cardinal Prefect of Propaganda desires an explanation.

2. A copy of the translations, in which His Eminence has read them.

3. The dogmatic propositions, which they have been represented as infringing or otherwise impairing.[32]

Sadly, nothing came of this appeal and the matter simmered on for some years. However it is significant that Newman asked for clarification regarding any 'dogmatic' issues which he might have infringed. Apparently he changed this from the word 'theological' in his original draft.[33] This is a distinction which Newman is later to use consistently and which needs to be constantly reaffirmed in Catholic life and letters.

---

[29] Newman to Bishop Ullathorne May 13 1859 Charles Stephen Dessain *The Letters and Diaries of John Henry Newman,* Volume XIX, (London: Nelson, 1969) p. 131.

[30] LD XIX p. 206 n. 3.

[31] A summary is to be found in Ian Ker *John Henry Newman A Biography* (Oxford: University Press, 1988) pp. 485-9 and numerous details in LD XIX p. 290 n. 2 and p. 333 n. 2.

[32] Newman to Cardinal Wiseman January 19 1860 LD XIX p. 289.

[33] LD XIX p. 289 n. 2.

The matter of *The Rambler* article also brought forth some typical Newmanesque lamentations which displayed the pain occasioned by the affair:

> I marvel, but do not complain, that, after many years of patient and self denying labour in the cause of Catholicity, the one appropriate acknowledgement in my old age should be considered to consist in taking advantage against me of what is at worst a slip of the pen in an anonymous un-theological paper. But I suppose it is a law of the world, that those who toil much and say little, are little thought of. [34]

A further challenge came with the publication of the Encyclical *Quanta Cura* and the accompanying *Syllabus of Errors*. This did not present a challenge to Newman personally, so much as pose a difficulty for Catholics in countries such as England. Undoubtedly the most embarrassing declaration, and the most frequently quoted, is the 80th and last of the errors condemned in the Syllabus: "The Roman Pontiff can, and ought to, reconcile himself, and come to terms with progress, liberalism and modern civilization."[35] In a society becoming more democratic and readily informed by the emerging popular press it lent itself to criticism and ridicule, to say nothing of confusion to Catholics. In order to be properly understood it needed to be read in the context of the document from which it was taken, a criticism of anti-Catholic policies being implemented by the government of Piedmont in the name of liberalism and democracy. Stated as blandly as it was in the *Syllabus*, it appeared highly contentious to the average English reader.

Newman commented that "we are bound to receive what the pope says, and not to speak about it ... there is little in what he says but would have been said by all high churchmen thirty years ago, or by the Record and Keble now." This indeed is to see the document in the wide sweep of ecclesiastical attitudes during the greater part of the century which often viewed political trends as harbingers of a repeat performance of the French Revolution. But Newman was also realistic enough to see that the document presented real problems: "The advisers of the Holy Father seemed determined to make our position in England as difficult as ever they can."[36] He was perplexed: "I don't understand its meaning or its worth ... The only point which makes it interesting to *us* is that it is addressed to the whole Catholic

[34] Newman to Cardinal Wiseman January 19 1860 LD XIX pp. 289-290.
[35] Taken from Allocution *Jamdudum cernimus*, March 18, 1861. Text in Internet site http://www.papalencyclicals.net/Pius09/p9syll.htm accessed 27/04/07.
[36] Newman to Ambrose St John January 8 1865 in Charles Stephen Dessain and Edward E. Kelly SJ (Eds) *Letters and Diaries of John Henry Newman*, Volume XXI (London:Nelson, 1971) p. 378.

world – there seems nothing else in it which looks like a theological decision." That being the case, Newman invoked his freedom in the matter: "If (a formal decision) is urged against me as such, I should (be) obliged to fall back on my liberty of opinion, *till* that liberty is *proved* to be taken away." [37]

Newman is content to take the wide sweep of history: "An impartial posterity (might) pronounce it to be a wise, bold, and necessary manifesto." [38] This was being very tactful indeed. He privately continued to think it "a heavy blow and a great discouragement to us in England." [39] In many ways the Syllabus was a prelude to the more intensely discussed issue of papal infallibility. He saw in it the hand of an "ultra party". [40] These were soon to be vigorously promoting the definition of papal infallibility.

There is every evidence that Newman personally had little difficulty with the idea of papal infallibility. As early as 1843 he wrote to Keble:

> In June and July 1839, near four years ago, I read the Monophysite Controversy, and it made a deep impression on me, which I was not able to shake off, that the Pope had a certain gift of infallibility, and that communion with the see of Rome was a divinely intended means of grace and illumination. [41]

While he constantly professed a belief in papal infallibility in practice, his dislike of the idea of a definition was shaped both by practical pastoral needs and also the manner in which the definition was promoted. "The fears of some unknown definition, when every thing is at rest is secretly distressing numbers. What heresy calls for a decision? What have we done that we can't be let alone?" [42] Such an attitude was to be made public when a very confidential letter to Bishop Ullathorne was leaked to the press by Bishop Clifford of Clifton. Newman lamented:

> When we are all at rest, and have no doubts, and at least practically, not to say doctrinally, hold the Holy Father to be infallible, suddenly there is thunder in the clear sky, and we are told to prepare for something we know not what to try our faith we know not how.

[37] Newman to William Monsell January 12 1865 LD XXI p. 385.
[38] Newman to Henry Nutcombe Oxenham January 25 1865 LD XXI p. 391.
[39] Newman to Ambrose Pjillips de Lisle February 13 1865 LD XXI p. 415.
[40] Newman to Sir John Simeon March 22 1865 LD XXI p. 436.
[41] Newman to John Keble May 4 1843 in Francis J. McGrath FMS and Gerard Tracey (Eds) *Letters & Diaries of John Henry Newman*, Volume IX (Oxford: University Press, 2006) p. 328.
[42] Newman to David Moriarty, Bishop of Kerry January 28 1870 in Charles Stephen Dessain and Thomas Gornall SJ *Letters and Diaries of John Henry Newman*, Volume XXV (Oxford: Clarendon Press, 1973) p. 17.

> No impending danger is to be averted, but a great difficulty is to be
> created. Is this the proper work for an Ecumenical Council?

Rather than being influenced by "the flattery of a clique of Jesuits, Redemptorists, and converts"[43] Newman would have preferred that "changes in thought (should not be) hurried, abrupt, violent – out of tenderness to souls …"[44] In the turbulent times during and immediately after the First Vatican Council, Newman was able to point to both the importance of this difference between doctrine and theology, and also the progress of his own development. After enumerating the many occasions when, as a Catholic, he had spoken on behalf of the Pope's infallibility, he added:

> This is quite consistent, in my way of viewing it, in my being most energetic against the *definition*. Many things are true which are not points of faith, and I thought the definition of this doctrine *most inexpedient*. And, as St Paul, though inspired, doubted whether his words might not do harm to his Corinthian converts, so do I now fear much lest the infallible voice of the Council may not do harm to the cause of the Church in Germany, England, and elsewhere.
>
> What I said in the private letter to my Bishop … was that the definition would unsettle men's minds. This anticipation has been abundantly fulfilled. I said moreover expressly that it would be *no* difficulty to me, but that it was making the defence of Catholicism more *difficult*. [45]

This would seem to be a fair account of his attitude throughout. First of all, it was consistently his view that if papal infallibility were defined at all, it would "only change it in my mind from an opinion to a dogma."[46] And throughout his discussions on the topic he kept a lively sense of his freedom in the matter until such time as there was no doubt as to its being pronounced as a dogma. Even after the final vote on July 18th, he told one correspondent that while he would accept the definition if called upon to profess it, "it cannot be denied that there are reasons for a Catholic, till better informed, to suspend his judgement on its validity." He cited the eighty Council Fathers who absented themselves from the final vote, and wondered whether there was the moral unanimity such as Pius IV had expected of the

---

[43] Newman to Bishop Ullathorne January 28 1870 LD XXV pp. 18-19.

[44] Newman to Richard Holt Hutton February 16 1870 LD XXV pp. 31-32.

[45] Newman to Alfred Plummer July 19 1872 in Charles Stephen Dessain and Thomas Gornall SJ *Letters and Diaries of John Henry Newman*, Volume XXVI (Oxford: Clarendon Press, 1974) p. 139.

[46] Newman to J T Seccombe January 2 1870 LD XXV p. 5.

Council of Trent.[47] He was still maintaining this attitude some weeks later when writing to Mrs William Froude he confided:

> As far as I see no one is bound to believe it at this moment, certainly not till the end of the Council. This I hold in spite of Dr Manning. At the same time since the Pope has pronounced the definition, I think it safer to accept it at once. I very much doubt if at this moment, before the end of the Council, I could get myself publicly to say it was de fide whatever came of it – though I believe the doctrine itself.[48]

There can be little doubt that Newman's concern for such liberty was motivated by a keen pastoral sense: to a lady having difficulty with it he wrote succinctly "Such confusion has been at other times ... Be calm – beware of dangerous steps ... Don't set yourself against the doctrine."[49] The Newman correspondence continued to show this sensitive pastoral sense, but by the end of the year he had came to the view that the "doctrine of Infallibility has now been more than sufficiently promulgated."[50] And of course Newman was relieved that the definition was so limited: "A Pope is not *inspired*; he has no inherent gift of divine knowledge, but when he speaks ex Cathedra, he may say little or much, but he is simply protected from saying what is untrue."[51] Such was Newman's acceptance of the definition that he defended it in his *Letter to the Duke of Norfolk*. This was occasioned by the exaggerated claims made by William Gladstone concerning the political implications of the definition. It offered Newman an opportunity to present a moderate view of papal infallibility against those Catholics who

> have conducted themselves as if no responsibility attached to wild words and overbearing deeds; who have stated truths in the most paradoxical form, and stretched principles till they were close to snapping; and who at length, having done their best to set the house on fire, leave to others the task of putting out the flame.[52]

So coupled with his pastoral sense was Newman's dislike (as he saw it) of the method of those promoting the definition: "the conduct of the *instruments* of the Definition ... was very cruel, and they would have to bear the responsibility of that cruelty."[53] Bishop Clifford apparently

---

[47] Newman to Ambrose Phillips de Lisle July 24 1870 LD XXV p. 165.
[48] Newman to Mrs William Froude August 8 1870 LD XXV p. 176.
[49] Newman to Mrs William Beckwith August 21 1870 LD XXV p. 189.
[50] Newman to Georges Darboy, Archbishop of Paris (one of the minority Bishops) End of 1870 (?) LD XXV p. 259.
[51] Newman to Mrs William Froude March 5 1871 LD XXV p. 299.
[52] J H Newman, *A Letter Addressed to the Duke of Norfolk on Occasion of Mr. Gladstone's Recent Expostulation* (London: 1874) p. 4.
[53] Newman to Emile Perceval August 15 1870 LD XXV p. 185.

advised him to "be perfectly quiet, lest the tyrant majority should do something more"[54] and while yet again professing his acceptance of the doctrine Newman reiterated that "the conduct of the promoters of the dogma has been simply cruel."[55]

Newman's consistent attitude, on the contrary, was to allow people space and time to develop. To a mother anxious about the progress of her son at school he feared lest "we should meddle with him too much, and make too much of little things"[56]; to another mother solicitous for the religious commitment of her young adult son, he suggested "leave him alone" as the wisest course[57]; to a lady who felt unduly pressured by her confessor to express ready agreement with the Vatican decrees, he commented that "some Bishops and Priests ... act as if they did not care at all whether souls were lost or not ... I deeply lament the violence which has been used in this matter."[58]

This sensitive pastoral care does not mean that Newman was unconcerned for the teaching of truth. From the time of the Oxford Movement his whole life witnessed to the need to proclaim Catholic Truth. But as well as being taught and articulated clearly, it also needed to have a power of attraction. He prayed:

> Teach me to show forth Thy praise, Thy truth, Thy will. Make me preach Thee without preaching – not by words, but by my example and by the catching force, the sympathetic influence of what I do – by my visible resemblance to Thy saints, and the evident fullness of the love which my heart bears to Thee.[59]

The way the Church proclaims the truth is inseparable from the way she deals with individuals. Clearly that power of attraction came from being close to the mystery of God, and attuned to that mystery in one's mode of living. Here, *cor ad cor loquitur*, and here is the most profound and effective exercise of Magisterium.[60]

---

[54] Newman to Ambrose St John August 21 1870 LD XXV p. 192.

[55] Newman to Lady Chatterton August 6 1870 LD XXV p. 174.

[56] Newman to the Duchess of Norfolk April 16 1862 Charles Stephen Dessain (Ed) *Letters and Diaries of John Henry Newman*, Volume XX (London: Nelson, 1970) p. 187.

[57] Newman to Lady Herbert of Lea October 6 1879, Charles Stephen Dessain and Thomas Gornall SJ (Eds) *Letters and Diaries of John Henry Newman*, Volume XXIX (Oxford: Clarendon Press, 1976) p. 181.

[58] Newman to Mrs Wilson October 20 1870 LD XXV p. 216.

[59] *Meditations and Devotions of the Late John Henry Cardinal Newman* (London: Longmans, Greene & Co., 1907) p. 365.

[60] Cf. the chapter 'Personal Influence' in C.S. Dessain *Newman's Spiritual Themes* (Dublin: Veritas, 1977) pp. 31–52.

Conclusion

Finally, one may ask whether Newman's attitude to the *Magisterium* holds any value for the contemporary Christian. There is surely a perennial value in Newman's appreciation of the clear distinction between doctrine and theology. There are certain basic realities and Newman was wonderfully consistent in his attachment to these. Late in life they were reiterated in *The Dream of Gerontius*: "Firmly I believe and truly". This is the moving *cantus firmus* which punctuates his whole life. This dogmatic basis is the bedrock, the solid ground, on which the whole subsists and which is the basis of our hope of final fulfillment.

But along with obedience to central doctrines, there is the area of freedom. To hold these two in a productive tension calls for a breadth of vision and a depth of charity. In a world which so often opts for polarization, a Catholic sense of unity and diversity in an atmosphere of mutual respect and love is surely the ideal.

And Newman was certainly committed to a sense of patient waiting for people to develop. The mystery of development is in a sense the secret of each one of us. Provided there is a basic good will, then growth will certainly take place. This is very reminiscent of that typically pragmatic English approach of an all too little known spiritual master, Walter Hilton. Hilton taught that there is a double conversion: that of faith (which takes place readily and is a basic orientation towards God) and the conversion of feeling, the slow purification of the bewildering complexity of affective facets of the human being.[61] It may be taken as a move from a notional assent to a real assent to the truths of the faith.

Finally, an appeal to development invites the educated Christian to move freely up and down the Christian centuries and be enslaved to none. Can this be of any use in an age when history is little valued and rarely taught? But Catholics have an almost innate sense of the doctrine of the communion of saints. If we know to whom to turn when things seem hopeless, or lost, why can we not also be made aware of Athanasius, champion of Christological orthodoxy; Basil, theologian of the Holy Spirit; Benedict, the master of a balanced life-style; Augustine, a classical case of conversion? The list is seemingly endless: this cloud of witnesses can attest to the beauty and value of the tradition. Maybe we need to re-think our approach to the ministry

---

[61] Walter Hilton, *The Ladder of Perfection*, (New York: Paulist Press, 1991) pp. 199-200.

of teaching and preaching and call more frequently on the experience of the Church. Newman apparently thought so. After admitting that it "requires time and learning" to see the whole of Catholicism in a systematic and complete manner, he added:

> But in the life of a Saint, we have a microcosm, or whole work of God, a perfect work from beginning to end, yet one which may be bound between two boards, and mastered by the most unlearned. The exhibition of a person, his thoughts, his words, his acts, his trials, his fortunes, his beginnings, his growth, his end have a charm to every one, and when he is a Saint they have a Divine influence and persuasion, a power of exercising and eliciting the latent elements of Divine grace in individual readers, as no other reading can claim.[62]

---

[62] 'Lives of the Saints,' Paper at the Oratory Archives, Birmingham and reproduced in Vincent Ferrer Blehl *The Essential Newman* (New York: New American Library, 1963) pp. 224-5.

Chapter 10

NEWMAN AND VATICAN II

by Jean Rencki

"Certainly, if I am obliged to bring religion into after-dinner toasts (which indeed does not seem quite the thing) I shall drink – to the Pope, if you please – still, to Conscience first, and to the Pope afterwards." Excerpt from Newman's *Letter to the Duke of Norfolk,* quoted by Cardinal Heenan at Vatican II in 1965.

The Second Vatican Council (1962-1965) opened more than seventy years after Cardinal Newman's death. Vatican II is a council which is too easily taken for granted, and its texts are only beginning to be known in their fullness and richness by the larger Catholic public. This chapter will attempt to demonstrate how the Council vindicated a number of Newman's stances.

In what sense can it be said that Newman was the prophet of Vatican II? As Dr Ian Ker, the great biographer of Newman, put it: "Newman has often been called the Father of Vatican II." Although his direct influence was not "deep and determinative", he was "undoubtedly a great pioneering figure towering in the background, of whom the principal theologians at Vatican II were very well aware. There is certainly no doubt that Vatican II upheld and vindicated those controversial positions which he espoused in his own time and so often at his own personal cost."[1] As suggested by the late Abbot of Downside, Dom Butler, who took an active part in Council debates, I would say that he "possessed a prophetic charism". Newman was a prophet in the sense that he was not only "able to diagnose the

---

[1] Cf. Ian T. Ker, *Newman and the Fullness of Christianity,* T & T. Clark, Edinburgh, 1993, 127 ff. Cf. also Ian Ker's definitive biography, *John Henry Newman: A Biography,* OUP, Oxford, 1988.

evils of his own day, but also to see beyond them,"[2] and mysteriously perceived God's plan as well as the needs and aspirations of the Church and the world.

To put Newman in the wider historical context of ecumenical councils, Jean Guitton, the contemporary French philosopher and great expert on the fellow of Oriel used to say that "councils are inspired by one [particular line of] thought: Nicaea [325] by Athanasius; Trent [1545-63] by Aquinas". One day, the philosopher added, it "will become evident that Vatican II was inspired by Newman – and Pope Paul VI had this clearly in mind."[3]

In this chapter, I have selected four fields in which Newman's writings anticipated some of the major themes of Vatican II.

The first field regards Christian doctrine, based on Scripture and Tradition, as a living and a developing Truth (I). The second field examines how this living Truth develops in the Church, the Body of Christ, the "Holy Spirit's especial dwelling place", the living community of all the faithful (II). The third field deals with the dignity of the human person – how, in the Church, the person experiences, in their conscience, the liberating link between freedom and authority, freedom and revealed Truth (III). And finally, the fourth field briefly explores how, firmly rooted in that Truth, our mission as baptised Christians includes dialogue with unbelievers and persons belonging to other religions (IV).

Before embarking on these four points, I must remind the reader that I always assume the unity of Newman's personal life-long spiritual development. Put it this way: Newman was a great apostle of the living Truth – the Truth he tirelessly pursued and found in the person of Christ, and his Body, the Church. Whether it be his Anglican period or the period following his reception into the full communion of the Catholic fold on October 9 1845, when he became convinced that "the modern Roman Communion was [actually] the heir and image of the Primitive Church"[4], his whole life sheds an interesting light on the development of his theological opinions.

---

[2] B.C. Butler, 'Newman and the Second Vatican Council', in Coulson and Allchin (eds), *The rediscovery of Newman: An Oxford Symposium*, London, Sheed and Ward, 1967, 245.

[3] O. Chadwick, *John-Henry Newman*, (préface de J. Guitton), Cerf, Paris, 1989, xv.

[4] *The Letters and Diaries of John Henry Newman*, C.S. Dessain ed., Oxford, 1973-77, XXIII, 288 (Hereafter referred to as LD).

Part I

Let us now extend our horizons to the development of that living truth he embraced in the history of the Church as a whole. This historical perspective of Newman is one of his greatest contributions to theology and to the understanding of how Christian dogma evolves, lives and develops. Thus one can say that Tradition is always to be understood as living, not as fossilised or stilted tradition in unchanging forms. But the question soon arises: to what extent is this developing tradition faithful to the original deposit of faith first transmitted by the Apostles, who witnessed the Resurrection of our Lord? And beyond the question, a fear – the fear that the further away we are from the spring, the muddier the stream, the fear that something foreign to the original data might be added, and might pervert its substance. A short passage from Newman's *Essay on the Development of Christian Doctrine* will make things clear as to what exactly he means by his theory of development:

> It is indeed sometimes said that the stream is clearest near the spring. Whatever use may fairly be made of this image, it does not apply to the history of ... belief, which on the contrary is more equable, and purer, and stronger, when its bed has become deep, and broad, and full. It necessarily rises out of an existing state of things, and for a time savours of the soil. Its vital element needs disengaging from what is foreign and temporary, and is employed in efforts after freedom which become more vigorous and hopeful as its years increase. Its beginnings are no measure of its capabilities, nor of its scope ... It [an 'idea' like that of Christianity] changes with them [changing historical circumstances] in order to remain the same. In a higher world it is otherwise, but here below to live is to change, and to be perfect is to have changed often.[5]

Here below, not being in eternity, the pilgrim Church – since the day of the Pentecost, when the Apostles received the Holy Spirit so that they might enter into the fullness of Truth, the fullness of Revelation, and until the day of the final recapitulation of all things in Christ at the end of time – is subject to history. Its changing circumstances and life provide the setting for legitimate developments of the deposit of faith – thus rendering explicit what was merely implicit in the minds of the Apostles. Thus, development conserves permanence, all newness having actually come in the Paschal Mystery of Christ's Passion and Resurrection, which fulfils the Old Covenant, which fulfils Scripture.

---

[5] J.H. Newman, *Essay on the Development of Christian Doctrine*, p. 40 (hereafter referred to as Dev.).

The Biblical idea of newness is akin to that of Newman's development: "The whole Bible is written on the principle of development. As the Revelation proceeds, it is ever new, yet ever old."[6] Old Testament typology – especially in the Prophets – abundantly exemplifies this. And as our Lord tells us in the New, he came "not to destroy, but to fulfil the Law and the Prophets." In Biblical terms, "new" does not mean "other", or "additional", but "fulfilled", "perfected". Thus John's "new commandment", is the old perfected and fulfilled by the act of Christ's giving up his life for the redemption of all mankind, thus completing, fulfilling, the rite of sacrifice "first enjoined by Moses." At Pentecost and till the end of time, the Holy Spirit is given to the Church so that she might be guided to the "whole Truth" (Jn 16:13), so that the Christ-event, to which nothing will be added, might unfold and develop in the minds and life of Christians of every age and culture.

These developments since Pentecost and the early Church need to be faithful and authentic. That is the reason why Newman proposes a series of seven "tests" or "notes" of faithful and genuine developments – as contrasted with corruptions. Thus a doctrine develops faithfully to the original:

> There is no corruption if it retains one and the same type (1), the same principles (2), the same organisation [or logical sequence] (4), if its beginnings anticipate its subsequent phases (5), and its later phenomena protect and subserve its earlier (6), if it has a power of assimilation and revival (3), and a vigorous action from first to last (7).[7]

Here, I will only illustrate the first note. As far as the preservation of the type is concerned, the clearest explanation is offered by the analogy of physical growth. A baby growing into a child, and then into an adult person, remains the same person from first to last, despite all the changes he undergoes. And the fully grown oak belongs to the same species as the acorn. Or, as Newman explained, "young birds do not grow into fishes."[8]

Newman, also being a great contemplative, invites us to contemplate Mary, Mother of God, Mother of the Church and Seat of Wisdom. He extols Mary, the *Sedes Sapientiae*, as the "pattern of Faith, both in the reception and in the study of Divine Truth."[9] In a famous University

---

[6] Dev., p. 65.
[7] Dev., p. 171.
[8] Dev., p. 172.
[9] J.H. Newman, *Oxford University Sermons*, XV, 313.

Sermon on the theory of development, he comments on Saint Luke's short sentence describing Mary after the birth of her Son ("She kept all these things, and pondered them in her heart" Lk 2:19): obediently she was letting herself be "impressed" by the "idea" of the mystery she was freely co-operating in the Incarnation and lovingly, with her biblical intelligence and memory, she was fruitfully expanding and developing it. Thus Newman argues,

> [Mary] symbolises to us, not only the faith of the unlearned, but of the doctors of the Church also, who have to investigate, and weigh, and define, as well as to profess the Gospel; to draw the line between truth and heresy; to anticipate or remedy the various aberrations of wrong reason; to combat pride and recklessness with their own arms; and thus to triumph over the sophist and the innovator.[10]

Therefore the original idea is fruitfully maintained throughout the changes of history.

The same dynamic climate is evident in *Dei Verbum*. The Vatican II constitution on Revelation is remarkable for its typically Newmanian historical perspective: the whole history of our salvation, fulfilled at the advent of Christ, constitutes the revelation of God to mankind. The Gospel uttered by our Lord, the "Word made flesh" is the unique "source" of the Revelation, of the Truth that saves us. The inseparability of Scripture and Tradition had always been held by Newman, but somewhat neglected by Catholics who after the Council of Trent (1545-63), (not during the Council itself though), insisted on there being "two sources" so as to oppose the Protestant *Sola Scriptura*. From the ecumenical point of view, this is obviously crucial. In *Dei Verbum*, the council fathers provide a thorough explanation of the dynamic link between Scripture and Tradition:

> There exists a close connection and communication between sacred tradition and Sacred Scripture. For both of them, flowing from the same divine wellspring, in a certain way merge into a unity and tend towards the same end. For Sacred Scripture is the word of God inasmuch as it is consigned to writing under the inspiration of the divine Spirit, while sacred tradition transmits the word of God entrusted by Christ the Lord and the Holy Spirit to the Apostles, and hands it on to their successors in its full purity, so that led by the light of the Spirit of truth, they may in proclaiming it preserve this word of God faithfully, explain it, and make it more widely known.[11]

---

[10] Ibid.
[11] Vatican II, *Dei Verbum*, § 9.

A paragraph earlier in the text, where Tradition is actually described in its life, its growth, Abbot Butler clearly perceives a Newmanian influence, with the same reference to Luke 2:19:

> The Tradition which comes from the Apostles *develops* under the Holy Ghost in the Church (the Latin *proficit* is here understood to mean "internal progress" and *not* "addition to the contents of the Deposit of Faith"): the understanding of the things and words handed down grows, through the contemplation and study of believers, who compare these things in their heart (cf. "ponders", the verb used in *Lk* 2,19.51), and through their interior understanding of the spiritual realities which they experience. The Church, we may say, as the ages pass, tends continually towards the fullness of divine truth, till the words of God are consummated in her.[12]

Part II

This fullness, this fruitful life of Christian Doctrine has a home: the Church. In this second point, I shall examine Newman's conception of the Church, as described in the letters and other writings of the 1870s, in which he commented on the developments at Vatican I, and prophesied Vatican II's constitution on the Church, *Lumen Gentium*.

Familiar as Newman was with the history of ecumenical councils, with the development, the growth, and the life of Christian doctrine, especially in the early Church, he reflected on the recent Council of the Vatican. He observed that, as on other occasions in the past, the recently defined doctrine of papal infallibility would have to be interpreted, "explained and completed". The Council had broken up as a result of the invasion of Rome by Garibaldi's troops in 1870, and the fathers had not had time to complete their agenda. As Leo, at the Council of Chalcedon (in 451), had "trimmed the balance" of the doctrine defined at the Council of Ephesus (where, in 431, the Virgin Mary had been given the title of *Theotokos* or "Mother of God") by completing it (thus ensuring that not only the divine nature of Christ but also his fully human nature was affirmed and defended), so would another pope convene "another council", as Newman put it, to "occupy itself in other points" which would have "the effect" of "qualifying and guarding the dogma of papal infallibility."[13]

A new balance was indeed needed to prevent what he feared would be an "alteration of the elementary constitution of the Church",

---

[12] Vatican II, *Dei Verbum*, § 8.
[13] Cf. LD XXIV, p. 330.

because it would encourage the pope to act alone without the bishops. For Newman, this constituted the "gravest innovation possible" – i.e. an unfaithful development. The creeping infallibility he had predicted actually occurred between the two councils. Cardinal Manning and the Ultramontanes, for instance, exaggeratedly extended the defined infallibility of the pope to include his teachings in general, which, as far as we can judge, the Vatican I definition itself does not allow:

> Faithfully adhering to the tradition received from the beginning of the Christian faith, ... with the approval of the sacred council, we teach and define as a divinely revealed dogma that, when the Roman pontiff speaks *ex cathedra*, that is, when, in the exercise of his office as shepherd and teacher of all Christians, in virtue of his supreme apostolic authority, he defines a doctrine concerning faith or morals to be held by the whole Church, he possesses, by the assistance promised to him in Blessed Peter, that infallibility which the divine Redeemer willed his Church to enjoy in defining doctrines concerning faith or morals.[14]

Eventually, in 1959, Blessed Pope John XXIII convened Vatican II which interpreted, in a fuller, broader sense, the doctrine arrived at under his predecessor Pius IX. Thus, the primacy of the pope and the infallibility he personally enjoyed were put into the wider context of the college of bishops and indeed within the framework of the whole Church, that is to say, within the whole body of the faithful of Christ. If we consider the first two chapters of *Lumen Gentium* – the Council's constitution on the Church – we realise that Newman's "prophecy" was "fulfilled" in a "magnificently comprehensive"[15] way. Never before had the Church presented itself to the world in such a fullness. Like Newman's writings, it resorted chiefly to Scriptural images and to the Fathers of the primitive Church. The Church was no longer merely presented first and foremost as a hierarchy (this only comes in Chapter III), but above all as a Mystery, as a "Sacrament", as Christ's mystical Body and Bride (in Chapter I), and as the "People of God" (Chapter II).

Referring to the whole community of the baptised, not just the laity *versus* the clergy, Newman boldly stated in an article published in 1859, entitled 'On Consulting the Faithful in Matters of Doctrine': "The body of the faithful is one of the witnesses to the fact of the tradition of revealed doctrine ... Their consensus through Christendom

---

[14] Vatican I, Constitution *Pastor Aeternus*, Chap. IV.
[15] Cf. Ian T. Ker, *Newman and the Fullness of Christianity*, T & T. Clark, Edinburgh, 1993, p. 128.

is the voice of the infallible Church."[16] In a letter of 1875, he referred to "the passive infallibility" of the whole body "(the *universitas*) of the faithful", as opposed to the "active infallibility" of the "Pope and the Bishops."[17]

Similarly, Vatican II, in *Lumen Gentium* (Chapter II) declares:

> The universal body of the faithful (the *universitas fidelium*) who have an anointing that comes from the Holy One cannot be mistaken in belief. It displays this particular quality through a supernatural sense of the faith (*sensus fidei*) in the whole people when, 'from the bishops to the last of the faithful laity', it expresses a universal consent in matters of faith and morals. Through this *sensus fidei* which is aroused through the Spirit of truth, the People of God, under the guidance of the sacred *magisterium* to which it is faithfully obedient, receives not the word of men but truly the word of God.[18]

Thus, a universal Catholic consensus of the faithful is a powerful indication of the orthodox faith of the Church.

Part III

Newman's balanced, Scripture-based, and personal treatment of the Church is reflected in a related matter: the subtle and complex relationship between freedom and truth (as entrusted to the guardianship and infallible authority of the Pope and the bishops). Scripture never separates the two: "the Truth will make you free", says the Lord (Jn 8:32). And, this is best experienced in the intimate "sanctuary" of our "conscience". Newman has often been called the "doctor of conscience", being a great advocate of the rights of conscience. How are we to understand this? And how does Vatican II's approach to the dignity of the human person and of religious freedom vindicate Newman's positions?

Newman's religious autobiography, his *Apologia pro Vita Sua* published in 1865, and his *Letter to the Duke of Norfolk*, ten years later, provide precious indications on that crucial and contemporary theme, which figures prominently in a number of Vatican II texts.

In the *Apologia*, freedom of thought is always inseparable from obedience to revealed Truth. Thus one can understand his staunch rejection of what he calls Liberalism:

[16] J.H. Newman, *On Consulting the Faithful in Matters of Doctrine*, Chapman, London 1961, p. 63 (referred to as Cons.).
[17] LD XXVII, p. 338.
[18] Cf. Vatican II, *Lumen Gentium*, § p. 12.

By Liberalism I mean false liberty of thought, or the exercise of thought upon matters, in which, from the constitution of the human mind, thought cannot be brought to any successful issue, and therefore is out of place. Among such matters are first principles ... of these the most sacred and momentous are especially to be reckoned the truths of Revelation. Liberalism then is the mistake of subjecting to human judgement those revealed doctrines which are in their nature beyond and independent of it.[19]

In the brilliant Chapter V of the *Apologia*, Newman, however, rejected the charge that obedience to the infallible Church constitutes a "degrading bondage" to an arbitrary power which can change the Creed at will. He first reminds us that infallibility is "a provision, adapted by the mercy of the Creator to preserve religion in the world ... and rescue freedom from its own suicidal excesses." He then argues – not only against some of his Anglican critics, but also against the extremist Ultramontane party – that:

Infallibility cannot act outside of a definite circle of thought, and it must in all its decisions, or definitions, as they are called, profess to be keeping within it. The great truths of the moral law, of natural religion, and of Apostolical faith, are both its boundary and its foundation. It must not go beyond them, and it must ever appeal to them. Both its subject-matter, and its articles in that subject-matter, are fixed. And it must ever profess to be guided by Scripture and by tradition. It must refer to the particular Apostolic truth which it is enforcing, or (what is called) defining. Nothing, then, can be presented to me, in time to come, as part of the faith, but what I ought already to have received, and hitherto have been kept from receiving, (if so,) merely because it has not been brought home to me. Nothing can be imposed upon me different in kind from what I hold already, – much less contrary to it. The new truth which is promulgated, if it is to be called new, must be at least homogeneous, cognate, implicit, viewed relatively to the old truth.[20]

To substantiate his affirmation, he refers to the dogmatic definition of the Immaculate Conception (defined by Pius IX in 1854). Contrary to received opinion in Protestant circles, Newman maintains that far from being "a tyrannical infliction on the Catholic world, the definition was received everywhere ... with the greatest enthusiasm" after six centuries of debate. To add further weight to his argumentation, he considers the history of the relations between freedom of debate and authority in the Church and concludes that its "infallible authority"

---

[19] J.H. Newman, *Apologia Pro Vita Sua*, p. 193.
[20] Ibid., p. 254.

has never destroyed the "independence of the mind", and that paradoxically, it has rather enhanced it. As he puts it, the "energy of the intellect does from opposition grow."[21]

In 1875, in his long open *Letter to the Duke of Norfolk*, Newman actually replies to Gladstone who, in a pamphlet had accused the Catholics of being "moral and mental slaves" of a foreign power, whose arbitrary infallibility, he said, prevented British Catholics from being loyal subjects. This outrageous accusation he easily dismisses, and points out to the former Prime Minister that, as already noted, the *ex cathedra* infallibility is narrowly defined and does not for instance extend to politics.

But more importantly, he serenely and majestically expounds the nature of conscience, rooting its dignity in our being created in the image of God. Therefore, popes can only defend the rights of conscience, because they have no right whatsoever over it – simply because the authority of conscience is more original than that of the successor of St Peter:

> Did the Pope actually speak against Conscience in the true sense of the word, he would commit a suicidal act. He would be cutting the ground from under his feet. His very mission is to proclaim the moral law, and to protect and strengthen that 'Light which enlighteneth every man that cometh into the world'.[22]

"Conscience has rights because it has duties", Newman goes on to explain in a passage of the same letter – which was famously quoted by the late Pope John Paul II. The very foundation of our freedom of conscience – properly understood – is our being created in the image of our Creator, and therefore called to respond to his loving initiative by obeying his commandment to love Him as well as to love our neighbour. Such is the basis of the "prerogatives" of conscience, which no other authority can found!

Negatively, these prerogatives do not consist in being one's "own master in all things", do not consist in pure "licence", or in the "right of self-will". A large number of Newman's contemporaries are wrong if they think "the very right and freedom of conscience" is "to dispense with conscience, to ignore a Lawgiver and Judge, to be independent of unseen obligations." That is why the "so-called liberty of conscience" of the liberals of his days – and ours – is here clearly rejected.

---

[21] Ibid., p. 252.

[22] J.H. Newman, *Certain Difficulties felt by Anglicans in Catholic Teaching*, vol. 2, London, Longmans, 1910, (hereafter referred to as Diff. II), p. 252.

Positively, "conscience is a stern monitor" constantly reminding us of our "duty", in "thought and deed" to the "Creator". As Creator he "implanted" his "Divine Law"- the "standard of right and wrong, a sovereign ... absolute authority in the presence of men and angels" – in "the intelligence of all his rational creatures." "The natural law" is an "impression" of that "Divine Light" in them, a "participation" of the "eternal law" in them. And "this Law, as apprehended in the minds of individual men, is called conscience," which has "the prerogative of commanding obedience." This "Divine Law is the rule of our conduct by means of our conscience." Hence, it is "never lawful to go against our conscience."

Far from being "a creation of man", conscience is the "voice of God", the "internal witness ... of the law of God", a "dictate", conveying "the notion of responsibility" and of "duty". Conscience is a "messenger from Him who ... teaches and rules us by his representatives." In that sense, one clearly understands that the authority of conscience – and for that matter, its very dignity – lies not in its being independent and autonomous, but in its being "the aboriginal Vicar of Christ".[23]

This famous quote, which – thanks to Cardinal Honoré – found its way into the recent *Catechism of the Catholic Church* (§1778), simply means that conscience is the first representative of Christ, and comes before the pope, who is traditionally referred to as the "Vicar of Christ". This is particularly important for all members of the human race for whom Christ has died and who know neither Him, nor His Church, nor obviously the Pope. And yet, by the grace of the Paschal Mystery, they mysteriously hear the call, in the sanctuary of their consciences, to lead moral lives.

In his moral teaching, the late Pope John Paul II constantly emphasised the dignity of the human person as rooted in Creation, and whose freedom cannot be understood independently from Truth. It is therefore quite natural that he should often have resorted to Newman, the "Doctor of Conscience", when discussing the dignity of conscience, which he said, was "the heart of the person where the relationship between freedom and truth, freedom and God's law is most deeply lived out."[24]

In § 34 of his encyclical on the Splendour of Truth, John Paul II used the Newman quote I have already alluded to, "Conscience has

---

[23] Diff. II, pp. 246-252.
[24] John Paul II, enc. *Veritatis Splendor*, § 54.

rights because it has duties", to comment on the close connection between freedom and truth in Vatican II texts. He quotes *Gaudium et Spes* (the Vatican II constitution on the Church in the World) and *Dignitatis Humanae* (the Vatican II declaration on Religious Freedom), in support of that point. John Paul II first quoted *Gaudium et Spes* on "genuine" freedom:

> Genuine freedom is an outstanding manifestation of the divine image in man. For God willed to leave man 'in the power of his own counsel' (cf. *Sir* 15, 14), so that he would seek his Creator of his own accord and would freely arrive at full and blessed perfection by cleaving to God. [25]

Recognising this "right to be respected in one's own journey in search of the truth", the late pope then articulates it with a reference to the "prior moral obligation ... to seek the truth and to adhere to it once it is known", referred to in *Dignitatis Humanae*:

> It is in accordance with their dignity as persons ... that all men should be at once impelled by nature and also bound by a moral obligation to seek the truth, especially religious truth. They are also bound to adhere to the truth, once it is known, and to order their whole lives in accord with the demands of truth. However, men cannot discharge these obligations in a manner in keeping with their own nature unless they enjoy immunity from external coercion as well as psychological freedom. Therefore, the right to religious freedom has its foundation not in the subjective disposition of the person, but in his very nature. [26]

He then confirmed this by introducing the quotation from Newman, "Conscience has rights because it has duties". He went on to describe the Cardinal as "that outstanding defender of the rights of conscience", and thus confirms "the dependence of freedom on truth" – as opposed to a freedom that tends to "create values". [27] Further discussing Newman, the pope also mentioned another – most central – passage of *Gaudium et Spes* on conscience:

> In the depths of his conscience, man detects a law which he does not impose upon himself, but which holds him to obedience. Always summoning him to love good and avoid evil, the voice of conscience when necessary speaks to his heart: do this, shun that. For man has in his heart a law written by God; to obey it is the very dignity of man; according to it he will be judged. Conscience is the most secret core and sanctuary of a man. There he is alone with

---

[25] Vatican II, *Gaudium et Spes*, § 17.

[26] Vatican II, *Dignitatis Humanae*, § 2.

[27] John Paul II, enc. *Veritatis Splendor*, § 34–35.

God, Whose voice echoes in his depths. In a wonderful manner conscience reveals that law which is fulfilled by love of God and neighbour.[28]

It could thus be maintained that, particularly on the subject of conscience, Newman not only anticipated Vatican II but also served as a guide to its proper reception by the People of God in the past forty years. Both John Paul II, who declared Newman 'Venerable' in 1991, and Benedict XVI, who were both active participants at Vatican II, have always had a clear cognisance of that.

On the occasion of the centenary of Newman's cardinalate in 1979, John Paul II marvelled at the visionary teaching of the Cardinal on conscience:

[Newman] who was convinced of being faithful throughout his life, with all his heart devoted to the light of truth, today becomes an ever brighter beacon for all who are seeking an informed orientation and sure guidance amid the uncertainties of the modern world — a world which he himself prophetically foresaw ... By insisting 'that the Church must be prepared for converts, as well as converts prepared for the Church', he already in a certain measure anticipated in his broad theological vision one of the main aims and orientations of the Second Vatican Council and the Church in the post-conciliar period.[29]

The American Jesuit Avery Dulles underlined Newman's guidance on the proper understanding of the nature of conscience in the post-conciliar period when he maintained that

the teaching of both Newman and Vatican II was based on a longstanding Catholic tradition. Recognizing the accord, Pope John Paul II in his encyclical *Veritatis Splendor* quoted Newman's *Letter to the Duke of Norfolk* to confirm the teaching of Vatican II.[30]

The current Pope — who was personally immersed in Newman's "theological Personalism" during his training — never fails to extol the merits of the fellow of Oriel whom he ranks as one of the "great teachers of the Church" whose teaching on conscience brought "a decisive contribution to the renewal of theology." For Benedict XVI, Newman's life and works taken as a whole actually constitute "a great commentary on the question of conscience."[31]

[28] Vatican II, *Gaudium et Spes*, § 16.
[29] John Paul II, *Letter on the occasion of the centenary of Newman's cardinalate*, 12 May 1979.
[30] A. Dulles, *John Henry Newman*, Continuum, New York, 2002, 162.
[31] *Benedict XVI and Cardinal Newman*, P. Jennings ed., Oxford, Family Publications, 2005, pp. 34-35.

Part IV

The fourth field I shall now briefly be considering deals with two closely related areas of dialogue to which Newman and the fathers of Vatican II were keenly committed: with non-Christians, and with atheistic rationalists.

As to pagan non-Christians or members of other religions, Newman was steeped in the writings of the fourth century Alexandrian school which had produced such luminaries as Origen and Athanasius, the great defender of the divinity of Christ. That theological school, known for its "allegorical" reading of Scripture, was keen to see in non-Christians pagan cultures, signs, images, elements that implicitly lead pagans to discover the Truth of Christ, for the very reason that they were a "dispensation" of the Creator himself. He describes that method of evangelisation, as practised for the first time by St Paul at Athens (see Acts 17), in his first book, published in 1834, *The Arians of the Fourth Century*:

> Instead of uttering any invective against their Polytheism, he began a discourse upon the Unity of the Divine Nature; and then proceeded to claim the altar, consecrated in the neighbourhood to the unknown God, as the property of Him whom he preached to them, and to enforce his doctrine of the Divine Immateriality, not by miracles, but by argument, and that founded on the words of a heathen poet.[32]

This example from Scripture, which the Alexandrians set before them in their intercourse with the heathen, served as a reference for subsequent intercourse with and mission to the heathen. This is exemplified by

> [the conversion of Gregory of Neocaesarea by Origen in AD 231 who], while professedly teaching him Pagan philosophy, ... insensibly enlightened him in the knowledge of the Christian faith. Then leading him to Scripture, he explained to him its difficulties as they arose; till Gregory, overcome by the force of truth, announced to his instructor his intention of exchanging the pursuits of this world for the service of God.[33]

This "Gospel preparation" or *preparatio evangelica*, evinced by many non-Christian cultural traits, is mentioned in a number of Vatican II texts. And quite naturally so, because they quote abundantly from early Church Fathers who were involved in that missionary approach.

---

[32] J. H. Newman, *The Arians of the Fourth Century*, p. 67.
[33] Ibid., p. 67.

Going beyond purely individual possibilities of salvation, Vatican II's positive inter-religious openness, especially its declaration on non-Christian religions, *Nostra Aetate*, is indeed remarkable for its recollection of Patristic teaching on non-Christian religions which contain "seeds of the Word" or *semina verbi*[34] – positive values which were natural endowments of human nature which enabled people to reach a valid natural knowledge of God that by itself was incapable of leading to salvation. These actually constituted a preparation, a *preparatio evangelica*.[35]

But Vatican II also considered seriously the intrinsic value of non-Christian religious traditions which contain "a ray of that Truth which enlightens everyone"[36] and elements of "truth and grace",[37] supernatural gifts of God conducive, in themselves, to salvation.

The second area of dialogue engages Christians with rationalist atheists who happen to hold, according to Newman and many a modern philosopher, a very narrow-minded view of reason – a reason limited to the production of logical visible objective grounds. Newman held that reason was much larger and wider than that. In his *Oxford University Sermons* in the 1830s, he engaged the difficult theme of the relation of reason to faith. In Sermon XIII, he was keen to show that one could reasonably believe without producing explicit grounds for doing so. Newman summed it up by saying that "all men have a reason, but not all men can give a reason. We may denote, then, these two exercises of mind as reasoning and arguing, or as conscious and unconscious reasoning, or as Implicit Reason and Explicit Reason."[38]

By referring to "implicit reason", Newman also had in mind all these "antecedent probabilities" or "presuppositions" which help us to attain certitude or real "assent" in religious belief. For instance, the powerful testimony of loving Christian parents. Newman also pointed out that similar antecedents also influenced apparently purely rationalistic and objective unbelief – and equally affected social, moral, and political convictions.

---

[34] Vatican II, *Ad Gentes*, § 11.

[35] Vatican II, *Lumen Gentium*, § 16.

[36] Vatican II, *Nostra Aetate*, § 2.

[37] Vatican II, *Ad Gentes*, § 9.

[38] J. H. Newman, *Oxford University Sermons*, XIII, p. 259.

By way of conclusion, it seems to me that Cardinal Newman's motto –
Cor ad cor loquitur (litterally "The heart speaks to the heart") – provides
a concise summary of the Newmanian themes I have broached in this
chapter in their relation to the Second Vatican Council. Such a motto
is highly appropriate for a great theologian and a very saintly person
who devoted his whole life to Truth – Truth in the Person of Christ,
and Truth in the close inter-personal communion of His Body, the
Church.

Translating it, Abbot Butler meditates:

> "*Cor ad cor loquitur* – not only, nor primarily, the heart of the
> religious man to the heart of God, but the heart of God to the heart
> of his faithful servant. This was Newman's motto; if ecumenical
> councils were given mottoes, this is the motto I would propose for
> the Second Vatican Council. *Cor ad cor loquitur*: the heart of God to
> the heart of his Church; the heart of the Church to the heart of her
> God, and therefore to the hearts of all men of good will."[39]

It is indeed only in this close relationship to God that the "Truth"
which is also our "Life" (cf. Jn 14:6) can be both received and given
to the world. In that sense – in keeping with his seventh "note" of
an authentic development, that of "chronic vigour" or simply life –
Newman would have delighted in the two chief traits of a truly pastoral
council. With Vatican II, the Church experienced both a *ressourcement*
(1) and an *aggiornamento* (2). To enable our contemporaries to have
"life to the fullest" (Jn 10:10), it was – and is still – necessary: (1) to
deepen and renew our relationship to the roots of our faith, Scripture
and Tradition, which point to the unique source of God's revelation
"the Word made flesh" (Jn 1:14); and (2) to open up the windows of
the Church to our very diverse world so as to be able to share the
treasure of the Gospel with all men of good will.

Thus, despite unfortunate misinterpretations in the 1970s, Vatican
II clearly paved the way for the missionary renewal launched by Pope
Paul VI's Apostolic Exhortation *Evangelii Nuntiandi* (1975). This was
considerably amplified by John Paul II's call for a "new evangelisation",
the first fruits of which Newman would no doubt have applauded as
a new "second spring",[40] this time not just for England but for the
whole world.

---

[39] B.C. Butler, *op. cit.*, 246.
[40] J. H. Newman, *Sermons Preached on Various Occasions*, 10, 169.

PART III

CONSCIENCE

Chapter 11

NEWMAN AND CONSCIENCE

by Luc Terlinden

The freedom to act in accordance with one's conscience has become a fundamental claim in our western societies. Subjects have a right to follow their conscience rather than to act under external constraint, as the Second Vatican Council stated.[1] But what does 'follow one's conscience' mean? What is conscience? Does 'following one's conscience' consist in letting oneself be guided by one's feelings? Is conscience one and the same thing as a person's desires and will? Or else, is conscience comparable to some sort of calculation, as is the case with utilitarians, who consider that the criterion for moral choices should be what is most useful to the individual and to society, or what is most likely to bring happiness to the greatest number? The current ethical debate about embryonic stem cell research provides us with a good example of the latter conception of conscience. For many of its proponents, the mere presumed utility for society of this type of research would suffice to make it ethically good.

Contemporary conceptions of conscience are indeed very diverse. Yet they very often have something in common: they get rid of any idea of conscience as an echo of the voice of God in man or as a manifestation of divine law. This is not new – over a century and a half ago, Newman already noted in his *Letter to the Duke of Norfolk*:

> When men advocate the rights of conscience, they in no sense mean the rights of the Creator, nor the duty to Him, in thought and deed, of the creature; but the right of thinking, speaking, writing, and acting, according to their judgment or their humour, without any thought of God at all. They do not even pretend to go by any moral rule, but they demand, what they think is an Englishman's prerogative, for each to be his own master in all things, and to

---

[1] See Vatican Council II, *Declaration on Religious Freedom* (Dignitatis Humanae), § 3.

profess what he pleases, asking no one's leave.[2]

The properly religious dimension of conscience, which is so often neglected, is however central in Newman's view. It is even the most fundamental dimension. For, according to him, conscience is inseparable from the voice of God which manifests itself in the heart of man. This appears clearly in the analysis he gives of conscience as a twofold feeling, a moral sense and a sense of duty.[3]

1. The twofold nature of conscience

1.1 Conscience as a moral sense

Newman adopted the notion of moral sense which was prevalent in the eighteenth century, but not without integrating it into a broader understanding of conscience. According to him, the moral sense is the act of the mind which enables it to distinguish between good and evil, but also to perceive certain principles which underlie our reasoning in matters of morals or religion.[4]

Good and evil are perceived in an immediate and spontaneous way by the moral sense. One action will be approved by it, whereas another action will be condemned. Through various experiences, the moral sense thus provides the first elements of morality, which reason will then be able to generalise and develop into a moral code.[5] The perception of good and evil is then not simply a matter of taste or personal feelings. The moral sense is always placed under the control of reason. Moreover, contrary to a passing feeling, the perception of good and evil is rooted in the nature of man:

> The cultivated moral perception ... is sometimes improperly termed, 'feeling', – improperly, because feeling comes and goes, and, having no root in our nature, speaks with no divine authority; but the moral perception, though varying in the mass of men, is fixed in each individual, and is an original element within us.[6]

The perception of good and evil imposes itself on the subject as an

---

[2] J. H. Newman, 'A Letter Addressed to the Duke of Norfolk on Occasion of Mr Gladstone's Recent Expostulation', in *Certain difficulties felt by Anglicans in Catholic Teaching*. Vol. II, London, Longmans Green and Co., 1907, p. 250.

[3] "The feeling of conscience ... is twofold: – it is a moral sense, and a sense of duty; a judgment of the reason and a magisterial dictate" (J. H. Newman, *An Essay in Aid of a Grammar of Assent*, London, Longmans, Green, and Co., 1870, p. 105).

[4] See J. H. Newman, *Fifteen Sermons Preached before the University of Oxford*, London, Longmans, Green, and Co., 1872, IV, p. 55, n. 3.

[5] See J. H. Newman, *A Grammar of Assent*, p. 106.

[6] J. H. Newman, *University Sermons*, IV, § 6, pp. 59-60.

inner moral law. This law of nature is the law of conscience. It exerts a supreme authority on a person, as the authority it claims does not come from man, but from Him who implanted it in him, and whom it represents.[7]

It is, however, all too obvious that the perception of good and evil can vary considerably from one individual to the next, and that there is never unanimous agreement as to the content of the law of good and evil. How is it possible then to affirm that the law of conscience exerts supreme and divine authority, if there are so many divergences in its content? It should be noted that the moral sense has to be formed and refined in each person, and it is only insofar as one obeys this inner law of good and evil that one becomes able to grow in expertness in the science of morals.[8] Besides, this science of morals extends to all details of thought and conduct. It is therefore to ignorance that the apparent relativity of the moral law should be attributed. Even among the saints, there can be found, beyond real defects, habits and differences of taste or talent which can modify the commands of an inner light which, in itself, is divine and infallible.[9]

If it is true that, in fact, the moral sense can diverge considerably from one person to the next, it remains however inseparable from another aspect of conscience – the sense of duty which is common to all.

1.2 Conscience as a sense of duty

The Anglican bishop Joseph Butler (1692-1752) had shown that ordinary people could be led to acknowledge that they not only have a faculty of judgment between good and evil (a moral sense), but that this faculty is also endowed with its own authority, which enables it to act in them as a guide and judge. In other words, actions are not only submitted to the approval or disapproval of a moral sense, they also come under the authority of conscience and its injunctions – an authority derived from the Author of the nature, who placed it within man.

For Newman too, conscience cannot be reduced to a moral sense. For conscience does not limit itself to pointing to a way, it commands with authority; it does not content itself with judging the morality of

---

[7] See J. H. Newman, *University Sermons*, IV, § 17, p. 69; VIII, § 2, p. 137.

[8] "Still, unformed and incomplete as is this law by nature, it is quite certain that obedience to it is attended by a continually growing expertness in the science of Morals." (J. H. Newman, *University Sermons*, II, § 11, p. 20)

[9] See J. H. Newman, *University Sermons*, V, § 11, p. 82.

an action or providing first principles, it also entails a sanction.[10] The sense of duty therefore implies a relationship between the soul and a superior authority, between the self and somebody who commands it. The latter, according to Newman, can be no other than God. To show this, he does not use a theoretical demonstration; rather, he prefers to start from experience.

The experience on which Newman relies to show that conscience implies a relationship with God, is the experience of feelings of pleasure or grief, of hope or fear, of serenity or remorse, which manifest good or bad conscience. For in the inner peace that accompanies a good action or in the confusion that pervades the soul after a serious fault, the self confusedly realizes that it is not alone, but that there is something, or rather someone, towards whom it is responsible. In its conscience, it perceives the echo of a voice, the voice of a Person whom it loves and venerates, a Governor and a Judge.

Newman has shrewdly described this manifestation of the voice of God through the sense of duty in conscience in his novel *Callista*, and the dialogue between his heroine and Polemo:

'Well,' she said, 'I feel that God within my heart. I feel myself in His presence. He says to me, 'Do this: don't do that.' You may tell me that this dictate is a mere law of my nature, as is to joy or to grieve. I cannot understand this. No, it is the echo of a person speaking to me. Nothing shall persuade me that it does not ultimately proceed from a person external to me. It carries with it its proof of its divine origin. My nature feels towards it as towards a person. When I obey it, I feel a satisfaction; when I disobey, a soreness – just like that which I feel in pleasing or offending some revered friend. So you see, Polemo, I believe in what is more than a mere 'something.' I believe in what is more real to me than sun, moon, stars, and the fair earth, and the voice of friends. You will say, Who is He? Has He ever told you anything about Himself? Alas! no! – the more's the pity! But I will not give up what I have, because I have not more. An echo implies a voice; a voice a speaker. That speaker I love and I fear.'[11]

The specific emotions of conscience such as fear, remorse, inner peace or lightness of heart should not be mistaken for ordinary feelings, because they imply the inner presence of a Person towards whom the subject feels accountable. In the *Grammar of Assent*, Newman thus shows how these specific emotions contribute to imprint in the self

---

[10] See J. H. Newman, *University Sermons*, II, §§ 7-11, pp. 18-21.

[11] J. H. Newman, *Callista. A Tale of the Third Century*, London, Longmans, Green, and Co., 1890, pp. 314-315.

the image of a supreme Governor and a just Judge.[12] The image, in the language of Newman, is what represents in the mind concrete things and facts, that is to say the "real".[13] The experience of conscience therefore makes a real and concrete experience of God possible. Far from being the distant and abstract god of the philosophers, this is the living and creating God who manifests himself in the heart of man, the God who had already revealed himself to the young Newman when, at the age of fifteen, he experienced the conversion which left him "in the thought of two and two only absolute and luminously self-evident beings, myself and my Creator."[14]

The experience of conscience refers to a real experience of God and to the personal relationship which develops with him. That is why it is the foundation of natural religion in the mind. Besides, this relationship with God, which is established through conscience, is so important that it will condition the whole moral and religious development of the person. For the person who is faithful to the voice of his conscience and who finds in it the voice of God, the person who lets this relationship with God go deeper, will be all the more sensitive to the injunctions of his conscience and its commandments. The more the voice of conscience is listened to, the more this voice will make itself heard clearly. It will also become more possible to welcome what God reveals of himself. In fact, listening to the voice of God which echoes deep in conscience is a preparation for welcoming Revelation. It prepares the mind to receive what God says in Scripture and in Tradition.

However, it is possible for man to ignore the voice echoing in his conscience, to deform it, to stifle it or to disobey it. Yet this voice remains present. Man cannot destroy it because it does not come from him.[15] And if it is true that the moral sense, that is to say the perception of good and evil, can differ considerably from one individual to the next, the sense of duty is common to all. Everybody can experience a good or bad conscience. According to Newman, in some cases it is even possible not to perceive any longer the immoral character of an act, while still keeping the feeling of having disobeyed when

---

[12] See J. H. Newman, *A Grammar of Assent*, p. 110.

[13] In the *Grammar of Assent*, Newman makes a distinction between the "real", which concerns the thing in itself, *res* in Latin, and the "notional", which is an abstraction and a generalisation, a creation of the mind. See J. H. Newman, *A Grammar of Assent*, pp. 9–12.

[14] J. H. Newman, *Apologia pro Vita Sua*, London, Longmans, Green, and Co., 1873, p. 4.

[15] See J. H. Newman, *Sermons preached on Various Occasions*, London, Longmans, Green, and Co., 1874, pp. 60–74.

accomplishing it.[16]

Is it not, however, contradictory to affirm that it is possible to keep a sense of obligation, if the moral sense is not there any more? For how is it possible to keep the feeling that some acts are morally forbidden, if the moral sense does not perceive them as morally bad? Faithful to his principle of the reality of things, according to which things have to be taken as they are, Newman might answer this objection by saying that it has to be admitted, through experience, that the sanction of a bad conscience does not necessarily disappear when the moral sense of a person is warped to the point of considering as good an action which is contrary to its moral nature. If the moral sense can be mistaken, the sense of duty does not disappear for that reason, because the voice of God which echoes deep in our hearts remains. Let us take an example. A person influenced by society and her environment can have such a flawed judgment about abortion that she fails to perceive in it an intrinsically evil act. This does not exclude the possibility that this person might experience the feeling of a guilty conscience if she had an abortion.

1.3 The sense of duty confronted with subjectivism

Newman's observation on the permanence of the sense of duty in conscience, despite the errors of the moral sense, takes on, in my view, a particular importance in an age increasingly marked by individualism and subjectivism. For today, even more than in the nineteenth century, the perception of good and evil varies greatly from one individual to the next. With the priority given to individual freedom in western culture, the desires and will of the subject have assumed such importance that they are often the only realities that matter any longer. It is therefore becoming more and more difficult to reach agreement on an objective order of the moral good and moral values. To guide his choices between good and evil, the individual falls back to his moral conscience understood above all in its subjectivity, that is to say as a freedom for the subject to choose his values himself. This reference to conscience therefore involves the risk of turning conscience into a power creating moral values, thus opening the door to unbridled subjectivism, each individual following but their own desires, to the detriment of the calling from others, and the Other.

However, the reference to conscience can also become an

---

[16] "Though I lost my sense of their moral deformity [of acts of dishonesty], I should not therefore lose my sense that they were forbidden to me." (J. H. Newman, *A Grammar of Assent*, p. 106)

opportunity for renewed attention to the voice of God manifested in the depth of the heart. By relentlessly approving of good and condemning evil, this voice, when it is perceived and listened to, may be the only voice today capable of prompting this "prick of conscience" which will lead contemporary people to understand that not all choices are good for them and that not all roads lead to life. There are also roads leading to death. The voice of conscience is a call to life, which, we dare hope, it is not possible to ignore for ever.

2. Conscience or reason?

Is the call to the sense of duty in conscience, which is manifested through certain emotions of fear, remorse or inner peace, always sufficient to oppose subjectivism? Rather, does not the 'emotional' character of conscience (as Newman sees it), run the risk of allowing too much room for subjectivity? Should not the rational dimension of conscience be stressed instead, as is the case in the Thomist tradition, which closely associates conscience and practical reason?[17]

It may seem surprising that Newman often sought to distinguish conscience and reason rather than to draw them closer to one another. In some of his works, like his *University Sermons*, he only gives a subordinate role to reason in the search for moral or religious truths. Reason is indeed an instrument in the service of spiritual discernment which is led by conscience. However, its use remains exterior or secondary, accidental, useful in its place but not necessary.[18] Indeed, "moral and religious truths ... fall under the province of *Conscience* far more than of the intellect."[19]

How can this dualism between conscience and reason which Newman seems to establish be understood? Should it be opposed to the Thomist tradition which considers conscience as an activity of reason? To understand properly Newman's originality and what makes him different from other traditions, it is important to start by situating his writings in context. Newman is a man of his time, and he used his own way of thinking and his own concepts when he endeavoured to meet the challenges which were confronting him.

---

[17] For Thomas Aquinas, conscience is, strictly speaking, an act and, more particularly, an activity of reason. See *Summa Theologiae*, Ia IIae, Q. 19, a. 5.

[18] See J. H. Newman, *University Sermons*, IV, § 2, p. 55; § 4, p. 58; § 9, p. 62; § 14, p. 67.

[19] J. H. Newman, *Parochial and Plain Sermons*. Vol. I, London, Longmans, Green, and Co., 1875, p. 224. See F. Attard, 'John Henry Newman. Advocacy of Conscience – 1825-1832 (*seguito*)', *Salesianum* 62 (2000) pp. 440-446.

One of the first challenges he had to meet was rationalism, which was beginning to pervade all aspects of life, including religion. This rationalism had been made possible by the new conception of reason which accompanied modernity and was fundamentally different from the approach of, for example, Thomas Aquinas.

2.1 The procedural conception of reason

The contemporary Canadian philosopher Charles Taylor shed light on the shift, brought about by modernity, from a substantial to a procedural conception of reason. According to the substantial conception of reason, which was prevalent from Antiquity to the Middle Ages, rationality is linked to the perception of a moral order. To be rational, by definition, is to have a substantially correct vision of the order and to conform to it. Practical reason was therefore defined in a substantial way: practical wisdom consisted in perceiving an order at work in nature. In the words of the traditional saying, *agere sequitur esse*, the action of things should follow their being, and lead them to perfection. To act rationally is to possess a true vision of the order of things, or in the case of Aristotle's phronêsis, to possess an ability to discern moral matters well.[20]

From Descartes onwards, however, the order will no longer be discovered by reason; rather it is reason itself which will construct its own order, according to its own norms.[21] Rationality is therefore no longer defined in terms of the order of being, but in terms of a procedure, of the norms according to which the orders are constructed in science and in life. To be rational consists in following the right procedure, even if different ways of approaching these procedures have been at odds during the modern period (such as the deductive, inductive or empirical approaches.)

This new procedural conception of reason encouraged the rejection of an ethical system based on an order of the good. Indeed, when the starting point for a definition of rationality is no longer the vision of an order, but a procedure, the temptation becomes great to reject the idea that the foundation of the good is on an order of being independent from the will. For, as we have said, the modern exaltation of freedom and autonomy has given priority to the desires or will of the subject when it comes to decide on what course of action is

---

[20] See C. Taylor, *Sources of the Self. The Making of the Modern Identity*, Cambridge, Harvard University Press, 1989, pp. 85-90.
[21] See C. Taylor, *Sources of the Self*, pp. 143-158.

good. Each individual chooses what is good for them, irrespective of an objective order of the good. In order not to fall into anarchy and to make life in society possible, it is however necessary to reach a certain agreement on common values and objectives. Hence the importance of finding rational methods or procedures which enable people to bring out these values and objectives. In this case, since procedural reason is no longer linked to the vision of an order of the good, it sometimes becomes itself the creator of moral values and ideals. The latter result from an all-embracing compromise between different positions rather than the outcome of an objective search for the good.[22]

2.2 Usurpations of reason

The distinction which Newman, unlike the Thomist tradition, establishes between conscience and reason, is therefore better understood in the light of the modern shift from a substantial to a procedural conception of reason. Reason is no longer defined in relation to the vision of an order of being, but in relation to a procedure or method. In England, this new conception of reason had led to the development of an empirical rationalism which subsumed all areas of knowledge and life. In the nineteenth century in particular, an increasingly influential trend was to try to deal with questions pertaining to morals or religion in the same way as questions pertaining to natural sciences (physics, chemistry, biology, etc.). Faith would have to rely on a form of logical demonstration, built from evidence in favour of Revelation. It would only be possible to believe on the basis of evidence, and all that cannot be demonstrated by reason would have to be left aside.

For Newman, however, it was clear that this attitude was undermining the very foundation of religion. It was challenging the dogmatic principle, according to which revealed truth is one and definitive: the mind has to submit to it and accept it as it is.[23] In other words, one has to accept what God says of Himself in conscience or in the Bible and in Tradition, and to welcome Him as He is, and not as one would like Him to be. By trying to submit the truths of religion

---

[22] The current debates about embryo research, euthanasia, etc. manifest the success of these ethical systems, known as procedural ethics, which have superseded the ethical systems based on the good or virtue.

[23] See J. H. Newman, *An Essay on the Development of Christian Doctrine*, London, Longmans Green and Co., 1878, p. 357.

to the authority of procedural and empirical reason, the aim was in fact to impose limits a priori to Revelation. Reason came to usurp a domain which actually comes under the province of conscience. For it is the role of conscience, as a moral sense, to discern between good and evil and to perceive the first principles which underlie reasoning in moral and religious matters.

Newman could not accept that reason could become the foundation for moral values and religious truths. Confronted with a modern conception of reason and the abuses that this could entail, he did not attempt to strip reason of its own excellence, nor of its legitimate authority in its own sphere.[24] He rather limited the use of that form of reason, by placing it within the context of a holistic understanding of the human person, an understanding which revolves around the ethical–religious experience of conscience.

2.3 The role of reason

In the field of morals and religion, reason acts as an instrument in the service of the other faculties of the mind. Reason is not a faculty used to perceive but to infer.[25] The validity of the reasoning process will depend on premises which reason does not give itself, but which it receives from elsewhere. In religious matters, these premises are provided by the moral sense, reason being but an instrument in the service of spiritual discernment, which is led by conscience. The role of reason is indeed to control the work of conscience, and it cannot substitute itself for conscience.[26]

Reason cannot either be reduced to formal logic or to explicit and conscious reasoning. Much reasoning, especially in practical matters, is performed by an instinctive inner faculty, implicit reason.[27] Reaching certitude in concrete circumstances is a personal act which is not limited to an abstract demonstration; for it is always a person who thinks, using their first principles, their beliefs, their opinions and other moral dispositions. As the Fathers of the Church have already stressed,

---

[24] "No one can deny to the intellect its own excellence, nor deprive it of its due honours; the question is merely this, whether it be not limited in its turn, as regards its range, so as not without intrusion to exercise itself as an independent authority in the field of morals and religion."(J. H. Newman, *University Sermons*, IV, § 3, p. 57).

[25] "Reason does not really perceive any thing; but it is a faculty of proceeding from things that are perceived to things which are not." (J. H. Newman, *University Sermons*, XI, § 7, p. 206)

[26] See J. H. Newman, *University Sermons*, X, § 14, p. 183.

[27] In the *Grammar of Assent*, Newman calls the perfection or the virtue of this implicit reasoning 'illative sense' See J. H. Newman, *A Grammar of Assent*, p. 361.

moral rectitude leads to intellectual rectitude, and not vice-versa.[28]

2.4 The rationalist and the religious man

By criticizing the usurpations of reason and by rehabilitating the role of conscience in moral and religious life, Newman brings to light two opposite attitudes: that of the rationalist and that of the religious man.[29] In the case of the rationalist, reason has become the measure of being and of religious truths. Reason is therefore no longer ready to submit itself to the real or to the injunctions of conscience: all truths in matters of morals or religion have to be of the same nature as mathematical or scientific truths. In his attempt to submit everything to his reason, the rationalist turns into a self-proclaimed judge of the works of God.

Because his heart is hardened, the rationalist becomes deaf to the voice of God. The teachings of conscience and the authority of Scripture are set aside. In particular, the sense of duty in conscience is neglected, and conscience is restricted to a sense of expediency or a moral sense, which in its turn is limited to an instinct of benevolence or an aesthetic sense. Then reason supersedes conscience, as is the case with utilitarians who want to reduce moral choices to a calculation aimed at reaching maximum utility, and who do not acknowledge the sense of duty which makes conscience an independent arbiter of the actions of the subject.

To this vision of the rationalist is opposed that of the religious man. In the latter, reason is integrated in the sphere of the subject, of the self and his essential relationship with God. The person in all his dimensions thinks and reasons. The experience of conscience influences, in particular, the work of reason. For the first principles, and the antecedents on which reasoning in concrete matters is based, depend on the faithfulness of conscience. Reason, however, is not left behind, since it has the task of developing a moral science and of allowing the moral sense to train and refine itself. Instead of the word 'opposition', it is better to use 'complementarity' between conscience and reason. In the *Grammar of Assent*, Newman describes

---

[28] "A certain moral state, and not evidence, is made the means of gaining the Truth, and the beginning of spiritual perfection" (J. H. Newman, *University Sermons*, XII, § 22, p. 237).

[29] For a more detailed description of the opposite attitudes of the rationalist and the religious man, see L. Terlinden, *Le conflit des intériorités. Charles Taylor et l'intériorisation des sources morales: une lecture théologique à la lumière de John Henry Newman*, Roma, Editiones Academiae Alfonsianae (Tesi Accademia Alfonsiana, 2), 2006, pp. 220-243.

the common work of reason and conscience in the act of faith and religious assent.[30]

The attitude of the religious man, built on faithfulness to his conscience, finds one of its best illustrations in the life of Newman himself. In his *Apologia*, he described the itinerary of the man who, in all his life, from his 'conversion' at the age of fifteen, to his final entry into the Catholic Church, passing through the Tractarian movement, sought to remain faithful to the One who lives in his conscience:

> I am a Catholic by virtue of my believing in a God; and if I am asked why I believe in a God, I answer that it is because I believe in myself, for I feel it impossible to believe in my own existence (and of that fact I am quite sure) without believing also in the existence of Him, who lives as a Personal, All-seeing, All-judging Being in my conscience.[31]

Once he had become a Catholic, Newman never renounced this faithfulness to conscience. In particular, the controversy surrounding the question of the Church's infallibility allowed him, on several occasions, to show that there is no opposition between conscience and Roman infallibility.[32] If the Church ever denied the right and the duty to listen to the divine voice which is expressed in conscience, it would undermine her own foundations. At the same time, the Church is at the service of conscience, which is often very frail and needs to be supported.[33]

Conclusion: Newman the precursor

Newman's teaching on conscience unites originality and continuity. His originality manifests itself especially with regard to the Catholic theology of his era. Through his Anglican background, Newman

---

[30] See T. Merrigan, *Clear Heads and Holy Hearts. The Religious and Theological Ideal of John Henry Newman*, Louvain, Peeters (Louvain Theological & Pastoral Monographs, 7), 1991.

[31] J. H. Newman, *Apologia*, p. 198.

[32] See O. de Berranger, 'Conscience et infaillibilité dans l'*Apologia* de Newman', in *Nouvelle Revue Théologique* 129 (2007) p. 177.

[33] "There is no scoffing of any Pope, in formal documents addressed to the faithful at large, at that most serious doctrine, the right and the duty of following that Divine Authority, the voice of conscience, on which in truth the Church herself is built. ... But the sense of right and wrong, which is the first element in religion, is so delicate, so fitful, so easily puzzled, obscured, perverted, so subtle in its argumentative methods, so impressible by education, so biased by pride and passion, so unsteady in its course, that, in the struggle for existence amid the various exercises and triumphs of the human intellect, this sense is at once the highest of all teachers, yet the least luminous; and the Church, the Pope, the Hierarchy are, in the Divine purpose, the supply of an urgent demand." (J. H. Newman, *A Letter Addressed to the Duke of Norfolk*, pp. 252-254).

belonged to a culture and a philosophical tradition, each of which was growing apart from the Catholic Church. Through dialogue – and often polemic – with his contemporaries, he was successful in handing on in a new language the contents of the faith and of religious experience. His doctrine on conscience, which was enriched by his own experience, used concepts drawn from his own time, although not without renewing them profoundly.

But if Newman is a man of his time, he is also deeply rooted in Scripture and Tradition. His insistence on a dimension of conscience, which is not only moral but also religious, allows him to draw near to the Biblical notion of the heart as an interior place where man meets God. Like the Fathers of the Church, he also developed an anthropology centred on this interior experience of God, which influences the complete intellectual and moral development of the person.

Encompassing both an authentic attachment to Scripture and Tradition and a dialogue with the culture of his time, Newman is at once a model for the enculturation of the faith and a precursor of the Second Vatican Council. But the man who was, as Paul VI thought, the inspirer of the Council, was so particularly because of his teaching on conscience. It suffices to read the description given in the constitution *Gaudium et Spes* to see the extent of the influence exercised by the great Cardinal on the conciliar Fathers:

> In the depths of his conscience, man detects a law which he does not impose upon himself, but which holds him to obedience. Always summoning him to love good and avoid evil, the voice of conscience when necessary speaks to his heart: do this, shun that. For man has in his heart a law written by God; to obey it is the very dignity of man; according to it he will be judged. Conscience is the most secret core and sanctuary of a man. There he is alone with God, Whose voice echoes in his depths. In a wonderful manner conscience reveals that law which is fulfilled by love of God and neighbour. In fidelity to conscience, Christians are joined with the rest of men in the search for truth, and for the genuine solution to the numerous problems which arise in the life of individuals and from social relationships. Hence the more right conscience holds sway, the more persons and groups turn aside from blind choice and strive to be guided by the objective norms of morality.[34]

---

[34] Vatican Council II, *Pastoral Constitution on the Church in the Modern World* (Gaudium et Spes), § 16.

Chapter 12

NEWMAN AND MORAL LIBERALISM

by Bernard Mahoney

Newman opposed moral liberalism, formulated in the nineteenth century Utilitarian Philosophy of Jeremy Bentham and John Stuart Mill, because it undermined the judgments of conscience. Utilitarianism based its morality on the principle that individuals and society should seek the greatest good for the greatest number of people. Thus, Utilitarianism rejected the traditional Christian foundation of morality based on the natural law, the foundation of the Christian conscience. For Newman says, in *A Letter Addressed to His Grace The Duke of Norfolk*, the conscience is "the voice of God, whereas it is fashionable on all hands to consider it in one way or another a creation of man."[1]

Part I

Moral Liberalism undermines the judgments of conscience because it tends to make all moral judgments the result of a personal preference, or public opinion, which John Stuart Mill listed in *The Utility of Religion* as "the love of glory; the love of praise, the love of admiration, the love of respect and deference; even the love of sympathy."[2] The judgments of conscience, in contrast, are based on the natural law for all human beings, which are a part of the laws of nature for all creation. The laws of nature begin with the axiom that the existence of everything in this universe is based on reason. Science, ancient and modern, studies the relationship of causes and effects; it attempts to find a reasonable explanation for an event or a series of events. The

---

[1] *Conscience, Consensus, and the Development of Doctrine.* Introduction and Notes by James Gaffney. (New York, Image Books, 1992) p.448.

[2] *http://www.la.utexas.edu/research/poltheory/mill/three/utilrelig.html*, p. 5.

intellectual tradition of the West, from the Ancient Greeks, through the Middle Ages, and into the present day, is founded on the use of reason to explain our universe, and the place of human beings in it. This tradition was eloquently expressed by Thomas Jefferson in the *Declaration of Independence* when he formulated a fundamental premise of the Natural Law that human beings would quickly recognize and respond to. He wrote: "We hold these truths to be self-evident, that all men are created equal, that they are endowed by their Creator with certain inalienable rights, that among these are life, liberty, and the pursuit of happiness." These rights are an essential part of Natural Law, and are the basis of the judgments of conscience. Moral Liberalism and the judgments of conscience, which Newman discusses at length in the *Grammar of Assent*, differ in some important ways. Moral Liberalism views human laws as subjective solutions to human situations, while, for Newman, the judgments of conscience search for objective conclusions from the Natural Law, which is a part of the Laws of Nature for all creation. Moral Liberalism forms its decisions from the majority opinion of the community, while Newman considers that the judgments of conscience are made for the good of the community in general. Moral Liberalism seeks to put some reasonable limit on our personal aims, while Newman maintains that the judgments of conscience search for the benefits to the common good. Moral Liberalism tries to find the least common denominator that will offend the majority, while Newman asserts that the judgments of conscience try to find common ground that will give reasonable conclusions for all to live by.

A part of the ongoing discussion about the conscience was the definition of the moral sense. The Third Earl of Shaftesbury introduced this term into the philosophical discussion in response to the emphasis by John Locke that all knowledge comes to us through our five senses. The Earl of Shaftesbury insisted that we have another sense, a sixth sense, which he called a "moral sense". This "moral sense" tells us what is right and wrong, good and bad. Because all university education was based on reading the classics of Greece and Rome in the original language, university graduates had a common language. They all understood that the search for "the true, the good and the beautiful" was the goal of classical philosophers, and this set of values was also a part of their vocabulary as they discussed the important issues of their day. This search was also applied to the search for beauty in poetry, literature, and art. But then, recalling the

Latin dictum *de gustibus, non est disputandum* (about taste, there is no dispute), the "moral sense" can then become the private property of the individual. One's preference for Michelangelo or Raphael could not be argued. Both of these artists had produced great works of art, and one's preference for one or the other was a personal matter. This kind of toleration was extended to moral issues as well. So the judgments of one's conscience then became a private matter, beyond dispute and argument.

Anthony Ashley Cooper, the Third Earl of Shaftesbury (1671-1713),[3] claimed that only humans have a "moral sense" in addition to our five senses. This sense involves both a capacity for reflection and a feeling by which we humans can discern both right and wrong.

> Rejecting the popular view that morality is based on the will of God, Shaftesbury maintains rather that morality depends on human nature, and he introduces the notion of a sense of right and wrong, possessed uniquely by human beings who alone are capable of reflection.[4]

Shaftesbury's "moral sense" was a reaction against the self-interest and egoism that Thomas Hobbes (1588-1679) claimed was a part of the "state of nature", which he called "the war of all against all."[5] Hobbes claimed that people were interested only in their own personal advantage. In contrast, the "moral sense" is a part of basic human nature and is a more benevolent response to the interests of the larger community. These perceptions of right and wrong are a part of the common language of human beings.

The "moral sense" went through a series of definitions by philosophers and theologians who both agreed and disagreed with one another, or amended and corrected one another. Francis Hutcheson (1694-1746), one of the fathers of the movement known as the Scottish Enlightenment, asserted a series of "internal" senses such as honor, sympathy, morality, and beauty. Since these internal perceptual responses concern intellectual concepts, they differ from the perceptions of the five physical senses, which react only to physical objects. But Hutcheson's attention was devoted primarily to the moral sense, which gives its judgment as if from instinct. We approve

---

[3] 'Shaftesbury', *The Cambridge Dictionary of Philosophy*. (Cambridge University Press, 1995) p. 732.

[4] 'Moral sense theory', *The Cambridge Dictionary of Philosophy*. (Cambridge University Press, 1995) p. 512.

[5] Samuel Enoch Stumph, *Philosophy, History and Problems*. (New York, McGraw-Hill, 1994) p. 231.

or disapprove of an action by another person even if that action has no immediate effect in our lives. He claims that goals promoted by such a benevolent person tend to produce the greatest happiness for the greatest number of people, a phrase which he uses in his *Inquiry concerning Moral Good and Evil* (sect. 3) that anticipates a key idea of Utilitarianism.[6]

David Hume (1711-1776) defined the "moral sense" in terms of his version of Empiricism. Certain dispositions, over time, have developed various practical rules in response to our own feelings and sentiments, as well as those of others, which come from our "moral sense". There is a cognitive content to responses of approval or disapproval, since we can judge the action of a person that has no influence on our lives. For example, I can pick a remote person in history that has no effect on my daily life, and judge that person's motives and character with approval or disapproval. Hume's "moral sense" is based primarily on feeling and sentiment. Hume made the claim that "reason 'is not sufficient alone to produce any moral blame or approbation.' What limits the role of reason in ethics is that reason makes judgments concerning *matter of fact* and *relations* whereas moral judgments of good and evil are not limited to matters of fact or relations."[7]

Although Hume realized that basing his "moral sense" on sentiment or feeling might cause some to consider such a judgment a matter of taste, he nonetheless asserted that these feelings were universal. He claimed that humans generally praise and blame the same actions, whether in different parts of the world or at different times in human history. The qualities that all humans approve of are "discretion, caution, enterprise, industry, economy, good-sense, prudence, and discernment." He adds that we all approve as well "the merit of temperance, sobriety, patience, constancy, considerateness, presence of mind, quickness of conception, and felicity of expression." For Hume, these qualities are *useful* and *agreeable*, not just for one individual, but for society in general. We see that our own interests are tied in with the interests of the community at large. "Thus self-interest is the original motive to the establishment of justice: but a sympathy with public interest is the source of moral approbation that attends that virtue."[8]

---

[6] 'Hutcheson, Francis', *The Cambridge Dictionary of Philosophy,* p. 351.
[7] Stumpf, p. 287.
[8] Stumpf, pp. 288-289.

Newman's answer to the "moral sense" is his Illative Sense, which he says is the power of judging and concluding.[9] It is equivalent to "common sense" or a "sense of beauty". His study of the *Nichomachean Ethics,* where he examined Aristotle's concept of the *phronesis* (practical judgment), gave him this original idea. The Illative Sense uses the inductive reasoning power of our intellect, which insight he credited to Francis Bacon.[10] This sense accumulates the observations of the five senses to come to a highly probable conclusion. For Newman, this important operation enables us to make conclusions about Natural Religion that will lead us to accept the truths of Revealed Religion. This Illative Sense will guide us to the conclusions our conscience will form, which Newman elaborates in Chapter X of the *Grammar of Assent.*

Jeremy Bentham (1748-1832) and John Stuart Mill (1806-1873) continued the discussion of the "moral sense" in their philosophy of Utilitarianism. Their basic premise of *usefulness* had already been stated by many of the Empiricist philosophers, such as Hobbes, Locke and Hume. But their ideas on practical reform, especially reform of the prison system in England, gave new emphasis to their philosophical ideas. Bentham began his *Introduction to the Principles of Morals and Legislation* with this famous sentence: "Nature has placed mankind under the governance of two sovereign masters, *pain* and *pleasure.* It is for them alone to point out what we ought to do, as well as determine what we shall do."[11] Using a mathematical concept, Bentham tried to formulate a *Pleasure-Pain Calculus* to enable us to make a suitable choice of action. This choice would be based on the quantitative amounts of pleasure or pain. This calculus, for Bentham, is useful not only for individuals, but for society in general. Thus, the purpose of our legal system is to provide for the greatest happiness of the greatest number of citizens.

In a rather lengthy footnote in *The Principles of Morals and Legislation,* Bentham claims the concept of "moral sense" used by previous philosophers is a bit vague. He lists this term along with "common sense", "understanding", "right reason", "nature's law", and "good order" among others, all of which, he asserts, tend to substantiate one's own personal opinion. Bentham thinks that each

---

[9] J.H. Newman, *An Essay in Aid of A Grammar of Assent.* (New York, Longmans, Green, and Co. 1947) Chapter IX, p. 268.

[10] *Grammar of Assent,* Ch. IX, p. 266.

[11] Jeremy Bentham, *An Introduction to the Principles of Morals and Legislation.* With an Introduction by Laurence J. Lafleur. (New York, Hafner Publishing Co. 1965) p. 1.

one of these terms is just another substitute for the "moral sense".[12] These concepts are simply a way of imposing one's own subjective opinion on others, which are different from what he asserts is the objective merit of his principle of utility, the clearest term that can describe the basis of his philosophy.

Bentham also sees a contradiction in the concept of natural rights because of what he says is confusion between what is and what ought to be:

> To say that men have inalienable rights is clearly false, when the assertion is made by way of protesting against a government that has in fact alienated rights ... On the other hand, if we take the doctrine of natural rights as statement of what governments ought to do, it will be found untenable. No government could continue to govern if it abstained from ever depriving any of it citizens of life, liberty, or property (still less of happiness), since taxation and punishment would then be impossible."[13]

Bentham also sees confusion in the concept of the natural law, which he says is actually not a law. The "supreme governors" who make the laws are also subject to the laws, so thus they cannot be above the law. The sanction of public opinion obviously limits what the lawmaker can actually accomplish.[14]

The weakness of his attempt to formulate the "moral sanction" of Utilitarianism is based on a moral right that he postulates in opposition to the "moral sense". Although he rejects the concept of natural rights, he then postulates another moral right, which is "to have one's happiness considered equally with that of other men." This turns out to be another form of egoism, which is what he asserts is the problem with the "moral sense".[15]

The *Pleasure-Pain Calculus* seems like a simple and direct method to help make a choice about mundane issues in everyday life, but Bentham does not offer any method by which pleasure can be calculated. Any calculus often fails to be impartial when the greatest good for the greatest number is in question. For example, legislators often include *their own* interests as a part of, or even instead of, the greatest good for the greatest number. Since Bentham's *Pleasure-Pain Calculus* is based solely on the amounts of pleasure or pain, it is all too

---

[12] Jeremy Bentham, *The Principles of Morals and Legislation,* p. 17.

[13] *Encyclopedia of Philosophy*, "Bentham Jeremy" D.H. Munro. (Macmillan Publishing Co. New York, 1967.) p. 284b.

[14] *Encyclopedia of Philosophy*, "Bentham, Jeremy" p. 284b.

[15] *Encyclopedia of Philosophy*, "Bentham, Jeremy" p. 285a.

often calculated to find a personal and individual benefit, especially when life and death issues are at stake.

Although John Stuart Mill added his own ideas to Bentham's Utilitarianism, he followed Bentham's lead in formulating a morality for a purely secular society:

> For many of the Benthamite 'philosophical radicals' of the late eighteenth and nineteenth century Christianity was an especially pernicious superstition. It fostered indifference or outright hostility to human happiness, the keystone of utilitarian morality. In addition, religious sanctions (e.g., the prospect of eternal damnation or eternal reward) impeded social and political reform – the Church thereby set itself in alliance with the privileged classes to limit the power of the masses . . . Moreover, in 'Utility of Religion' he contends that Christianity weakens the intellect by asking its adherents to accept a flawed theology, fosters selfishness for the majority with its doctrine of heaven and hell, and places questionable moral exemplars before its believers, including a God who seems to act arbitrarily by keeping grace from the millions who lived and died without ever hearing of Christ.[16]

Since Christian Theology upheld a moral code based on the Ten Commandments, which reflect the Natural Law, Bentham and Mill's Utilitarianism attempted to formulate a new code of conduct. Christian notions of sin and redemption were considered archaic and destructive to the new social order. Utilitarianism attempted to offer a new set of values that would displace the Christian morality based on the Natural Law.

With his Utilitarianism, Bentham thought he had measured the amount of pleasure by his "calculus," and said that the "quantity of pleasure being equal, pushpin is as good as poetry."[17] Mill's Utilitarianism contradicted the simple quantification of Bentham's Utilitarianism by factoring quality into the equation. Mill objected to the notion that an adult's pleasure of poetry was on the same level as the child's pleasure with the game of pushpin or "Pin the tail on a donkey." In response, he asserted that "it is better to be a human dissatisfied than a pig satisfied; better to be Socrates dissatisfied than a fool satisfied."[18]

For Mill there was an important difference between qualitative pleasure and quantitative pleasure that Bentham's *Calculus* didn't

---

[16] Colin Heydt, "Narrative, Imagination and Religion of Humanity in Mill's Ethics." *Journal of the History of Philosophy*, vol. 44 no. 1 (2006) 99-115.

[17] 'Bentham, Jeremy', *Encyclopedia of Philosophy* p. 283a.

[18] John Stuart Mill, *Utilitarianism*, Vol. 43. *Great Books of The Western World*. (Chicago, Encyclopedia Britannica, 1952.) Chapter 2, p. 449c.

consider. Quantitative pleasure was primarily physical, while qualitative pleasure was intellectual and emotional. Mill wanted to make his "moral sense", or conscience, more than simply a matter of taste, and so asks some penetrating questions: "What is its sanction? What are the motives to obey it? Or more specifically, what is the source of its obligation?"[19] The "moral sense" or the conscience, as Mill names it here, makes its choices based on various external sources, such as "the hope of favour, and the fear of displeasure, from our fellow creatures or from the Ruler of the Universe..."[20] But there is also an internal sanction:

> Whatever our standard of duty may be, is one and the same – a feeling in our own mind; a pain, more or less intense, attendant on violation of duty, which in properly cultivated moral natures rises, in the more serous cases, into shrinking from it as an impossibility. This feeling, when disinterested, and connecting itself with the pure idea of duty, and not with some particular form it, or with any of the merely accessory circumstances, is the essence of Conscience; though in that complex phenomenon as it actually exists, the simple fact is in general all encrusted over with collateral associations, derived from sympathy, from love, and still more from fear; from all the forms of religious feelings; from the recollections of childhood an all of our past life; from self-esteem of others, and occasionally even self-abasement.[21]

This explanation was Mill's attempt to bypass any reference to the Christian conscience. He considered Christian morality too restrictive and even passé. Science was providing some new answers to old questions, especially with the publication of Charles Darwin's *The Origin of Species* in 1859. The increasing wealth of the nouveau riche made earthly pleasures of greater importance than any concern for eternal happiness; and the popularity of the philosophy of Deism made Christian morality unimportant. The image of a clock was the popular metaphor that scientists used to describe the Universe:God, the Clock-maker, having set the Universe in motion was simply too far removed to have any concern about people's daily and personal problems.

Placing one's moral beliefs in the Utilitarian framework would lead one to see them in a new light. Utilitarianism forces one to relate morality not to God's will, the soul's salvation, and blessedness

---

[19] John Stuart Mill, *Utilitarianism*. Chapter 3, p. 457c.

[20] John Stuart Mill, *Utilitarianism*. Chapter 2, p.458a.

[21] John Stuart Mill, *Utilitarianism*. Chapter 2, p. 458b–c.

JOHN HENRY NEWMAN DOCTOR OF THE CHURCH

in another life, but to man's desires, human happiness, and increasing satisfactoriness of life on earth. The feeling that moral principles and rules are awesome and imposing dictates from on high

> is replaced by an attitude which takes them as one of the many devices that men construct, as they work together for the general welfare. Morality is felt to be an instrument in our hands, to be used by us and for us, to be changed or not as facts demand and we see fit.[22]

Mill's definition of conscience is primarily a feeling that comes from many different internal motivations, which is in contrast to Newman's definition that it is a response to a person outside ourselves. The human responses to the choices we have to make in our daily lives can sometimes be altruistic, but they can also be individual and personal. Although self-abasement is a common feeling when we have made a spectacle of ourselves in front of other people, it hardly merits a universal judgment of conscience. Our religious feelings can also be personal and individual. When we try to reassure ourselves that God has forgiven a particular sin of ours, often we are privately embarrassed by our poor choice. Merely identifying our common feelings and responses to embarrassing situations from other human beings is hardly a sound definition of the conscience, which for Newman is the guide for our moral choices. The kind of definition of conscience that Mill formulated in his *Utilitarianism* was rejected by Newman in his Note A on 'Liberalism' in his *Apologia*:

> There are rights of conscience such, that everyone may lawfully advance a claim to profess and teach what is false and wrong in matters, religious, social, and moral, provided that to his private conscience it seems absolutely true and right.[23]

Part II

In his *An Essay in Aid of a Grammar of Assent*, Newman specifically rejects the concept of the Moral Sense:

> Half the world would be puzzled by what was meant by the moral sense, but everyone knows what is meant by a good or bad conscience ... however, Taste and Conscience part company; for the sense of beautifulness, as indeed Moral Sense, has no special relation to persons, but rather contemplates objects in themselves;

---

[22] *Mill's Ethical Writings*. Edited, with an Introduction by J.B. Schneewind. (New York Collier Books, 1965) p. 38.
[23] J.H. Newman, *Apologia Pro Vita Sua*. (New York, Longmans, Green and Co. 1947) p. 267.

conscience, on the other hand, is concerned with persons primarily, and with actions mainly viewed in their doers ...

And again, in consequence of this prerogative of dictating and commanding, which is of its essence, Conscience has an intimate bearing on our affections and emotions, leading us to reverence and awe, hope and fear, especially fear, a feeling which is foreign not only to Taste, but even to Moral Sense, except in consequence of accidental associations.[24]

Newman rejected the rather academic definitions of the conscience, such as described by Mill, and gave expression to his own insights. Since the conscience reaches beyond itself, and recognizes a sanction is connected with its decisions, "... hence we are accustomed to speak of conscience as a voice ... or the echo of a voice, imperative and constraining ..." The sense of the beautiful is universal to human beings, but it has no compelling commands. We enjoy "the specimens of the beautiful simply for their own sake."[25] These statements contrast with those famous last lines from John Keats' poem, *Ode on a Grecian Urn*.

'Beauty is truth, truth beauty, – that is all
Ye know on earth, and all ye need to know.'

Unlike the Moral Sense, or the sense of beauty, the Conscience is always emotional. He says that inanimate objects cannot cause an emotional reaction in us; only a person causes an emotional reaction. Our reaction to the voice of conscience implies that we are responding to a person. Newman continues:

We feel responsibility, are ashamed, are frightened, at transgressing the voice of conscience, this implies that there is One to whom we are responsible, before whom we are ashamed, whose claims upon us we fear. If, on doing wrong, we feel the same tearful, broken-hearted sorrow which overwhelms us on hurting a mother; if on doing right, we enjoy the same soothing satisfactory delight which follows praise from a father, we certainly have within us the image of some person, to whom our love and veneration look, in whose smile we find our happiness, for whom we yearn, towards whom we direct our pleadings, in whose anger we are troubled and waste away.[26]

This forceful, and lyrical, statement by Newman was reiterated in his response to the Duke of Norfolk. Cardinal Newman gives his

[24] J.H. Newman, *An Essay in Aid of A Grammar of Assent.* (New York, Longmans, Green, and Co. 1947) Chapter V, pp. 81–82.
[25] J.H. Newman, *An Essay in Aid of A Grammar of Assent.* p. 82.
[26] J.H. Newman, *An Essay in Aid of A Grammar of Assent.* p. 8.

definition of conscience in his famous *A Letter Addressed to His Grace the Duke of Norfolk on the Occasion of Mr. Gladstone's Recent Expostulation* in 1874:

> The rule and measure of duty is not utility, nor expedience, nor the happiness of the greatest number, nor State convenience, nor fitness, order and the ... *pulcrum* (beautiful). Conscience is not a long-sighted selfishness, nor a desire to be consistent with oneself; but it is a messenger from Him, who, both in nature and grace, speaks to us behind a veil, and teaches and rules us by His representatives. Conscience is the aboriginal Vicar of Christ, a prophet in its informations, a monarch in its peremptoriness, a priest in its blessings and anathemas, and even though the eternal priesthood throughout the Church could cease to be, in it the sacerdotal principle would remain and have a sway.[27]

This *Letter* was a response to a pamphlet, *The Vatican Decrees in Their Bearing on Civil Allegiance,* written by William Gladstone in 1874, the Liberal Prime Minister of Britain. *The Decree on Papal Infallibility* was one of the few documents voted on at The First Ecumenical Council of the Vatican, which convened in the summer of 1870 in Rome. The discussions of the lengthy agenda were cut short by the political revolution that summer in Italy, which finally unified the peninsula for the first time since the Ancient Roman Empire collapsed in the fifth century. The physical safety of the delegates to the Council from around the world was threatened, and so the Council was hastily adjourned. But before it did close, this important document on Papal Infallibility received an affirmative vote by a very large number of the Cardinals and Bishops. Although there were, and are, sound theological reasons for the affirmative vote, the political overtones of the revolution in Italy clouded the issue. And Gladstone took a most negative response to this document.

Certain Catholics in England identified themselves as *Ultramontanes*, literally translated as "beyond the mountains". These Roman Catholics took the issue of Papal Infallibility to the extreme. The Document from Vatican I states that the Pope is infallible in those issues concerning "faith and morals". But the Ultramontanes wanted to include every statement the Pope made, including those of his private opinions. Newman rejected this false definition, and used this opportunity to respond not only to Gladstone, but also to the Ultramontane Catholics.

One of the striking parts of Newman's definition of conscience

---

[27] John Gaffney, *Conscience, Consensus, and the Development of Doctrine.* p. 449.

is quoted in the *Catechism of the Catholic Church*. The *Catechism* first makes a reference to Saint Paul's Letter to the Romans where he says that the Gentiles do not have the demands of the law given to Moses, but they do have "the demands of the law written in their hearts." (Rom 2:15)[28] Newman identifies this voice as "the aboriginal Vicar of Christ."[29] The basic principles of the natural law are a part of the mind and heart of each person. Newman quotes both Saint Augustine and Saint Thomas Aquinas to support his claim. His quote from Saint Augustine says: "The eternal law is the Divine Reason or Will of God, commanding the observance, forbidding the disturbance, of the natural order of things." And his quote from Saint Thomas states, "The natural law is an impression of the Divine Light in us, a participation of the eternal law in the rational creature."[30] Since the conscience is an essential part of the Natural Law, which prefigured the Law of Moses, and since the Old Law of Moses prefigured the New Law of Christ, Newman can then refer to the Conscience, which "speaks to us behind a veil" as "the aboriginal Vicar of Christ." The *Catechism* reaffirms this point: "When he listens to his conscience, the prudent man can hear God speaking."[31]

For Newman, the Conscience is one of the mental acts of the human mind, on a level with the memory, reasoning, and imagination. The conscience has a prominent part in our affections and emotions, "leading us to reverence and awe, hope and fear, especially fear, a feeling that is foreign for the most part, not only to Taste, but even to the Moral Sense ..."[32] Newman differentiates the Conscience from both Taste and the Moral Sense, as well as our sense of the beautiful, because "inanimate objects cannot stir our affections; these are correlative with persons."[33]

> If, as is the case, we feel responsibility, are ashamed, are frightened, at transgressing the voice of conscience, this implies that there is One to whom we are responsible, before whom we are ashamed, whose claims upon us we fear.[34]

For Newman, human beings were a direct creation by a Creator. Charles Darwin published his *Origin of Species* in 1859 amid a huge

---

[28] *Catechism of the Catholic Church,* 1777. (New York, Image Books, 1995).

[29] CCC, 1778.

[30] John Gaffney, p. 448.

[31] CCC, 1777.

[32] J.H. Newman, *An Essay in Aid of A Grammar of Assent,* Ch. 5, p. 82.

[33] J.H. Newman, *An Essay in Aid of A Grammar of Assent,* Ch. 5, p. 83.

[34] J.H. Newman, *An Essay in Aid of A Grammar of Assent,* Ch. 5, p. 83.

furor of rejection by Christians of all denominations. Newman was not formally involved in any response to this publication, and he would unquestioningly accept that human beings were created in the image and likeness of God, as is stated in the Book of Genesis 1:29. Whether or not one ever read the Bible, or even heard of Christianity, Newman stated that these feelings we have obviously require a response to an intelligent being. He says that we do not treat a stone with affection, nor do we feel shame before a dog or a horse. And we have no remorse for breaking a mere human law. He concludes that since nothing in the visible world can cause such reactions, the Conscience is giving us a "picture of a Supreme Governor, a Judge, holy, just, all-seeing, retributive ..."[35] This fundamental response in human nature gives Newman a reason for the voice of his Conscience.

The obvious question to ask is how can one be certain that the voice of the Conscience is speaking to us. Newman's answer was the Illative sense in contrast to the Moral Sense of Mill and the Utilitarians, which he explains at great length in his *Grammar of Assent*.[36] The *Grammar of Assent* begins with the analysis of apprehension, where a good Empiricist would always start. The two kinds of apprehension are notional and real. We give notional apprehension to concepts and ideas, but we give real apprehension to the choices that one must make in everyday real life. Notional assent is given to intellectual and scientific concepts that might take time to comprehend and understand fully. Real assent is given to choices that we must make immediately in our daily lives. We use the syllogism to come to conclusions that a scientist can understand and explain. The scientist has the time and the temperament to be able to formulate a series of inductive observations into a set of premises, which will then be used in a syllogism. These premises may even be amended by more observations. But, given the premises of a syllogism, the conclusion must be certain. Newman says that our daily lives demand a much quicker answer than the one the measured and rigid logic of the syllogism provides, and the methodical approach that a scientist demands.

Instead, we use the rule of converging probabilities to come to practical decisions in our daily lives, which is identical with the process of induction. He uses the geometrical example of Newton's

---

[35] J.H. Newman, *An Essay in Aid of A Grammar of Assent*, Chapter V, p. 84.

[36] The word 'Illative' comes from the past participle of the Latin word inferro, inferre, intuli, illatus, which is the root for the English word 'infer', to come to a conclusion.

lemma as his example on *Informal Inference*.[37] The *lemma* is made of straight lines of a polygon that become shorter and shorter, so that the polygon vanishes before it has coincided with the circle. For example, each one of us is certain that one day we will die. The only proof we have is the accumulated instances of death in the history of human affairs, and so we conclude that we too will one day die, as a result of these "converging probabilities". The conclusion from inductive reasoning is only probable, and in the case of our death so very highly probable that we can accept it as a certainty. Newman contends that this is how we make most of our practical decisions in our everyday life, and especially the judgments of our Conscience.

Newman's insight into the place the conscience has in our lives began with his study of Aristotle's *Nichomachean Ethics* as a student in Trinity College at the University of Oxford, where he matriculated on December 14 1816. Until the middle of the nineteenth century, Aristotle's *Nichomachean Ethics*, in the original Greek, was a part of the core curriculum for every student. Oxford, founded in the twelfth century, and modelled after the University of Paris, emphasized the study of Aristotle. In Book VI of the *Nichomachean Ethics*, Aristotle's concept of *phronesis* became an essential part of Newman's explanation of how the conscience is certain that it is hearing the voice of his Supreme Judge. Newman's own text of the *Nichomachean Ethics* had his notes on the interleaves, from his student days when he wrote his Degree Examination on February 21 1822 until the publication of *A Grammar of Assent* in 1870.[38] His detailed knowledge of Aristotle's *Ethics* provided him with a sound base for his analysis of the certainty we have about the judgments of the conscience. He discusses Aristotle's concept of the *phronesis*, which is the basis for his definition of the Illative Sense. Newman points out that an ethical system "may supply laws, general rules, guiding principles, a number of examples, suggestions, landmarks, limitations, cautions, distinctions, solutions of critical or anxious difficulties," but we need a living intellect for an authoritative oracle.[39] There are only two choices, our own, or another's. We do not need a decision in some hypothetical situation, or help in deciding what to do ten years from now. The Illative Sense comes to practical conclusions for the here and now. First, the Illative

---

[37] J.H. Newman, *An Essay in Aid of A Grammar of Assent*, Ch. VII, p. 244.

[38] Rev. Bernard J. Mahoney, *Newman and Aristotle: The Concept of the Conscience.* A Thesis submitted for the Degree of Doctor of Philosophy in the University of Birmingham, England. October 1967.

[39] J.H. Newman, *An Essay in Aid of A Grammar of Assent*, Ch. IX, p. 269.

Sense functions the same way in all "concrete matters", whether chemistry, law, or morality. Second, the Illative Sense is attached to "definite subject-matters." Thus, one person may have it in history, and another have it in philosophy. Third, the Illative Sense uses the method of "converging probabilities" to come to its inductive conclusion. Fourth, the Illative Sense is always the final judge of truth or error.[40]

Newman used this kind of reasoning to clarify the conclusions we reach from our Illative Sense to explain how the conscience is vital to our understanding of natural religion. He refers to that event from the Acts of the Apostles where Saint Paul speaks to the Athenians about the "Unknown God", which Saint Paul said was a preparation for understanding the God of Revelation. The "Unknown God" can be as vague a definition as used by the theists who can speak of an *anima mundi,* a life of the world, wherever life came from. Newman adds some distinctive prerogatives about the "Unknown God", such as "numerically One, ... Personal, ... the Life of Law and Order, the Moral Governor ... which I ascribe unconditionally and unreservedly to the great Being whom I call God."[41] It is this God who is the voice of the conscience.

Part III

Newman maintained the inviolability of the judgments of conscience. The conscience speaks to us about the natural law that is of the essence of a human being. The natural law's basic command is "to do good and avoid evil." The function of the conscience then is to force us, "by threats and by promises that we must follow the right and avoid the wrong."[42] The laws of nature determine how the cosmos we live in operates, but the natural law, which follows from the laws of nature, requires our understanding and cooperation. Although the conscience can be ill trained and uninformed, and although we can use our prejudices and superstitions for certainties, the voice of the conscience can speak the truth to us. The voice, or sanction, of the conscience will enable us to determine the difference between a bad choice and a good choice.

Although, for Newman, our conscience suggests many things, "its cardinal and distinguishing truth, is that He is our Judge."[43] In his

---

[40] J.H. Newman, *An Essay in Aid of A Grammar of Assent*, Ch. IX, p. 272.
[41] J.H. Newman, *An Essay in Aid of A Grammar of Assent*, Ch. V, p. 77.
[42] J.H. Newman, *An Essay in Aid of A Grammar of Assent*, Ch. V, p. 81.
[43] *An Essay in Aid of A Grammar of Assent*, Ch. X, p. 2.

Proof of Theism, an unpublished monograph from his notes that was finally published in 1961, Newman says:

> Conscience implies a relation between the soul and something exterior, and that, moreover, superior to itself; a relation to an excellence which it does not possess, and to a tribunal over which it has no power.[44]

He continues that the very existence of the conscience

> carries on our minds to a Being exterior to ourselves; for else whence did it come? And to a being superior to ourselves; else whence its strange, troublesome peremptoriness? ... Its very existence throws us out of ourselves and beyond ourselves, to go and seek for Him in the height and depth, whose voice it is.[45]

The conscience, then, is the voice of God, "the Aboriginal Vicar of Christ", that speaks to each one of us and prepares us to receive the fullness of Revelation.

Conclusion

Joseph Cardinal Ratzinger, now Pope Benedict XVI, in his article *Conscience and Truth*, quotes the famous line of Cardinal Newman in his *Letter to the Duke of Norfolk*:

> Certainly, if I am obliged to bring religion into after-dinner toasts, (which indeed does not seem quite the thing), I shall drink to the Pope, if you please – still, to the conscience first, and to the Pope afterwards.[46]

He says that Newman correctly conceived of a papacy that not only is not in opposition to the conscience but also is based on it and guarantees it. Cardinal Ratzinger began his article discussing the erroneous conscience by questioning whether the SS Troops of Nazi Germany could use their erroneous consciences to escape blame for their murderous deeds, since they thought they were doing something good and right by their slaughter of the Jews, and other non-Aryans. This seemed so preposterous that he had to find another explanation. He finds his answer in Saint Luke (18:9-14) in the parable about the pharisee and the tax collector. The contrast is not between the sins of the tax collector, which were sins, or the good deeds of the

[44] Adrian J. Boekraad and Henry Tristam, *The Argument from Conscience to The Existence of God.* (Louvain, Editions Nauwelaerts, 1961) p. 113.
[45] *The Argument from Conscience to The Existence of God.* pp. 114, 116.
[46] Joseph Cardinal Ratzinger, "Conscience and Truth," in *Crisis of Conscience*, ed. John M. Haas. (New York, The Crossroad Publishing Company, 1996) p. 8.

pharisee, which were good deeds. The tax collector knows that he is a sinner, but the pharisee does not recognize his guilt, thinking that he has a clear conscience. The point of the parable is that the pharisee's erroneous conscience does not excuse him from guilt. He is still responsible for his sins. Moral Liberalism imitates the pharisee. However, "firm, subjective conviction and the lack of doubts and scruples which follow there-from do not justify man."[47] Cardinal Ratzinger concludes:

> Newman embraced an interpretation of the papacy, which is only correctly conceived when it is viewed together with the primacy of the conscience – a papacy not put in opposition to the primacy of the conscience but based on it and guaranteeing it.[48]

[47] Joseph Cardinal Ratzinger, *Conscience and Truth*, p.5.
[48] Joseph Cardinal Ratzinger, *Conscience and Truth*, p. 8.

PART IV

DEVELOPMENT OF DOCTRINE

Chapter 13

NEWMAN, TRADITION AND DEVELOPMENT

by James Pereiro

Newman's influence in Vatican Council II has long been a matter of debate. He may not have been the major inspiration in the Council that some have claimed, but there is no doubt that, at least in the area of doctrinal development, the Council made its own ideas he had coined and put into circulation in his 1845 *Essay*.[1] While it is unlikely that any significant number of Council fathers were familiar with this work, a number of the *periti* and other theologians involved in the work of the Council had studied in detail some of the issues raised by Newman about the development of Christian doctrine.[2] Besides, the attention that the topic had attracted from the late nineteenth century onwards guaranteed that even those Council fathers unfamiliar with his classical treatise on the subject were not unaware of the issues involved.

The topic of doctrinal development does not loom large in the Council documents. Paragraph 8 of the Constitution *Dei Verbum* – the main explicit reference to the subject – brings together Tradition and development in a text whose shortness is inversely proportional to its relevance. Christ, the Constitution teaches, is the only source of revelation. The Gospel is not just a message; it is the fullness of the self-communication of God (Truth and Life) to man,[3] and the

---

[1] J.H. Newman, *An Essay on the Development of Christian Doctrine* (London, 1845).
[2] For a general study of the authors who had focused their attention on Newman's *Essay* see A. Nichols, *From Newman to Congar. The Idea of Doctrinal Development from the Victorians to the Second Vatican Council* (Edinburgh, 1990).
[3] Vatican II, *Dei Verbum*, 9.

Church – the mystery of communion between God and man – is the guardian of this deposit and the agent of its transmission: "in her doctrine, life and worship, [she] perpetuates and transmits to every generation all that she herself is, all that she believes." In other words, the Church is both the agent and the content of Tradition. Invoking Vatican Council I, the Constitution goes on to stress that Tradition is a living principle, and that the idea of progress is an integral part of it: "The Tradition that comes from the apostles makes progress in the Church, with the help of the Holy Spirit. There is growth in insight into the realities and words that are being passed on." *Dei Verbum* adds that this dynamism of the Church transcends time: she is "always advancing towards the plenitude of divine truth, until eventually the words of God are fulfilled in her."[4] Within that process, Tradition acts as the living principle of revelation, pointing towards an eschatological realization in the fullness of knowledge and love at the end of time, "when everything has been subjected to him, then the Son himself will be subjected to the One who has subjected everything to him, so that God *may be all in all*" (1 Cor 15:28).

1. Development and Tradition

"From the time I became a Catholic, of course I have no further history of my religious opinions to narrate. In saying this, I do not mean to say that my mind has been idle, or that I have given up thinking on theological subjects; but that I have no variations to record."[5] A superficial reading of Newman's words in the last chapter of his *Apologia* might suggest a rather unpromising future for development within the Catholic Church. Did he think that the fullness of divine truth the Catholic Church claims to possess put an end to the possibility of doctrinal development within it? Nothing could be further removed from Newman's mind, who in the *Essay* had described development as a permanent law of the Church, one not to be arrested until her eschatological fulfilment. With that sentence in the *Apologia* he wanted to clarify the difference between 'variations' and 'development', between 'development' and 'evolution'. Newman's fundamental concerns during the long years of study leading towards the *Development* had been continuity and identity. The differences between the present–day Church and Primitive Christianity were

---

[4] Vatican II, *Dei Verbum*, 8.
[5] J.H. Newman, *Apologia pro Vita Sua* (London, 1913), p. 238.

such as to make it difficult to appreciate the identity between the two, and led to questions regarding the continuity in time of the Church founded by Christ. Did Christ's Church still exist? If so, which among the different claimants was its true continuation? How to account for the differences between the early Church and that of the nineteenth century? The *Development of Christian Doctrine* was the result of years of study and intellectual struggle to answer those questions.

One thing was clear to Newman from the very beginning: development was not evolution, as Darwin would later understand it. Their respective theories were separated by more than the decade that elapsed between the publication of the *Development* and that of the *Origin of Species*: they were concerned with different phenomena and described different processes. Evolution involves a diversification of the original organism, bringing forth new life forms that belong to genera or species totally different from the original, and so genetically diverse that the latter are no longer able to interbreed with the parent species (were this still to exist).[6] Newman did not contemplate the possibility of a diversity of true churches evolving from an original and originating Church, professing incompatible doctrines, and following irreconcilable practices. Development, as Newman described it, represents the organic growth of a living being towards adulthood, while preserving its identity and original nature; doctrinal developments do not supersede the original truth, they only illustrate and reinforce it.

During most of his Anglican period Newman had defended the continuity and identity of the Christian Church on the basis of the Vincentian canon: *quod semper, quod ubique, quod ab omnibus* (the faith that has been believed 'always, everywhere, and by all'). The faith of the primitive Church was the faith of today's Church; Christians in the nineteenth century did not believe something different from what was believed in the early Church, neither did they believe more. Catholicity, Antiquity, and the consent of Fathers, constitute the proper evidence of the Apostolicity of any professed tradition.[7] The primitive Church, Newman explained, is the sufficient authority and guide in matters of faith.[8] The present-day Church may impose

---

[6] For this distinction see for example S. Jaki's introduction to Newman's *An Essay on the Development of Christian Doctrine* (Pinckney, 2003), pp. xiii ff.

[7] J.H. Newman, *Lectures on the Prophetical Office of the Church* (new edn, London, 1897), p. 51.

[8] Newman, 'Third Letter to Jager', in L. Allen, *John Henry Newman and the Abbé Jager*

nothing to be believed as of necessary faith but what the early Church taught, founded on Scripture. He therefore rejected the possibility of any doctrinal developments adding new truths to be believed by the faithful. At this point, he clearly stated his case against Rome: she had continued adding to the fundamentals of the faith, and had declared as necessary for salvation doctrines founded on the sole authority of Tradition.[9]

Newman and the early Tractarians had a somewhat ambivalent relationship with Tradition. They acknowledged that it preceded Scripture in the definition and communication of the Faith: the writing of Scripture presupposes the foundation of churches, and the foundation of churches in its turn presupposes the delivering of the faith on which they were built. The oral teaching of the Apostles was the sole rule of faith before Holy Scripture was written, and it remained such until the books of the New Testament were not only written, but also collected into a canon and received by all the churches (for not every book contains all things necessary for salvation): a process that might have lasted till the end of the second or even the beginning of the third century AD. Nor did Tradition's role end once the Scriptures had been written, for the latter were interpreted within the Tradition the churches already possessed.[10] At this point, however, the Tractarians were confronted by a thorny question. They recognised that Apostolic authority (divinely granted) embraced and underwrote all their teaching, whether later contained in the sacred books or not. Had this authority been superseded by the writing of the Scriptures? The Tractarians hinted at times that this was not the case; on other occasions, they retreated into the Anglican principle that Scripture contained all that was to be believed. The question, then, was: were Christians supposed to believe more before the Scriptures were written than after they were complete? The conundrum was never solved satisfactorily.

Newman's firm rejection of the possibility of doctrinal development was shaken by Wiseman's 1839 article on the Donatists in the *Dublin Review*.[11] There, Wiseman had quoted St Augustine's dictum: *securus iudicat*

(London, 1975), p. 122.

[9] Newman, 'First Letter to Jager', in Allen, *Newman and Jager*, p. 45; see also *Prophetical Office*, pp. 212, 236 et al.

[10] See for example H.E. Manning, *The Rule of Faith* (London, 1838), pp. 27–8.

[11] N. Wiseman, *The High-Church Claims: or, a Series of Papers on the Oxford Controversy*, n. 5, Catholic Institute Tracts, n. 19 (London, n.d.), pp. 96ff.

TRADITION AND DEVELOPMENT

orbis terrarum, paraphrasing it as follows: "any Church, in one portion of the world, could not possibly be allowed to be right, while protesting against the union of other Churches over the rest of the world. The very fact of its being in such position, at once condemns it and proves it to be in schism."[12] Those words had seismic effects for Newman in the areas of Church unity, Antiquity and doctrinal development. He had decided to go by Antiquity, and here one of its main oracles was advancing a rule to settle doctrinal questions different from that of Vincent of Lerins and in apparent contradiction to it. "Antiquity," he would later write, "was deciding against itself."[13]

The outcome of the following months of spiritual and intellectual turmoil involved the reconciliation between the Vincentian *quod semper* and the Augustinian *securus*, probably on the basis of a new understanding of the former along the lines hinted at in his *Tract 85*. There, while maintaining that all things necessary for salvation are contained in Scripture, Newman added that points of faith might lie under the surface of Holy Writ.[14] This seems to have offered him the stepping-stone he needed towards admitting the possibility of doctrinal developments. In his 1843 university sermon he would clearly maintain that any new doctrine or doctrines adopted and proposed by the Church to be believed by the faithful were implicitly included in the primitive creed, and thus held by earlier Christians. If one of these doctrines were "now to be received, as surely it must be, as part of the Creed, it [the doctrine in question] was really held everywhere from the beginning, and therefore, in a measure, held as a mere religious impression, and perhaps an unconscious one."[15]

Newman's older concept of *realizing* was also an integral part of his newly conceived theory of development. His *Parochial and Plain Sermons* had dealt with a particular dimension of *realizing*: the passing from *notional* to *real* knowledge. In the *University Sermons* – in the 'Theory of Developments' (1843), in particular – Newman concentrated his attention on another, closely related aspect of the same

---

[12] Wiseman, *High Church Claims*, p. 97.

[13] Newman, *Apologia*, p. 117.

[14] [J.H. Newman], *Lectures on the Scripture Proof of the Doctrines of the Church*, *Tracts for the Times* n. 85 (London, 1838), pp. 14 et al.

[15] J.H. Newman, 'Theory of Developments', in *Sermons chiefly on the Theory of Religious Belief. Preached before the University of Oxford* [*US*] (London, 1843), p. 324; these words resemble the ones he had previously used when speaking of the Roman theory of development.

process of *realizing*: the progress from *implicit* to *explicit* knowledge. The Church's progressive *realizing* of revealed truths grows in 'intenseness', manifesting itself in verbal expression, theological treatment, and dogmatic definition.[16] Particular doctrines are more or less present (*realized*) to the consciousness of the Church: doctrines dogmatically defined are more realized than non-defined revealed truths, and those expressed in words are more realized than those that are not.

2. Development and 'ethos'

The concept of *realizing*, however, cannot be understood fully if it is not presented within Newman's theory of knowledge, of which it is an important part. The Tractarians felt that a knowledge involving a practical dimension could neither progress properly, nor be free from distortion, if the known truths were not to influence the life of the student. An education that led students to view subjects that were essentially practical in the light of mere theories, or solely as a way to academic distinction, involved a profanation of the discipline in question, and could lead to excessive self-confidence, arrogance, and intellectual rationalism.[17] And rationalism, when dealing with supernatural realities, was the intellectual equivalent of the blind leading the blind: they were bound to fall into the ditch of error. The Tractarians transferred to the knowledge of faith the Aristotelian concept of *phronesis*: that it is impossible to be practically wise – i.e. to discern the good to aim at, and the means to achieve it – without also being morally upright; the virtuous man possesses a certain instinct to detect what is ethically good. The principle, when translated from the practical to the intellectual level, professes that those who are faithful to the truth – who receive and incorporate it into their lives – have a special divine assistance to help them along the path of Christian knowledge. This moral temper or *ethos* involves openness to God's action in the soul and a humble disposition of mind and heart – opposed to the self-sufficiency of rationalism or the self-righteous confidence of private judgement; it also implies a generous spirit, capable of following a radical ideal. It might be said, indeed, that

---

[16] Newman's distinction between Apostolic and Prophetical Traditions did not constitute a step towards the conception of the theory of development. As a matter of fact, the concept was coined to deny doctrinal development. Prophetical Tradition finds its role here, as part of the process generating doctrinal developments.

[17] See for example F. Oakeley, *Remarks on the Study of Aristotelian and Platonic Ethics as a Branch of the Oxford System of Education* (Oxford, 1837), pp. 14-15.

there are no purely intellectual lights: every truth involves a certain giving of direction for present or future action. Newman considered that holiness (love of God) was the eye of faith, and the words of Scripture seemed to confirm this contention: "a good will to do His Will shall know of the doctrine if it is from God" (Jn 7:17). A right heart preserves clear the vision of its object, and acts as the safeguard of faith, protecting it against the vicious extremes of heresy or superstition. The words of an earlier sermon, though set in another context, describe well what Newman came to feel with increasing force in the late 1830s: "in him who is faithful to his own divinely implanted nature, the faint light of Truth dawns continually brighter; the shadows which at first trouble it, the unreal shapes created by its own twilight-state, vanish."[18]

The process of *realizing* is a complex one. *Dei Verbum* 8, when speaking about the progress of Tradition, adds that it comes about "through the contemplation and study of believers, who ponder these things in their hearts. It comes from the intimate sense of spiritual realities which they experience. And it comes from the preaching of those who have received, along with their right of succession in the episcopate, the sure charism of truth." Newman's *Essay* offers a richer description of the process as such and of the possible ways in which development may take place. To start with, Newman was very reluctant to over-stress the dependence of doctrinal development on a logic process, the piling up of conclusions on primary and original truths by way of syllogism. As a matter of fact, he was somewhat suspicious of mere logic – 'paper logic', as he called it. He felt that, for the most part, we gain new truths (natural or supernatural) without being fully conscious of the intermediate states. "We cannot tell when we first held this, or first held that doctrine." Men "are gradually modifying and changing their opinions, while they think they remain stationary."[19] Newman described the manner of this development in his novel *Loss and Gain*, when portraying the religious evolution of his main character, Charles Reding. Charles had turned his thoughts away from religious controversy but, unknown to himself, his religious views had continued progressing all the while: the slow spontaneous action of the mind had helped ideas take shape, find their place and establish connexions with previously held notions, putting forth new

---

[18] Newman, 'Personal Influence, the Means of Propagating the Truth' (22 Jan. 1832), US, p. 66.
[19] J.H. Newman, 'Difficulty of Realizing', *Parochial and Plain Sermons* [PPS], vi (London, 1899), pp. 102.

shoots.[20] Then, one day the new truth or truths burst unexpectedly into his consciousness.

The sudden and unexpected moment of *realizing* involves the perception and subsequent conceptual expression of a 'new' truth, as the result usually of a long process: the slow maturing of principles already held, accompanied by a deep and vital appropriation of such a truth. There is no one way in which this *realizing* may occur: it might be granted directly by God's illumination; it might take place while meditating or reading the Scriptures, when its sense suddenly breaks upon the reader as it had never done before; it might be mediated through a person, introducing another to truths he did not know or helping him understand previously half-understood ones; it might result from the application of principles to particular circumstances or problems.[21] The list is not an exhaustive one. In any of these or in other ways, the individual in question comes to perceive, at the appropriate time and according to his personal dispositions, new dimensions of already held principles, corollaries of known truths, the path he is to follow, and so on. Logic, in Newman's view, plays second fiddle in this process. It may be called now to establish the connexions between the truth formally held and those newly perceived, or to be the record of what has already taken place and to analyse what had been a process of implicit (non-logical) reasoning, complete in itself. Newman could even say that Faith is not 'compatible' with logical processes; these cannot bring about the *realizing* which characterizes the true act of Faith.[22]

This process of development, besides, is not uniform and continuous, for it is dependent not only on the work of the Holy Spirit but also on man's openness to His action. As we have seen, Newman thought that development owed less to formal logic than to the moral character (*ethos*) of the individual. The latter is the result of his ethical history – i.e. of his actions and the habits that have arisen from them – and of his experience of reality. A particular *ethos* manifests itself in a series of basic intellectual 'prejudices' (or principles) governing thought and action. Within this general structure, the predominant principle or tendency governs the interplay of the other principles and their respective influences, and defines the character and thought of a person. As a result, an idea or argument might strike two minds very differently, awake dissimilar

---

[20] J.H. Newman, *Loss and Gain. The History of a Convert* (13th edn, London, 1898), p. 202.

[21] Newman, 'Divine Calls', PPS, viii [1899], pp. 24–5, 28–30, et al.

[22] Newman, Apologia, p. 169; see also 'Explicit and Implicit Reason', US, p. 258ff.

associations, and even lead to opposite conclusions, depending on their respective intellectual principles, which, in their turn, rest ultimately on the dominant moral ones.

Newman considered that doctrines also have their own proper principles, in which they live and develop: the "life of doctrines may be said to consist in the law or principle which they embody," and doctrines "are developed by the operation of principles, and develop differently according to those principles."[23] As a result, the principles of a specific individual could harmonise or enter into conflict with those of a particular truth; if in conflict, the resolution of this tension in favour of the principles of the doctrine or of those of the individual in question would determine the direction of the development. Newman thought that a truth (natural or revealed) held without its corresponding principles would at best remain barren, a 'sham' supported by circumstances external to it; at worst – as in the case of a doctrine developed on the basis of an alien principle – it would generate error or heresy. A true development, on the other hand, would retain "both the doctrine and the principle with which it started."[24] In this sense, principle is a better test of heresy and orthodoxy than doctrine; the doctrines of heresy are transient but its principles are permanent.[25]

Thus, for Newman, a person experienced in the life of virtue and desirous to do good would have a sort of instinct for truth, making him or her more able to detect the bent of a particular doctrine. This was part of God's providential plan. Keble would say: "it has been God's will to constitute uprightness, rather than ability, judge of the truth on the highest of all subjects."[26] On the other hand, as St Paul had written to Timothy, "evil men and seducers shall wax worse and worse, deceiving and being deceived" (2 Tim 3:13). Newman and his Tractarian friends thought that there is a sort of blinding power in moral disease, particularly in pride, leading those affected by it along an inexorable descent from error into further error; a sliding into heterodoxy which could only be arrested by spiritual conversion.

Present-day academic pressures to publish, combined at times with a

---

[23] Newman, *Development*, pp. 67 and 71 [178 and 180]. Newman introduced numerous changes in the 3rd and definitive edition of the *Essay*; the pages in brackets correspond to the 1909 reprint of it.

[24] Newman, *Development*, p. 72 [181].

[25] Newman, *Development*, p. 72 [181].

[26] Keble, 'Implicit Faith Recognised by Reason,' in *Sermons Academical and Occasional* (London, 1847), p. 42.

desire to make a name for oneself by revisionist novel approaches, have exacerbated the danger of discordance between the principles of revealed truth and those of the academic theologian. The connexion between the search for sanctity and theological investigation which was the mark of the Fathers and of the great theologians like Thomas Aquinas, Bonaventure and others is no longer seen as part of the *bene esse* (well-being) of theology. For Newman it was of its very essence. Otherwise, he thought, theology would lose its character of sapiential knowledge and become mere 'erudition'; and mere erudition would open the door to a rationalism that would end by reviving heresies long dead and often condemned. Newman considered that theology, to be truly such, needs to keep alive its original driving force: the love of God as the impulse behind the search for the knowledge of the divine other.

3. Development and Faith

If charity was for Newman a fundamental ingredient in the makeup of the theologian, so was humble faith. Revealed truth rejects the proud effort of those who try to impose on it human categories, while revealing itself to the humble.[27] Like the wise scribe of the gospel (Mt 13:52), Tradition brings out of the storehouse of revelation things both old and new, truths confessed for generations and others which had been hidden in the depths of faith and practice, lived out but without being formally acknowledged or finding explicit formulation. Development involves a deeper apprehension and a more lucid enunciation of the original dogma. Newman never lost the anchor of faith provided by the Vincentian *quod semper*, and had accepted the idea of development only after discovering that it implied the preservation of the original truth: development did not change truth, but only perfected it. His concept of doctrinal development was as far removed from rationalism as from any form of historicism involving a development without roots, without the anchor of Holy Scripture and Tradition. He also rejected a concept of Tradition fossilized in a particular era of Church history. This kind of 'traditionalism' would involve the betrayal of Tradition's very nature; it would put a stop to the growth of the Church towards its final fulfilment and, in denying truth its natural growth, would not even be able to protect the truths it claimed to defend. As Newman wrote,

---

[27] Mt 11:25: "I bless you, Father, Lord of heaven and earth for hiding these things from the learned and the clever and revealing them to little children."

one of the causes of "corruption in religion is the refusal to follow the course of doctrine as it moves on, and an obstinacy in the notions of the past."[28] A living organism prevented from its natural growth and constrained by unnatural pressures is eventually deformed, and ends up misshapen and monstrous.

A deformation may also result when revelation is forced into the mould of a philosophy which does not respect revelation's fundamental metaphysical principles about the world and man. The pluralism of today's philosophical speculation, which provides many different – and at times conflicting – accounts of reality, seems to make it difficult to establish a common conceptual and linguistic foundation for theology. The theologies emerging from such disparate philosophies might, as a result, become closed in themselves. Would this, as some have suggested, spell the end of development? Like the much-talked-of 'end of history', the announcement of the demise of doctrinal development is in fact premature. On the one hand it ignores divine providence, which leads the Church and history towards its fulfilment. On the other hand, the fact that some current philosophic-theological trends have led many theologians into an intellectual cul-de-sac does not imply that there is no way forward. But progress may require turning round and retracing one's steps until a point is reached (clearly mapped and solidly founded) that offers a reliable basis for renewed development. As far as philosophy is concerned, theological development would no doubt be facilitated by a return to the basic principles of the philosophy of Thomas Aquinas, as recommended by Vatican II and John Paul II. Such a philosophy not closed into a rigid scholasticism but able to assimilate the positive contributions of other philosophical systems, would offer a common intellectual foundation on which to build dialogue and theological development. Newman is himself an example of this: his theory of knowledge, while being highly personal, is in general agreement with Aristotelian – Thomist principles, and it adds new and positive insights into the nature of knowledge in general and of religious knowledge in particular.[29]

At this stage, Newman would also have introduced – as he does in the *Essay* – the need for some authority to arrange and authenticate the various expressions and results of theological enquiry, separating true theological developments from corruption and error.[30] The

[28] Newman, *Development* (1845), p. 61 [177].

[29] L. Richardson, *Newman's Approach to Knowledge* (Leominster, 2007).

[30] Newman, *Development of Doctrine* (1845), 116-7 [77-8].

reopening of a proper path for development requires a 'rediscovery' of the role of the Magisterium (both solemn and ordinary) in the process of doctrinal development. However, the panorama of much recent theological speculation offers few grounds for optimism in this respect. Dogma is often resented as a shackle, a limit in the construction of theology, rather than a window opened upon the infinite.[31] In addition, the sustained rejection of the ordinary Magisterium of the Church has become one of the features of much post-Vatican II theology. Theologians have dramatically devalued its role. At times, they have done this indirectly by patronizing the Magisterium, treating it with the condescension with which a professor might regard the arguments of a wayward pupil's essay. Other theologians have adopted a novel view of the teaching Church: its role, in their opinion, is merely to give conceptual form and promulgate the *sensus fidelium*, the consensus of believers. Newman offered them unintentional protection under the wings of his 'On Consulting the Faithful in Matters of Doctrine', a paper few have read but many are ready to misrepresent (as they did in the Cardinal's time). He was far from those sentiments and often insisted on the importance of the *pietas fidei*: rejecting the ordinary Magisterium on the grounds that it is not infallible would be not only sinful but even unreasonable, given the Holy Spirit's general assistance to the Church.[32]

It has also been claimed that today's Magisterium cannot pronounce on present-day theological questions; it is bound by its very nature to be perpetually unable to 'catch up with' theological developments. This has always been the case. The principal role of the Magisterium, however, is not that of a standards agency, providing a hallmark for theological speculation before it is offered to the public. Jansen may have died three years before his doctrines were censured by Rome; still, his errors (adopted by some) were condemned long before they seriously affected the faith of the mass of the faithful, lay and clerical. It is true that present-day hurried and superficial media coverage makes the Magisterium's task of scrutinising new theological trends and propositions doubly difficult; it also makes it that much more necessary. This task would be greatly simplified if the theologians were

---

[31] J. Ratzinger, *Milestones. Memoirs 1927-1977* (San Francisco, 1997), 52; *The Ratzinger Report* (Leominster, 1985), 72.

[32] See for example his letter to Flanagan, 15 Feb. 1868, in J.D. Holmes (ed.), *The Theological Papers of John Henry Newman on Biblical Inspiration and on Infallibility* (Oxford, 1979), p. 155; and Newman's 'Letter to the Duke of Norfolk', in *Certain Difficulties felt by Anglicans in Catholic Teaching*, ii (London, 1898), pp. 257-8, 339, 345.

to pay greater consideration to preceding magisterial pronouncements (solemn and ordinary). Not a few theological propositions being put forward nowadays have already been the object of more than one magisterial declaration: present-day renewals of Arian Christological errors and heresies condemned in the early centuries of the Church bear testimony to the fact.

Most aspects of Newman's theory of development are by now common theological patrimony, in particular his notes of true doctrinal developments. The deeper implications of some of these notes, however, have not been fully understood, as a result of neglecting their intellectual background. The genesis of Newman's theory of development reveals the fundamental role played in it by his ideas about religious knowledge and its dependence on moral temper (*ethos*). This is perhaps Newman's most interesting contribution to present theological endeavours: the insight that the right *ethos* is the only adequate stimulus to initiate theological enquiry, and a necessary guide for its development. The present descent of Theology faculties towards Religious Studies status, and eventually towards inclusion (as seems only too likely) into the Sociology faculty is one of the results of neglecting this basic principle. Theology for Newman is an act of faith, of openness to God's communication to man; it is an act of charity, a yearning for a deeper communion with the Truth and the Life of God; it is also an act of humility, as the acknowledgement of man's intellectual limitation before the greatness of the mystery helps him to avoid imposing a rationalist reductionism on revelation and to accept the guidance provided by God through the Magisterium. True, the theologian must be a man of scholarship, but he must also be a man of prayer.[33] Theology was for Newman a sapiential knowledge, not an exact science; as such, the moral temper of the individual plays a determining role in the direction of his thought. This was a lesson he never tired of repeating. At the distance of one hundred and sixty years from the publication of the *Essay*, Newman keeps reminding us about it.

---

[33] This has a second dimension. Cardinal Ratzinger wrote often about how the theologian, while paying attention to the developments in history and scholarship, should pay even more attention to the testimony of the saints, their experience of the reality of God in prayer (J. Ratzinger, *To look on Christ. Exercises in Faith, Hope and Love* (New York, 1991), p. 33).

Chapter 14

NEWMAN, TRADITION AND NINETEENTH-CENTURY PROTESTANT THEOLOGY

by Edward Enright

I. John Henry Newman

Tradition is integrally tied up with history. Divine revelation, God's own self-communication, took place in key historical events, the Exodus for the Jews, Jesus for the Christians, continuity as well as change having taken place during the course of these events and the events that took place both before and after them. This revelation was, according to Jewish and at least some Christian interpretations, passed on to generation after generation in both oral and written forms, some official and some unofficial. Tradition, whether both written and oral or just written, is by its very nature historical; if something is passed to different generations in different places, time and culture have necessarily to be involved. Tradition, therefore, has been understood to include the process of handing on, and the content of that process, the content being molded by the time and place, the very culture of the process. Both the process and the content of tradition are temporally and culturally bound; in other words, historically bound.

On the whole the Protestant interpretation of tradition has included, at least in its content, both the Patristic and the Reformation interpretations of Scripture, the process of tradition of course being presumed. While the magisterial Reformation would have ideally desired Spirit-guided individual interpretation of Scripture, Luther and Calvin, at least, came to understand that the interpretation of Scripture needed some guidance, which they were more than willing to offer, for example, in Luther's *Small Catechism* and Calvin's *Institutes of the Christian Religion*. They both engaged with the Fathers of the Church in their theological writings, and while not allowing the Fathers to be understood as a source of revelation, their interpretations of Scripture were understood to be helpful and, therefore, to be respected, if not necessarily taken as the last word. The Bible would, of course, be the ultimate source for the record of revelation and, therefore, of faith and doctrine.

Newman's interpretation of tradition was honed by his writings in response to issues, ideologies, and movements both within and outside the Church. Newman's thought on tradition was stated in a number of writings during his Anglican period. In fact, anything written on the subject as a Catholic was, more or less, a repetition in pastoral circumstances of what he had already proposed before his conversion to Roman Catholicism. Except for filtering out the anti-Catholic statements in later additions of his works, he maintained a consistency between the Anglican and Roman Catholic phases of his life.

Often Newman has been studied either in isolation, or in the context of his British contemporaries. But he lived and wrote in a time when much theological and historical thinking was happening on the Continent as well. With the exception of the Catholic Tubingen School at the beginning of the century and the Roman Catholic Modernists at the end of the century, the only creative (and some would question whether it was creative) theological writing besides that of Newman by Roman Catholics during the nineteenth century was done by Thomists, the most important being Johann Baptist Franzelin, Joseph Kleutgen and Matthias Joseph Scheeben, the first two Jesuits, and the last one a diocesan priest, but all Germans. Otherwise, the nineteenth century is the century of Protestant theology. To name just a few, there were Schleiermacher, Baur, Ritschl, Harnack, Hermann, the early Troeltsch, and of course Kierkegaard. So, Newman has some pretty impressive company in the development of ideas that set the theological agenda for the twentieth century and beyond. The present author will only be able to look at Newman in relation to Schleiermacher, the 'Father of modern liberal Protestant theology', and Adolf von Harnack, the 'Father of modern church history. Newman had some knowledge of Schleiermacher's thinking, his *Christian Faith* having been translated fairly early on.

Even though, neither Newman nor Harnack had any knowledge of the other, both have been compared because they have so much in common in their thought on development, though they, of course, differ as well.

To one degree or another both the two Protestant theologians and Newman held that tradition was to be understood under two headings: the relationship between Scripture and tradition, and the development of doctrine. Consequently, after exposing Newman's ideas on both of these themes, with the greater emphasis on the first during the 1830s (limited to *Essays Critical and Historical* and *Lectures on the Prophetical Office of the Church*) and the second during the 1840s (limited to *An Essay on the Development of Christian Doctrine*), the same will be done with Schleiermacher, and Harnack. A major difference in the following presentation of Newman in contradistinction to the two Protestant theologians, is that, because Newman can be counted among the greatest rhetoricians in history and his way with language being so colorfully descriptive and creatively poignant, the author will allow Newman to speak mostly for himself. The positions of the two Protestant theologians, due to lack of space, will be summarized, with notation as to where the reader can turn to make their own take on these thinkers. The conclusion will make clear the similarities and differences between and among Newman and the two Protestant thinkers.

A. Essays Critical and Historical

Dedicated to his friend, William Froude, Esq., FRS, whose brother Hurrell, an even closer friend, had died in 1836, the collection entitled *Essays Critical and Historical*, published in 1871, is made up of a number of Newman's Anglican essays composed between 1828 and 1846. The piece most pertinent for us is 'Apostolical Tradition', composed in 1836. Newman in an appended note advises the reader that "it was written before Dr Hampden's appointment to the Regius Professorship of Divinity" at Oxford University in February of that year. Newman writes that it was "a continuation of a series of protests conscientiously made against his [Dr Hampden's] theology by the author and others from the date of November, 1834."[1] In his defense of what he believed to be the authentic view of Anglican doctrine,

---

[1] *Essays Critical and Historical* (London: Longmans, Green and Co., 1919) 1, p. 137. R.D. Hampton was a good example of the anti-dogmatic liberals that Newman and the Oxford Movement challenged theologically.

Newman argued that it is true that "Scripture has one, and but one, teaching, one direct and definite sense, on the sacred matters of which it treats, and that it is the test of revealed truth." However, he goes on to say about Scripture, that

> as Anglicans, we maintain that it is not its own interpreter, and that, as an historical fact, it has ever been furnished for individuals with an interpreter which is external to its readers and infallible, that is, with an ecclesiastical Tradition, derived in the first instance from the Apostles – a Tradition illuminating Scripture and protecting it; moreover, that this Tradition, and not Scripture itself, is our immediate and practical authority for such high doctrines [Trinity and Incarnation].[2]

Newman is very emphatic here in his disagreement with the Latitudinarians in the Church of England, and with Protestantism in general, that the interpretation of Scripture is not to be left to private judgment. On a practical level, furthermore, he is saying to his addressees in so many words, "you have got to be kidding if you think that the ordinary people in the pew have learned about their fundamental Christian beliefs from studying and interpreting Scripture on their own". "To the millions for whom Redemption has been wrought, creeds and catechisms, liturgies and a theological system, the multitudinous ever-sounding voice, the categorical, peremptory incisiveness, the (so to say) full chime, of ecclesiastical authority, is a first necessity, if they are to realize the world unseen." In fact, he notes that if interpretation of Scripture is left to the individual's private judgment, then it would be impossible to agree universally on "any certainties in Revelation whatever."[3]

Newman, being one of the leading authorities in England at the time on the Fathers of the Church, and believing that their interpretations of Scripture were essential to the belief system of the Church of England, is going to wonder what one of his opponents is doing ironically when he turns to the Fathers to support what he believes he has discovered by his own individual lights. Newman's question is to ask, why would one or more of the Father's interpretations be supportive of the meaning of the Scriptures? The answer for him, he feels, should be obvious. That support, "that testimony comes close upon the Apostles, and thereby is more likely to convey to us their sense of a Scripture passage." Such a testimony, he firmly believes,

---

[2] Newman, *Ess.* 1, p. 103.
[3] Newman, *Ess.* 1, pp. 121, 104.

JOHN HENRY NEWMAN DOCTOR OF THE CHURCH

"has a certain Apostolical authority in explaining Scripture." What would have really startled his opponents would be his belief that that testimony "is a source of Christian truth in some sense independent of Scripture – a guide to a certain extent superseding the need of private judgment." Without this apostolic authority, the interpretation of one of the Fathers would be just another opinion, no better than anyone else's. So, why bother consulting the Fathers at all![4] Newman later argues that if the Bible is considered to be the one and only authority, then the ordinary Christian will define him/herself as a believer in a book rather than the doctrine that is found in the book.[5]

What Newman has been writing so far in this essay has been leading up to the climax of his position, that is, the doctrines of the Church of England about the Trinity and the Incarnation did not come from the private interpretation of Scripture by individuals but the tradition flowing without interruption from the time of the Apostles. Furthermore, it is his belief that these doctrines were passed on orally by various and sundry means, such as "conversations, catechizings, preachings, ecclesiastical determinations, prayers,"[6] as well as in the biblical writings. He goes so far as to say that, even if there had been no Scriptures, the doctrines Anglicans believe in would have come down to them over the centuries by all of the above means, and then some. In support of this position, he quotes St Robert Bellarmine, as well as certain Fathers and Vincent of Lerins, but also noting that Bellarmine would agree that, with regard to Scripture, tradition can be understood as interpretation, as well as distinct from Scripture. Newman then quotes Jacques-Bénigne Bossuet to bring the two distinct but mutually related views of tradition together, Bossuet saying, Newman agreeing, that the authority of both the unwritten word and the written word, having come from Jesus Christ, "makes us receive with *equal veneration* all that has been taught by the Apostles."[7]

Newman spends much of the remainder of the essay proving his point by studying the continuity from the Apostles through to Nicaea and beyond, and doing so, as is fitting with his thinking generally and the nineteenth century approach to knowledge both in theory and in

---

[4] Newman, *Ess.* 1, pp. 107,108.

[5] Newman, *Ess.* 1, p. 111.

[6] Newman, *Ess.* 1, pp. 112,115.

[7] Newman, *Ess.* 1, p. 118; Bossuet was one of Louis XIV's court bishops and one of the great apologists for Christianity during the seventeenth century. Newman is quoting from Bossuet's *Expositions of Catholic Doctrine on Matters of Controversy*.

practice, by taking a view of history.[8] There are three points within this discussion that should be noted. The first is his reference to a deposit of faith: "A body of doctrine has been delivered by the Apostles to their successors, and by them in turn to the next generation, and then to the next." He quotes approvingly from Vincent of Lerins that a deposit is "that which hath been intrusted to you, not that which thou hast discovered; what thou hast received, not what thou hast thought out; a matter, not of cleverness, but of teaching, not of private handling, but of public tradition."[9] The second point is his use of what he would eventually call the convergence of probabilities. Here he makes use of such terms as 'catholicity', 'unanimity', and 'joint testimony'. With regard to the decision made at the First Council of Nicaea in 315 AD about Our Lord's divinity, Newman wrote, that it was "not merely the decision of a majority; but simply and plainly the joint testimony of many local bodies, as independent witnesses to the separate existence in each of them, from time immemorial, of that great dogma in which they found each other to agree."[10] The third and final point is his naive belief at this time that the "theory of a development" from the Apostles to Nicaea I with regard to Christ's divinity "is not tenable." Newman wrote: "Nor can it be successfully maintained that an identity of doctrine, such as is found in AD 325, in such various quarters of Christendom, was the gradual, silent, insensible, homogeneous growth of the intermediate period, during which the vague statements of Apostles, parallel to those in Scripture, were adjusted and completed."[11]

The essay comes to a close with Newman's use of arguments from William Paley, an Anglican, to further bolster his position that Scripture and tradition working together provide a firm foundation for any Anglican's faith in the doctrines that they have been taught to believe.[12]

B. Via Media

Moving on to *Lectures on the Prophetical Office of the Church Viewed Relatively to Romanism and Popular Protestantism*, published in the next year, 1837, and constituting the first volume of his *Via Media*,

---

[8] Newman, *Ess.* 1, pp. 122 - 130 passim.

[9] Newman, *Ess.* 1, pp. 125,126; Newman is quoting from Vincent's well-known treatise entitled the *Commonitorium*.

[10] Newman, *Ess.* 1, p. 128.

[11] Newman, *Ess.* 1, p. 129.

[12] Newman, *Ess.* 1, pp. 131-134 passim.

the reader finds Newman making a distinction he had not made in *Essays Critical and Historical,* that is, a distinction between what he calls 'Episcopal Tradition' and 'Prophetical Tradition'. Before going into this distinction, Newman discussed the notion of tradition more generally. While much of what has already been said in the *Essays* we have perused can be found here, there are some additional points that require looking at. One in particular would belie Newman's denial in the *Essays* that no theory of development has been involved in the movement of a Christian teaching from the time of the Apostles up to and beyond Nicaea I. He does not use the word 'development', but he does make use of words that will become prominent in his not-too-distant writings on doctrinal development. If you will, his later position is 'latent' in his position here adumbrated in the *Lectures.*

Newman begins with a typical (for him) comparison of the Roman Catholic, Anglo-Catholic, and Protestant approaches to use of the Bible (note that he makes a clear distinction between the Anglo-Catholic and the Protestant traditions). He does this concisely in a single paragraph, mentioning the difference between the Anglican and Roman positions on the relationship between the creed and the Bible. While the Roman Catholic would say quite publicly and at any time that he or she can prove the articles of the creed from Scripture, the Anglican would "take this ground only in controversy, not in teaching our own people or in our private studies." Furthermore, he writes that none of the Christian denominations who claim to base their faith on Scripture alone actually does so. Rather, none of them "embraces the whole Bible, none of them is able to interpret the whole, none of them has a key which will revolve through the entire compass of the words which lie within. Each has its favourite text, and neglects the rest." On the other hand, the Anglo-Catholic turns to "Antiquity to strengthen such intimations of doctrine as are but faintly, though really given in Scripture." And then, there is Protestantism. His polemics come out here when he writes that Protestantism "considers it a hardship to have anything clearly and distinctly told it in elucidation of Scripture doctrine, an infringement of its right of doubting, and mistaking, and labouring in vain."[13]

He returns then to his presentation on Roman Catholics and, in doing so, uses an analogy with his own idea found particularly in his writings on faith and reason, that no one can express all at once what

[13] *The Via Media of the Anglican Church Illustrated in Lectures, Letters and Tracts written between 1830 and 1841* (London: Longmans, Green, and Co., 1899) 1, pp. 28-9, 159, 239.

they know about such and such, but reveals what he or she does know on a particular topic when called upon to do so. What Newman approves here in the Roman Catholic position is that the Apostles could not possibly have put everything they knew and wanted to say into writing: "No one you fall in with on the highway, can tell you all his mind at once; much less could the Apostles ... digest in one Epistle or Treatise a systematic view of the Revelation made to them." The Romans, he said, argue that the New Testament is "an incomplete document," lacking "harmony or consistency in its parts." Furthermore, the New Testament does not offer us any legal code, or a "list of fundamentals." It is in what is written later in the *Lectures* where hints of his acceptance and proposal of doctrinal development begin to emerge. Tradition "is latent, but it lives. It is silent, like the rapids of a river, before the rocks intercept it. It is the Church's unconscious habit of opinion and sentiment; which reflects upon, masters, and expresses, according to the emergency." He goes on to say what he said in the *Essays*, that all Christians come to "receive through Tradition both the Bible itself, and the doctrine that it is divinely inspired," and that in fact Christians "derive their faith" from tradition and not from Scripture.[14] Newman, however, did not let Roman Catholics off easily. Like Protestants and his fellow Anglo-Catholics, he chastises Roman Catholics for substituting "the authority of the Church for that of Antiquity." As far as he is concerned, Catholicism's emphasis on Catholicity is not enough. Christianity must be rooted in Antiquity, "and the consent of the Fathers," not on some doctrinal matters, but on all. For him, Catholicism tends to pick and choose what it likes from the Fathers by way of support of its teachings. His reasoning for this criticism, is that "History is a record of facts" and that the Fathers "are far too ample to allow" such picking and choosing.[15]

Having dealt with tradition in its relationship to Scripture, Newman went on to make his unique distinction between 'Episcopal Tradition' and 'Prophetical Tradition'. It should be made clear at this point that there is overlap between what he says in this part of the *Lectures* and what has already been said in the previous discussion of his views on tradition more generally. He is very clear that the source of 'Episcopal Tradition' is the Apostles. The 'Episcopal Tradition' is what he has already discussed as 'Apostolical Tradition'. Where the overlap comes in is in his discussion of 'Prophetical Tradition', by which is meant the

---

[14] Newman, *Via Media*, 1, pp. 31–4, 281, 244.
[15] Newman, *Via Media*, 1, pp. 49, 51, 56, 71, 107, 38.

usual Protestant, but here also Anglo-Catholic, view of tradition as the interpretation of revelation as recorded in the Scriptures. He writes that such tradition is a "body of Truth, pervading the Church like an atmosphere." It exists "primarily in the bosom of the Church itself, and recorded in such measure as Providence has determined in the writings of eminent men." It is interesting to note here that it is this kind of tradition that, for Newman, is most subject to corruption and, therefore, any doctrines that flow from such a tradition "are entitled to very different degrees of credit."[16] These phrases forecast his view of development as a movement from the implicit to the explicit, the implicit being so much a part of the Church that it is like fragrant odors pervading one's clothing (the author's analogy).

C. An Essay on the Development of Christian Doctrine

An exposition of Newman's thought on doctrinal development is now in order. Inspite of his disavowal of doctrinal development in the piece from *Essays Critical and Historical*, published in 1836, in fact Newman had already begun to consider it in *Arians of the Fourth Century*. He continues to broach the subject and develop his ideas in the *Parochial and Plain Sermons*, the two books (again in spite of his disavowal therein) we have already taken a look at, and most of all before the *Essay on Development*, in the last of his *University Sermons*, 'The Theory of Development in Religious Doctrine', of 1843. Since, however, his fullest thoughts as an Anglican, which were confirmed as a Catholic,[17] are to be found in *An Essay on the Development of Christian Doctrine*, the following reflections will be taken from there. Published in 1845, with a second edition the next year, and a final revised addition in 1878,[18] Newman considered the *Essay* to be an unsystematic attempt to convey a 'view' of doctrinal development that would be "an hypothesis to account for a difficulty." The difficulty was whether the Roman Catholic Church of his own day could be substantively the same as the Church of the Fathers in spite of what

[16] Newman, *Via Media*, 1, pp. 250-2.

[17] For reading in his Catholic writings, turn to *De Catholici Dogmatis Evolutione* (translated into English), *The Idea of a University, Historical Sketches*, Vol. III, *Tracts Theological and Ecclesiastical, The Theological Papers of John Henry Newman on Biblical Inspiration and Infallibility, Apologia pro vita sua, An Essay in Aid of a Grammar of Assent, Discussions and Arguments on Various Occasions, Certain Difficulties Felt by Anglicans in Catholic Teaching*, and the 1877 'Preface' to the reprinting of the *Lectures on the Prophetical Office of the Church*.

[18] *An Essay on the Development of Christian Doctrine*. John Henry Newman (Notre Dame, Indiana: University of Notre Dame Press, 1989). From here on, it will be referred to in the notes as Dev.

at least appeared to be additions or innovations or even corruptions. Firmly believing in the historicity of Christianity, he puts the form of the difficulty in these words:

> Our using in controversy the testimony of our most natural informant concerning the doctrine and worship of Christianity, viz. the history of eighteen hundred years. The view on which it is written has at all times, perhaps, been implicitly adopted by theologians ... that the increase and expansion of the Christian Creed and Ritual, and the variations which have attended the process in the case of individual writers and Churches, are the necessary attendants on any philosophy or polity which takes possession of the intellect and heart, and has any wide or extended dominion; that, from the nature of the human mind, time is necessary for the full comprehension and perfection of great ideas; and that the highest and most wonderful truths, though communicated to the world once for all by inspired teachers, could not be comprehended all at once by the recipients, but, as being received and transmitted by minds not inspired and through media which were human, have required only the longer time and deeper thought for all their elucidation. This may be called the *Theory of Development of Doctrine*.[19]

Now, the author could stop right here, because almost all of the essentials of what Newman involved in his view of doctrinal development can be savored in this passage. The reader can certainly pick out the similarities from the previous readings on tradition. There are, however, some other elements that have to be considered. What Newman means by the word 'idea' needs to be established, because his view is about the development of an idea.

What the reader will notice in the following passage is the multiplicity, the variety, the organic relationship of the elemental dimensions of an idea. The reader should also take note of the comparisons with everyday life of which Newman was so fond. And so, he wrote that:

> The idea which represents an object or supposed object is commensurate with the sum total of its possible aspects, however they may vary in the separate consciousness of individuals; and in proportion to the variety of aspects under which it presents itself to various minds in its force and depth, and the argument for its reality. Ordinarily an idea is not brought home to the intellect as objective except through this variety; like bodily substances, which are not apprehended except under the clothing of their properties and results, and which admit of being walked round, and surveyed

---

[19] Newman, Dev., pp. 29-30.

on opposite sides, and in different perspectives, and in contrary light, in evidence of their reality. And, as views of a material object may be taken from points so remote or so opposed, that they seem at first sight incompatible, and especially as their shadows will be disproportionate, or even monstrous, and yet all these anomalies will disappear and all these contrarieties be adjusted, on ascertaining the point of vision or the surface of projection in each case; so also the aspects of an idea are capable of coalition, and of a resolution into the object to which it belongs and the *prima facie* dissimilitude of its aspects becomes, when explained, an argument for its substantiveness and integrity, and their multiplicity for its originality and power.[20]

In this passage we see Newman the Romanticist coming fully alive, with his very organic notion of a real idea. This is where his theory of the convergence of probabilities comes into play. All aspects of an idea converge into an organic whole. If one applies this point to a revelatory idea, one can easily see Newman's appreciation of an idea as mystery, which is so other than what the human mind can comprehend, that this mind, while needing to express what is revealed in some intelligible way, must also be aware that its expressions can never pigeon-hole the transcendent. Even before one attempts to formulate by reason one's understanding of a revealed idea, both the individual and the Church must be grasped by the idea, or, to put it in active voice, to take possession of it, to own it; otherwise the formulation is virtually nominal, and ceases, if it even begins, to be effective in the life of the individual or the Church.[21]

Having assessed what an idea is in Newman's mind, how does he understand the development of such an idea? He wrote that it is the bringing of "the aspects of an idea into consistency" that is "its development, being the germination and maturation of some truth or apparent truth on a large mental field." But after describing in a nutshell the meaning of development, he then warns that "this process will not be a development, unless the assemblage of aspects, which constitute its ultimate shape, really belongs to the idea from which they start." The dynamism of this development is so powerful it seems to become creatively destructive, as it were. But at the least it modifies and incorporates "existing modes of thinking and operating."[22] He tells us then, and this should not be a surprise, given what he has written thus far about the dynamism of an idea's development, that:

---

[20] Newman, Dev., pp. 34-5.
[21] Newman, Dev., pp. 35-6.
[22] Newman, Dev., p. 38.

> The development ... of an idea is not like an investigation worked out on paper, in which each successive advance is a pure evolution from a foregoing, but it is carried on through and by means of communities of men [sic] and their leaders and guides; and it employs their minds as its instruments, and depends upon them, while it uses them. And so, as regards existing opinions, principles, measures, and institutions of the community which it has invaded; it develops by establishing relations between itself and them; it employs itself, in giving them a new meaning and direction, in creating what may be called a jurisdiction over them, in throwing off whatever in them it cannot assimilate. It grows when it incorporates, and its identity is found, not in isolation, but in continuity and sovereignty ... It is the warfare of ideas under their various aspects striving for the mastery, each of them enterprising, engrossing, imperious, more or less incompatible with the rest, and rallying followers or rousing foes, according as it acts upon the faith, the prejudices, or the interest of parties or classes.[23]

These lines clearly give us an idea's development in its very active sense. Is there a passive sense, in which an idea as it develops is on the receiving end? The answer is yes, especially in that it is influenced by its context: "[A]n idea ... is modified, or at least influenced, by the state of things in which it is carried out, and is dependent in various ways on the circumstances surrounding it."[24] Newman spells out the details of what he means about this very important point to do with context, but to summarize it one could write that any idea is subject to all the socio-economic, political, psychological, philosophical, and religious aspects of any given context. Newman wanted his readers to know that no idea worth its salt is going to have an easy time of it when it is in the process of developing.

Newman makes two other major points before proceeding to explain the various notes (tests in the 1845 version). They are that developments are to be expected, and that they are guided by an infallible authority. With regard to the first point, it is Newman's contention that any idea that is great, living, real should be expected to produce developments. This contention is applied to Christianity: "If Christianity is a fact, and impresses an idea of itself on our minds and is a subject-matter of exercises of the reason, that idea will in course of time expand into a multitude of ideas, and aspects of ideas, connected and harmonious with one another, and in themselves determinate and immutable, as is the objective fact itself which is thus represented."

[23] Newman, Dev., pp. 38-9.
[24] Newman, Dev., p. 39.

With uncanny insight into how the mind learns, he noted that when we learn we do so a bit at a time; we are not able to comprehend a reality in all its richness in a single mental act. "[W]hole objects do not create in the intellect whole ideas," Newman wrote, "but are ... thrown into series, into a number of statements, strengthening, interpreting, correcting each other, and with more or less exactness approximating, as they accumulate, to a perfect image." He anticipates in what he says about the way we learn, how we need to approach a reality such as the Trinity, one person at a time, a point he makes in his exposition of his theology of the Trinity in *An Essay in Aid of a Grammar of Assent*, published in 1870. He is also approaching the point he so often makes in his writings of the cumulation or convergence of probabilities; we come to the truth of a subject by the power of the illative sense telling us when enough probabilities have converged to do so. The Church does the same thing in formulating its doctrines. In another statement he advises us to be careful not to identify any one aspect of a subject with the subject itself, which is much more complex and organic.[25] Being so often at least a century ahead of his time, Newman, when applying this organic view of reality to Christianity, seems to have a more global sense of reality as well. He noted that:

> If Christianity be an universal religion, suited not simply to one locality or period, but to all times and places, it cannot but vary in its relations and dealings towards the world around it, that is, it will develop. Principles require a very various application according as persons and circumstances vary, and must be thrown into new shapes according to the form of society which they are to influence.[26]

His understanding of development as growth can be inferred from this statement. Reminding ourselves that for Newman the great and living ideas are first found in Scripture as the first explicit expression of the idea of Christianity impressed upon the imagination, Newman voiced his concern for the natural questions that will emerge from contemplation of this inspired source which, however, is not self-interpreting as he had previously noted, writing "that questions exist in the subject-matter of which the Scriptures treat, which Scripture does not solve; questions so real, so practical, that they must be answered, and, unless we suppose a new revelation, answered by the means of the revelation which we have, that is, by development."[27]

---

[25] Newman, Dev., p. 55.

[26] Newman, Dev., p. 59.

[27] Newman, Dev., p. 60.

In other words, since there can be no new revelation, according to Newman, who is in line with traditional Christian belief, if new questions arise, then the only way the original revelation can speak to them is by development of what is already contained in the revelation, especially as it is explicated initially in Scripture. Scripture needing "completion, the question is brought to this issue, whether defect or inchoateness in its doctrines be or be not an antecedent probability in favour of a development of them."[28] Newman concluded his thinking on developments of ideas being expected by using Scripture as the primary example.[29] One sees development going on in Scripture itself, most especially in the way Christianity in the New Testament interprets Christ, for example, by making use of Old Testament characteristics applied to but deepened, expanded, and enriched in the God–Man.

Taking up the second point on the infallible guide, Newman thinks that logically, "if the Christian doctrine, as originally taught, admits of true and important developments ... this is a strong antecedent argument in favour of a provision in the Dispensation for putting a seal of authority upon these." For him, this "seal of authority" is an infallible one, since "Christianity ... is a revelation which comes to us as a revelation, as a whole, objectively, and with a profession of infallibility."[30] Therefore, "if then there are certain truths, or duties, or observances, naturally and legitimately resulting from the doctrines originally professed, it is but reasonable to include these true results in the idea of revelation itself, to consider them parts of it, and if the revelation be not only true, but guaranteed as true, to anticipate that they too will come under the privilege of that guarantee. Christianity ... is an objective religion, or a revelation with credentials."[31] In fact, Newman believed that "a revelation is not given, if there be no authority to decide what it is that is given." Newman was certain in his own mind that "the notion of development under infallible authority," accounts "for the rise of Christianity and the formation of its theology."[32]

Since the seven tests or notes of true or false development have already been covered, the exposition of Newman's ideas on the relationship between Scripture and tradition, and the understanding

[28] Newman, Dev., p. 62.
[29] Newman, Dev., pp 64–68 passim.
[30] Newman, Dev., p. 79.
[31] Newman, Dev., pp. 79–80.
[32] Newman, Dev., pp. 89, 92.

of tradition as development, will close by saying that it was Newman's belief that existing developments of doctrine are the probable fulfillment of the antecedent expectation that they will occur.

Having previewed Newman's thinking on tradition and doctrinal development, the reader is now set for an exposition of the two Protestant thinkers chosen for this chapter.

II. Friedrich Schleiermacher

Born in Breslau, Germany, November 21, 1768, Friedrich Daniel Ernst Schleiermacher was the son of a Prussian army chaplain of the Reformed or Calvinist persuasion. He was educated by the Moravians who had instilled in him the Pietist spiritual approach to Christianity. The Pietists constituted a movement within eighteenth-century Protestantism that countered the Enlightenment emphasis on reason with their own emphasis on religion as experiential; more a matter of the heart than of the mind. Although he moved on intellectually from his childhood education, Schleiermacher never abandoned an experiential approach to religion and theology. Considered the 'Father of modern liberal Protestant theology', he made use of the Romantic ethos that had taken over in a good sense so many of the cultural dimensions of society in the late eighteenth and early nineteenth centuries. The essence of Romanticism, whether applied to theology, philosophy, literature, music, art, and even architecture was about the organic interrelationship of the transcendent and the immanent, the divine, on the one hand, and the human and the natural, on the other, in more pedestrian terms. Schleiermacher, who taught first at the University of Halle and then at the new University of Berlin, where he spent the last twenty four years of his life, understood religion as the immediate self-consciousness of the infinite in the finite and the eternal in the temporal. This was an intuitive experience of the presence of the divine in the human and the natural. Faith is, therefore, a matter of absolute dependence by the human on the divine. This organic interrelationship is experienced subconsciously almost like a white mass, as this author describes it, and the distinct elements in this relationship begin to emerge slowly into consciousness, moving from an experience of the distinctions but maintaining the organic whole to the possibility of reflecting on each element independently of the other. However, if one does not continue to keep in mind that all elements of the whole are organically involved, then all of them become disconnected and this leads to the loss of their integrity; this is what Schleiermacher defines as 'sin', God-forgetfulness. As an example, the reader might be interested to learn that for Schleiermacher only Jesus had full God-consciousness, that is, perfect consciousness of the organic interrelationship of the divine, the human and the natural; that the divine is present in the human and the natural; that he was absolutely dependent on God. Therefore, redemption is understood by him as Jesus transforming the sinner into becoming increasingly more God-conscious; increasingly more conscious of the organic nature of reality.

Where does Schleiermacher's understanding of the organic nature of reality fit in with tradition and doctrinal development? As would be expected, the Christian must always be in relationship with Christ; Christ is the Christian's center from whom all that is identified as Christian is organically related. The Church is the community of these Christ-centered individuals living in communion with one another; communion is natural to the God-conscious. The Church's theology is the 'speech' that the God-conscious community speaks to express in language the intuitive experience of absolute dependence. If you will, the experience and its language expression are in dialectic with one another. Insofar as the Christian community lives in different times and places, the language of theology and, therefore, of doctrine, is historically contextualized. Doctrinal tradition, therefore, is a matter of the God-conscious community, especially through the explorations of its theologians, interpreting the past, in a way that speaks to the community of the present in all its historical dimensions and, therefore, allowing for the necessary contemporary speech expressions of God-consciousness to actually engage that consciousness in a way that will bring the individual and the community closer to its salvific center, Jesus Christ. Doctrine keeps the community in contact with the past without replicating the past.

One would expect that a Protestant theologian would consider Scripture as the foremost body of language in which the Church's God-consciousness would be best expressed. But for Schleiermacher the confessional documents of Protestantism coming out of the Reformation should be studied first, not as superior to or supplanting Scripture, but as being the best place to define Protestantism over Catholicism. Resorting to Scripture is important for demonstrating that the doctrine proposed is in fact Christian. Scripture is, of course, indirectly present in the confessional statements of the different Protestant persuasions. The fact that the confessional statements are as important as has been stated shows Scleiermacher's respect for tradition.[33]

III. Adolf von Harnack

Born in Dorpat, Estonia in 1851, Adolf von Harnack was the son of a theology professor at the university there, who was also a Lutheran Pietist. Educated as a youth at Dorpat and Erlangen, the 'Father of modern church history' studied at the University of Leipzig, where his teaching career also began. He taught respectively at the University of Giessen and the University of Marburg, and then accepted a chair at the University of Berlin where he remained until his death. A prolific author, he is best known for two books: *History of Dogma* and *What is Christianity?* His thought on tradition and doctrinal development is best stated in the first of these two books.

Even more than his mentor, Ritschl, another important Protestant historical theologian who put the study of Christianity primarily in the hands of the historian, Harnack understood Christianity and its doctrines from a purely historical interpretation. There would be no truck with philosophy or religious experience. The historical-critical method was the only way to go. What he does share Schleiermacher is the connection of the past with the present. The past should be studied only if it could in some way be of value to the present.

For our purposes at this time, Harnack's *History of Dogma* is the place to start. The history of dogma came to an end with the Reformation, for Harnack. In fact, if Christianity was going to be liberated so as to make an impact on the modern world, the world in which he lived, the need for dogma would have to have ended. He firmly believed, in fact, that one had to study dogma so as to be free of it. Turning to the study of dogma, he contended that there were no dogmas in the very earliest centuries of Christianity, so why did dogma all of a sudden appear? He went on to say that the development of dogma was necessary to the growth of Christianity. Even though it was not until the hellenization of Christianity took place, that dogma emerged on the Christian scene, it helped to define Christianity over against the various heresies that would distort the truth of Christianity; dogma set the boundaries. He felt similarly

---

[33] For further reading, see Schleiermacher, *Brief Outline on the Study of Theology* Trans, Terrence N. Tice (Atlanta, Georgia: John Knox Press, 1977, 3rd edn); *The Christian Faith* (any recent edn); and *On Religion: Speeches to Its Cultured Despisers* (any recent edn). The reader should begin with the latter and then go to the *Brief Outline*, and lastly to *The Christian Faith*.

about the Christian retention of the Old Testament. As an historian of dogma, he knew that the earliest Christians turned to the Old Testament, the only Scripture available to them at the time, to help them better understand who Jesus was. Like our previous Protestant thinkers, Harnack would be naturally moved to see Protestantism in opposition to Catholicism (he found himself later in a contrary position when Alfred Loisy, one of the most famous Roman Catholic Modernists, wrote *The Gospel and the Church*, in response to Harnack's restricting Christianity to a narrow essence). His main complaint about the development of dogma in antiquity was that it was an expression of an ecclesial form, Catholicism, which, as authoritarian, he believed, was alien to the primitive Gospel which was liberating. Dogma and its necessity came to an end when Luther unshackled Christianity from its former imprisonment by Rome. Harnack was rather typical of liberal thinkers from the Enlightenment in that Catholicism had kept humankind in a state of childhood, but that it was Luther that made it possible for humankind to take responsibility for itself.

In spite of his great love for Luther and what he thought Luther had wrought for humanity, Harnack, nevertheless, taught that no one particular form of Christianity could pin down the essential reality of Christianity. Even so, Christians would not be able to uncover the essence of Christianity without its historical forms. The desire to uncover the essence of Christianity was a common theme of nineteenth-century theology, mostly but not exclusively Protestant. Here, once again, a thinker is making the point that the essence of this divinely given reality is in dialectical relationship with its historical forms. The essence could be extracted from the historical forms, or, to use Harnack's own language, the 'kernel' could be extracted from its 'husk'. This could be misunderstood, if it were not for the fact that Harnack insisted that the credibility of the past is no longer possible in a new cultural situation. Continuity could, therefore, be construed by the reader as unimportant; previous husks, so to speak, have no permanent value at all.

For Harnack, the essence of Christianity is the gospel of Jesus Christ, as he described it in *What is Christianity?*. Repeating his previous point about no historical form being able to box in the essential reality of Christianity, he wrote that just the opposite is true. The gospel of Jesus Christ is to critique any and all historical forms it takes on. Otherwise, and here is where the idea of tradition is revealed, tradition will take control of Christianity. This gives one the sense that for Harnack, tradition is a distortion of the original primitive gospel of Jesus Christ. He was up front in saying that the content of this essence is more difficult to determine, but he did say that it is not some intellectual construct, but a living reality. No matter what historical form the essence may take, it is necessary for the Christian who wants to be in touch with the reality that Christianity is all about that he or she needs to penetrate the historical form to embrace this essence, however it is understood. One of the most important stresses he puts out to the reader is that the essence, the gospel of Jesus Christ, is Christ himself, a personal reality, and not some notional object for intellectual discussion. This being the case, the need for dogma as a protection for the essence is not necessary. One simply lives a gospel life.[34]

IV. Conclusion

What do Newman, Schleiermacher, and Harnack have in common? First of all, they approached theological issues by historical methodology, and all had, at least to some extent, pastoral concerns. For all of them Jesus Christ was the center of Christianity, which, of course, should be obvious. But the motive of their work was to put the individual Christian as well as the Christian community in touch with that center. Therefore, the correlation between the past and the present was necessary without question. The historical and cultural context for interpreting the history of the Church and its teachings was manifest in their writings as well. Where Newman and Schleiermacher are very much in the same mold is on the matter of the Romantic theme of the organic wholeness of reality. For both, all of doctrine centered on Jesus Christ is organically integrated, even if the starting point of each of these theologians differs. For Schleiermacher, that starting point is the experience of absolute dependency because of God-consciousness; doctrine being an expression of this experience. For Newman, that starting point is a real grasp of the divine reality expressed by the doctrine. Before going in to other differences, let it be noted that what both Newman and Schleiermacher also have in common on the matter of the relationship between the individual and doctrine is that it happens within the ecclesial community. About all three theologians it can also be concluded that they take history

---

[34] Although there many of Harnack's works in English, the most important for further reading would be his multivolume *History of Dogma* trans. Neil Buchanan (New York: Dover Publications, 1961), and *What is Christianity?* Trans. Thomas Bailey Saunders (New York: Harper, c1957), and Outlines of the History of Dogma. Trans. Edwin Knox Mitchell. (Boston: Beacon Press, 1959).

and, therefore, change very seriously. The issue of continuity in the midst of change is a central topic for all of them, as well. However, they differed to one degree or another as to how to understand this.

How do they differ? Starting with the issue of continuity, one can say that Newman thought in terms of an evolutionary approach. For Newman, the Holy Spirit would be involved, at least implicitly, in the development of doctrine. There was an unfolding of historical divine revelation throughout the history of the Church, even though as an Anglican he would place the emphasis on the patristic period. The stress on early antiquity both Newman and Harnack had in common, but Harnack was able to take development to the Reformation, when it comes to an end, and Newman, by the time he wrote *An Essay on the Development of Christian Doctrine*, believed that the Roman Catholic Church of the nineteenth century was the Church of the Fathers in the midst of all the change over the years. Revelation does not cease to unfold, as far as he is concerned. The Protestants can give the impression that each historical period is a discreet entity unto itself, even if they want to allow for some connection from period to period.

At this point it would be pertinent to include the difference between Newman, Schleiermacher, and Harnack on the role of tradition in relation to Scripture. It is clear that for Newman, while Scripture is the ultimate source of doctrine, Scripture is not self-interpreting. The role of tradition is to be the necessary interpreter. He grew, however, to believe that tradition could also be understood as including the oral stage of apostolic teaching, because the Apostles and the succeeding ecclesial community could not put all of the historical revelation into words. Absorbing tradition into doctrinal development, he would view tradition's role as biblical interpreter in an ongoing dynamic relationship as long as the Church continues to live in history. The two Protestant theologians would only allow tradition to be an interpreter of Scripture, and limited to patristic interpretation of Scripture, as long as it confirmed what was already in Scripture. We know too that Harnack held to the belief that doctrine of any kind was no longer needed after Luther, so that we study the history of dogma in order to be free of it.

While all three would say that critical study of Scripture and doctrine should be done by the historical method, Newman would not have limited tradition to interpretation of Scripture, even though that was one of its functions. The Historical–critical method, he would

271

say, should also study the non-written tradition, such as liturgy, prayer, and pastoral practice, to name only a few. Where Harnack is perhaps most different is that, unlike Newman and Schleiermacher, he went in search of the essence of Christianity in the midst of the facts. This is the theme of his *What is Christianity?* Newman was not interested in discovering any narrowly restricted essence. Only the truth found in the doctrines infallibly guided by the Church's teaching authority is worth the search.

What the reader has taken in as he or she has contemplated the contents of this chapter should lead hopefully to a further study of Newman and the nineteenth-century Protestant historical theologians. Newman is always fascinating on his own, but putting him into the context of his own century, whether in Great Britain or on the Continent, brings greater gratitude for his life and work, and the respect that all students should have for a thinker who was so far ahead of his own time. It would take Catholicism some time in the twentieth century to fully accept the idea that doctrine develops.

Chapter 15

NEWMAN AND THE CRISIS OF MODERNISM

by Charles Talar

In the fall of 1907 Wilfrid Ward was worried. That September Rome had issued the encyclical *Pascendi dominici gregis* which condemned Modernism as the "synthesis of all heresies."[1] The document had done some synthesizing of its own in order to present Modernism as an orderly system, exposing its philosophical roots and the extent of its reach into multiple areas of Catholic intellectual and practical life. What caused Ward no little anxiety was a perception that the encyclical had done its work all too well. In its creation of a Modernist system its net had been cast rather widely – to the point where some of Newman's positions could appear to have been caught. Moreover, the concerns that Ward was expressing in private correspondence were being aired publicly by defenders of Modernism. In doing so their strategy was to debunk *Pascendi*'s characterization of Modernism by declaring that a censure that struck at Newman said less about any doubtful orthodoxy on his part and more about the adequacy of the encyclical's understanding of what was at stake in the first place. In turn defenders of Newman sought ways to demonstrate that, despite apparent similarities in language between Newman's writings and those of recognized Modernists, underlying differences rendered them worlds apart. Given Newman's importance among English Catholics, this public discussion of his relation to Modernism was followed with interest. A measure of reassurance emerged in the form of a letter from Pope Pius X to the Bishop of Limerick in the spring of 1908,

----

[1] The text of the encyclical can be found in Claudia Carlen, IHM, ed. *The Papal Encyclicals* Vol. 3 (Raleigh: Mc Grath Publishing Company, 1981), pp. 71-97.

distancing Newman from any taint of Modernist error.[2] However, in the repressive atmosphere that followed upon the condemnation of Modernism,[3] suspicions lingered, at least in some minds. And even if positions were not clearly erroneous, they still could be considered dangerous.

What, then, was this Modernism that posed a threat to Newman's reputation? Despite the sense of crisis that it aroused at the turn of the twentieth century, it is hardly familiar to the vast majority of present-day Catholics. Like most 'isms' (with the possible exception of Catholicism, depending on whom one is talking to!) it carries a vaguely negative scent. And indeed the severity of its condemnation in 1907, positioning it as going a step beyond Protestantism and poised on the brink of atheism, confirms and deepens that impression. Modernism's partisans were represented as driven by inordinate curiosity and pride, whose consequences were destructive for the very life of the Church.

As is often the case, the historical reality is far more complex than its schematic synthesis. Rather than the coordinated conspiracy alleged by the encyclical, Roman Catholic Modernism was a loosely structured movement that encompassed a series of initiatives that aimed at bringing Catholicism into a more positive relation with the modern world. It arose out of a concern on the part of a number of priests and laity that minds formed by modernity needed to be addressed in a form that spoke to that formation; the language of scholasticism constituted a barrier rather than a bridge to the truths of the faith. In consequence, the times called for reform: intellectual reform in philosophy (especially as that bore upon apologetics), in biblical and historical studies (utilizing historical critical method), with implications for the understanding of dogma and its development; and structural reform insofar as the Church needed to come to terms

---

[2] Ward's reactions are set out in Maisie Ward, *The Wilfrid Wards and the Transition* vol. 2 *Insurrection versus Resurrection* (London: Sheed & Ward, 1937), ch. 14. See also Dom Paschal Scott, *Out of Due Time: Wilfrid Ward and the "Dublin Review"* (Washington, DC: The Catholic University of American Press, 2006), pp. 69-79. The pope's letter to Bishop O'Dwyer is available in Latin and English at: http://www.newmanreader.org/canonization/popes/acta10mar08.html.

[3] When, in 1922, Friedrich von Hügel wrote to Dom Cuthbert Butler, urging him to do some work on Christian origins, Butler replied, "In regard to what you say about your regret that I am not giving myself up to early Christian things,—years ago I recognized that these things—Xian origins, New Testament, History of Dogma, etc.—have been made impossible for a priest, except on the most narrow apologetic lines.... When the Biblical Commission got underway, and the Lamentabili and Pascendi were issued, I deliberately turned away from all this work." Quoted in Alec R. Vidler, *20th Century Defenders of the Faith* (London: SCM Press, 1965), pp. 36-37.

with democratic forms of organization.

The consequences of such reforms would be far reaching. The question then became how much of the ancient tradition of the Church would endure. The sense was 'too little' and Modernist initiatives were rejected, their advocates sanctioned, their works Indexed, vigilance committees erected, and in 1910 an oath against Modernism imposed that endured until the 1960s. Likewise, the consequences of condemnation would also be far reaching, setting a climate in which theological work was conducted for succeeding decades.

If the truth were more simple, it would be possible to position Modernists as reformers out of due time, Vatican II Catholics who had the misfortune of arriving on the scene several decades too soon. Equally and alternatively, it would be possible to simply affirm *Pascendi*'s portrait as adequate without remainder. Here the truth is, as in so many cases, much more complex. While reformers had the courage to face and engage the questions, they did not always possess the requisite resources to adequately address them. While, as we shall see, there was a great deal of diversity among partisans of renewal, at least in some cases positions they advocated would have been corrosive of a transcendent faith. Thus the condemnation of Modernism was not entirely off the mark and *Pascendi* put its finger on a number of issues that constituted a danger to the historical faith. However, in its attempt at a synthesis of a variety of initiatives the encyclical imputed an organization, both intellectual and structural, to a movement that in fact it did not possess. Moreover, real differences between rationalist extremists, centrists and more moderate progressives were elided, with unfortunate consequences for representatives of the progressive wing especially.[4]

At the time of the Modernist crisis, two of the neuralgic questions that engaged Newman's work concerned the development of doctrine and the grounding of faith. To provide focus in this chapter only the

---

[4] There is a considerable body of literature on Modernism. Especially useful are Gabriel Daly, OSA. *Transcendence and Immanence: A Study in Catholic Modernism and Integralism* (Oxford: Clarendon Press, 1980); Darrell Jodock, ed. *Catholicism Contending with Modernity: Roman Catholic Modernism and Anti-Modernism in Historical Context* (Cambridge: Cambridge University Press, 2000). Marvin O'Connell's *Critics on Trial: An Introduction to the Catholic Modernist Crisis* (Washington, DC: Catholic University of America Press, 1994) needs to be read critically, as it largely accepts *Pascendi*'s characterization of the movement. For the impact of Modernism and its condemnation on various regions of the Church see the issue of *US Catholic Historian* 25/1 (2007) which is devoted to the topic.

first of these will figure, and the discussion of development will be confined to France. In many ways France appeared to contemporaries of the crisis as the epicenter of Modernism.[5] For present purposes it was home to a variety of responses to Newman's work that provide access to the diversity of interpretation that his writings evoked.

Newman's conversion in 1845 catalyzed French interest in him and in his writings. Given the relative lack of knowledge of English among Roman theologians, Newman was understandably concerned over the accuracy of any French translations of those writings, in particular over the *Essay on the Development of Christian Doctrine*. Despite those concerns, he did not have any input into the translation of the *Essay* made by Louise Boyeldieu d'Auvigny. Published in 1847 as *Développement de la doctrine chrétienne, preuves de la foi catholique*, its defects went far beyond incautious renderings of particular phrases. Jules Gondon, whose authorized translation appeared the following year, catalogued his predecessor's inadequacies in a translator's forward. They were legion, extending to the omission of negatives, giving the impression that Newman held positions that he in fact rejected; to the omission of quotation marks, leading to possible attribution to Newman of positions he was retrieving – and at times opposing; to a near comical confusion of names; and to serious lapses in the comprehension of English.[6]

Fortunately, immediate French reactions to the *Essay* were based on the comparatively superior (or less inadequate) translation made by Gondon. Even so, they manifest divergences that emerge from the nature of the work itself, and not simply from its translated form. As Aidan Nichols observes, "In the last resort, the *Essay* is a difficult work to interpret, so much so that we may be tempted to apply to it J. A. Froude's description of history: 'a child's box of letters with which we can spell any word we please'."[7] Though the book garnered praise from the Bishop of La Rochelle and from a future Archbishop of Paris, on a more ominous note it could also be seen as "valuable proof

[5] Cf. Alec Vidler, *A Variety of Catholic Modernists* (Cambridge: Cambridge University Press, 1970), p. 20.
[6] See Jules Gondon, "Avant-propos du traducteur" in J H Newman, *Histoire du développement de la doctrine chrétienne* (Paris: Sagnier et Bray, 1848), pp. i-xvi. As a staff member of *L'Univers* charged with English works, Gondon was in a better position to interpret Newman to French readers – though his own translation is not without its shortcomings.
[7] Aidan Nichols, *From Newman to Congar. The Idea of Doctrinal Development from the Victorians to the Second Vatican Council* (Edinburgh: T & T Clark, 1990), p. 57.

of the widespread invasion of rationalist ideas."[8]

If, through his involvement in the Oxford Movement and especially through his conversion, Newman gained a measure of familiarity in France, by 1870 that interest had declined – to the point where his attitude toward the Vatican Council went unremarked there and the *Grammar of Assent* went completely unnoticed. (The *Grammar* would not receive an integral translation until 1907.) Only as the century drew to its close did French interest in Newman revive.

While a number of biographical studies brought attention to Newman – Paul Thureau-Dangin's three-volume *Renaissance catholique en Angleterre au XIXe siècle* began appearing in 1899, Lucie Félix-Faure's *Newman, sa vie, ses oeuvres* was published in 1901, and Henri Brémond's *Newman, essai de biographie psychologique* in 1906[9] – there are signs of renewed engagement with Newman's thought earlier in the 1890s. Discussions surrounding doctrine and its development drew upon his work and Newman's name once more came before a larger public. That is not to say that he was entirely forgotten in France. John Hogan, a Sulpician of Irish origin, cultivated seminarians at Saint-Sulpice in Paris who showed intellectual promise. In stimulating them to think beyond the confines of the manual theology that served as the staple of the seminary curriculum, he exposed them to Newman's writings. The *Essay on Development* figured prominently among those and, on the testimony of several of those he mentored, made a profound impression on their minds. Several of the names that will figure significantly in the controversies surrounding Modernism felt Hogan's influence: Eudoxe Irénée Mignot, future Bishop of Fréjus and ultimately Archbishop of Albi; Pierre Batiffol, eventual collaborator with Marie-Joseph Lagrange OP on the *Revue biblique* and future rector of the Institut catholique de Toulouse; and Marcel Hébert, whose philosophical interests Hogan would broaden beyond scholasticism and who would assume direction of the École Fénelon in Paris. Certainly Hogan held no monopoly of access to Newman for the generation that would become prominent in the initiatives for intellectual renewal that led to the condemnations in *Pascendi*. Henri

---

[8] Respectively: Clément Villecourt in *L'Ami de la religion* 136 (1848): 461-467, 549-552; Georges Darboy in *Le Correspondant* 23 (1848): 281-293; and Émile Saisset in *La Liberté de penser* 1 (1848): 337-357.

[9] Thureau-Dangin's trilogy appeared in English translation in two volumes as *The English Catholic Revival in the Nineteenth Century* (New York: E P Dutton, s. d.). Brémond's biography was published under the title *The Mystery of Newman* (London: Williams and Norgate, 1907) with an introduction by George Tyrrell.

Brémond gained his exposure to Newman during his years of Jesuit formation in Britain. Alfred Loisy found stimulus in the Cardinal's writings for lines of thought he was already developing from other sources. That said, Hogan played a notable role in preserving and extending Newman's ideas among French ecclesiastics.

The question of how doctrine may be understood to develop in a way that provided continuity while allowing for difference provided a natural bridge to Newman's work. Although the issue was already under discussion among French Catholics in the 1890s, the publication of the liberal Protestant Auguste Sabatier's *Esquisse d'une philosophie de la religion d'après la psychologie et l'histoire* late in the decade (1897) gave additional stimulus.[10] *La Vie du dogme catholique*, published the following year by André de la Barre SJ, Professor at the Paris Institut catholique, remains within the then dominant scholastic framework of understanding development. From that perspective Sabatier's formulation of evolutionary development comes under heavy criticism. While Newman is not central to de la Barre's study in the way that Sabatier is, the *Essay on Development* is taken up and – relative to this chapter's interests – assimilated to a scholastic take on the problem. By the 1890s 'evolution' had become a key term in theological discussion of development. The question becomes, how did de la Barre understand that term? And how did that understanding set the terms of his interpretation of Newman?

The Foreword to *La Vie du dogme catholique* contains a transparent reference to Sabatier's views, in its taking note of those who fail to recognize the divine element in the conservation and ongoing life of dogma, reducing it to an essentially natural phenomenon, a product of human consciousness. This sets evolution at odds with authority. By contrast, within the ranks of Catholic conservatives there are fideists who concede too little significance to the human element in dogma. In their case evolution becomes the problematic aspect. For de la Barre, authority and evolution are not to be seen in opposition, but as complementary. Evolution contributes a dynamic element, while authority brings a directive principle of order.[11]

In a scholastic understanding revelation constitutes a body of truths (the 'deposit of faith') confided to the Church. Over the course

---

[10] Translated as *Outlines of a Philosophy of Religion* (New York: George H Doran, s. d.; reprinted Harper Torchbooks, 1957). This is another case of a translation suffering at the hands of a translator. The English abridges the original in places, rendering the development of the thought incoherent.

[11] André de la Barre, *La Vie du dogme catholique* (Paris: P. Lethielleux, 1898), pp. 2-5.

of time these truths emerge from a more lived and thus more implicit understanding to achieve more articulate expression in explicit formulas. Thus, contrary to fideism there is a legitimate role to be accorded to philosophy. It provides terminology to bring revealed truths into more refined expression in dogmatic definition. Through application of logical deduction philosophy assists the process of bringing to a level of conscious awareness the implicit truths contained in the unformulated and undefined portions of the deposit of faith. And through its role in systematizing the scattered data of revelation it lends further clarity to truths now seen in relation rather than in relative isolation. Thus the development of dogma amounts to a logical development, coming about slowly over time within the social consciousness of the Church reflecting on revealed truth, and coming to fruition in dogmatic definition. Contrary to any imputation of a process of naturalistic evolution, here the human effort that prepares the way for explicit definition of what was held implicitly is internal to development, not something imported from without. Likewise, the authority which guarantees that the formula resulting from this preparatory work constitutes a legitimate interpretation of scripture is interior to the organism of the Church as the soul of this society.[12] This, in broad outline, is de la Barre's reconciliation of the immutability of dogma with its life, authority with evolution.

While Sabatier's *Esquisse* provides points of contrast with de la Barre's position, Newman's *Essay* instead invites comparison. The Jesuit acknowledges that some of Newman's expressions have been disputed and that even the overall theological value of his general conception has been questioned. Nonetheless, in de la Barre's estimation the substance remains compatible with Catholic teaching, although expressed poetically rather than in more familiar scholastic terms.[13] From his discussion of the *Essay*'s chapter on the power of assimilation of ideas, it is clear that de la Barre assimilates the organic perspective that pervades the book to the logical framework of scholasticism. He dwells on the capacity of ideas to form logical systems, in which some ideas emerge as dominant and acquire the power of assimilating to themselves secondary ideas, as planets revolve around a central sun. The more an idea grows stronger and becomes more clear in the course of the progress of human intellectual development, the more dominant it becomes – "and this is what Newman understood by the

---

[12] De la Barre, pp. 171-172.
[13] De la Barre, pp. 175 n. and 177.

assimilative power of the idea."[14]

This way of reading Newman is consistent with the overall tenor of *La Vie du dogme catholique*. Evolution is understood as a process of the implicit becoming explicit, from being obscurely held to dogmatically defined by the ecclesiastical magisterium, and from being loosely coordinated to systematically connected to other truths so clarified. Thus truth as "a seed which germinates in developing its content" can serve to express "the veritable notion of logical evolution."[15] It is an interpretation that will find resonance with other scholastics and thus serves to represent one strand of utilizing Newman's work.

It is telling, however, that de la Barre's reading of the *Essay* evoked professed surprise from one reviewer of *La Vie du dogme catholique*. It was not clear why development had to be understood as purely logical, on the model of a geometrical system. Nor was the attenuation of Newman's contributions to the power of the assimilation of the idea, understood so narrowly, allowed to pass unquestioned. While de la Barre may

> very well show that the evolution of a truth is compatible to that of a seed which sprouts in developing its content, why not add what is already contained implicitly in this comparison, that 'Christian development must be conceived as profound, vital, real, as considerable in its order as that of animal life from birth to adulthood, implying, in consequence, the identity of the being under all the transformations that are at work in it according to the law of its institution, but excluding as a state of death the absolute immobility of the form once acquired?' Why not in particular insist again with Newman on this idea that the essential condition and principal mark of a true development is the maintenance of unity of type throughout the most profound transformation, and that the identity of a living being is not purely external and material but one that is personal?[16]

The reviewer is quoting an article published under the name of 'A Firmin' that appeared in the *Revue du clergé français* in 1898. "Le développement chrétien d'après le cardinal Newman" was in actuality the work of Alfred Loisy, already known for his exegetical studies on the Old and New Testaments and histories of the development of the biblical canon. This alternative reading of Newman indicates that the diversity of interpretation that surfaced in France over the

---

[14] De la Barre, p. 176.
[15] De la Barre, p. 169 (emphasis omitted).
[16] "Notes et critiques" in *Bulletin de littérature ecclésiastique* 1 (1899): 27-33, citing p. 31.

publication of the translations of the *Essay* resurfaces at the turn of the century, and will constitute a contributing factor to the Modernist crisis. Since Loisy's *L'Évangile et l'Église* (1902) may be said to have precipitated that crisis, not least through its portrayal of development, his positioning of Newman becomes significant.

By the early 1890s Loisy seemed well on his way to establishing a career as a Catholic biblical scholar. His classes at the Institut catholique in Paris provided material for a growing body of publications. However, in the sensitive atmosphere surrounding the encyclical *Providentissimus Deus* (1893)[17] his published views on biblical inspiration were judged overly daring and he was dismissed from his position. Installed as a chaplain at a convent school in a Paris suburb, he turned his energies toward formulating an apologetic for Catholicism that would speak to the needs of modernity, producing a lengthy manuscript from which he began to quarry articles for publication in the *Revue du clergé français*. The one on Newman and development initiated the series.

In this commentary on Newman's *Essay on Development*, Loisy appears as a competent expositor of its thought.[18] It becomes apparent, however, that a primary concern is to develop Newman on development. To meet the needs of the present, the theory has to be taken beyond the point to which Newman brought it – from the history of doctrine to its origin in revelation. The interval of half a century has posed the question in different terms than Newman faced when writing the *Essay*. Its theory can be extended to provide a developmental model of revelation itself. While Loisy is willing to interpret the *Essay* in organic terms closer to the understanding of evolutionary development put forth in Sabatier's *Esquisse*, he judges Newman's work superior to the latter, "reflecting a more complete religious experience, a more open and more impartial mind."[19] Those seeking "a broad conception of the history of dogmas and of Christian development, a truly scientific conception, in which can be arbitrated all the legitimate conclusions of historical criticism"[20] need look no farther than Newman.

In *L'Évangile et l'Église* Loisy thought to put this broad conception to good use, in proposing what may be termed an historical apologetic

---

[17] See Carlen, ed. *The Papal Encyclicals* Vol. 2, pp. 325-339.

[18] Nicholas Lash, "Newman and 'A. Firmin'" in Arthur Hilary Jenkins, ed. *John Henry Newman and Modernism. Newman-Studien* Vol. XIV (Sigmaringendorf: Glock und Lutz, 1990), pp. 56-73.

[19] A Firmin [Alfred Loisy], "Le développement chrétien d'après le cardinal Newman" in *Revue du clergé français* 17 (1898): 5-20, citing p. 20.

[20] Firmin, p. 20.

for Catholicism. A developmental framework pervades the entire book. The chapter devoted to Christian dogma brings it to the fore. He attempts to show that development has been present throughout the history of Christianity as a fact. In a more historically conscious age there is more explicit awareness of that fact and, consequently, a felt need to account for it in a theologically satisfactory way. As Loisy expressed it:

> It is easy to say that the Catholic Church does not even recognize the existence of this development, and condemns the very idea of it. Perhaps it would be nearer the truth to say that she has never had consciousness of it, and that she has no official theory concerning the philosophy of her own history. That which is taught by Vincent de Lérins, modern theologians (except Cardinal Newman) and the Council of the Vatican, touching the development of dogma, applies in reality to the definitely intellectual and theological phase of its development, not to the first budding and formation of beliefs, or at least includes in an abstract definition, much work for which this definition is no adequate expression. It is just the idea of development which is now needed, not to be created all at once, but established from a better knowledge of the past.[21]

He continues in terms that stand in marked contrast to the conception of development advanced by de la Barre. Dogmas

> were not contained in primitive tradition, like a conclusion in the premises of a syllogism, but as a germ in a seed, a real and living element, which must become transformed as it grows, and be determined by discussion before its crystallization into a solemn formula.[22]

Initial reactions to *L'Évangile et l'Église* were not unfavorable. Shortly after its appearance Wilfred Ward wrote to Baron Friedrich von Hügel, praising the book for "showing a perfect knowledge of what Newman wanted and intended."[23] It was not long, however, before Loisy's essay in apologetics came under strong criticism.[24] As was the case with Sabatier, his way of presenting development was perceived to naturalize the process, rendering it a purely human product. He

[21] Alfred Loisy, *L'Évangile et l'Église* (Paris: Alphonse Picard, 1902), pp. 161-162. Eng. Trans. *The Gospel and the Church* (London: Isbister, 1903), pp. 213-214 (Reprinted 1976 by Fortress Press).
[22] Loisy, pp. 162 and 214 of the French and English versions respectively.
[23] Alfred Loisy, *Mémoires pour servir à l'histoire religieuse de notre temps* Vol. 2 (Paris: Nourry, 1931), p. 173.
[24] For representative critics and their critique see C J T Talar, *Metaphor and Modernist: The Polarization of Alfred Loisy and His Neo-Thomist Critics* (Lanham, MD: University Press of America, 1987), ch. 2.

defended his positions in *Autour d'un petit livre* (1903) which merely served to deepen dissatisfaction on the part of his critics. Later that year the Holy Office condemned five of the exegete's books, these two included in their number. Little wonder that at the time of Modernism's condemnation in 1907 Ward would exhibit considerable anxiety over the ability of Catholics to distinguish between Newman's approach and those of Modernists.

While Loisy played an important role in shaping French perceptions of Newman, Henri Brémond also proved influential through his publication of Newman texts for the series 'La Pensée chrétienne.' His *Newman I. Le développement du dogme chrétien* (1904, 1906) contained a translation of the Oxford University Sermon on development, together with excerpts from the *Essay* interspersed with Brémond's summaries and commentary. *Newman II. Psychologie de la foi* (1905) drew from a greater range of Newman's writings, while highlighting the *Grammar* and the *Oxford University Sermons* on faith.[25] *Newman III. La vie chrétienne* (1906) presented translations of a selection of the *Parochial and Plain Sermons*.

When Brémond agreed to contribute to 'La Pensée chrétienne' on Newman, he was aware that the *Essay on Development* had earlier been translated into French. Unfortunately, he was not then aware that this had been done twice, so he merely requested a French edition of the work from a bookseller – and received Boyeldieu d'Auvigny's. It did not take him long to discern its deficiencies but, given the time at his disposal, it was not feasible to redo the translation from scratch. Thus he decided to retain this version as a basis for his own presentation of Newman, revising it to a point where it could be considered passable. He also decided to follow the structure of the revised edition of the *Essay* published in 1878. So *Le développement du dogme chrétien* was not a simple cut and paste appropriation of Boyeldieu's attempt, coupled with Abbé Deferrière's more competent translation of the Oxford University sermon.

Despite Brémond's efforts, sow's ears do not furnish good material for silk purses, and a quantity of his predecessor's lapses passed over into his own pages.[26] While Deferrière's rendering of the sermon

---

[25] For background on Brémond's exposure to Newman's writings and reception of his compendium of Newman texts on faith see C J T Talar, "Assenting to Newman: Henri Brémond's *Psychologie de la foi*" in *Downside Review* 121 (2003): 251-270.

[26] In his review of *Le développement chrétien* (*Études* 104 [July-Sept. 1905]: 259-260), Léonce de Grandmaison listed several errors to be found in a single chapter and wondered over Brémond's use of d'Auvigny, given the existence of Gondon's less imperfect translation. Brémond would

apparently passed muster, at least one reviewer questioned Brémond's italicizing of certain portions of the text. While the practice would be permissible in a citation or in an analysis, to do so in the text was to mix and confuse editor and author.[27] However, as Brémond himself acknowledged, it was his introduction to the volume that raised the sharpest objections.

At the outset of his introduction Brémond portrays Newman as one whose thought is understood only in understanding the man. Brémond thus cautions his reader that this initial volume of Newman texts is limited to only one aspect of the cardinal's thought and that subsequent volumes will provide greater familiarity with Newman himself. At the very beginning of his projected series, then, Brémond sought to forestall any tendencies to see Newman's ideas as corrosive of Christian beliefs. If those ideas can be bracing, even at times disconcerting, their force is tempered by his "contagious faith."[28]

In the substantive portion of his introduction Brémond argued for areas of agreement between Newman's position on development and that of the seventeenth-century paragon of Catholic orthodoxy, Jacques-Bénigne Bossuet.[29] Despite apparent differences in their views, Brémond found points of reconciliation – thus assimilating Newman to classic Catholic thinking on this issue. Nonetheless, given the alternatives of Bossuet or Newman, it is clear that Brémond saw the way forward as residing with the latter. He found it not without significance that Auguste Sabatier took Newman, rather than Bossuet, as the Catholic theologian who must be answered. To cling as a Catholic to Bossuet would be to leave Sabatier unanswered – and beyond him, the evidence amassed by disciplined research. By contrast, a disciple of Newman can engage a work such as Sabatier's, and others like it, unafraid.[30] Not that Newman has spoken the last word on development. The *Essay* is "useful as an initiation into new methods" – which for Brémond is already saying a great deal. "It

---

use Gondon as the basis of his second edition of *Le développement du dogme chrétien*, which appeared in 1906.

[27] J-V Bainvel, review of *Le développement chrétien* in *Revue de philosophie* 6 (1905): 188-189, citing 189n. In the 1906 edition Brémond defended his italicizing the sermon on the strength of wanting to draw attention to the differences which he believed to exist between the still hesitant ideas of the 1843 sermon and the "firm doctrine" of the *Essay* in 1845. Henri Brémond, *Newman I. Le développement chrétien* (Paris: Librairie Bloud, 1906), pp. xxiv-xxv.

[28] Brémond, *Développement* (1904), pp. vi-viii; (1906), pp. 2-4.

[29] Bossuet's views on doctrinal progress are set out in Owen Chadwick, *From Bossuet to Newman. The Idea of Doctrinal Development* (Cambridge: Cambridge University Press, 1957), ch. 1.

[30] Brémond, *Développement* (1904), p. xiv and (1906), p. 10.

is another *Discourse on Method* and a necessary discipline for anyone who wants to tackle the history of Christian dogmas."[31] However, Brémond shared with Loisy the conviction that the *Essay* itself was in need of further development by future theologians.

While obviously intended to calm Catholic fears over the use of Newman, Brémond's introduction was not entirely successful. Once again, Wilfrid Ward may serve as a perceptive critic. Part of the difficulty Ward experienced he attributed to the combination of Newman's style of expression and the very nature of Brémond's project. Newman is not a linear thinker. His tendency rather is to survey "many aspects of the mental phenomena he is studying – which seem at times logically irreconcilable."[32] In consequence, great care is required on the part of an interpreter wishing to represent Newman accurately. "His sentences are physiologically and not mechanically united, and to isolate one is like amputating a limb. In his writing, a paragraph has almost the same indivisible character as a sentence in the writing of others."[33] Thus any attempt to condense a writing such as the *Essay* risks doing less than justice to the "many aspects" of development Newman considers there. On a smaller scale, distortion of meaning resulted from selective quotations from portions of a work. A distortion compounded by interpreters bent on clarifying Newman's thought by supplying what he must have intended but did not state in so many words. This last procedure in particular drew Ward's ire.

He focused upon Brémond's summation of Newman's perspective as that was set out in the introduction:

> In this book's initial pages are found these extraordinary words: 'Great ideas evolve at the risk of being corrupted. In the other world it is otherwise, but here below to live is to change: the more a doctrine is perfect, the more often it has had to change.'[34]

In these few sentences Ward was able to find a mare's nest of problems. In his introduction Brémond had used the passage to elaborately contrast Newman's position with Bossuet's adherence to the

---

[31] Brémond, *Développement* (1904), p. xiii and (1906), p. 9.

[32] Wilfrid Ward, "Newman Through French Spectacles" in *The Tablet* 108 (21 July 1906): 86-89, citing 86.

[33] Ward, "Newman Through French Spectacles," p. 86.

[34] Brémond, *Développement* (1904), p. x and (1906), p. 6. The French text reads: "Dès les premières pages de ce livre, on rencontre ces extraordinaires paroles. 'Les grandes idées évoluent sous peine de se corrompre. Il n'en va pas ainsi dans l'autre monde, mais ici-bas vivre c'est changer; plus d'une doctrine est parfaite, plus souvent elle a dû changer.'"

unchangeableness of Catholic dogma. However, as an accurate basis for Newman's actual position, the quotation simply will not do, as Ward made clear via comparison with the original text. He provided a lengthy quote, heeding his own admonition about the importance of providing adequate context to Newman's expression. The part that directly relates to Brémond's excerpt reads

> old principles reappear under new forms. [The idea] changes with them in order to remain the same. In a higher world it is otherwise, but here below to live is to change, and to be perfect is to have changed often.[35]

Brémond has omitted the sentence which insists on the unchangeableness of Christian truth; has proffered instead a sentence whose approximate equivalent Ward could not find in the *Essay*; and has substituted doctrine for the original, more general discussion of living ideas in the history of the world. Moreover, the text is accurately rendered by Brémond in the translation of the *Essay* that follows, making the changes in the introduction's version all the more curious. Such distortion of Newman's thought Ward considered serious at a time when the ideas contained in the *Essay* were being denounced in France as dangerous.

The appearance of Edouard Le Roy's explosive article, "Qu'est-ce qu'un dogme?" in *La Quinzaine* (1905) rendered discussions of dogma and its development all the more volatile. Le Roy's republication of the article, together with criticism it had received and its reply in 1907 as *Dogme et critique* kept the controversy on dogma alive.[36] In the midst of these debates appeared the second series of Pierre Batiffol's *Études d'histoire et de théologie positive* (1905), which focused on the eucharist, more specifically on the real presence and transubstantiation. An earlier series of studies bearing the same title had been published in 1902, examining the historical evolution of the sacrament of penance and the primitive hierarchy. Common to both volumes was the conviction that this evolutionary development raised real doctrinal problems, not all of which were perceived by the early theologians. A modern critic, however, could not ignore them. The two series of studies also adopted a common approach,

---

[35] Ward, "Newman Through French Spectacles," p. 88, citing *Essay on Development* (1897), p. 40.
[36] An English translation of the original article may be found in Joseph Fitzer, ed. *Romance and the Rock: Nineteenth-Century Catholics on Faith and Reason* (Minneapolis: Fortress Press, 1989), pp. 347-373. On the controversy aroused by Le Roy see Guy Mansini, OSB, *"What Is A Dogma?" The Meaning and Truth of Dogma in Edouard Le Roy and His Scholastic Opponents* (Roma: Editrice Pontificia Università Gregoriana, 1985).

which Batiffol characterized as "taking the texts, situating them in their time and context, trying to interpret them by themselves, then grouping their assertions according to their affinities, and, once this empirical classification is made, discovering, with the continuity of a central idea, the slow elaboration of dogmatic reflection."[37] This way of proceeding was in conformity with Newman's approach, and Batiffol acknowledged his dependence. In these studies he found "a verification of Newman's law, more convincing perhaps, than any of the historical examples proposed by Newman himself."[38]

Batiffol made it clear that he regarded Newman's *Essay* as providing a synthetic view of what he had expressed historically in his tracing of the stages of development of the real presence in the second volume. Here there arose a difficulty. Batiffol's claim to Newman's mantle did not prove successful in neutralizing the book's doctrinal shortcomings as those were perceived by subscribers to the logical notion of development characterized earlier. Though Batiffol introduced revisions into the text, the third edition of his book was placed on the Index in July of 1907, the same month in which the antimodernist syllabus *Lamentabili sane exitu* was promulgated. The decision of the Congregation of the Index was not made public, although word of it leaked out.[39]

Among those who linked Batiffol's removal from the rectorship of the Institut catholique de Toulouse in 1907 with the unconfirmed report of his book being placed on the Index, questions would naturally arise. Were Vatican reservations linked to Batiffol's own use of development? Or did neo-Thomism, with its emphasis on logical forms of development, or at least explanation via analogies from logic, intend to exclude an approach such as Newman's, which "proclaimed the logical explanation to be insufficient, and in so doing admitted the possibility of a more drastic change in the history of dogma than Thomism could possibly allow?"[40]

Within the movement for renewal that came to be censured under the label of 'Modernism' Batiffol occupied a position on the right,

[37] Pierre Batiffol, "Pour l'histoire des dogmes" in *Bulletin de littérature ecclésiastique* 7 (1905): 151–164, citing p. 158.
[38] Batiffol, "Pour l'histoire des dogmes," p. 158. Indeed, Batiffol cautioned that, absent a familiarity with Newman's *Essay on Development* and Oxford University Sermon of 2 February 1843, a potential reader may be advised against trying to assimilate the contents of the 1905 volume.
[39] See Marcel Bécamel, "Comment Monseigneur Batiffol quitta Toulouse à la Noël 1907" in *Bulletin de littérature ecclésiastique* 72 (1971): 258–288 and 74 (1973): 109–138, at 111–114.
[40] Chadwick, *From Bossuet to Newman*, p. 193.

among the 'progressives' (or 'progressistes' as they sometimes styled themselves).[41] Loisy – and Brémond, taking into account George Tyrrell's influence, especially where Newman is concerned – may be seen to occupy a centrist position. We may conclude this survey with a brief look at a representative of the left wing, Marcel Hébert.

Unlike Loisy and Batiffol, whose interests were strongly (though far from exclusively) historical, Hébert early developed an interest in philosophy. Through exposure to Kant in particular, he migrated from a convinced Thomism to a position of evolutionary naturalism that led him to a loss of his faith and his separation from the Church in 1903.

Though aware of Loisy's work and influenced by it, the pressures upon traditional understandings of dogma Hébert experienced were primarily philosophical in nature. Unable to reconcile the presence of evil in the world with the existence of a personal God, Hébert sought a *modus vivendi* in a symbolist reading of dogma. On this interpretation dogmas provided images that spoke to the heart, not objective depictions of reality. This gave images a provisional character, given their inevitable inadequacy to the reality they engaged. The Kantian influence is apparent in Hébert's affirmation that, "after having formed ideas, concepts, there is a mistake and an immense danger in generalizing from the data of the senses or of psychological consciousness, in applying those to Reality as it is *in itself* and not as it *appears* in our fragmented, imperfect experiences."[42] Yet, images remained necessary – they tied the abstract idea to the heart of the believer. Hence for a period while he remained within the Church, he thought that criticism, both historical and philosophical, could purify dogmas, recreate, reinvent them, investing them with new forms, less material and more psychological. This species of pragmatist fideism gave ground before Hébert's evolutionism, to the point that his *L'Évolution de la foi catholique* (1905) could well be titled 'Evolution *beyond* the Catholic Faith.'

In this book Hébert viewed Catholic dogma as caught between the jaws of a vice, pressured from one side by critical philosophical thought and from the other by historical criticism. The pressure had been steadily mounting and Catholicism must inevitably break,

---

[41] See François Laplanche, *La crise de l'origine. La science catholique des Évangiles et l'histoire au XXe siècle* (Paris: Albin Michel, 2006) for treatment of progressive Catholic scholarship in the period following the Modernist crisis.

[42] Marcel Hébert, "La Dernière Idole. Étude sur la personalité divine" in *Revue de Métaphysique et de Morale* 10 (1902): 397–408, citing p. 406 (italics in original).

for the escape proffered by symbolism had been rejected with the condemnation of Loisy's works in 1903. Hébert traced the roots of the symbolist interpretation of dogma back to Kant, who discerned the moral symbolism conveyed by dogma. However, it was necessary to go beyond Kant to acknowledge that dogmas were equally symbols of metaphysical hypotheses.[43] To do this it was necessary to go beyond the transitional nature of 'loisyste' Catholicism and extend that symbolic awareness to the very fundamentals of Christianity, not excluding the mythical image of divine personality. The impossibility of Christianity's making this admission without self-destructing limited it to a now outdated, if fruitful and interesting, stage in the evolution of human consciousness. The challenge remained to find what was good and efficacious in Christianity, gained over the course of its historical development, and incorporate that into the current progress of humanity.[44] While the psychological needs of humanity exhibited continuity, the forms of satisfying those have undergone a shift in the transition to modernity. To minds increasingly free from socialization into the traditional dogmatic language, simpler and more effective expressions would need to be found as alternatives to Christian myths and imagery. L'Évolution de la foi and its successor volume, Le Divan (1907), were designed to build upon the accomplishments of Loisy and Sabatier and find a way forward in these "obscure hours of transition."[45]

In the end, for Hébert, Newman and his successors do not go far enough in their application of evolution. For those formed by modernity and thus capable of distinguishing between image and idea, there is more real change and less continuity than Newman – or even Sabatier –would allow. The question is no longer that of preservation of type within Christianity, but rather seeing Christianity itself as one of a number of types of belief created by human consciousness over the course of centuries, a type that is being surpassed as humanity transitions to its next phase of development.

This survey of some French responses to Newman's writings on development has yielded several 'Newmans.' There is the Newman compatible with the logical theory of development set forward by André de la Barre; the Newman who gives more systematic expression to the historical particularities unearthed by Pierre Batiffol; the

---

[43] Marcel Hébert, L'Évolution de la foi catholique (Paris: Félix Alcan, 1905), pp. 164-165, 150-155.
[44] Hébert, L'Évolution de la foi catholique, p. 3.
[45] Hébert, L'Évolution de la foi catholique, p. 210.

Newman who points the way forward to a theory of development that needs to address questions that he did not foresee in his own time, a Newman on development requiring development in his turn, advanced by Alfred Loisy and Henri Brémond; lastly, a Newman left behind, together with his Modernist exponents, by the evolutionary advance of human consciousness, posited by Marcel Hébert. How may these varieties of Newmans be explained? What was it about the man's work, or the times themselves, that called forth so many and such incompatible representations?

Elements of an answer are suggested in the work of two scholars who have intensively studied Newman's writings on development. First, Aidan Nichols has indicated a shift in the question asked at the time of the Modernist crisis in comparison to that which Newman engaged. Identifying "two great questions which cannot be answered without some consideration of doctrinal development" as "How is the confession of the Catholic Church to be justified, vis-à-vis other Christian churches, and how is the primitive Creed, the Creed of the early Church, to be justified, over against alternative readings of Christian origins," he sees Newman and his contemporaries largely concerned with the first, while Modernists and neo-Thomists primarily engaged the second.[46]

Second, Nicholas Lash has also pointed out a difference between Newman's focus and that of later interpreters:

> To him, as a pioneer, it was the *fact* of 'development' which he offered as a 'hypothesis', as an alternative to 'immutability', on the one hand, and 'corruption' on the other. He took into consideration many widely differing types of 'development', both because the complexity of the historical evidence demanded this, and because his heuristic conception of 'development' as the key to the problem was not further implemented in the form of any single 'theory of development', in the modern sense, at all.[47]

In Lash's view, Newman's *Essay on Development* did not present a single theory of development, but rather "the seeds of a number of such theories."[48] Depending on which aspect of development interpreters fastened upon, their more systematic elaboration of it could – and did – assume diverse forms, not always compatible with one another, and not all of which would have been regarded by Newman as legitimate

---

[46] Nichols, *From Newman to Congar*, pp. 12-13.
[47] Nicholas Lash, *Newman on Development* (Shepherdstown, WV: Patmos, 1975), p. 56 (emphasis in original).
[48] Lash, *Newman on Development*, p. 56.

offspring of his *Essay*.

If from each side there were differences in focus, and from Newman's side resources for constructing and legitimating a number of theories of development, from the Modernist side there were differences operative in that construction that stemmed from contrasting conceptions of the nature of knowledge and the process of human knowing. The left wing of the reformers is characterized by the tendency to privilege history at the expense of suppressing orthodoxy. This 'rationalist' response to the problems raised by historical consciousness may be seen as the mirror image of the 'dogmatist' tendency to reconcile orthodoxy and history at the expense of history, as seen in logical theories of development.[49] For Hébert, as for a number of others who were involved in the movement, the dogmas of faith were but a transitory step in the evolution toward a truer knowledge of human life in the world.

Batiffol, reflecting progressives on the right more generally, hoped to distinguish in orthodoxy an essential, static element, and an element clarified by ecclesial reflection. This distinction could not be identified independently of applied research on the part of historical theology, a domesticated historical criticism, so to speak. While the second element has a history the permanent element does not. Thus, despite a change in the concept of orthodoxy, historical theology "rests in this serene knowledge of the essential that cannot be affected by history."[50]

In Christoph Théobald's judgment, rationalism and progressivism share a common preoccupation with the essential (accepted by the progressive and refused by the rationalist) while holding contrasting judgments about its relation to history. Thus the real question would not be the entry of history into the religious universe. Rationalism, progressivism, and dogmatism are all aware of that. What distinguishes Loisy, Brémond and others such as Mgr Mignot is a new way of conceiving history that goes beyond the parameters set by the foregoing positions.

Unlike Batiffol, for whom the practice of criticism would reveal an essential, permanent element in dogma distinguishable from the historical forms dogma had assumed, for Loisy the scientific work of

---

[49] The terms are those of Christoph Théobald, who develops them in "L'Entrée de l'histoire dans l'univers religieux et théologique au moment de la crise 'moderniste'" in Jean Greisch et al., *La Crise contemporaine. Du modernisme à la crise des herméneutiques* (Paris: Beauchesne, 1973), pp. 10–13.

[50] Théobald, "L'Entrée de l'histoire," p. 16.

the recent past had introduced a schism between the ancient religious universe and modern historical consciousness. The latter has the effect of dissolving the essential element rather than bringing it more clearly into focus. Attempted preservation of the traditional formulae results in incomprehension, eventually in incredulity. A work of translation is necessary, but one that is more than a matter of language. What is required is a translation of ideas.

The justification for this work of reconstruction took the form of a new conception of truth, that of 'relative truth' or historical relativity. Truth – or error – must always be viewed in relation to an historical situation. For Loisy, "the efforts of a healthy theology should be directed to a solution of the antinomy, presented by the unquestionable authority faith demands for dogma, and the variability, the relativity, the critic cannot fail to perceive in the history of dogmas and dogmatic formulas."[51] This relativity reveals a distance between the interpreter's location in time and that of the historical object.

Loisy has been judged more successful in revealing the 'great ugly ditch' of history than in resolving the problem it raised. Nonetheless, his work does represent an advance over the progressives, who did not succeed in posing the question of historical interpretation in viable form. However, further advance would necessitate greater awareness of the relativity imposed by the interpreter's location in history, not only the text's. "Loisy highlights the historical relativity and the finitude of the religious phenomenon. He veils those in the historian's own work."[52]

Turning from the larger implications of controversies over development during the Modernist period for theology, and back to Newman, it can be said that, at least in France, Ward's worries were justified. Despite Vatican disclaimers that Newman was not in view in the condemnations of Modernism, his reputation suffered. For several decades his name would once again be under a cloud, until his work would be taken up by a new generation of Catholic scholars and impact Vatican II.

---

[51] Loisy, *L'Évangile et l'Église*, p. 163; *Gospel and the Church*, p. 215 (translation modified).
[52] Théobald, "L'Entrée de l'histoire," p. 42. The same can be said of Hébert and other 'rationalists.'

Chapter 16

NEWMAN ON DEVELOPMENT IN THEOLOGY AND NATURAL SCIENCE

by Thomas Ryba

Introduction

Because we live in an age dominated by the success of the natural sciences, among the most pressing questions for the contemporary Catholic believer is "What is the proper understanding of the relation between science and religion?" It is evidence of the prescience of John Henry Newman to have provided answers to this question over one hundred and sixty years ago, answers which, when re-examined today, have a satisfying and decidedly contemporary character. Newman's answers are of two kinds. First, there is the answer to the question: "Where does theology fit into the architecture of the sciences?" Second, there are the answers Newman gives to the question: "What are the similarities that allow us to establish resemblances between the sciences?"

The answer that Newman gave to the first question was intentional and self-conscious. Newman had a clear understanding of the significance of the question, and he succeeded in answering it with some finality. Because issues connected with it had already been raised at the time Newman lived, but have continued to be raised since Newman offered an answer to it, his intent was to offer a sort of perennial solution whose general features were set, even though newly emergent details remain to be worked out anew by each generation.[1]

---

[1] For a survey of these issues, consult J. H. Newman, *The Idea of a University*. New York: Image Books, 1959 [1853 & 1858], especially the following lectures or essays: 'Theology a Branch of Knowledge,' 'Bearing of Theology on Other Knowledge,' 'Bearing of Other Knowledge on Theology' and 'Christianity and Physical Science.'

Though Newman also provides answers to the second question, the difference here is that it was not that he *intended* to provide them, nor was he necessarily even aware of the significance of the second question. Rather, these answers come as by-products of his other investigations, and though they function as answers to the questions we ask today, but are different from the questions Newman intentionally answered, they are, just for this reason, testimonies to Newman's amazing prescience. The value of Newman's answers is shown especially in the relevance of these questions to contemporary discussion of scientific development.

Ian Barbour on the relations between Religion and Natural Science

In his Gifford lectures (1989-1991), *Religion in an Age of Science*, the Anglo-American philosopher of science, Ian Barbour, provides an analysis of the possible relations between science and religion which has become one of the root formulations for the science–religion dialogue.[2] Apparently using, as his point of departure, the various relations between Christ and culture which H. Richard Niebuhr discussed in his classic Christology, Barbour suggests that there are four possible relations between natural science and religion.[3] These are either: conflict, independence, dialogue, or integration.

Religion and natural science are in conflict when both make "rival literal statements about the same domain ... so that one must choose between them."[4] Barbour thinks that whenever either religion or science oversteps its boundary, it may come into a false conflict with the other. When a Christian believer moves from his interpretation of

---

[2] Ian Barbour, *Religion in an Age of Science*. The Gifford Lectures (1989-1991). Volume 1. San Francisco: Harper San Francisco, 1990, pp. 3-30.

[3] Barbour does not say the source of his analysis of the relations between science and religion is H. Richard Niebuhr's Christology, but other references show that he is, nevertheless, familiar with Niebuhr's theology. The match between Barbour's analysis and Niebuhr's analysis is not perfect, but this is probably explicable because: Barbour (more reductively) takes religion and science to be sectors of culture, while Niebuhr takes Christ as transcendent to culture, throughout. Barbour constructs his analysis on the basis of only four of Niebuhr's relations. Whereas Niebuhr has Christ *against* culture, Christ *of* culture, Christ *above* culture, and Christ and culture *in paradox*, Barbour has religion and science *in conflict*, religion and science *in integration*, religion and science *in dialogue*, and religion and science *as independent*. Omitted is a correlative to Niebuhr's fifth relation, Christ *as transforming* culture. On these similarities compare Barbour's discussion to H. Richard Niebuhr's discussion in *Christ and Culture*. New York: Harper and Row, 1956, pp. 45-189.

[4] Barbour, *Religion in an Age of Science*, p. 4.

the Bible to correct science or when a scientist moves from a scientific theory to propose a universal materialist metaphysics that excludes religious realities, this falsely places science and religion into conflict. Religious believers err when they imagine that their interpretation of a scriptural passage can correct a scientific fact. Scientists err when they believe that their interpretation of a scientific theory excludes faith.

On the other hand, the attempt to avoid conflicts between religion and science by segregating them into hermetically sealed domains and making them speak entirely different languages means that they can never be brought into any relation to one another; it means that the search for a unitary reality which unites faith and science is a pipedream.[5] This view is tantamount to saying that, for all practical purposes, religion and science result in two different, incompatible conceptions of truth.

Dialogue is an attempt to resolve the oppositions of the first two approaches. Its purpose is to explore the significance of the points at which natural science and religion are in apparent conflict or correlation and to explain the significance of both. Dialogical stances are truthful to the degree to which they avoid seeing the points of contact between natural science and religion as either purely conflictual or correlative. By over-emphasizing the conflictual, they move close to the view that natural science and religion define completely exclusive domains of experience. But though they may move close to this view, they must ultimately draw back, for were this extreme reached, dialogue would be *impossible*. On the other hand, by over-emphasizing the correlative, dialogical stances move close to the view that natural science and religion are the same thing, but – again – they may only move close to this view, for were this extreme reached, natural science and religion would be collapsed into one-another, and dialogue would be *unnecessary*. The latter is an outcome which clearly cannot be achieved, given the different techniques and ends of each.[6]

For Barbour, the desideratum of the exploration of the relations between science and religion is to arrive at a unified view of the world which is consistent with both. This is the goal of the integrative approach: to find an encompassing theory of the world – a metaphysics – which will allow the compatibility of religion and science.[7] But it is a goal which is only susceptible to provisional fulfillment. Because

---

[5] Barbour, *Religion in an Age of Science*, pp. 10, 16.
[6] Barbour, *Religion in an Age of Science*, pp. 16–23.
[7] Barbour, *Religion in an Age of Science*, pp. 28–30.

religion and science are perpetually growing, there can be no ultimate integration which is not subject to revision. Therefore, there can never be a metaphysics which will represent the compatibility of science and religion with finality.

If we think of Barbour's description of the relations between natural science and religion as a sequence that represents *a dialectic*, then a few observations from a Catholic perspective are especially relevant.[8] First, neither the first nor the second position represents the mainstream position of our tradition. Catholics are neither biblical positivists – like some of our fundamentalist brethren – nor do we accept a view of the universe that fragments it into hermetically sealed compartments, like the various neo-Kantian philosophers of science. The positions in Barbour's dialectic that most properly represent Catholic view are the last two, but its contemporary stance may be framed more precisely as: *dialogue leading to a unified worldview*.

It has not always been so. At one time – during the western medieval period – the Catholic tradition could rest with confidence in the view that a unifying synthesis had been accomplished between the sciences and metaphysics. That synthesis, and the confidence which accompanied it, were short-lived. Since the rise of the scientific world view, the Catholic tradition has struggled against Barbour's first two relations, from a position within the third, but with hope that the fourth might again be possible.

It is my purpose in this essay to argue that Newman's criteria of what constitutes the development of doctrine opens up new avenues in the dialogue between natural science and religion because of the questions his thought answers. What I hope to show is that the old claim that theology is science is renewed in its plausibility, when one compares John Henry Newman's view of doctrinal development with Imre Lakatos' view of scientific development. In making this claim, I hope to avoid the pitfalls of dialogue to which Barbour has alerted us. I am well aware that theology is not identical to natural science, as I am aware that they are not so radically exclusive to make all conversation between them impossible. My position is a bit more subtle. I hope to show that the similarities between Newman's notion of genuine doctrinal development and Imre Lakatos' notion of progressive scientific development lend additional weight to the idea

---

[8] By 'dialectic' I mean a process of intellectual engagement and wrangling by which the truthful features of unworkable ideas or standpoints are preserved in improved or more realistic ideas and standpoints.

that though not identical, *both* have claim to be classified as science. But before we can proceed to this comparison, I think it is necessary to clear up a point having to do with the terms of the comparison.

The terms of comparison: Religion and Science or Theology and Science?

Up to now, I have alternatively spoken about the relations between natural science and religion and natural science and theology. Although both Barbour and Newman leave the word 'religion' relatively undefined and quite underdetermined in its meaning (sometimes associating it with the widest range of practices and beliefs but sometimes associating with what is more properly theology), we would do well, at this point, to make a distinction between religion and theology that neither thinker supplies.[9]

---

[9] A quick comparison of Newman and Barbour's definitions, with the definitions I have proposed, suggests uniform compatibility.

Newman speaks, in various works, at great length, about the propositions which comprise the content of natural and monotheistic theology. He does not, however, attempt to specify its general features across the various religions, as do the provisional definitions I have proposed. Newman does give these general characteristics: (1) Theology is the science of God "or the truths we know about God put into a system" but whose fullness is beyond any system (*Idea*, pp. 96-97); (2) "theology is precise and consistent in its intellectual structure; ... [it is] one idea [that of God] unfolded in its just proportions, carried out upon an intelligible method, and issuing in necessary and immutable results; understood indeed at one time and place better than another, held here and there with more or less of inconsistency, but ... where it is found, the evolution, not of half-a-dozen ideas, but of one" (*Idea*, pp. 100-101); (3) theology enters into all other orders of knowledge and leads to a "connected" view of things (*Scope*, pp. xxxviii, 15, 31-34); (4) theology is about notional assent and notional apprehension; religion is about real assent and imaginative apprehension (*Grammar*, pp. 98, 120); (5) theology apprehends propositions "for the purposes of proof, analysis, comparison" as expressing notions, but religion apprehends propositions for the purposes of devotion as "the image of a reality" (*Grammar*, p. 119); (6) natural theology can stand as "a substantive science ... without religion," but "religion cannot maintain its ground without theology" (*Grammar*, p. 121). See: J. H. Newman, *On the Scope and Nature of University Education*, New York: Dutton, 1965 [1852]. *The Idea of a University*. New York: Image Books, 1959 [1852 & 1858] and *An Essay in Aid of a Grammar of Assent*. Westminster, MD: Christian Classics, 1973 [1870].

Barbour conducts his comparisons between science and religion without providing precise definitions of either 'religion' or 'theology.' He does say that theology is "critical reflection on the life and thought of the religious community" and that it "deals primarily with religious beliefs, which must always be seen against the wider background of religious traditions that include formative scriptures, communal rituals, individual experiences, and ethical norms" (*Age*, p. 3). Barbour concentrates especially on characterizing religious experience in its six forms: (1) numinous experience, (2) unitive mystical experience, (3) transvaluative experience, (4) courage in the face of suffering and death, (5) the moral experience of obligation, and (6) the experience of mundane order and creativity (*Age*, pp. 36-38). See: Ian Barbour, *Religion in an Age of Science*. The Gifford Lectures (1989-1991). Volume 1. San Francisco: Harper San Francisco, 1990.

We may stipulate that religion is belief in an *Ultimate* (or *Eternal*) and the actions, objects and thoughts which result from this belief. Belief can be induced by *transcendental* experiences or profound feelings (awe, mystery, guilt, joy, subservience, fear, etc.) which can occur in the presence of cultic objects, rituals, symbols, holy persons, or in the presence of nature, itself. Such belief both *gives rise to* and *results from*: (1) distinctions between the transcendental and the mundane (sacred and the profane), (2) moral codes, (3) world views, (4) personal transformations, (5) rituals, (6) symbols, (7) cultic objects, and (8) a social group bound together by all the above. Belief can also be induced by theology, which is *rational reflection upon* and *argumentation about* all of the above. Theology is not simply equivalent to religion but it may be considered a supplemental part of religion.[10]

As a supplement, theology is a reasoned "second story" to a religion; it takes the content of that religious belief and practice as its subject matter, and it is directed to the intellectual support, testing and refinement of the system of belief. A theology functions as a legitimation of some particular religion. As such, theology is a form of religion-based knowledge which is partisan, reflective, critical, defensive, analytic, and systematic and which results in reasoned interpretations, criticisms, defenses, orderings and conclusions of that religion.[11] Finally, in its capacity as a legitimation, theology has a dual reference: (a) it treats the objective features of the religion, and (b) it treats the subjective/anthropological features of the religion. Likewise its arguments can be directed objectively (extrinsically) and subjectively (intrinsically).

Theology is a proper part of the Christian religion, and an especially prominent proper part of the Catholic tradition. What applies to the Christian religion vis-à-vis natural science therefore *especially* applies to Christian theology vis-à-vis natural science. To put it another way, whatever similarities one finds between religion and natural science should be all the stronger when the terms of the comparison are theology and science. In fact, one wonders whether the latter comparison isn't really the more appropriate one, owing to theology's systematic and rational orientations.

---

[10] This is a freely modified version of the definition of 'religion' provided by William Alston in his article "Religion" in *The Encyclopedia of Philosophy*. Paul Edwards, Editor. Volume 7. New York: Macmillan, 1972, pp. 141b–142a.

[11] This also is a freely modified conflation of the definitions of 'theology' presented by Roger Schmidt, *Exploring Religion*. Belmont, California: Wadsworth, 1980, pp. 22-25, 283-285 and Alister McGrath, *Christian Theology: An Introduction*. London: Blackwell, 2006, pp. 1-4, 99-120.

Theology as Science

But is theology a science? It is only since the Enlightenment that this question has had saliency. Before the eighteenth century, the question would not have been raised because no one would have thought to doubt that the answer to this question was anything other than "Yes". Theology had been classically defined both as *scientia* (science) and as *epistēmē* (certain knowledge) and was viewed as one of the oldest varieties of rigorous inquiry. It is especially since the Enlightenment, with its critique of knowledge and the dominance of the empirical-scientific worldview, that theology's status as science has come to be questioned. Since then, whenever the question has been posed, (more often than not) it has been answered in the negative. Thankfully, such important questions are not decided by ideological consensus. As Catholics, we are under a proscription not to follow the spirit of the age, unthinkingly. But when we, as thinking Catholics, buck a prevalent trend, we *are* expected to give our reasons for doing so.

Because space is limited, I cannot undertake an argument which will convincingly establish the scientific status of theology in all particulars. That must wait for a book.[12] What I can do, however, is to sketch some of the most suggestive similarities between what Newman describes as the robust development of Christian doctrine and what Imre Lakatos describes as the robust development of natural science. There is a well-worn saying that "if it walks like a duck, and it quacks like a duck, and it looks like a duck, then it probably is a duck." Like most popular, over-used expressions it hides an important generalization. I suggest that the same might be said for the features that qualify a discipline as a science. About the question of theology's being science, I would like to argue that theology behaves in such a way that, though this behavior is far from clinching the case that it is *unequivocally* science, nevertheless, its behavior in a number of respects – one of which is the character of its development – does add credence to that conclusion.

It seems to me that the similarities between Christian theology and natural science suggest an alternative to the four possible relations that Barbour described. That fifth alternative is that both natural science and theology, though differing methodologically and with respect to their objects of study, are both expressions of a common

---

[12] In my unpublished 2006 Hutton lecture, *Dogma, Theology, and Scientific Structure*, I have outlined some of the analogous structures to be treated in this future book. My Hutton lecture will be forthcoming, with necessary changes, in the *Toronto Journal of Theology*, sometime in 2009.

underlying form of inquiry in which they both share. It is that common, broader, underlying form which has as much right to the name 'science' as anything exclusively characterized by the methods of the natural sciences. If we ask the question "What is the origin of this underlying form?" I would argue that it is the complement to the nature of reality.[13] In other words, the complex nature of the real world is such that it demands a form of science broader than natural scientific reductionists are able to supply. It seems to me that Barbour's search for a unifying worldview or metaphysics is an attempt to provide a description of the reality which grounds this general form of inquiry.

Here, I think we are greatly helped in our reasons by the thought of John Henry Cardinal Newman, who in his *Essay on the Development of Christian Doctrine* gave an incredibly prescient description of genuine development which allows us to see the unity of theology and the empirical sciences according to a particular characteristic. It is a measure of Newman's prescience to have anticipated – by over one hundred years – many of the same features that Imre Lakatos would associate with progressive natural scientific programs, but Newman found those features not in natural science but in the development of Christian doctrine.

John Henry Newman on the Nature and Development of Doctrine

One important question concerns the unit of analysis to which Newman applies his analysis of development. Although his work treating development is entitled *An Essay on the Development of Christian Doctrine*, the units which Newman attempts to gauge by his criteria of development are variable: they consist of individual ideas, doctrines, theologies, and the Christian tradition itself.[14] Lakatos' analysis, too, seems to drift between research programs and theories with a certain imprecision. But, I would argue neither analysis is very much compromised by this ambiguity.

The Units of Newman's Analysis

Newman begins his essay with a discussion of ideas which he takes to be the *elemental* units which undergo development. This understanding

---

[13] This follows from the Thomist principle of intellectual adequation: that the intellect is adequate to its objects.

[14] J. H. Newman's *An Essay on the Development of Christian Doctrine* was first published in 1845.

of an idea's relation to the reality it represents is a brilliant anticipation of Husserl's phenomenology.[15] Newman says that the idea representing "an object or supposed object is commensurate with the sum total of its [the object's] possible aspects" as these aspects "vary in the separate consciousnesses of individuals" and "in proportion to ... [the idea's] force and depth, and the argument for its reality."[16] The problem with the aspectuality of ideas is that the views of ideas may be taken from so many different stances and under so many different conditions that "they [may] seem at first sight incompatible, ... disproportionate or even monstrous" until an argument for their "coalition, resolution, substantiveness, integrity, originality and power" is produced.[17] In part, the argument for the harmonization of the aspects of an idea is both synchronic (it makes this harmonization of the idea at a particular time, across all views of it) and diachronic (it makes this harmonization of the idea across all times, across all views of it). It is the purpose of the *Essay* to accomplish the latter.[18]

However, the *Essay* is not directed to the harmonization of a single idea but to the harmonization of a more complicated complex of ideas by explaining that set of ideas, developmentally. For Newman, Christian doctrine, at large, is composed of a set of theologies which themselves are sets of ideas. Christian doctrine is nothing less than

---

[15] Edmund Husserl calls these aspects "perspectives" and recommends a kind of analysis called "perspectival variation", a method roughly anticipated in Newman's discussion of ideas both in his essay on development and the *Grammar of Assent*. Husserl's formulation of phenomenology in the 20th century was anticipated by a number of figures who paved the way for its mature realization in his thought. For a rehearsal of this antecedent development and a description of the Husserlian phenomenology, see: Thomas Ryba, *The Essence of Phenomenology and Its Meaning for the Scientific Study of Religion*. Toronto Studies in Religion. New York: Peter Lang, 1994.

[16] John Henry Cardinal Newman, *An Essay on the Development of Christian Doctrine*. New York: Image Books, 1960 [1878 revision], 1:1:2: p. 58.

[17] J. H. Newman, *An Essay on the Development of Christian Doctrine* [1878], 1:1:2: p. 58.

[18] Newman's analysis in his *Essay* and my analysis in this essay represent only half of a possible phenomenological analysis. There are *noetic* (the act of consciousness) as well as *noematic* dimensions (the object of such acts) to the development of doctrine and natural scientific research programs. In this chapter, I concentrate on the noematic dimension in the comparison between theology and natural science, this dimension having to do with the way ideas objectively refer to realities. But it would also be possible to compare theology and scientific research programs with respect to the way theologians and scientists subjectively relate to their ideas. For Newman, the tools for such a noetic analysis are provided in the *Grammar of Assent*, where he treats, *in extenso*, the subjective acts that condition our objective understanding of the world. We sometimes forget that in natural science questions of warrant, observation, choice, etc., are bound up with human will, desire and emotions and these sometimes account for the way scientists comport themselves. In the Lakatosian description of science, we must recognize the stubbornness of scientists who, in their commitment to a particular program of research, refuse to let contradictory evidences undermine their program and who may or may not have good reasons for doing so.

the comprehensive view of the total set of intellectual views of the content of the Christian faith. It is, therefore, Christian doctrine as a whole that is Newman's real unit of analysis.

Because Newman takes Christian doctrine as his unit, this means that anomalies between aspects of Christian doctrine will be dissolved when their development is understood, but this harmonization also would seem to require that any false views must be identified and excluded. Likewise according to Imre Lakatos, the business of the natural scientific research program is the elimination of false natural scientific views, in the long run.

Newman cannot hope to harmonize every aspect of this whole. He chooses certain "leading ideas" but with the stipulation that no leading idea be taken as an "aspect deep enough to exhaust the content of a real idea," that "no one term or proposition will serve to define it."[19] Though "it is allowable" when dealing with complex ideas "to consider [a complex idea's] ... distinct aspects as if [they were] separate ideas," these leading ideas can only be used "as a central idea for convenience, in order to group others around it."[20] In Newman's opinion, this core-periphery structure means that the Incarnation becomes the "central aspect" of Christianity, as long as all other aspects of doctrine are brought to a unity with it.[21] Although Newman's understanding of the structure of Christian doctrine is not worked out with the precision of Lakatos' understanding of the structure of natural scientific research programs, Newman toys with a core-periphery structure for doctrine which Lakatos finds as normative for the natural sciences.

Newman's desire to bring Christian doctrine into a harmony of aspects is accomplished through the criteria that define "healthy development". Healthy development is contrasted with corruption. Corruption entails that an organized thing – something with its own function, direction, aim, nature and laws – "loses its unity" and "breaks apart" into "constituent parts" and "loses its unity" prior to its mutation or "dissolution" and "termination".[22] In corruption, the organism's "principle of life and growth" is lost and it is resolved into other "ideas which take its place."[23] In sum, any "development is to be

[19] J. H. Newman, *An Essay on the Development of Christian Doctrine* [1878], 1:1:3: p. 58.
[20] Ibid., 1:1:3: pp. 58–59.
[21] Ibid., 1:1:3: p. 59.
[22] Ibid., 5:0:3: p. 176.
[23] J. H. Newman, *An Essay on the Development of Christian Doctrine*. New York: Penguin, 1973 [1845 edition], 1:3:1: pp. 120-121. From this point on, I alternate between the two editions of

considered a corruption which *obscures or prejudices its essential idea*, or which *disturbs the laws of development* which constitute its organization, or which reverses its course of development."[24]

In contrast, Newman calls the characteristics of "healthy" or "genuine" development variously "notes" or "tests" of development.[25] He understands the tests of genuine development as also the tests of substantial unity.[26] There are seven of these notes or tests: (1) preservation of idea or type, (2) continuity of principles, (3) power of assimilation, (4) logical sequence, (5) early anticipation or anticipation of its future, (6) preservative additions or conservative action on its past, and (7) chronic continuance or vigor.[27] Newman summarizes what comprises a healthy or genuine development in contrast to a corruption as follows:

> To guarantee its own substantial unity, it must be seen to be one in type, one in its system of principles, one in its unitive power toward externals, one in its logical constructiveness, one in its witness of its early phases to its later, one in the protection which its later extends to its earlier, and one in its vigor with continuance, that is, in its tenacity.[28]

Imre Lakatos on the Structure and Progress of Scientific Research Programs

Writing some one hundred and twenty three years after Newman's *Essay*, the Hungarian philosopher of science, Imre Lakatos, proposed a description of scientific change which has remarkable resonances with Newman's description of genuine development. Because Lakatos devotes much of his time in his classic essay to the description of the structure of scientific theories, and not simply to a description of what constitutes legitimate development, and because that structure figures in his description of what constitutes scientific development, it is necessary to give a brief description of that structure.

Without raising all of the issues in the philosophy of science Lakatos' theory was designed to address, let me simply say that it was pitched against the irrationalist interpretation of Thomas Kuhn's

Newman's *Essay*, depending upon which version presents his argument in greatest detail.

[24] J. H. Newman, *An Essay on the Development of Christian Doctrine* [1845], 1:3:1: pp. 121-122.

[25] 'Tests' is the earlier stronger claim of the first edition, 'notes' is the later weaker claim of the second edition, though he at points uses 'notes' and 'tests' interchangeably in the second edition.

[26] The substantial unity refers, of course, to the organic unity of Christian doctrine.

[27] Compare the alternative phrasings in the edition of 1845 and 1878.

[28] J. H. Newman, *An Essay on the Development of Christian Doctrine* [1878], 5:7:4: pp. 206-207.

theory of scientific revolutions. According to the Lakatos view, Kuhn was right to describe paradigm shifts as new scientific perspectives but irrationalist when he – or others – suggested that they were to be viewed as radical discontinuities requiring "mystical conversion."[29] Lakatos' purpose was to provide a persuasive reconstruction of how paradigm shifts occur which did not imply that they were radically discontinuous mystical leaps of faith.

Deviating from the philosophies of Karl Popper and Thomas Kuhn, Lakatos argued that the unit of analysis for scientific progress was neither paradigms, nor conjectures and refutations, nor theories, but *research programs*. For Lakatos, scientific rationality is "the specification of a criterion of choice between competing 'research programs'."[30] For Lakatos, this criterion determines whether the scientific program is progressive or regressive (or "degenerating" as he puts it).

For Lakatos, a research program possesses the following features:

(1) A hard core of established scientific principles,
(2) A belt of auxiliary, protective hypotheses,
(3) A negative heuristic[31] associated with the hard core, and
(4) A positive heuristic associated with the auxiliary belt.

The negative heuristic associated with the hard core constitutes a prohibition by which the hard core is immunized from the application of *modus tollens* as a rule of falsification.[32] To protect the central core, a belt of auxiliary hypotheses are thrown up so as to be the alternative, possibly disprovable, intermediaries that deflect falsification. In an immature or insufficiently organized research program, the belt of auxiliary hypotheses will be thrown up helter-skelter, and may not be effective at deflecting falsification of the core of the program, but in a mature (or highly organized) research program, there will be a positive heuristic which consists of a series of "suggestions or hints

---

[29] Lakatos cited in John Losee. *A Historical Introduction to the Philosophy of Science*. Third Edition. Oxford: Oxford University Press, p. 229.

[30] Nancey Murphy. *Theology in an Age of Scientific Reasoning*. Ithaca: Cornell University Press, 1993, p. 59.

[31] A heuristic is a methodological path. A positive heuristic is a methodological path to pursue; a negative heuristic is a methodological path to avoid. Imre Lakatos, 'The Methodology of Scientific Research Programs' in *Criticism and the Growth of Knowledge*. Edits., Imre Lakatos and Alan Musgrave. Cambridge: Cambridge University Press, 1988 [1970], p. 47.

[32] The logical form of *modus tollens* is $[A \supset B] \supset [\sim B \supset \sim A]$. In theories of science that take the falsification of predictions to be decisive, *modus tollens* is taken as showing the hypothesis has been falsified. For example if a scientist were to say that a hypothesis 'H' predicted the existence of some phenomenon 'P' and P was not found, then according to these theories of falsification, the hypothesis would be disproven. Lakatos argues, to the contrary, that hypotheses are rarely abandoned simply because some phenomena are falsely predicted.

on how to change, develop the refutable variants of the research programme," that is ,"how to modify" or "sophisticate the 'refutable' protective belt."[33] These features are represented in the diagram below.

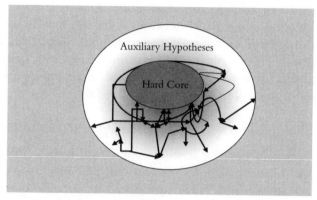

The Structure of Scientific Theories according to Lakatos

Auxiliary Hypotheses

Hard Core

There are two things to consider in the above diagram: (1) The various sentences of the research program are more compact (interconnected) as one approaches its core; (2) The core is maintained as stable because of the research program's ability to throw up a barage of hypotheses (arrows) which are particularizations of it and deflect its direct falsification.

Three conditions must be met for a research program to be considered progressive:

(1) Every new version of the central core and auxiliary hypotheses must preserve the un-refuted content of its predecessor research program, with which it is continuous;

(2) Every new version must have a larger empirical content over its predecessor; in other words, it must predict novel facts up until now not explained;

(3) *Some* of these predictions must be corroborated.[34]

Consistency is still expected to be a regulative principle in research programs but it is not to be an idol. The mere proliferation of observational anomalies rarely stops a progressive research program. More likely, anomalies are simply put into temporary quarantine either until other related inconsistencies build so precipitously to make them worthy of liberation or until they are dissolved by the explanatory capabilities of the program.

---

[33] Imre Lakatos, 'The Methodology of Scientific Research Programs [1970]', p. 135.

[34] Nancey Murphy. *Theology in an Age of Scientific Reasoning*. Ithaca: Cornell, 1990, p. 59.

Lakatos also recognizes three intentional stances of those who work in research programs – conservative, anarchic and rationalist – which also bear a surprising similarity to the intentional stances of theologians. Conservatives tend to want to halt the program until inconsistencies are worked out; the conservatives also tend to focus (diligently) on demonstrating the continuities between old versions and new versions of the program. Anarchists revel in mixed foundations and extol weak inconsistency as a property of the real world. Of the three, the rationalist approach has, historically, been the most fruitful. The rationalist will take inconsistencies seriously but will also work hardest to throw up a cloud of positive hypotheses to protect the core of the research program.[35]

Doctrinal and Natural Scientific Development Compared

Comparing their respective accounts of doctrinal and scientific change, it is possible to see the similarities that unite the two conceptions.

(1) Preservation of Type: Newman argues that in genuine development the various definitive parts of the doctrine of a religious tradition – its *"essential idea"* – will be preserved, though with variation in external form and extent. An inner essential unity will be maintained even as superficial external features may vary greatly.[36]

In the Lakatosian understanding of the development of scientific research programs, there is an analogous preservative operation. In Lakatosian scientific development, the scientific program is preserved, if the conceptual framework is preserved, even while allowing superficial changes to take place. Lakatos believes that the positive and negative heuristics taken together provide a "rough (or implicit) definition of the conceptual framework (and consequently the [characteristic] language [of the program])."[37] For Lakatos, there is no meaningful difference between the metaphysical and non-metaphysical statements in a program's conceptual framework. Both work together to define it.

(2) Continuity of Principles: Principles are the constant, unchanging, laws that are present in doctrines. Principles resemble eternal truths (or Platonic forms), which instantiate themselves according to place

---

[35] Imre Lakatos, 'The Methodology of Scientific Research Programs' in *Criticism and the Growth of Knowledge*, pp. 144–146.

[36] J. H. Newman, *An Essay on the Development of Christian Doctrine* [1878], 5:1:1–5:1:9: pp. 177–183; J. H. Newman, *An Essay on the Development of Christian Doctrine* [1845], 1:3:2: p. 124.

[37] Imre Lakatos, "The Methodology of Scientific Research Programs [1970]," p. 47, note 1.

and time in doctrines, while doctrines are the adaptations to time and circumstance of eternal principles. Doctrines are constituted by principles in combination with facts and concrete historical circumstances and may develop, their development being equivalent to the unfolding of the principles which they embody. Though the formulation and style of expression of doctrines can change, the principles they manifest are permanent. "Doctrines stand to principles ... as fecundity viewed relatively to generation" and the "life of doctrines may be said to consist in the law or principle which they embody."[38] Principles are thus the eternal generative rules for doctrines.

Together, principles and circumstances are responsible for the development of theological systems. "Systems live in principles and represent doctrines."[39] Either change in, or elimination of, these principles constitutes degeneration or corruption in doctrine. Such corruption results in theological systems which are not viable. For a theological system to be robust, there must be continuity in the principles of its doctrines.

There is a corresponding continuity in Lakatos' understanding of scientific development. Whereas, for Newman continuity must be maintained in principles, which are the ineluctable assumptions behind doctrines, for Lakatos continuity must be maintained in the series of successive theories; it is this continuity which "welds them into *research programmes*."[40] These theories are primarily connected with the positive heuristic of the scientific program. It is the positive heuristic which "defines problems, outlines the construction of a belt of auxiliary hypotheses, foresees anomalies, and turns them into examples all according to a preconceived plan."[41] It is the positive heuristic of a scientific program which dictates the problems the scientist will address, it is not the anomalies that raise problems that seem to contradict the theory which define this problem set.[42] The continuity of the constituent theories entails that a common set of research problems will be recognized.

(3) Power of Assimilation: The healthy development of a doctrine entails that that doctrine will be able to absorb or assimilate other challenging ideas into its unity, make them nurture its powers, serve

[38] J. H. Newman, *An Essay on the Development of Christian Doctrine* [1878], 5:2:1–5:2:2: pp. 183–184.
[39] J. H. Newman, *An Essay on the Development of Christian Doctrine* [1878], 5:2:1: p. 183.
[40] Imre Lakatos, 'The Methodology of Scientific Research Programs [1970]', p. 47.
[41] Imre Lakatos, 'The Methodology of Scientific Research Programs [1970]', pp. 110-111.
[42] Imre Lakatos, 'The Methodology of Scientific Research Programs [1970]', p. 111.

its purposes, and expand its content.[43] The stronger the doctrine is, the more it will trust its agility in the confrontation and absorption of what is good in challenging ideas.[44]

For Lakatos, the ability to absorb anomalies which seem contrary to the series of theories defining a research program is the means by which a viable research program is distinguished from which is non-viable. The way this absorption is accomplished is through the auxiliary core of hypotheses. Because the "hard core" of a program prohibits the application of the logical law of *modus tollens* to the content of that core, a band of auxiliary hypotheses is thrown up to account for anomalies that may appear as errors in observations, etc. If these hypotheses are ingeniously constructed, then they will be verified experimentally and lend greater support to the core of the program.[45] The increase in the size of this set of hypotheses, especially as they successfully absorb anomalous data, means a general increase in the content of the research program and, consequently, an improvement in its ability to answer objections.

(4) Logical Sequence: Though the consequences and meanings of doctrines may remain implicit and crabbed in their early forms, through time – according to Newman – they will be unfolded according to a logical structure and sequence. From time to time, the hidden wealth of doctrines held unexamined in the depths of consciousness will be elicited "into formal statement" and "logic [will be] ... brought in to arrange and inculcate what no science was employed in gaining."[46] The resulting logical conclusions and sequence will provide insights into the original doctrine and they will show the continuity of the later development with the original.[47]

Lakatos rejected the logical positivists' attempt to reduce the process of scientific discovery to an axiomatic deductive form in the same way that Newman rejected the reduction of natural reasoning to "paper logic".[48] But Lakatos' rejection of the formalization of natural

---

[43] J. H. Newman, *An Essay on the Development of Christian Doctrine* [1878], 5:3:1-5:3:4: pp. 189-191.
[44] Ibid., 5:3:5: pp. 191-192.
[45] Imre Lakatos, 'The Methodology of Scientific Research Programs [1970]', pp. 48-49.
[46] J. H. Newman, *An Essay on the Development of Christian Doctrine* [1878], 5:4:1: p. 193.
[47] Ibid., 5:4:5: p. 197.
[48] "It is the concrete being that reasons; pass a number of years, and I find my mind in a new place; how? the whole man moves; paper logic is but the record of it" (*Apologia*, p. 264). The term 'paper logic' comes from the *Apologia*, but Newman takes up the idea in many places as the description of the representation of reasoning taken as its reality. He describes paper logic at length in the Grammar : "I said just now that an object of sense presents itself to our view as one whole, and not in its separate details: we take it in, recognize it, and discriminate it from

science did not mean he rejected all attempts at representing those processes formally, after the fact. Like Newman, he stipulated that such formalization must not confuse the representation with the reality.

Also, Lakatos does not rule out consistency as a principle governing the evaluation of progressive science. For science to aim at truth, it must aim at consistency, but that does not mean that consistency must "immediately stop the development of a research program."[49] It is at times admissible, on the basis of a program's success and robustness, to allow inconsistencies to exist until the theory grows sufficiently to dissolve them or until the cloud of anomalies is so great as to call core assertions into question.

(5) Anticipation of Its Future: The healthy growth of a doctrine is always accompanied by the anachronistic anticipation of ideas which emerge prematurely only to take fuller form later.[50] These anticipations take the form of presentiments, intimations, and foreshadowings of later ideas which will become constitutive of doctrines at a later stage in its development.

---

other objects, all at once. Such too is the intellectual view we take of the *momenta* of proof for a concrete truth; we grasp the full tale of premises and the conclusion, *per modum unius,* – by a sort of instinctive perception of the legitimate conclusion in and through the premises, not by a formal juxtaposition of propositions. ... It is this distinction between ratiocination as the exercise of a living faculty in the individual intellect, and mere skill in argumentative science, which is the true interpretation of the prejudice which exists against logic in the popular mind, and of the animadversions which are leveled against it, as that its formulas make a pedant and a *doctrinaire,* that it never makes converts. ... Such maxims mean, when analyzed, that the processes of reasoning which legitimately lead to assent, to action, to certitude, are in fact too multiform, subtle, omnigenous, too implicit, to allow of being measured by rule, that they are after all personal, – verbal argumentation being useful only in subordination to a higher logic" (*Grammar,* pp. 301-303). In Sermon XIII, paragraph 9, of the *Oxford Sermons* ("Implicit and Explicit Reason"), Newman succinctly summarizes the distinction between paper and living logic as the distinction between explicit and implicit reason: "All men reason ...; but all men do not reflect upon their own reasonings. ... In other words all men have a reason, but not all men can give a reason. We may denote, then, these two exercises of mind as conscious and unconscious reasoning, or as Implicit Reason and Explicit Reason." J. H. Newman, *Apologia Pro Vita Sua.* New York: Image Books, 1962; *An Essay in Aid of a Grammar of Assent.* Westminster, MD: Christian Classics, 1973 [1870]; and *Fifteen Sermons Preached Before the University of Oxford (1826 – 1843).* Notre Dame: University of Notre Dame Press, 1997 [1872 edition].
Lakatos makes a similar point in the form of his favorite 'joke': The "history of science is frequently a caricature of its rational reconstructions; ... rational reconstructions are frequently caricatures of actual history; and ... some histories of science are caricatures both of actual history and its rational reconstructions." See: Imre Lakatos, "History of Science and Its Rational Reconstructions" in *The Methodology of Scientific Research Programmes.* Vol. 1. John Worrall and Gregory Currie, Editors. Cambridge: Cambridge University Press, 1986, p. 138.
[49] Imre Lakatos, 'The Methodology of Scientific Research Programs [1970]', p. 58.
[50] J. H. Newman, *An Essay on the Development of Christian Doctrine* [1845], 1:3:6: pp. 133-134; J. H. Newman, *An Essay on the Development of Christian Doctrine* [1878], 5:5:1: pp. 197-198.

Likewise, according to Lakatos, what allows the scientist or the philosopher of science to judge which of two competing natural scientific programs is superior to another is that the superior one possesses theories with the ability to predict novel facts which are neither predicted nor disallowed by the other program. The superiority of a research program's theories is proven as far as these novel facts are confirmed. It may be that the facts predicted by the superior theory will not find corroboration or further theoretical development for years, but once they do, then the theory from which they issue will be judged superior to the theory which did not predict them. Also, a superior research program will be able to do more. It will anticipate novel auxiliary theories.[51]

(6) *Conservative Action on Its Past:* This test is complementary to the fourth and fifth tests and describes the action of a genuinely developing doctrine on earlier stages of its growth. Because a developed doctrine is an outgrowth from an earlier form, it is not discontinuous with its earlier form but is a sublimation of it; "it is an addition which illustrates, not obscures, corroborates, not corrects, the body of thought from which it proceeds."[52] This is the ongoing perfection of what has been laid down doctrinally, neither its mutation nor destruction.[53]

Similarly, Lakatos negatively reinforces Newman's point, when he stipulates that what constitutes a break between a scientific research program and contemporary or antecedent programs is a discontinuity in its "hard core" which marks it as a new development not continuous with those programs. When such a break occurs, the new program cannot in any meaningful sense – except in terms of historical sequence or shared history – be considered continuous with the other programs. So great will be the difference between different research programs that their "hard cores", as well as their negative and positive heuristics, the facts predicted by each, as well as their explanation of anomalies, will make them incompatible.

(7) *Chronic Vigor:* A healthy or genuine development will endure through time. It will be tenacious in its vitality and durability and, though challenged by different historical circumstances, it will not be destroyed by them.[54]

Similarly, the strength of a research program is also measured by its durability, its superior ability to adapt and to offer plausible explanations

---

[51] Imre Lakatos, 'The Methodology of Scientific Research Programs [1970]', p. 88.

[52] J. H. Newman, *An Essay on the Development of Christian Doctrine* [1878], 5:6:1: p. 201.

[53] Ibid.

[54] Ibid., 5:7:1–5:7:3: pp. 204–206.

DEVELOPMENT IN THEOLOGY AND SCIENCE

for observational anomalies, and to be fruitful in anticipating a wider field of facts, than any of its competitors.[55]

On the basis of a cross-comparison of Newman's tests and Lakatos' criteria, it is possible to summarize the correspondences in a table.

COMPARISON OF NEWMAN'S TESTS AND LAKATOS' CRITERIA			
Newman's Tests/Notes:	Meaning of Newman's Tests/Notes	Meaning of Lakatos' Criteria	Lakatos' Criteria:
Preservation of Type	The essential idea of the doctrine must be preserved through time.	The conceptual framework of the program must be preserved through time.	Preservation of the Conceptual Framework
Continuity of Principles	The generative truths of doctrine are invariant through time.	Continuity in the constituent theories of a research program is maintained.	Continuity in Scientific Theories
Power of Assimilation	Doctrine will be able to absorb challenging ideas.	The research program will be able to absorb challenging anomalies.	Absorption of Anomalies
Logical Sequence	The development of doctrine will be unfolded through logical form and sequence.	The development of the program will be consistent.	Progressively Consistent
Early Anticipation	Doctrine, in its history, will show instances of anticipating later ideas.	The research program will possess the ability to anticipate new facts and theories.	Anticipation of Novel Facts and Novel Auxiliary Hypotheses
Preservative Additions/ Conservative Action	Earlier theologies/ideas will be preserved in later expansions.	The "hard core" of the program will be preserved by the expansion of protective hypotheses.	Preservation of the Hard Core of the Theory.
Chronic Vigor	The doctrine will endure and grow through time.	The research program will endure, adapt, and expand through time.	Chronic Strength
Healthy Growth	Doctrine preserves its substantial unity as defined by the above notes.	The research program preserves its conceptual unity as defined by the above criteria.	Progressive Growth

---

[55] Imre Lakatos, 'The Methodology of Scientific Research Programs [1970]', p. 88.

Conclusions

The above comparison of Newman's theory of the development of doctrine and Lakatos' theory of the development of scientific research programs concentrates on similarities in order to make the point that these resemblances add further weight to the contention that theology, though certainly not natural science, is nevertheless a science-like discipline. In attempting to specify how to identify viable doctrine, Newman anticipated a number of criteria that have analogues in Lakatos' criteria for the viability of natural scientific research programs. This suggests that when a kind of human endeavor develops viably and succeeds, it does so because it possesses the same features as other kinds of human endeavor which similarly develop and succeed. When these endeavors each claim to be a kind of knowledge, and each also claims viability *as knowledge*, then this lends plausibility to the idea that each possesses this viability because of some common underlying shared nature.

Although I do not think that the resemblances (outlined above) finally decide the case that Christian theology is worthy of being classed as science according to a common meaning that includes natural scientific research programs, I *do* think that they move the case toward this conclusion. If this case is ever made unequivocally, it will be – in part – because of John Henry Newman's incisive powers of analysis, powers which enabled him to complete a diagnosis whose features, today, are profoundly important to an understanding of the similarities between science and religion. But at the time he wrote, he could not have predicted this. The final irony is that the prescience of the applicability of the "tests" of doctrinal development to natural scientific research programs stood in direct proportion to Newman's ignorance of it.

APPENDIX

The Biglietto Speech

Vi ringrazio, Monsignore, per la participazione che m'avete fatto dell' alto onore che il Santo Padre si è degnato conferire sulla mia umile persona –

And, if I ask your permission to continue my address to you, not in your musical language, but in my own dear mother tongue, it is because in the latter I can better express my feelings on this most gracious announcement which you have brought to me than if I attempted what is above me.

First of all then, I am led to speak of the wonder and profound gratitude which came upon me, and which is upon me still, at the condescension and love towards me of the Holy Father in singling me out for so immense an honour. It was a great surprise. Such an elevation had never come into my thoughts, and seemed to be out of keeping with all my antecedents. I had passed through many trials, but they were over; and now the end of all things had almost come to me, and I was at peace. And was it possible that after all I had lived through so many years for this?

Nor is it easy to see how I could have borne so great a shock, had not the Holy Father resolved on a second act of condescension towards me, which tempered it, and was to all who heard of it a touching evidence of his kindly and generous nature. He felt for me, and he told me the reasons why he raised me to this high position. Besides other words of encouragement, he said his act was a recognition of my zeal and good service for so many years in the Catholic cause; moreover, he judged it would give pleasure to English Catholics, and even to Protestant England, if I received some mark of his favour. After such gracious words from his Holiness, I should have been insensible and heartless if I had had scruples any longer.

This is what he had the kindness to say to me, and what could I want more? In a long course of years I have made many mistakes. I have nothing of that high perfection which belongs to the writings of Saints, viz., that error cannot be found in them; but what I trust that I may claim all through what I have written, is this, – an honest intention, an absence of private ends, a temper of obedience, a willingness to be corrected, a dread of error, a desire to serve Holy Church, and, through Divine mercy, a fair measure of success. And, I rejoice to say, to one great mischief I have from the first opposed myself. For thirty, forty, fifty years I have resisted to the best of my powers the spirit of liberalism in religion. Never did Holy Church need champions against it more sorely than now, when, alas! it is an error overspreading, as a snare, the whole earth; and on this great occasion, when it is natural for one who is in my place to look out upon the world, and upon Holy Church as in it, and upon her future, it will not, I hope, be considered out of place, if I renew the protest against it which I have made so often.

Liberalism in religion is the doctrine that there is no positive truth in religion, but that one creed is as good as another, and this is the teaching which is gaining substance and force daily. It is inconsistent with any recognition of any religion, as true. It teaches that all are to be tolerated, for all are matters of opinion. Revealed religion is not a truth, but a sentiment and a taste; not an objective fact, not miraculous; and it is the right of each individual to make it say just what strikes his fancy. Devotion is not necessarily founded on faith. Men may go to Protestant Churches and to Catholic, may get good from both and belong to neither. They may fraternise together in spiritual thoughts and feelings, without having any views at all of doctrine in common, or seeing the need of them. Since, then, religion is so personal a peculiarity and so private a possession, we must of necessity ignore it in the intercourse of man with man. If a man puts on a new religion every morning, what is that to you? It is as impertinent to think about a man's religion as about his sources of income or his management of his family. Religion is in no sense the bond of society.

Hitherto the civil Power has been Christian. Even in countries separated from the Church, as in my own, the dictum was in force, when I was young, that: "Christianity was the law of the land". Now, everywhere that goodly framework of society, which is the creation of Christianity, is throwing off Christianity. The dictum to which I have referred, with a hundred others which followed upon it, is gone, or is going everywhere; and, by the end of the century, unless the Almighty interferes, it will be forgotten. Hitherto, it has been considered that religion alone, with its supernatural sanctions, was strong enough to secure submission of the masses of our population to law and order; now the Philosophers and Politicians are bent on satisfying this problem without the aid of Christianity. Instead of the Church's authority and teaching, they would substitute first of all a universal and a thoroughly secular education, calculated to bring home to every individual that to be orderly, industrious, and sober, is his personal interest. Then, for great working principles to take the place of religion, for the use of the masses thus carefully educated, it provides – the broad fundamental ethical truths, of justice, benevolence, veracity, and the like; proved experience; and those natural laws which exist and act spontaneously in society, and in social matters, whether physical or psychological; for instance, in government, trade, finance, sanitary experiments, and the intercourse of nations. As to Religion, it is a private luxury, which a man may have if he will; but which of course he must pay for, and which he must not obtrude upon others, or indulge in to their annoyance.

The general character of this great *apostasia* is one and the same everywhere; but in detail, and in character, it varies in different countries. For myself, I would rather speak of it in my own country, which I know. There, I think it threatens to have a formidable success; though it is not easy to see what will be its ultimate issue. At first sight it might be thought that Englishmen are too religious for a movement which, on the Continent, seems to be founded on infidelity; but the misfortune with us is, that, though it ends in infidelity as in other places, it does not necessarily arise out of infidelity. It must be recollected that the religious sects, which sprang up in England three centuries ago, and which are so powerful now, have ever been fiercely opposed to the Union of Church and State, and would advocate the un-Christianising of the monarchy and all that belongs to it, under the notion that such a catastrophe would make Christianity much more pure and much more powerful. Next the liberal principle is forced on us from the necessity of the case. Consider what follows from the very fact of these many sects. They constitute the religion, it is supposed, of half the population; and, recollect, our mode of government is popular. Every dozen men taken at random whom you meet in the streets has a share in political power, – when you inquire into their forms of belief, perhaps they represent one or other of as many as seven religions; how can they possibly act together in municipal or in national matters, if each insists on the recognition of his own religious denomination? All action would be at a deadlock unless the subject of religion was ignored. We cannot help ourselves. And, thirdly, it must be borne in mind, that there is much in the liberalistic theory which is good and true; for example, not to say more, the precepts of justice, truthfulness, sobriety, self-command, benevolence, which, as I have already noted, are among its avowed principles, and the natural laws of society. It is not till we find that this array of principles is intended to supersede, to block out, religion, that we pronounce it to be evil. There never was a device of the Enemy so cleverly framed and with such promise of success. And already it has answered to the expectations which have been formed of it. It is sweeping into its own ranks great numbers of able, earnest, virtuous men, elderly men of approved antecedents, young men with a career before them.

Such is the state of things in England, and it is well that it should be realised by all of us; but it must not be supposed for a moment that I am afraid of it. I lament it deeply, because I foresee that it may be the ruin of many souls; but I have no fear at all that it really can do aught of serious harm to the Word of God, to Holy Church, to our Almighty King, the Lion of the tribe of Judah, Faithful and True, or to His Vicar on earth. Christianity has been too often in what seemed deadly peril, that we should fear for it any new trial now. So far is certain; on the other hand, what is uncertain, and in these great contests commonly is uncertain, and what is commonly a great surprise, when it is witnessed, is the particular mode by which, in the event, Providence rescues and saves His elect inheritance. Sometimes our enemy is turned into a friend; sometimes he is despoiled of that special virulence of evil which was so threatening; sometimes he falls to pieces of himself; sometimes he does just so much as is beneficial, and then is removed. Commonly the Church has nothing more to do than to go on in her own proper duties, in confidence and peace; to stand still and to see the salvation of God.

Mansueti hereditabunt terram,
Et delectabuntur in multitudine pacis.

NOTE ON THE CONTRIBUTORS

FR ROBERT BARRON was ordained in the Archdiocese of Chicago in 1986. He holds a Master's degree in philosophy from The Catholic University of America and a PhD in theology from the Institut Catholique de Paris. Fr Barron is professor of systematic theology at the University of St Mary of the Lake - Mundelein Seminary outside Chicago. He has published extensively on theology and spirituality.

FR KEITH BEAUMONT, CO, was born in 1944 in Melbourne, Australia. He has a PhD in French literature and a Master's degree in theology. A lecturer at Leicester University from 1970 to 1991, he was received into the Catholic Church in 1986 and ordained priest of the French Oratory in 1996. He is currently a student chaplain and engaged in teaching and writing on Newman and the history of spirituality. He is also the President of the *Association Française des Amis de Newman*.

DR ARNELLA FRANCIS CLAMOR obtained her Doctorate in systematic theology from the Katholieke Universiteit Leuven in Belgium. She is presently teaching theology and philosophy in the Jesuit University of Ateneo de Manila, and in Mother of Life Center, a school for the formation of catechists from all over the Philippines.

FR AUSTIN COOPER, OMI, lectures in Church history and Christian spirituality at Catholic Theological College, Melbourne. He was Master of the College for three separate terms and in 2004 was awarded the Order of Australia for services to theological education. He has published numerous articles related to the Oxford Movement.

CARDINAL AVERY DULLES, SJ, is the Laurence J. McGinley Professor of Religion and Society at Fordham University. He was made a cardinal by Pope John Paul II in recognition of his service to the Church as a theologian. The author of over 800 articles on theological topics, he has also written twenty-three books including a book about Newman. He is the first United States-born theologian who is not a bishop to be created a cardinal.

FR EDWARD J. ENRIGHT, OSA, received his STD from The Catholic University of America, with a doctoral dissertation on Newman. He teaches Church history and modern historical theology in the Department of Theology and Religious Studies at Villanova

University, Pennsylvania. Fr Enright is currently writing a book, tentatively entitled "History and Doctrine: Newman's Thought on Development in Modern Theological Context."

FR DAVID GRÉA is a diocesan priest of Lyon, France. He has studied Newman in Oxford and in Rome and is currently completing a PhD on Newman's Catholic Ecclesiology during the years 1846-1851. He is a member of the *Association Française des Amis de Newman*.

FR BERNARD J. MAHONEY was ordained priest for the Diocese of Austin, Texas in 1953. He gained his PhD from the University of Birmingham, England in 1967 on "Newman and Aristotle, The Concept of the Conscience", under the guidance of Fr Stephen Dessain of the Oratory and Professor Ninian Smart.

DR EDWARD JEREMY MILLER completed a double doctorate at Louvain under the renowned Newman scholar, Jan Walgrave. Before taking his present position at Gwynedd Mercy College in suburban Philadelphia, he was professor of Roman Catholic theology at Emory University in Atlanta. He has published on Newman, Aquinas, and topics in systematic theology.

DR ANDREW NASH read English at Cambridge. He later taught at the Oratory School (founded by Newman) and in 2000 became the first doctoral graduate of the Maryvale Institute. He has published a critical edition of Newman's *Lectures on the Present Position of Catholics in England*. Since 2001 he has been Headmaster of St Edward's School, Cheltenham.

PROFESSOR RICHARD PENASKOVIC is Professor of Religious Studies and Immediate Past Chair of the University Senate and University Faculty at Auburn University in Alabama. He wrote the book *Open to the Spirit: The Role of the Laity in John H. Newman*, and his articles on Newman have appeared in *Louvain Studies*, *Augustinian Studies*, and *Priests and People*.

FR JAMES PEREIRO, a priest of the Opus Dei Prelature, is chaplain of Grandpont House, Oxford and a member of the History Faculty of Oxford University. He has published extensively on ecclesiastical history of the nineteenth century, and among his publications is *Cardinal Manning* (Oxford, 1998). OUP is also publishing his *Ethos and the Oxford Movement*.

FR JEAN RENCKI, born in 1968, was ordained for the Archdiocese of Paris in 2002. As a deacon, he spent two terms at Oxford, exploring the life and works of Newman. He has since developed an interest in the missionary aspects of Newman's works and has given lectures on that topic to various audiences. He is now a parish priest in the diocese of Evry. He is also a member of the *Association Française des Amis de Newman*.

DR JANE RUPERT holds a PhD in English Literature from the University of Toronto. She has written a number of articles on John Henry Newman and is presently completing a book on "Literary Rationality and the Battle of Methods".

DR THOMAS RYBA is Notre Dame Theologian-in-Residence at the Saint Thomas Aquinas Catholic Center at Purdue University, Adjunct Professor of Philosophy, and Adjunct Professor of Jewish Studies at Purdue University. Author and editor of several books and many articles on theology, he is currently at work on three books, one of which is about the thought of John Henry Cardinal Newman and is tentatively entitled "Newman for New Millennium".

FR CHARLES J.T. TALAR, a priest of the Diocese of Bridgeport, Connecticut is Professor of Systematic Theology at the Graduate School of Theology of the University of Saint Thomas in Houston, Texas. He has published extensively on nineteenth-century Catholicism.

FR LUC TERLINDEN is a priest of the Archdiocese of Malines-Bruxelles in Belgium. He holds a Licentiate Degree in Economic Sciences, as well as a Licentiate and a Doctorate from the Alphonsian Academy in Rome. His doctoral thesis was on Charles Taylor and moral theology in the light of John Henry Newman. He is presently involved in pastoral ministry and teaches moral theology in various institutes of his diocese.